True Stories
from the American Past

Volume II: Since 1865

YA
50¢

THIRD EDITION

True Stories from the American Past

VOLUME II: SINCE 1865

EDITED BY

William Graebner
State University of New York
College at Fredonia

Boston   Burr Ridge, IL   Dubuque, IA   Madison, WI   New York
San Francisco   St. Louis   Bangkok   Bogotá   Caracas   Kuala Lumpur
Lisbon   London   Madrid   Mexico City   Milan   Montreal   New Delhi
Santiago   Seoul   Singapore   Sydney   Taipei   Toronto

McGraw-Hill Higher Education

A Division of The **McGraw-Hill** Companies

TRUE STORIES FROM THE AMERICAN PAST, VOLUME II: SINCE 1865

Published by McGraw-Hill, a business unit of The McGraw-Hill Companies, Inc., 1221 Avenue of the Americas, New York, NY, 10020. Copyright © 2003, 1997, by The McGraw-Hill Companies, Inc. All rights reserved. No part of this publication may be reproduced or distributed in any form or by any means, or stored in a database or retrieval system, without the prior written consent of The McGraw-Hill Companies, Inc., including, but not limited to, in any network or other electronic storage or transmission, or broadcast for distance learning. Some ancillaries, including electronic and print components, may not be available to customers outside the United States.

This book is printed on acid-free paper.

1 2 3 4 5 6 7 8 9 0 FGR/FGR 0 9 8 7 6 5 4 3 2

ISBN 0-07-241754-4

Publisher: *Lyn Uhl*
Senior sponsoring editor: *Steven Drummond*
Developmental editor: *Kristen Mellitt*
Project manager: *Karen Nelson*
Production supervisor: *Susanne Riedell*
Coordinator of freelance design: *Jenny El-Shamy/Mary E. Kazak*
Photo research coordinator: *Nora Agbayani*
Photo researcher: *Robin Sand*
Cover design: *Lodge Design*
Typeface: *10/12 Palatino*
Compositor: *Techbooks*
Printer: *Quebecor World Fairfield Inc.*

Library of Congress Cataloging-in-Publication Data

True stories from the American past/edited by Altina L. Waller, William Graebner.-- 3rd ed.
   p. cm
   Contents: v. 1. To 1865 -- v. 2. Since 1865
   ISBN 0-07-241752-8 (v. 1 : alk. paper) -- ISBN 0-07-241754-4 (v. 2 : alk. paper)
   1. United States--History. I. Waller, Altina L. (Altina Laura), 1940- II. Graebner, William
E178.T86 2003
973--dc21   2002035768

www.mhhe.com
Cover image: © *Los Angeles Times Photographic Archives, Department of Special Collections, Charles E. Young Research Library, UCLA.*

ABOUT THE AUTHORS

BETH BAILEY is professor of American studies and Regents Lecturer at the University of New Mexico. She is the author of *From Front Porch to Back Seat: Courtship in 20th Century America* (1988); *Sex in the Heartland* (1999), about the sexual revolution in Kansas; and, with David Farber, *The First Strange Place: Race and Sex in World War II Hawaii* (1992).

LARRY E. BURGESS holds a Ph.D. in history from Claremont Graduate School, where he specialized in the history of the West. He is the Director of the A.K. Smiley Public Library in Redlands. With James A. Sandos, he is the author of *The Hunt for Willie Boy: Indian-Hating and Popular Culture* (1994), which won a Gustavus Myers Center Award for an "Outstanding Book on Human Rights in North America" in 1995.

LEONARD DINNERSTEIN is professor of history at the University of Arizona. He specializes in American ethnic history. Among his books are *The Leo Frank Case* (1968), *America and the Survivors of the Holocaust* (1982), and *Antisemitism in America* (1994). He has also coauthored *Ethnic Americans,* with David Reimers (1988), and *Natives and Strangers: A Multicultural History of Americans,* with Roger L. Nichols and David Reimers (1996, forthcoming in a new edition, 2003.). He is currently doing research for a book on the Holocaust, the survivors, and the memories.

DAVID FARBER is professor of history at the University of New Mexico. He is the author of *Chicago '68* (1988); *The Age of Great Dreams: America in the 1960s* (1994); *Sloan Rules: Alfred P. Sloan and the Triumph of General Motors* (2002); and, with Beth Bailey, *The Columbia Guide to America in the 1960s* (2001) and *The First Strange Place: Race and Sex in World War II Hawaii* (1992).

WILLIAM GRAEBNER is professor of history at the State University of New York, College at Fredonia. He has written on a variety of aspects of twentieth-century American history. His books include *A History of Retirement* (1980), *The Engineering of Consent: Democracy and Authority in Twentieth-Century America* (1987), *Coming of Age in Buffalo* (1990), and *The Age of Doubt: American Thought and Culture in the 1940s* (1991). He is Associate Editor of *American Studies.*

WALTER LAFEBER is the Andrew and James Tisch Professor at Cornell University. His recent books are *The Clash: U.S.–Japan Relations Throughout History* (1997), and *America, Russia, and the Cold War, 1945–2001* (ninth revised edition, 2002). He currently serves on the editorial board of *Political Science Quarterly*.

GEORGE LIPSITZ is professor of ethnic studies at the University of California, San Diego and the author of *Rainbow at Midnight* (1994), *Dangerous Crossroads* (1994), *Sidewalks of St. Louis* (1991), *Time Passages* (1990), and *A Life in the Struggle: Ivory Perry and the Culture of Opposition* (1988 and 1995).

GERALD MARKOWITZ is professor of history and chair, Department of Thematic Studies at John Jay College of Criminal Justice and professor of history at the CUNY Graduate center. He was a recipient of the Viseltear Prize from the Medical Care Section of the American Public Health Association for "Outstanding Contributions" to the history of public health. He has co-authored and edited with David Rosner numerous books and articles, including *Deadly Dust: Silicosis and the Politics of Occupational Disease in Twentieth Century America* (1991, 1994); *Children, Race, and Power: Kenneth and Mamie Clark's Northside Center* (1996); *Dying for Work* (1987); and *"Slaves of the Depression," Workers' Letters about Life on the Job* (1987). He and David Rosner have recently published *Deceit and Denial: The Deadly Politics of Industrial Pollution* (2002).

ELAINE TYLER MAY is professor of American studies and history at the University of Minnesota. Her publications include *Great Expectations: Marriage and Divorce in Post-Victorian America* (1980); *Homeward Bound: American Families in the Cold War Era* (1988, new edition 1999); *Pushing the Limits: American Women, 1940–1961* (1996); and *Barren in the Promised Land: Childless Americans and the Pursuit of Happiness* (1997). She is also co-editor of *Here, There and Everywhere: The Foreign Politics of American Popular Culture* (2000).

MICHAEL MAY is a freelance writer and producer living in Austin, Texas. He is the former editor of *Responsive Philanthropy*, the quarterly of the National Committee for Responsive Philanthropy, and holds a B.A. in history from Grinnell College. He has written and produced stories for National Public Radio, Public Radio International, the *Austin Chronicle*, and others. As a domestic and foreign correspondent he has covered politics and culture from the United States, Russia, Peru, Cuba, and the War Crimes Tribunal at The Hague for broadcast and publication.

STUART CREIGHTON MILLER is emeritus professor of social science and history and director of the social science program at San Francisco State University. He is the author of *The Unwelcome Immigrant: The American*

Image of the Chinese, 1785–1882 (1969), the runner-up for the 1970 Bancroft Prize, and *"Benevolent Assimilation": The American Conquest of the Philippines, 1899–1903* (1982). His current research is on immigration history, focusing on cultural pluralism as a romantic quest.

STEPHEN NISSENBAUM teaches history at the University of Massachusetts at Amherst. His most recent book, *The Battle for Christmas* (1996), was a finalist for the Pulitzer Prize. He has also written *Salem Possessed: Social Origins of Witchcraft* (with Paul Boyer, 1974); *Sex, Diet and Debility in Jacksonian America* (1980); *The Pursuit of Liberty* (third edition, 1996), a multiauthored textbook; and *All Over the Map: Rethinking American Regions* (1996), with Edward L. Ayers, Patricia Nelson Limerick, and Peter Onuf. Active in the public humanities, he has served as member and president of the Massachusetts Foundation for the Humanities.

DAVID ROSNER is professor of history and public health at Columbia University and Director of the Center for the History of Public Health at Columbia's Mailman School of Public Health. He received his doctorate from Harvard in the History of Science and formerly was University Distinguished Professor of History at the City University of New York. He has been awarded the Distinguished Scholar's Prize from the City University and recently, the Viseltear Prize for Outstanding Work in the History of Public Health from the APHA. He is author of *A Once Charitable Enterprise* (1982, 1987) and *Health Care in America: Essays in Social History* (with Susan Reverby). In addition, he has co-authored and edited with Gerald Markowitz numerous books and articles, including *Deadly Dust: Silicosis and the Politics of Occupational Disease in Twentieth Century America* (1991, 1994), *Children, Race, and Power: Kenneth and Mamie Clark's Northside Center* (1996); *Dying for Work* (1987) and *"Slaves of the Depression," Workers' Letters about Life on the Job* (1987). He and Gerald Markowitz have recently authored *Deceit and Denial: The Deadly Politics of Industrial Pollution* (2002).

JAMES A. SANDOS is the Helen and Vernon Farquhar Professor of the Southwest at the University of Redlands. He specializes in the Indian history of the region, especially in California. With Larry E. Burgess, he is the author of *The Hunt for Willie Boy: Indian-Hating and Popular Culture* (1994), which won a Gustavus Meyers Center Award for an "Outstanding Book on Human Rights in North America" in 1995.

CARLOS A. SCHWANTES is the St. Louis Mercantile Professor of Transportation Studies and the West at the University of Missouri–St. Louis. He is the author of 15 books, including *Coxey's Army: An American Odyssey* (1985) and *Railroad Signatures Across the Pacific Northwest* (1993). His most recent book project is a study of how transportation transformed the twentieth-century West.

RICKIE SOLINGER is a historian, the author of *Wake Up Little Susie: Single Pregnancy and Race before* Roe v. Wade (1992); *The Abortionist: A Woman Against the Law* (1994); and *Beggars and Choosers: How the Politics of Choice Shapes Adoption, Abortion and Welfare in the United States* (2001). She is the editor of *Abortion Wars: A Half-Century of Struggle, 1950–2000* (1998), and co-editor, with Gwendolyn Mink, of *U.S. Welfare Policy: A Documentary History* (2002). Rickie Solinger works with artists and photographers to make exhibitions associated with her books.

RONALD STORY is professor of history at the University of Massachusetts at Amherst. Story's work includes *Generations of Americans* (1976), *The Forging of an Aristocracy* (1980), *Sports in Massachusetts* (1991), *Five Colleges, Five Histories* (1992), and *A More Perfect Union*, 4th edition (1995). He has also produced a CD-ROM on the Civil War and a website on Jackie Robinson and the desegregation of baseball.

ALAN TRACHTENBERG is Neil Gray, Jr. Professor Emeritus of English and American Studies at Yale University. He is the author of *Brooklyn Bridge: Fact and Symbol* (1965), *The Incorporation of America: Culture and Society in the Gilded Age* (1982), and *Reading American Photographs: Images as History, Matthew Brady to Walker Evans* (1989).

ALTINA L. WALLER is professor of history at the University of Connecticut. She received her doctorate from the University of Massachusetts at Amherst and has taught at West Virginia University and Rhodes College in Memphis, Tennessee. Her first book was *Reverend Beecher and Mrs. Tilton: Sex and Class in Victorian America* (1982). Her second book, *Feud: Hatfields, McCoys and Social Change in Appalachia, 1860–1900* (1988), is the basis for her story about the feud.

CONTENTS

PREFACE

True Stories is a special kind of reader. Each of its two volumes consists of fifteen stories, thoroughly researched and impeccably crafted by scholars who are authorities in their respective fields. In this volume, each story deals with a significant and compelling episode in the history of the United States since the Civil War. Every decade of that history is represented by at least one story.

In selecting the stories, I have been moved by the sense that the American past is too rich and varied to be bound and contained by the traditional and comfortable narratives with which most historians are conversant. Nonetheless, some of the stories—the story of the nation's imperial adventure in the Philippines, or the account of Francis Townsend's confrontation with Franklin D. Roosevelt's New Dealers over pensions for the aged—will be generally familiar to instructors, if not students. Other episodes, including the opening of Disneyland and the story of Sherri Finkbine's efforts to secure an abortion after having taking a drug known to produce fetal deformity, will have resonance for many Americans, yet received their first serious historical treatment in *True Stories*. Still others, including the story of the 1909 manhunt for the Indian Willie Boy, concern issues and incidents that are not even mentioned in survey textbooks. After surveying readers of the second edition, I have added the Willie Boy story—really a story about stories—and chosen stories for the 1960s and 1990s that deal with gender and racial issues. I hope readers will appreciate the remarkable diversity of *True Stories*.

Together, the stories cover a wide variety of fields of inquiry, many of them new to the study of history in the last two or three decades. These include popular culture, the history of medicine, women's history, the history of African Americans, the aged, the mass media, and the history of science and technology. Most important, each episode was selected because it promised to make, well, a good *story*.

Why use stories to study and learn history? The idea is not as unusual as it might seem. We live in a culture steeped in stories: the myths of ancient Greece, Biblical narratives, bedtime stories, fairy tales, newspaper accounts, Hollywood epics, neighborhood rumors, one's personal account of the day's events after a hard day at school or at the office. Even the standard history textbooks are essentially stories—longer, more general, more familiar, and more generally accepted stories than the ones found in this book—but stories, just the same.

The accounts that make up *True Stories* are obviously not myths, or fairy tales, or rumors. They are a certain kind of story that we easily recognize as "history." Indeed, history might be understood as a set of analytical stories about the past whose authors think are "true." When we read a historical account, we expect it to be balanced, to be based on historical research and "facts," and to show respect for the past; by these standards, the stories in *True Stories* certainly qualify as history. But this is not quite the history one finds in a history textbook. *True Stories* features people who live and act in specific places and times and in precise historical circumstances. Its flesh and blood protagonists—some of them resembling mythic heroes or antiheroes—build bridges, march on the nation's capitol, take money to throw baseball games, justify the marketing of hazardous substances, publicly accuse a Supreme Court nominee of sexual harassment, engage in armed combat with the federal government, or confront the nation's racist heritage on the sidewalks of World War II Hawaii. In short, one function of any story—and one purpose of *True Stories*—is to put people, and people's deeds, back into history.

There is another lesson to be learned from these stories, one that has to do with what a story is. Although the stories presented here often involve individuals acting in specific situations, they have significance that goes far beyond the setting or the actors. The people in *True Stories* (indeed, all of us) inevitably live their lives on the stage of history. The things that they do—even the odd, eccentric, or criminal things—are ultimately historical deeds, carried out within the economic, political, social, and cultural frameworks of a particular historical era. Therefore, a good story provides the insights of the traditional textbooks, though in a very different form.

Sometimes it can be difficult to see the connections between a story and history, between the text and its context. When one sees a movie, or watches the 11 o'clock television news, one does not easily or automatically think of these "stories" as part of history; and making the connections between a specific event and the larger past can be more difficult when the event occurred decades ago. To help students make these connections, and to see the need for making them, each episode concludes with an interpretive section that pulls together the themes in the story and links the story proper with some larger and familiar historical context. For example, the epic hill-country feud between the Hatfields and the McCoys in the 1880s emerges as a product of industrialization and urbanization; and the Iranian hostage crisis that began in 1979 is shaped as a moment in America's decline as a world economic and political power.

Each episode, then, has two distinct parts. The first part is the narrated story. Our goal was to keep this story section as free as possible from analysis and interpretation, in the hope that students would fashion their own perspectives once freed, if only relatively and momentarily, from the learned authority of the historian. The second part of the episode is a shorter interpretive conclusion, where the authors have been given free reign to bring their considerable analytical skills to bear on the body of the story.

As students and instructors will discover, the attempt to separate narrative and interpretation has been only moderately successful. Even the most rudimentary collections of "facts" and the simplest narratives begin with preconceptions, proceed from moral and ethical premises, and imply interpretive frameworks. So do our "true stories." Despite our efforts to put these elements in the background, they inevitably appear in the stories. Indeed, one purpose of the collection is to draw attention to the inescapable subjectivity of historians. Nonetheless, we also believe that the effort made here to separate narrative and analysis can assist students in generating their own readings of the past and, by doing so, in becoming active participants in the complex process of understanding and creating their own history.

Acknowledgments

The editor wishes to thank Phil Cantrell, West Virginia University; Jonathan Chu, University of Massachusetts–Boston; Virginia Noelke, Angelo State University; Michael Topp, University of Texas–El Paso; David Trevino, Texas A&M–Kingsville; and Gary Trogdon, University of Nebraska, for their helpful reviews of the second edition of this book.

William Graebner

1

AN INSURRECTION THAT NEVER HAPPENED: THE "CHRISTMAS RIOTS" OF 1865

Stephen Nissenbaum

At the end of the Civil War there remained the unresolved question of what was to be done about the more than three million African-Americans who had been freed from slavery. White Southerners were fearful about their own economic futures, to say nothing of fears for their physical safety if their former slaves united in retribution. Freed slaves had every reason to expect that a government that had been willing to sacrifice over 300,000 lives to end the slave system would also be willing to provide them with the essential economic means—land—to allow them to become contributing members of society. Yet the fate of both white Southerners and freedmen and freedwomen was in the hands of Northern politicians who had never been able to agree that the rights of freedpeople were a high priority in the war. What was universally celebrated at war's end was the subjugation of the South and the preservation of the Union. Considering that so many lives had been sacrificed, it was almost inevitable that the Union had become a "holy" cause, couched, by the President himself, in terms of a religious cleansing that would lead to a sanctified nation.

This emphasis on the preservation of the Union rather than the rights of African-Americans was clear from the beginning of the war right through to the end. Lincoln's Emancipation Proclamation, for example, was a very controversial, politically sensitive document. The President stood to lose much of his support for the war if he were to issue it in the early stages; such a proclamation only became feasible when the Union was in a militarily strong position after the bloody battle of Antietam. Even then the proclamation did not free slaves in slave states that had sided with the Union—Delaware, Maryland, Kentucky, and Missouri. In the South, of course, with the Confederacy in control, the proclamation had no effect until the military situation changed. Another example is the decision to use African-American troops in the Northern army. Northerners demonstrated their racism by initially denying the right of free blacks in the North to fight for the Union cause. Even when it became clear that enthusiasm for the war was waning and conscription was necessary to fill the ranks of the army, there was resistance to allowing African-Americans to fight. Only because of that shortage of men combined with extensive politicking and lobbying on the part of African-American leaders such as Frederick Douglass did black regiments become grudgingly acceptable to Northerners. Despite the not inconsiderable accomplishment of ending slavery as an institution, the still rampant racist attitudes in the North made the future of African-American freedpeople in the South very precarious.

Stephen Nissenbaum's story of the rumored Christmas insurrection reveals much about the immediate aftermath of the Civil War, when the hopes of freedpeople soared and white Southerners' fears reached almost hysterical proportions—emotions that were exacerbated by contested and ambiguous Northern policies. But this story also explores the nature of human relations in the plantation South before the war; the human give-and-take that was impossible to avoid, even though whites attempted to deny the essential humanity of their slaves. Embedded in the rituals of Christmas was reinforcement of the unequal and oppressive power hierarchy juxtaposed with the potential for resistance and the ultimate destruction of that hierarchy. What we know now is that despite the sacrifices of the Civil War, the Reconstruction era was not to overturn the hierarchy at all; that would have to wait another hundred years.

This is the story of an insurrection that never happened—a revolt that was never even planned. It is a story that would never have taken place at all except for the convergence of three elements, each involving a different kind of "history." The first element, one of *military history,* was the defeat of the South at the end of the Civil War. The second element, one of *political and economic history,* was the liberation of slaves and a new federal policy that promised them their own land. The third and final element, one of *social and cultural history,* was Christmas.

It is that final element, Christmas, which requires the most explanation. The Christmas season had long been a special occasion in the American South for both white and black people. And for the most part the season did not involve what we might expect—church services, or elegant balls, or Santa Claus. Instead, this was a season of hard drinking, noisemaking, and generally rowdy behavior. (It can best be considered as a New Year's Eve, Mardi Gras, and Halloween, all rolled into one.) Christmas was a time when the ordinary rules that governed social behavior simply ceased to operate, or when those rules were actually turned upside down. Children were allowed to demand gifts from grown-ups, women from men, and the poor from the rich. This was an occasion when "the world turned upside down." And those who really controlled Southern society—wealthy adult males—were generally willing to go along with this topsy-turvy state of affairs: They knew it would last only a short time.

As early as 1773, one visitor recorded in his diary on Christmas day that "I was waked this morning by Guns fired all around the House." In 1823, a rural white Southerner attacked the Christmas season for being a "general scene of dissipation and idleness." Some folks spent the time making "rough jokes." "Apprentice boys and little negroes" fired guns and crackers. And everyone—"parents, children, servants, old, young, white, black, and yellow"—drank hard. "And if you inquire what it is all for, no earthly reason is assigned . . . , except this, 'Why man! It is Christmas.'" More than three decades later, a teenage Virginia girl named Amanda Edmonds was awakened "by the repeated blows of the firecrackers, and the merry voices shouting 'hurr[a]y for Christmas,' and then the nog was on the wing until the eggs were foaming, in went the milk and all ingredients poured together; lastly it was foaming in our glasses, till they were drained of the contents."

Everybody commented at the time about how much Southerners drank during the Christmas season. It is clear that people—women and even children among them—commonly began drinking at breakfast. Teenager Amanda Edmonds began Christmas Day in 1857 drinking "glass after glass" of spiked eggnog. Once again, in 1861, the first thing Edmonds did in the morning was to have "a joyful eggnog drink—I really got tight. The first signs of Christmas that I've seen."

The American South was not unique in celebrating the Christmas season in such a fashion. In much of the North, and in Europe, too—in most early agricultural societies—late December was taken as a time of carnival. Here was the one time of the year in which there was fresh food and drink aplenty from the recently completed harvest and an extended period of leisure in which to consume it—leisure that followed hard upon months of grueling and intensive labor. (In a way, it was much like the same holiday season in modern college communities, in which the conclusion of final examinations is similarly celebrated with boisterous drinking and letting off steam.)

But in one important particular, Christmas in the antebellum South was unique. For, in that society, all those carnivalesque holiday rituals extended across the color line—they encompassed black slaves as well as their white masters. If Southern society was "turned upside down" at Christmas, that inversion involved not simply age, class, and gender (as it did in other places); above all, it involved race.

First of all, Christmas in the slave quarters meant *freedom*—for a little while. Christmas was the one time of year when slaves were released from the obligation to work, usually for several days in a row. Slaves became, in a sense, free—free from labor, free to do whatever they wished, free even to travel off their masters' property. One Northerner, living on a plantation as a tutor to the owner's children, reported that "[t]hroughout the state of South Carolina, Christmas is a holiday, together with 2 of the succeeding days . . . especially for the negroes. On these days the chains of slavery . . . are loosed. A smile is seen on every countenance."

Slaves employed their freedom in a variety of ways, from visiting friends and family members to participating in religious meetings. But perhaps the activities that were most often reported involved revelry: eating, drinking, dancing, making noise, and making love. Solomon Northup, a free black who was kidnapped into slavery in Louisiana, later wrote of Christmas as "the times of feasting, and frolicking, and fiddling—the carnival season with the children of bondage . . . the only days when they are allowed a little restricted liberty, and heartily indeed do they enjoy it." A white Southerner used the same term, calling Christmas "the time of the blacks' high carnival," while another white man described the period as "times of cramming, truly awful. [T]hey stuffed and drank, and sang and danced." The wife of ex–U.S. President John Tyler wrote in 1845 that the family's slaves "have from now a four days' holiday and have given themselves up completely to *their* kind of happiness—drinking, with nothing on earth to do."

It seems clear that sex was involved in all this, too. More than one visitor explicitly described the slave Christmas as a modern version of the old Roman Saturnalia, an orgiastic occasion. One writer who did so employed language whose euphemisms were not intended to conceal the author's meaning: "From three to four days *and* nights are given as holiday, during which every indulgence and license consistent with any subordination and safety are allowed."

Christmas misrule entailed even more than leisure and "liberty." It also meant a symbolic turning of the tables between masters and slaves. Christmas was the one occasion of the year when slaves were actually allowed to demand gifts from their masters, even to do so in an aggressive fashion that might have led to a whipping at any other time of the year. One common seasonal ritual was termed "Christmas Gift." "Christmas Gift!" usually amounted to a boisterous wake-up call combined with a demand for presents. A former slave described one version of the ritual: "The cock crowing for sunrise is scarcely over when the servants steal into the Big House on tiptoe so they can catch everybody there with a shouted 'Christmas Gift!' before the kitchen fire is even started or the water put on to boil for the early morning coffee." In response, each member of the white family who is thus "captured" must hand over a gift to the slave who has "caught" her. Years later, a planter's daughter, Susan Dabney Smedes, described the game with nostalgic affection:

> On Christmas mornings the servants delighted in catching the family [i.e., the owner's family] with "Christmas giff!" "Christmas giff!" betimes in the morning. They would spring out of unexpected corners and from behind doors on the young masters and mistresses. At such times [she adds in explanation] there was an affectionate throwing off of the reserve and decorum of every-day life.

Young Amanda Edmonds, the same teenager who got tight on eggnog at breakfast, wrote to her diary in 1857 that " 'Christmas Gift' was heard from every tongue this morning before we hardly saw the first gleam of morning in the far east." The recollections of a one-time slave, a Georgia field hand named James Bolton, suggest that the custom was not always limited to house servants: "We runned up to the big house early Christmas morning and holler out, 'Morning, Christmas Gif!' Then they gave us plenty of Santy Claus, and we would go back to our cabins to have fun till New Year's Day."

Christmas was the one occasion of the year on which plantation owners would formally offer presents to their chattel slaves. It was a rare planter who did not give something to his slaves at Christmas. At a minimum, the gifts were small—the kinds of things we might dismiss today as "trinkets" but which the slaves had good reason to value: sugar, tobacco, or hats, along with ribbons, bandannas, and other decorative items for the women. Some slaveholders distributed money. An especially lavish (and ostentatious) example of this practice was reported by Richard Jones, a former slave from South Carolina, whose account also reminds us how demeaning such ritualized generosity could be:

> Marse allus carried a roll of money as big as my arm. He would come up to de Quarter on Christmas, July 4th and Thanksgiving, and get up on a stump and call all the chilluns out. Den he would throw money to 'em. De chilluns got dimes, nickels, quarters, half-dollars and dollars. At Christmas he would throw ten-dollar bills. De parents would take de five and ten dollar bills in change, but Marse made dem let de chilluns keep de small change. I ain't never seed so much money since my marster been gone.

On many plantations slaves were asked to approach the Big House to receive their gifts in person from their master and his family (along with the family's best wishes). More often, it was masters and their families who visited the slave quarters to attend the slaves' own party there. But wherever these scenes took place, in the quarters or the Big House, some planters and their families used the occasion to make elaborate gestures of deference to their slaves. Oftentimes they joined in the festivities themselves, at least symbolically. Just as often, they prepared the party meal themselves, or they personally superintended its preparation. Occasionally, a master even made the ostentatious gesture of serving part of the meal to the slaves himself. One North Carolina slaveholder centered his version of the ritual on the preparation and distribution of eggnog: after the drink was "pronounced right," it was ceremoniously placed out on the piazza (on a beautiful mahogany table that came from the Big House). At this point the slaves assembled and were ceremoniously handed one glass apiece:

> My grandfather knew every one of his negroes, big and little, by name; and his greeting was always personal to each. They came up in couples, according to age and dignity, and the unvarying formula was: "Sarvant, Master; merry Christmas to you, an' all de fambly, sir!" "Thank you, Jack; merry Christmas to you and yours!"

Whites were aware of the symbolic significance of these gestures of deference, gestures that demonstrated that they were playing their part in the expected seasonal ritual in which the world was briefly and symbolically "turned upside down." They would refer to the unprecedented degree of "familiarity" between masters and slaves on this occasion. One Tennessee slaveowner claimed that at Christmas his "people" were "as happy as Lords." Another man wrote: "Here all authority and all distinction of colour ceases; black and white, overseer and book-keeper, mingle together in the dance." Another planter stressed how different Christmas was from the only other holiday he permitted his sixty slaves—the Fourth of July: "The one in July is celebrated with a dinner and whiskey. The Christmas holiday is a very different thing. It lasts from four to six days, and during this *jubilee* it is difficult to say who is master. The servants are allowed the largest liberty."

Dressing for the Carnival (1877). The great American artist Winslow Homer painted this large oil canvas while traveling in southern Virginia at the very end of Reconstruction. An immensely respectful and dignified portrayal, it shows a man being dressed for the John Canoe Christmas ritual by his wife and another woman as the children watch in fascination. (The Metropolitan Museum of Art, Amelia B. Lazarus Fund, 1922)

"It is difficult to say who is master." That was surely an exaggeration. But it was also the very point at which the meaning of Christmas in the slave South became potentially *political*—the point at which, under certain circumstances, slaves might think about becoming their own masters for real. In fact, some black people used Christmas to take *permanent* control of their lives. For example, the season offered unique opportunities for escaping slavery altogether by running away, taking advantage of the common Christmas privilege of freedom to travel (and along roads that might now be crowded with unfamiliar black faces). Christmas also presented a tempting occasion for more aggressive forms of resistance. Sanctioned disorders could always step across the bounds and edge over into violence, riot, or even revolt. A striking number of actual or rumored slave revolts were planned to take place at Christmas—nearly one-third the known total, according to one historian. Reports of Christmas insurrection were especially rampant in 1856; in that year revolts were reported in almost every one of the Southern states.

That was in slavery times. But the most serious rumors of planned insurrection at Christmas (rumors that amounted, in the end, to very little) came just *after* the slaves were finally emancipated, with the end of the Civil War, in December 1865. Here was the point at which the memory of the traditional rituals of the Southern Christmas converged with a moment of serious political crisis in the lives of both black and white Southerners.

Some political history, then. If ever there was a time when the hopes of African-Americans were at fever pitch, it was in 1865. Those hopes had been raised by a set of executive orders and congressional acts, passed during the war itself and for essentially military purposes. The Union army of General William Tecumseh Sherman had marched irresistibly through Georgia late in 1864, finally taking Savannah in late December. (Sherman telegraphed President Lincoln a famous message, offering him Savannah as a "Christmas present.") Sherman's march had created a refugee army of slaves, tens of thousands of newly liberated slaves who were now impoverished and homeless and who turned for assistance to the Northern troops. To deal with the army of refugees, in January 1865, General Sherman issued a proclamation that would have important consequences: Special Field Order No. 15. This proclamation set aside for the freedmen any lands (in the area of his recent march) that had been confiscated by the Union army or abandoned by their white owners. These lands, to be divided into 40-acre lots, included some of the best real estate in Georgia and South Carolina.

A few months later, in March 1865, the U.S. Congress established a new federal agency, the Freedmen's Bureau, designed to deal more systematically with the difficult but imminent transition to freedom. The Freedmen's Bureau adopted Sherman's policy and extended it to the entire Confederacy. In late July, the head of the Freedmen's Bureau, General Oliver O. Howard, issued to his staff Circular No. 13 (a circular was a memorandum designed to circulate to all agents of an organization). Circular No. 13 contained a set of procedures that would divide abandoned or confiscated Southern plantations into 40-acre lots and distribute them to black families. Each of these families would receive a written certificate of possession. (The policy became associated with the catchphrase *forty acres and a mule*.)

But in the summer of 1865, with the war over and Andrew Johnson in the White House, federal priorities in Washington underwent a significant change. President Johnson decided that the most important task facing the United States was not that of dealing with the freed slaves but rather that of reestablishing the loyalty of white Southerners. To do so would involve "restoring" abandoned lands to their former owners. The President now instructed General Howard to reverse his policy and to withdraw Circular No. 13. The Freedmen's Bureau was ordered to persuade the former slaves to abandon their hopes for land—and to sign labor contracts for the coming year with their former masters.

Both blacks and whites knew this was a crucial issue. Each side knew that the key to the future lay not just in legal freedom from slavery but also in the linked questions of land and labor. Whoever was able to own the one would also be able to control the other. Without working on land that belonged to them (or that they could later purchase), the freedmen and their families would be at the mercy of their former owners. And both sides knew that plantation owners would never voluntarily sell their land to blacks. Without land reform, the freedmen could never control their own labor. They would be working under conditions almost identical to those imposed by slavery itself.

The situation was profoundly muddled during the fall of 1865. Most agents of the Freedmen's Bureau (but not all of them) dutifully spent the fall of 1865 trying to extinguish the very hopes they had earlier helped to spread. In reality the cause of land reform was lost. But many freedmen could not bring themselves to believe that they were being betrayed by the very people who had just liberated them.

At this time of mixed and confusing messages, large numbers of Southern blacks came to pin their lingering hopes on the coming Christmas season. Word passed through the African-American community, often spread by Union soldiers, that when Christmas arrived in 1865, the government would provide them with land and the other necessities of economic independence. An ex-slaveholder from Greensboro, Alabama, wrote to his daughter that the Union troops who were stationed near his plantation had assured his former slaves "that our lands were to be divided among them at Christmas," and he added in frustration that they had already ceased doing any work. "Almost all are living along thoughtless of the future" and paying no attention to "what they will do after Christmas, when all will be turned adrift."

It should not be surprising that the freedmen chose to hold such high hopes for the Christmas season, since for African-Americans Christmas had long been associated with the symbolic inversion of the social hierarchy—with grand gestures of paternalistic generosity by the white patrons who had always governed their lives. In 1865 those white patrons happened to be the government of the United States. To intensify black hopes still further, the Thirteenth Amendment to the U.S. Constitution (abolishing slavery) was due to take effect on December 18, one week to the day before Christmas.

Black Refugees Crossing the Rappahannock River, 1862. Even relatively early in the Civil War, before emancipation, many African-American slaves fled their legal places of residence, especially in areas such as this one in northeastern Virginia, where Union troops were located nearby. Note the heavily laden cart drawn by oxen in this photograph. (Library of Congress)

By mid-November 1865, Southern newspapers were publishing stories about these Christmas dreams. One story (titled "The Negroes at Christmas Time") reported that blacks throughout the South entertained expectations of "being furnished, about Christmas, by the Government, with the necessaries of 'housekeeping' . . . waiting in a life of ease and idleness, for the jubilee. . . ." A newspaper in Mississippi reported that "wildly credulous and wildly hopeful of men are . . . awaiting the millennium of the 25th of December, who expect a big division of land and plunder on that day." And the *New Orleans Daily Picayune* editorialized that "it has seemed to be impossible to eradicate from their minds the belief that about Christmas they were to have lands partitioned among them; and their imaginations have been heated with the expectation of becoming landholders, and living as their old masters used to do without personal labor."

Without personal labor . . . a life of ease and idleness . . . awaiting the millennium . . . waiting for the jubilee. For white Southerners these were also code words. What they meant was that many blacks had not returned to work for their old masters at war's end (in fact, the crops of the 1865 season had gone mostly unharvested) and that they were refusing to sign degrading labor contracts with their former masters for the coming season. Alabama landowner Henry Watson reported that "Not a solitary negro in the country has made a contract for next year. The soldiers told them not to make them, that if they did they would be branded and become slaves again!" Their refusal posed a serious threat to the regional economy and especially to the well-being of the planter class.

It also indicated that the freedmen might be politically organized. Whites tended to interpret the hopes of the freedmen as aggressive and threatening, a sign that they were ready to turn to violence. And whites, like blacks, looked to the Christmas season as the time when matters would finally come to a head. Interpretations varied as to precisely how, and for what reason, violence would break out. Some whites thought it would happen spontaneously. An Atlanta newspaper warned that the holiday might start out as a "frolic" but that it would soon turn into something considerably more menacing. Emboldened by alcohol and encouraged by "bad white men," the blacks could be easily "persuaded to . . . commit outrage and violence." A planter from South Carolina told a visiting reporter that "some families will be murdered and some property destroyed," and he concluded ominously, *"It will begin the work of extermination."*

The fears of the one race were commingling in volatile fashion with the hopes of the other. As December approached, an increasing number of Southern whites became convinced that the freedmen were actively plotting an organized insurrection. All across the South, "apprehensions" of such a planned insurrection during the Christmas holidays were reported (and spread) by newspapers. In mid-November a Louisiana newspaper reported that "there is an increasing dread of what may turn up in the future. The negroes are, by some means, procuring arms, and are daily becoming more insolent." Toward the end of the month the *Cincinnati Daily Enquirer* headlined a story "A Negro Conspiracy Discovered in Mississippi" and explained that "a conspiracy had been organized among the blacks, extending from the Mississippi River to South Carolina, and that an insurrection was contemplated about Christmas." Such stories were printed and reprinted by newspapers throughout the South. Some of the rumors were quite detailed. A letter printed in the *New Orleans True Delta* cited a "reliable" report that blacks would collectively revolt "on the night before Christmas" and "wreak their vengeance" on whites whose names had already been chosen. The victims were to be identified to their attackers "by signs and marks placed on each house and place of business"—these marks would consist of coded numbers, as well as the letters X and O "set in chalk marks."

It was largely to the Freedmen's Bureau that there fell the task of persuading the freedmen that Christmas would not be ushering in the "jubilee," that further disruption of the Southern economy would harm them as well as whites, that the signing of labor contracts was now their best available recourse—and that insurrection would be futile. Under orders from President Johnson himself, the head of the Freedmen's Bureau, General O. O. Howard, spent the late fall touring the South in order to communicate these points. On November 12, General Howard sent a policy statement to his staff:

> It is constantly reported to the Commissioner and his agents that the free[d]men have been deceived as to the intentions of the Government. It is said that lands will be taken from the present holders and be divided among them on next Christmas or New Year's. This impression, wherever it exists, is wrong. All officers and agents of the Bureau are hereby directed to take every possible means to remove so erroneous and injurious an impression. They will further endeavor to overcome other false reports that have been industriously spread abroad, with a purpose to unsettle labor and give rise to disorder and suffering. Every proper means will be taken to secure fair written agreements or contracts for the coming year, and the freedmen instructed that it is for their best interests to look to the property-holders for employment. . . .

On another occasion, General Howard warned the freedmen directly that there would be "no division of lands, that nothing is going to happen at Christmas, that . . . [you] must go to work [and] make contracts for next year. . . . [I]nsurrection will lead to nothing but [your] destruction." Most agents of the bureau dutifully (if reluctantly) passed along the word that the freedmen's Christmas hopes were nothing but a pipe dream—or, as a Memphis newspaper put it, "a la mode Santa Claus." Colonel William E. Strong, the bureau's inspector general, addressed a group of Texas freedmen in plain language:

> I have been sent here from Washington, to make a speech to the colored people. I have little to say, and that is in plain words. Winter is coming on—go back to your former masters, work, be obedient, and show that you are worthy of freedom. You expect the Government to divide your late master's lands out to you, and about the first of January you will get buggies and carriages; but you are mistaken. You will not get a cent. It all belongs to the former owners, and you will not get anything unless you work for it. It is true that rations have been given to some of you, but you will not get any more. You have had good masters, I know. I have been through here long enough to find out for myself.

But white Southerners were skeptical about whether such a cautionary message would be heeded by the black community. What was needed, one newspaper argued (in a sarcastic reference to the abolitionist leanings and the New England background of many Freedmen's Bureau officials), was straight talk from "imposing" men "who were born at least one thousand miles distant from Cape Cod." Of course the planters themselves reiterated the message to their ex-slaves. But the slaves would not heed *their* warnings, either. As one Mississippi newspaper conceded, "It amounts to nothing for former masters and mistresses to read these orders to negroes. . . . They do not believe anything we can tell them."

Some whites consciously manipulated the fear of an insurrection as a way of convincing state and federal authorities to allow Southern whites to rearm themselves—and to disarm (and harass) the freedmen. An Alabama official used just such an argument in a letter to the governor of that state: "I am anxious to organize the local company. It is feared the negroes will be troublesome about Christmas unless there is some organization that can keep them in subjection."

But many whites were truly fearful. The mistress of one plantation near Columbia, South Carolina, later recalled how she was terrified by the nocturnal singing that came from what until recently had been her slave cabins—singing that evoked "expectations of a horde pouring into our houses to cut our throats and dance like fiends over our remains."

It is possible that some African-Americans were indeed harboring thoughts of (if not making plans for) a Christmas revolt. But those plans could hardly have amounted to a coordinated conspiracy. What is far more likely is an explanation that places both white fears and black hopes in the context of the intense expectations that normally surrounded Christmas on the slave plantation. For if Christmas was a time when slaves expected gestures of paternalist largesse, it was also a time when slaves were used to acting up. (In that sense, the Atlanta paper may have been shrewd in suggesting that the Christmas insurrection might begin as a "frolic.")

What was happening in late 1865 was that a serious, contested set of political and economic issues—issues involving the radical redistribution of property and the radical realignment of power—chanced to converge with a holiday season whose ordinary rituals had always pointed, however symbolically, to just such a redistribution of property and just such a realignment of power. On both sides of the color line there was a shared mythos about Christmas that made the holiday loom with ominous weight in the watershed year of white defeat and black emancipation.

There was no insurrection. Confrontations, yes—even, in a number of cities, violent riots. The most serious of these was in Alexandria, Virginia, where two people were killed. But it soon transpired that the Alexandria riot was actually initiated by whites and that both victims were black. By December 28 or 29, it was clear that the danger had subsided. "The *ides* of Christmas are past," one Southern paper proclaimed, "without any insurrection of the colored population of the late slave holding states. There is no probability of any combination of freedmen for hostile purposes; neither are they likely to combine, at present, for political or industrial objects." Another paper simply reported that "some cases of collision between blacks and whites occurred on Christmas, but there was no organized demonstration on the part of the former."

It was now possible to reinterpret the events of December 25, to put them back into the old, familiar antebellum categories. Newspapers reassured their readers that such "collisions" as did occur were "isolated" events and that they were not even political in nature but merely a function of old-fashioned Christmas rowdiness—occasioned by alcohol, not ideology. The Virginia correspondent of a Washington newspaper reported with relief that "a few brawls in Norfolk and Portsmouth were the result of whiskey, and had no political significance whatever." "Too much whiskey," claimed one paper; "much bad whiskey," added another; "some colored men, very much under the influence of bad whiskey," chimed in a third. And the newspapers now reported arrests for drunkenness and disorderly conduct by placing their notices in the police log, not the political columns. The racial identity of the offenders now hardly mattered. The *Richmond Daily Whig* reported on December 27 that "Christmas was celebrated in this city with unprecedented hilarity."

> It was more a street than a home celebration. "King Alcohol" asserted his sway and held possession of the town from Christmas eve until yesterday morning. Liquor and fire-crackers had everything their own way. A disposition was manifested to make up for lost time. This was the first real old fashioned Christmas frolic that has been enjoyed in the South for four years. The pent up dissipations and festivities of four Christmas days were crowded into this one day. . . .

By December 29, the *New Orleans Daily Picayune* even chose to use humor as a way of marginalizing the racial content of the violence that had indeed erupted in that city on Christmas day. Under the heading "Every one ought to be eloquent in his own defense," the paper reported that one white man, arrested on Christmas for rowdy behavior, testified in his defense: " 'Your honor, I am charged with being a disturber of the peace. It is a mistake, your honor. I have kept more than a hundred niggers off the streets these Christmas times. May it please your honor, I have a bad cold.' " The man's case was dismissed.

The crisis past, it was now possible for white Southerners to return to the underlying problem—the collective refusal of the freedmen to work for their old masters. That would take care of itself, the *New Orleans Daily Picayune* explained, as the freedmen came to understand that their "true friends" were the Southern planter class, not the Northern demagogues who had falsely promised them land. When that truth at last dawns upon them—as it inevitably will—"they will learn where to learn their own true interest and duty."

The same editorial went on to explain bluntly just what that would mean:

> As the season passes by, without bringing them the possessions they coveted, and the license to be idle, which they expected with them, and they learn that they must look for support to themselves—for the government will decline to help those who do not help themselves—the relations of labor to capital will begin to be freed from one of the most perplexing of the elements that have kept them unsettled; and to adjust themselves upon the natural basis of the mutual dependence of planter and freedmen on justice to each other for their mutual prosperity.

In other words, the freedmen would soon be forced back into virtual slavery. A newspaper in Richmond even resorted to a nostalgic evocation of the old interracial Christmas rituals, along with a rueful acknowledgment that the planters were unable to perform the part of patrons in the gift exchange. Not only would the freedmen fail to receive their masters' land, but they might even have to do without the "usual presents" they customarily received on this occasion. However, that was an aberration, indicating only that the planters were temporarily impoverished, not that race relations had changed:

> Heretofore every one of these four millions of beings expected and received a Christmas present, and partook of the master's good cheer. Now, alas, that former master is penniless, and he who depended upon his bounty is a homeless wanderer. The warm blanket, the cheerful fire, the substantial fare, the

Emancipated Negroes Celebrating the Emancipation Proclamation of President Lincoln. Like the bleak illustration on page 9, this woodcut, which appeared in March 1863 in a French magazine, *Le Monde Illustre,* shows African-American refugees accompanying an ox-drawn wagon (there were also two horses behind the oxen). But the few months that had passed since that earlier photograph made all the difference in the world to these refugees: they were now legally free. (*Le Monde Illustre,* March 21, 1863). (The New York Public Library)

affectionate greetings, and the gifts they have been accustomed to receive at the hands of old and young will, we fear, be sadly missed.

The Richmond editor summed up the prospect by referring to the eclipse of an old tradition—a tradition we have already encountered at the beginning of this story: "The familiar salutation of 'Christmas gift, master,' will not be heard." (That was the ritual in which slaves awakened their masters' families with a demand for gifts.) But the real object of nostalgia here was the *master's* loss, not the disappointment of his former slaves. That point came across clearly enough in the editor's concluding shot, an expression of hope that in another year or so things would be back to normal for the freedmen—"that their future condition may be better than their condition is at present, and that the next Christmas may dawn upon a thrifty, contented and well regulated negro peasantry."

Even now, with the Civil War lost and the black population legally free, the capital city of the Confederacy was continuing to link rituals of Christmas misrule with the maintenance of the antebellum racial hierarchy. A "contented and well regulated negro peasantry" was, after all, just what was needed to sustain a prosperous class of white planters. The cry of "Christmas gift!" would be music to their ears.

AN INTERPRETATION

The story of the "Christmas Riots" of 1865 is a microcosm of the entire period that became known as Reconstruction, the years between 1865 and 1877. It was a period of great hopes for the freedmen, hopes that were dashed, then raised, and then dashed once again.

As we have seen, with the war over, President Johnson quickly placed his highest priority on restoring the states of the late Confederacy to their former place in the federal Union. The new President rescinded Field Order No. 15. With his tacit encouragement, the Confederate states attempted to act as if little had been changed by their military defeat. They passed "Black Codes," requiring freedmen to sign annual contracts (those who refused were subject to arrest by any white man) or stipulating that unemployed blacks had to pay a "vagrancy" fine—and if they were unable to pay the fine, they could be bound out to work for anyone who paid it for them.

The South seemed to be reestablishing slavery in all but name. The defiance of a few states was especially brazen: Mississippi and Texas would not recognize the Thirteenth Amendment, and South Carolina actually refused to nullify its secession ordinance. When the South held elections at the end of 1865 to choose men who would go to Washington to serve in Congress (once again, with President Johnson's approval), the men they chose included former Confederate leaders: more than fifty members of the old Confederate legislature, nine Confederate generals, six members of Jefferson Davis's cabinet, and even the vice president of the Confederacy, Alexander Stephens!

This time they had gone too far, and there was a Northern backlash. To begin with, the Republican-dominated Congress simply refused to seat the newly elected representatives of the ex-Confederacy. Soon President Johnson completely lost control of the process, and Congress itself took charge. Beginning in 1866 it embarked on a program that became known as "Congressional Reconstruction" (to distinguish it from the brief preceding period of "Presidential Reconstruction"). The President vetoed several of the bills that reached his desk, but Congress passed them over his veto. By 1868, Johnson's authority was so low that he was actually impeached by the House of Representatives, and the Senate fell only a single vote shy of the two-thirds majority necessary to convict him, and thereby remove him from office!

The first three years of Congressional Reconstruction, from 1866 to 1869, were the most militant. Bolstered by the 1866 elections, which brought large majorities in both houses for the Republicans (majorities that were, of course, enhanced by the absence of representatives from the Confederate states), Congress embarked on a program designed to make certain that the states of the Confederacy would have to make radical changes before they were readmitted to the Union. Over President Johnson's veto, it passed a Civil Rights Bill and a law granting broader power to the Freedmen's Bureau. The following year, 1867, Congress passed the Fourteenth Amendment, which guaranteed the right of American citizenship to the former slaves and barred states from depriving any citizen of "life, liberty, or property without due process of law." In 1867, too, Congress passed a series of new laws designed to rein in the defiant South. The Old Confederacy was now divided up into five military districts, each overseen by a U.S. general. This military occupation was to be the cornerstone of the new process by which the individual states would be readmitted to the Union. First, the occupying armies were given the task of registering all eligible voters—adult white males who had not been disenfranchised by the Fourteenth Amendment, together with all adult black males. Next, those voters would choose delegates to constitutional conventions, conventions that would draft new state constitutions (those constitutions would be required to ratify the Fourteenth Amendment and to guarantee blacks the right to vote). Third, the new constitutions would be ratified by popular vote. Finally, then—and only then—could regular elections be held for representatives and senators who would at last be admitted as members of the U.S. Congress.

This was the process by which, one by one, the states of the Confederacy actually reentered the Union. By 1869, with black voters playing a central role, every one of the Confederate states had been readmitted—all with Republican majorities. That same year Congress passed the Fifteenth Amendment, which explicitly granted the right to vote to all adult black males. For the first time in Southern history (and, as it happened, the last time for another century), black people were exercising real political power. The African-American community greeted the suffrage with as much fervor as they had earlier greeted emancipation itself. They voted in large numbers, and many of them were elected to office. All in all, fourteen black men were elected to the U.S. House of Representatives and two to the Senate. (On the state level, though, the situation was different: not a single state had a black governor during the Reconstruction years, and only in South Carolina was there ever a black legislative majority.) Still, even this degree of black political power represented a startling change in Southern—and American—life.

Such radical change came about in part because many Northern Republicans were truly concerned with the rights of African-Americans. But it also depended on the support of *other* Northern Republicans, so-called moderates whose support for black suffrage came chiefly from the desire to punish the South for the terrible war it had waged or to make sure that when the Southern states finally *were* readmitted to the Union, the political power of the national Republican party would not be weakened by the election of Southern Democrats. These moderates knew that almost 80 percent of the Republican voters in the South were African-Americans.

In part for this reason, Congressional Reconstruction had its limits. Above all, it addressed not at all the one issue that had been responsible for rumors of the "Christmas Riots" of 1865: the confiscation and redistribution of lands formerly belonging to wealthy white slaveowners. Instead, the legislation of the period of Congressional Reconstruction was focused on black political equality. Despite the efforts of more radical Republicans, it ignored the need for black economic rights. No laws like Field Order No. 15 or Circular No. 13 were ever passed—even though one proposal that would have provided the freedmen with rights in land nearly managed to make it through Congress, only to be dropped at the very end.

In any case, Reconstruction was not to last or even to generate much enduring change. In one state after another during the 1870s, political power fell back into the hands of the Democratic party—into the control of "unreconstructed" Southern whites. The term used by Southern whites to name this process was *redemption* (a word ordinarily used to refer to the ransoming of hostages or, alternatively, to the salvation of souls). But the "redemption" of the South meant the restoration of power to wealthy ex-slaveholders and the subsequent denial of political rights to the black community.

Reconstruction ended for a variety of reasons. In most Southern states, blacks did not amount to a majority of the population. Three of these states—Tennessee, North Carolina, and Virginia—were "redeemed" as early as 1870. And where blacks were more numerous, they were systematically intimidated, notably by the Ku Klux Klan. The Klan (founded in 1866) directed terror attacks against black schools and churches and also against black economic and political leaders. The Ku Klux Klan was responsible for many hundreds of political murders across the South. These attacks were not random; instead, they were part of an attempt to undermine black autonomy and to destroy the infrastructure of the Republican party in the South.

In several states, election times regularly produced something approaching civil war. In Mississippi, the situation in 1875 was so tense that the state's Republican governor asked for federal military help. But by now most Northern Republicans had wearied of the battle. Former Union general Ulysses Grant (who had succeeded Andrew Johnson as President) refused to intervene in Mississippi, declaring that "the whole public are tired of these annual autumnal outbreaks in the South." The result was that the Democrats regained control of Mississippi. By the beginning of 1876 only South Carolina, Florida, and Louisiana remained in Republican control.

The presidential election of 1876 put a final end to Reconstruction. The two major candidates, Republican Rutherford B. Hayes and Democrat Samuel J. Tilden, ended up in an electoral deadlock (Tilden actually won the popular vote). Hayes finally managed to win the election by agreeing to remove all the remaining federal troops from the South—in exchange for the disputed electoral votes of three crucial Southern states. With the implementation of that bargain in 1877, the South was at last fully "redeemed."

Let this story end on a personal note. When I myself was in graduate school, during the 1960s, one of the first books I was assigned to read was about the end of Reconstruction. It was a well-known and respected book with an inspiring title, *The Road to Reunion.* On the front cover of this book was a picture that showed two hands entwined in a mutual handshake. The hands represented, of course, the two sections of the United States that had so recently been at war with each other: the North and the South. What I failed to notice, until a classmate pointed it out, was the color of those two hands. They were both white.

Sources: There is no full-fledged study of the "Christmas Riots"; this story was written mostly from contemporary newspapers. The one article on the subject is Dan T. Carter, "The Anatomy of Fear: The Christmas Day Insurrection Scare of 1865," in *Journal of Southern History,* vol. 42, 1976, pp. 345–364. Useful books include William McFeely, *Yankee Stepfather: General O. O. Howard and the Freedmen* (New Haven: Yale University Press, 1968), and Claude F. Oubre, *Forty Acres and a Mule: The Freedmen's Bureau and Black Land Ownership* (Baton Rouge: Louisiana State University Press, 1978), especially pp. 1–89. The Civil War origins of a potential land-reform policy are discussed in LaWanda Cox, "The Promise of Land for the Freedmen," *Mississippi Valley Historical Review,* vol. 45, 1958, pp. 413–440. A splendid study of the entire period is Eric Foner, *Reconstruction: America's Unfinished Revolution, 1863–1877* (New York: Harper & Row, 1988).

2

BUILDING THE BROOKLYN BRIDGE

Alan Trachtenberg

It took 15 years to build, but when the bridge spanning 1,600 feet of East River between Brooklyn and Manhattan was opened in 1883, it was undeniably one of the great engineering and scientific feats of the age—the equivalent, perhaps, of the development of the atomic bomb in the 1940s, the construction of the nation's system of interstate highways in the 1950s, or the drive to place a man on the moon in the 1960s. But, although these were all entirely public projects, carried out by the national government with public funds, the Brooklyn Bridge was begun and partially built by a private company—chartered, to be sure, by the state government, as nearly all corporations were—but for the most part beyond the purview of the public. Even after the mid-1870s, when legislation recognized that the people deserved a larger role in the project, key decisions were made by corporations and politicians who paid only lip service to the public trust. And so it was altogether appropriate that the opening of the bridge involved bestowing the structure on the public—that is, granting it not to equals but to supposed inferiors. In this and other ways, as Alan Trachtenberg's story reveals, the bridge was a product of a transitional era in American history. It was an era in which large corporations and big factories were still the exception rather than the rule, millions of ordinary Americans worked in the skilled trades, and government played a limited role in encouraging and policing the economy.

But in other ways the bridge looked toward the future, and shunned the past. After generations of sectional conflict, culminating in a traumatic Civil War, many Americans longed for an end to division and discord. They built bridges across the Ohio and the Mississippi. In 1869, they celebrated the joining of the Union Pacific and the Central Pacific railroads at Provo, Utah, and with it the linking of the coasts. And in the aftermath of the disputed national election of 1876, the major parties laid aside the ideological politics and disagreements on questions of race that had helped bring on the Civil War and fostered the bitterness of Reconstruction, and agreed to a historic compromise—the Compromise of 1877—that gave the election to Republican Rutherford B. Hayes and signaled a final end to the involvement of the federal government in helping black people in the South secure their legal and political rights. (Among those who had a hand in this process was Abram S. Hewitt, the campaign manager of the Democratic candidate, Samuel J. Tilden; a few years later, Hewitt would be a featured speaker at the opening of the bridge.) Uniting two land masses in one giant span, the Brooklyn Bridge stood as a symbol of a desire for unity that went well beyond the two cities that stood to gain the most from its construction. The unity embodied in the bridge was not just geographical, but social and economic: the unity of rich and poor, haves and have-nots; and the unity of the unified and uniform national market being created not just by bridges across the Ohio, Mississippi, and East rivers, but by the proliferation of giant corporations.

The story of the bridge is also the story of corruption so far-reaching that even the structure's enormous cables were braided with defective wire. Despite this sordid reality, contemporaries did not succumb to the cynicism that marks the present. Unlike the current generation of Americans, who believe themselves to be at the mercy of dark forces beyond their control, the generation of Americans who built the Brooklyn Bridge saw their creation as a wondrous sign that the world would yield—surely and inevitably—to their knowledge, their expertise, and their desire.

Before the Brooklyn Bridge, which opened to the public on May 24, 1883, ferry boats provided the sole means of crossing the East River between the boroughs of Manhattan and Brooklyn. A leisurely ride, open to fresh breezes as it moved diagonally upstream from the foot of Fulton Street in Brooklyn to its landing near South Street in Manhattan, the ferry offered thrilling vistas of the two shorelines. By the 1850s lower New York had already become a crowded commercial and manufacturing center, its shorelines hemmed with tall-masted ships. While Manhattan had expanded rapidly into a world center of trade, a center of wealth with an increasingly visible population of wage-laborers without personal wealth or property, Brooklyn enlarged at a slower pace. Even at midcentury it retained the look of a village, its residential hills and open spaces tempting many middle-class New Yorkers to seek homes there. The ferry ride seemed to many people, such as the poet Walt Whitman, a native of Long Island and Brooklyn who loved the streets of Manhattan, a perfect way to make the transition from village to metropolis. Whitman's poem, "Crossing Brooklyn Ferry," written in 1856, sang of the beauty of the views, of the sun sparkling on the water, and the pleasure of mingling with the crowds of working people passing to and fro across the river.

But the ferry had its shortcomings. It did not always provide so pleasant and relaxing a ride. Really a tidal strait rather than a true river, the lower East River is often shrouded in fog and churns with treacherous currents, and in winter it can be gorged with jagged chunks of ice. The winter of 1851 to 1852 was notably severe, and voices of exasperation arose demanding relief. Why not throw a bridge over the river, a quicker, surer, more reliable method of getting from one shore to the other? The idea was not new; an East River bridge had been proposed as early as 1811. By the 1840s and 1850s, when the idea revived, Brooklyn businessmen became increasingly serious about the prospect of more reliable and efficient connections with the financial and commercial markets of Manhattan; the growing numbers of people commuting to jobs in New York concurred. But would such a bridge, spanning about a mile between the shores, be feasible? No bridge of such magnitude had yet been constructed anywhere in the world. Most commonly bridges in America and Europe still employed the time-honored materials of wood and stone carved into arches. Recently, engineers had applied iron in the making of trusses, a rigid framework formed of separate members such as bars or rods, to build trestles for railroads. Chain links were employed in America and Europe to suspend roadways from stone towers, as in the Clifton Bridge (1859) at Bristol, England, by I. K. Brunel. But metal had not yet been tested in structures of the magnitude necessary to span the East River.

During that frigid winter of 1852, a German-born engineer, who placed great value on promptness, sat fuming at the inconvenience of being stuck on an ice-bound ferry boat in midstream. John Augustus Roebling began at once to imagine how a bridge might be built to replace or supplement the inefficient ferry. He had been trained as a civil engineer at the Royal Polytechnical Institute of Berlin; blocked in his career by the Prussian bureaucracy, he emigrated to western Pennsylvania in 1831 with a group who shared utopian ideals. They founded the agricultural community of Saxonburg. With the increase in commerce the construction of canals, railroads, aqueducts, and bridges soon became a necessity in the region. Roebling eventually found opportunities to put his training to practical use. By 1849 he had built a few aqueducts and small bridges in cities such as Pittsburgh. He added the manufacture of wire rope to the activities of Saxonburg, and then established a plant near Trenton, New Jersey, for the production of wire to be used in spinning cables for suspension bridges, the form to which he particularly applied himself.

From the beginning of his career Roebling pioneered in developing techniques for building suspension bridges. The form appealed to him for its simplicity and beauty. Combining several distinct elements, the suspension bridge embodied a philosophical principle especially attractive to Roebling. Along with engineering he had studied philosophy in Berlin with G. W. F. Hegel, who taught that opposition or contradiction lay at the base of nature, society, and mind. In a suspension bridge a cable is hung over two piers or towers and then anchored at each shore. The towers and anchorage represent force in compression, solid masses planted firmly on a solid base or ground; the cable, meanwhile, hangs in extension, approximating a catenary curve (the curve formed when you hold, say, a cord at each end and allow it to hang loosely). The entire structure represents, then, opposite forces, compression and extension, in harmonious balance. Using this form bridge builders are able to suspend upwardly curving central spans between the two towers, thus allowing for unhindered river traffic beneath the bridge. With the additional possibility of making such a bridge rigid enough to carry railroad trains, the suspension form seemed to Roebling an ideal solution to America's bridge-building needs.

At the time he was stranded in the ice-bound river, Roebling was at work on just such a railroad bridge over Niagara Falls, completed in 1855. In 1857 he wrote to Horace Greeley, editor of the New York *Tribune,* proposing "a wire suspension bridge crossing the East River by one single span at such an elevation as will not impede the navigation." Greeley responded enthusiastically and the engineer began to sketch his plans. But the time was not yet ripe. After the dramatic success of the Niagara bridge, Roebling was called on to build what would then be the world's longest suspension bridge, between Cincinnati and Covington over the Ohio River, a project that kept him occupied through the years of the Civil War. The bridge opened in 1867. Roebling then turned all his energy to the task of persuading people of wealth and influence in New York and Brooklyn that an East River bridge was both necessary and feasible.

In 1865, just after the Civil War in which his son Washington, also an engineer, served as a Union colonel, Roebling approached several Brooklyn businessmen to see if a private company might be established to recruit public support and money for such a bridge. Roebling preferred to deal directly with private capitalists rather than approach elected municipal officials. His experiences during the 1840s and 1850s taught him that public financing of construction projects often proved inefficient and expensive; politicians, he learned, tended to offer costly contracts in exchange for bribes. As early as 1860 Roebling anticipated similar problems in dealing with the city halls of New York and Brooklyn, and wrote that it was not "desirable to add to the complication and corruption of the governmental machinery of these cities" by seeking their official sponsorship for his proposed bridge.

In fact the problem of financing public projects had proved a complicated matter throughout the "internal improvements" period in the decades before the Civil War. One especially troubling issue concerned the respective roles of private capital and public funds raised by the sale of bonds. The issue centered on the question of ownership and control: Should private people or corporations, for example, be entitled to collect tolls on roads or bridges serving the public interest? The New York–Brooklyn situation was further complicated by the fact that the state government at Albany held final authority over the financing of public projects in both cities. The situation opened room for irregularities and corruption, exactly what Roebling feared.

In 1865 Roebling met with a dynamic Brooklyn contractor, William C. Kingsley, who in turn persuaded State Senator Henry C. Murphy to introduce a bill to charter the New York Bridge Company. The fact that the winter of 1866 to 1867 was one of the severest yet on record aroused popular support for the bill. Passed in April of 1867, the law fixed the capital of the Company at $5 million and endowed it with the power to raise more funds. It also authorized the cities of New York and Brooklyn to subscribe to the capital stock of the Company to the extent of 60 percent. The arrangement thus resulted in a "mixed" enterprise, joining private and public funds in a project too large and costly to be undertaken alone by either the private or public spheres. Yet the Company was chartered as a *private* enterprise, with unlimited control over public funds. The charter allowed the cities to "guarantee the payment of the principal and interest" of Company bonds; yet only by an amendment in 1869 were city officials assured seats on the board of directors, and then only as a small minority. To be sure, the charter gave the cities the right to take full control of the project if they wished, for a price: the full value of "the said bridge and appurtenances," plus $33\frac{1}{3}$ percent of that value, to be paid directly to the Company.

No wonder suspicions arose. They appeared initially because the cities of New York and Brooklyn, and indeed the legislature in Albany, were then under the control of a group known as the Tweed Ring, after its leader, William Marcy "Boss" Tweed. Although not himself a holder of high office, Tweed, like other big city bosses in the post–Civil War era, exercised vast power through a system of graft and favoritism. Elected officials loyal to Tweed or indebted to him for their office, frequently through rigged elections, awarded contracts for public buildings and utilities to contractors willing to "kick back" a certain amount of cash. Tweed came to power in the late 1860s through the local New York Democratic Party club known as Tammany Hall. When the Ring was disbanded and Tweed indicted in 1871, it was estimated that his crew had stolen as much as $30 million. One of the Ring's typical devices for tapping the public purse was to arrange for delays in construction of public projects, resulting in higher expenses padded to include kick backs. The Chambers Street Courthouse was one of their most notorious schemes.

Was Brooklyn Bridge another? Doubts surfaced periodically throughout the lengthy 16-year interval between the approval of the charter in 1867 and the opening of the bridge in 1883. One newspaper listed the bridge among "the seven fraudulent wonders of the New World," and wrote: "Conceived in inequity and begun in fraud, it has been continued in corruption." And indeed, in 1878 Tweed confessed that in 1867 he took a bribe of $60,000 from Kingsley to help push the chartering bill through the legislature, and, further, that the deal allowed Tweed himself to buy shares at an 80 percent reduction, and gave Kingsley a 15 percent cut on all purchases of construction materials. Overpayment to Kingsley, the principal shareholder, had been publicly revealed as early as 1872, at which time the contractor promised to make repayment.

Was the problem merely the greed of evil people, or was the charter itself at fault for allowing a private corporation full control over a public enterprise? The legislative act set no controls over the decisions of the Company, no process of public review. It was an act "to incorporate the New York Bridge Company, for the purpose of constructing and maintaining a bridge over the East River, between the cities of New York and Brooklyn." The law empowered the Company "to purchase, acquire and hold as much real estate as may be necessary for the site of the said bridge," and to fix rates of toll. It also set a handsome limit of 15 percent per annum as allowable net profits for investors. Typical of such private corporations contrived to fund public projects in the antebellum era, the Bridge Company was free of accountability to the public whose funds it solicited. Only the federal government required obedience to any regulation; Congress in 1869 granted that the proposed bridge might receive status as a lawful post road, provided it met standards of height appropriate to river traffic as recommended by a commission of the Army Engineers.

John Augustus Roebling (1806–1869). Roebling's piercing eyes were
perhaps his most memorable physical feature. (Library of Congress)

In May of 1867, the Company appointed John A. Roebling as Chief Engineer.
Given his role in initiating the project, his reputation as the world's master-
builder of the modern suspension bridge, and his known doggedness in seeing
his projects through to the finish, the choice was inevitable. The 61-year-old
engineer, industrialist, inventor, and philosopher applied himself at once to
surveying the site and drawing up plans. By September his report to the New
York Bridge Company was ready.

Roebling wrote the report not only as a plan but as an argument to meet
any possible objection to his design. In the preface he set the tone of cold,
irrefutable logic mixed with appeals to civic pride.

> The contemplated work, when constructed in accordance with my designs,
> will not only be the greatest Bridge in existence, but it will also be the greatest
> engineering work of this continent, and of the age. Its most conspicuous fea-
> tures, the great towers, will serve as landmarks to the adjoining cities, and they
> will be entitled to be ranked as national monuments.

Roebling's report addressed an audience primarily of businessmen, shareholders
in the New York Bridge Company who wanted to know if the bridge would pay
in the short and long run. Most telling were his strategic comments about a change
about to occur on completion of the Union Pacific Railroad (which occurred 2 years
later, in 1869) in America's commercial relations with the world, a change of vast
significance for business, especially for the commercial interests of New York:

This change will at first be very slow, but the breadth and depth of the commercial channel will increase with every coming year, until at last the city of New York will have become the great commercial emporium, not of this continent only, but of the world.

The East River bridge, he argued, would be a major link within a national and eventually international system of transportation, communication, and trade, and would enhance the flow of wealth into the coffers of New York. One use of the spaces within the approaches to the bridge, he suggested, might be as vaults for accumulated gold and silver.

The public was more concerned with safety than profits, and justifiably so, given the unprecedented length of the bridge and its several novel features. Roebling's report envisioned a bridge almost 1,600 feet in length, one half again as long as the Cincinnati Bridge. It would replace that bridge as the longest in the world. The roadway of the new bridge, to be held in place by four cables 16 inches in diameter, would bear 18,700 tons. A multipurpose roadway, it would allow for cable car traffic and horse-drawn traffic in side-by-side lanes in each direction, and an elevated promenade for pedestrians above the noise and dirt of the vehicular traffic; with benches and lamps and balconies around the base of each tower, the promenade was Roebling's particular pride. The granite towers, each pierced with two immense Gothic arches, would rise 276 feet and compete with the spire of Trinity Church on Wall Street as the tallest structures in New York at the time.

Roebling explained that theoretically "any span inside of three thousand feet is practicable." The only vital question was safety, and this was simply a question of cost. At this point Roebling estimated a cost of $7,000,000 exclusive of the amount necessary to acquire the land, about $3,800,000; the final cost (including the land) was closer to $15,500,000, largely a result of modifications such as raising the height of the bridge and increasing its width. Roebling explained the system of supports he had devised which, if followed according to his plan, would guarantee complete peace of mind about the stability of the structure:

> To guard against vertical and horizontal oscillations, and to insure that degree of stiffness in the flooring which is absolutely necessary to meet the effects of violent gales in such an exposed situation, I have provided six lines of iron trusses which run the whole length of the suspended floor from anchor wall to anchor wall. . . . I am not disposed to underrate the great force of a severe gale. . . . But my system of construction differs radically from that formerly practiced, and I have planned the East River Bridge with a special view to fully meet these destructive forces. It is for the same reason that, in my calculation of the requisite supporting strength, so large a proportion has been assigned to stays [diagonal wire supports, like the stays on sailing vessels] in place of cables. . . . The supporting power of the stays alone will be 15,000 tons; ample to hold up the floor. If the cables were removed, the Bridge would sink in the center but would not fall.

The confidence that speaks here, that the bridge would survive all imaginable traumas, persuaded the Company. But in order to obliterate all remaining doubts (absolute thoroughness being his style), Roebling convened a select board of eminent engineers to review his plans in meticulous detail, and to examine his other bridges on site. Their unanimous confirmation of his design and calculations in May, 1869, signaled that work could then commence.

Within 3 weeks there occurred a trauma Roebling's report did not anticipate: his own sudden death, the result of injuries when a boat crushed his right foot on the Brooklyn wharf as he surveyed the position of the main piers. He died horribly, of lockjaw, on July 22, 1869. The bridge had taken its first and most tragic toll.

Responsibility for the project now passed to Roebling's 32-year-old son, Colonel Washington A. Roebling, appointed in August to supervise construction of the bridge according to his father's design. A graduate of Rensselaer Polytechnic Institute and an engineer with the Union Army of the Potomac during the Civil War, Colonel Roebling's main experience had been as assistant to his father on the Cincinnati Bridge. In October, presumably to free his mind from all distractions but actual construction, the Executive Committee of the Company relieved Roebling of all responsibility for the awarding of contracts—and indeed of attending meetings unless specifically requested to—and appointed William Kingsley as General Superintendent precisely to perform that function. Colonel Roebling assembled his own youthful staff of assistants, whose age averaged 31 years in that year. E. F. Farrington, who had worked on the Cincinnati Bridge, was later named Master Mechanic. Among Colonel Roebling's responsibilities was the presentation in writing of exhaustive periodic reports on progress in construction to the Executive Committee of the Bridge Company.

Roebling's first dramatic step as Chief Engineer was the launching of the pneumatic caisson for the Brooklyn tower. While on a European tour after the Civil War, directed by his father to learn as much as he could about new building techniques, the younger Roebling studied closely the use of caissons for laying firm foundations for weight-carrying piers. Caissons are essentially large airtight boxes tapered into an open cutting edge on the bottom. For excavating the floor of the East River Roebling contrived a caisson with a timber roof 15 feet thick. Weighing 3,000 tons and measuring 168 feet long and 102 feet wide, his caissons would be the largest ever used. An enormous chamber using compressed air, the caisson was designed to provide breathing space for the workers, known as "sand-hogs." They dug away at the mud and clay on the river bottom while masons laid the granite of the tower on the roof of the caisson. The weight of the stone combined with the digging sunk the caisson through the river bed to bedrock, where the finished tower would find absolutely solid support.

An intricate construction balancing a number of elements—an airlock into the work area, supply shafts, water shafts to make possible the removal of debris without loss of air pressure—the caisson was as hazardous as it was essential. If the water shafts were not kept tightly sealed, blowouts could shower stone and mud into the air. There was the constant threat of fire; explosives were often used to break up compacted materials on the river floor, and because electric lighting was not yet available, lighted candles served as illumination. One newspaper account described them as "submarine giants [which] delve and dig and ditch and drill and blast." They performed their work around the clock.

For the sand-hogs the work was often unbearable. "The work of the buried bridge-builder," wrote one newspaper, "is like the onward flow of eternity; it does not cease for the sun at noonday or the silent stars at night. Gangs are relieved and replaced, and swart, perspiring companies of men follow each other up and down the iron locks, with a dim quiet purpose." The interior was hot, the air foul, and sickness quite common. Work shifts were reduced to 4 hours or less, at $2 a day for ordinary labor, increased to $2.25 a day as the caisson reached deeper below the river floor. The work crew for the Brooklyn caisson numbered 112 during each of the day shifts, and 40 at night; the New York caisson crew ranged from 50 to 125 during the day and 15 to 30 at night. Work crews for this relatively unskilled but extremely punishing labor were recruited mainly from Irish, German, and Italian immigrants, many undernourished and desperate for work. The turnover was enormous: 2,500 different workers for the Brooklyn caisson alone. In 1872, the entire New York caisson crew walked off the job, insisting on higher pay for such hazardous, fatiguing work: $3 for a 4-hour day. The strike lasted several days before the men settled for less of an increase than they demanded.

No serious accident occurred until December 2, 1870, when a burning candle ignited the oakum caulking lining the inside of the caisson; the fire was driven by air pressure deep into the caisson, but out of sight. Colonel Roebling rushed to the scene and helped fight the fire for 7 hours, until he lost consciousness. The caisson was finally flooded, and the water expelled some days later. The "Great Fire" caused no deaths but delayed work for 3 months. By March 1871, excavation for the foundation was finally complete, the caisson filled with concrete, and the Brooklyn tower began to rise layer by layer, the first above-water sign that a monumental bridge was in the making. In October of 1871, the New York caisson was launched, and it reached bedrock in May of 1872.

Just at this time, in 1871, Tweed's empire began to unravel. Spearheaded by upper-class figures like Abram Hewitt, son-in-law of the revered Peter Cooper and partner in his iron business, and Samuel Tilden, who would be the Democratic candidate for president in the controversial election of 1876, a movement developed against the corruption and fraud that was draining the city's resources. Campaigns in the press and public meetings led to Tweed's downfall and arrest. Called "reformers," such upper-class figures sought to replace corrupt party politicians with qualified political figures drawn from the class of "the best men," the rich, the cultivated, the socially respectable. Investigative committees appeared in both cities, and in June of 1872, the old Tammany representatives on the Bridge Company were replaced by figures with names like Vanderbilt, Aspinwall, Appleton, Hewitt, names of older wealthy and propertied families who viewed themselves as responsible for the civic health of the cities. Hewitt himself led an internal investigation on behalf of the Bridge Company, which resulted in exacting Kingsley's promise for repayment of funds, redefining his responsibilities, and essentially exonerating him and the Company of any fundamental wrong-doing. A report by Colonel Roebling assured the directors of the Company that all contract awards had resulted in the finest materials at the lowest costs; this proved decisive in dispelling the suspicion that the physical integrity of the bridge had been compromised.

The issue of accountability remained unresolved. Was the Company truly a *private* corporation, like a railroad company, free to do its business however it wished? Or, considering that the cities of New York and Brooklyn were both large stockholders, did the Company not have a special responsibility to the publicly elected bodies of those cities? These more critical views were advanced by Demas Barnes, chairman of the Committee of Investigation appointed by the board of the Company, who issued a separate report calling for board meetings open to the public. Hewitt and others agreed the charter should be amended to dispel ambiguities in the original document that made it seem an invitation to theft, but no changes were made at this time. After 3 years of construction, the jailing of Tweed, and the chiding of Kingsley, the Bridge Company remained under a cloud of suspicion.

Then another sudden event profoundly affected the project. At the end of May 1872, after spending long hours in the depths of the New York caisson, Colonel Roebling collapsed. Mysterious symptoms of paralysis had already attacked a number of the workers, and Roebling had asked a medical specialist to investigate. Little was then known about the sudden onset of caisson disease or "the bends," an affliction of the nervous system caused by living and working too long under atmospheric pressure much greater than normal. By 1883 the surgeon of the Bridge Company reported 110 cases of the disease, three of which were fatal, at that point. Roebling himself remained paralyzed the rest of his life, perhaps the result as much of a nervous disorder exacerbated by the strain of his position as of the bends. He never returned to the construction site, although he retained his position, making detailed drawings and writing out meticulous instructions that his wife Emily delivered to his staff, and following progress at the site through binoculars from his home nearby.

In June of 1874, the state legislature passed an amendment urged by Barnes requiring that the Bridge Company accept membership on its board of a significant number of representatives of the cities of New York and Brooklyn. The following year the legislature dissolved the original New York Bridge Company altogether; the bridge was now understood to be "a public work, to be constructed by the two cities for the accommodation, convenience and safe travel of the inhabitants." The change made a difference in the public's relation to the still ghostly structure slowly materializing into the shape of a bridge before their eyes—although the personnel of the actual day-by-day management remained the same.

What remained of the construction tasks were the completion of the towers and the two anchorages on each shore to which the four central cables would be attached. The Brooklyn tower reached its full height in May of 1875, and the New York tower in July of 1876. Then the real artistry of labor would commence—the spinning of the four main wire cables. By August of 1876, with the saddles designed to carry each cable over the top of each tower in place, the spinning itself began.

Apart from the drama of scandal and injury, the building of the bridge had provided another kind of daily spectacle: sheer physical work of the most demanding kind among new, odd-shaped pieces of machinery such as caissons, hoisting machines, cable saddles, the intricately arranged anchor plates. Through the press and firsthand observation, the public witnessed the skilled work of carpenters, machinists, masons, blacksmiths, sand-hogs, iron-workers, and seamen engaged to lash the diagonal stays to the vertical suspenders attaching the roadway to the main cables. At one time as many as 600 men worked together at the site, making this perhaps the largest outdoor concentration of a multiple-craft work force yet assembled in one site in the United States. It is impossible to say exactly how many workers lost their lives; estimates range from 20 to 40. Others suffered lasting effects from caisson disease.

None of the skilled tasks attracted as much attention as the spinning and wrapping of the four main cables. On August 14, 1876, a scow ran a rope across the river, which was then hoisted into position over and between the towers. Not until then could the structure be called a bridge. Now two cities were joined, or as a newspaper headline put it, "wedded." The next dramatic step would be for someone to cross the structure on the rope, and Master Mechanic E. F. Farrington was selected to make the historic venture in a boatswain's chair. The date was Friday, August 25, 1876, and to the cheers of workers swarming on the towers, crowds on both shores and on boats in the river, Farrington made the first trip via bridge from Brooklyn to New York; it took 22 minutes. A footbridge of slatted wood was soon added for less adventuresome passage by workers and occasional visitors.

Just when the end of construction seemed in sight, further delays caused by charges of corruption and recrimination among the principals almost brought the entire project to a permanent standstill. By September of 1876, with the actual spinning of the cables ready to proceed, Roebling submitted his detailed specifications for cable wire to the Executive Committee, as required, for their approval. Abram Hewitt, vice president of the board and himself a dealer in wire, judged the specifications "eminently wise," but insisted that no bids for the wire contract be accepted from any person or firm with a direct interest in the bridge. He declared that he himself would refrain from bidding, and he insisted that Colonel Roebling, an owner along with his brothers of the cable wire manufactory his father had founded near Trenton, be especially forbidden from entering a bid.

Indignant, the incapacitated Chief Engineer instantly penned an angry letter of resignation. In his reply to the board's refusal of the resignation, Roebling wrote:

> I was publicly and specifically singled out by name by Mr. Hewitt, as if I had spent my whole life in concocting a specification which I alone could fill or as if I were a thief trying to rob the bridge in some underhanded manner and against whom every precaution should be taken.

Washington Roebling became an increasingly remote and mysterious figure after his illness. He is depicted here, on the occasion of the opening of the bridge, as a somewhat grim but thoughtful Victorian gentleman, restraining his emotions of pride as his father's bridge nears completion. (*Frank Leslie's Illustrated Newspaper*, May 26, 1883). (The New York Public Library)

Then he added:

> As you seem to be deeply impressed with Mr. Hewitt's action in declining to become a competitor for this wire, I desire to say that his magnanimity is all a show, as the firm of Cooper and Hewitt have no facilities for making the steel wire, and if you receive a bid from Mr. Haigh of South Brooklyn, it will be well for you to investigate a little.

And to be sure, the award was made to a Mr. Haigh of South Brooklyn.

Roebling's suspicion of venality on the part of Hewitt deepened as a result of another disastrous event. In July, 1877, spinning of the cables began by means of a huge mechanical device that traveled from anchorage to anchorage, taking about 10 minutes each way. In November a wire snapped, and on examining the broken pieces, Roebling judged the wire, supplied by Haigh, to be defective. The following June two men were killed when another wire rope snapped, raising even more public anxiety about the safety of the bridge into which some $9 million had already been poured. Among New York Democrats who wished to distance themselves as far as possible from the lingering taint of Boss Tweed, a number agitated to cut off all further money to the bridge. On July 22, 1878, Roebling presented board president Henry Murphy with physical proof that Haigh had been supplying the bridge with consistently defective wire, fraudulently returning rolls of wire that had been already rejected on regular inspection. Roebling informed Murphy that "the distressing point of this affair is that all the rejected wire which has come to the Bridge has been worked into the cables, and cannot be removed." The Executive Committee chose to hush up a scandal potentially fatal to the completion of the bridge; it may be, though no certain evidence exists, that Haigh's friends, including Hewitt, insisted on the cover-up. The board was relieved to hear from Roebling, however, that because the cables had been designed with a sufficient margin of safety (six times beyond the tensile strength actually required), the damage was inconsequential—although the Chief Engineer did require that each cable be strengthened by 150 more strands of tested wire. On October 5, 1878, the spinning of the cables was completed—"this desirable event," remarked Master Mechanic E. F. Farrington, "was marked by no demonstrations, save the sounding of a steam whistle, and the raising of a United States flag on the Brooklyn tower." In later years Haigh was imprisoned in Sing Sing for passing bad checks.

The tasks that remained consisted chiefly of assembling the complex roadway, tying it into place by the diagonal stays John A. Roebling had designed to guarantee the security of the span, and the construction of the terminals at either end of the bridge. But in the face of continuing threats from New York to close out its funding of the project and rapidly deteriorating relations between an increasingly impatient and snappish Roebling and the board of directors, almost 5 years would elapse before these relatively undemanding objectives could be accomplished. As late as 1882 a move was launched to replace the Chief Engineer because of his physical disability; his position was saved partly by the eloquence of his wife in pleading with the board against such a move. When Abram Hewitt, a congressman and future mayor of New York, wrote to Colonel Roebling requesting information he might use in his Opening Ceremonies oration, the blunt-speaking engineer replied: "It took Cheops twenty years to build his pyramid, but if he had had a lot of Trustees, contractors and newspaper reporters to worry him, he might not have finished by this time. The advantages of modern engineering are in many ways overbalanced by the disadvantages of modern civilization."

On May 24, 1883, the Hon. J. S. T. Stranhahan, a "leading citizen" of Brooklyn, and a trusted trustee of the New York and Brooklyn Bridge Company from the start, presided over the Opening Ceremonies of the Great Bridge—a public drama the central act of which would be performed by officials: the bestowing of the bridge directly to the people. As the souvenir publication of the Opening Ceremonies put it, "It was a holiday for high and low, rich and poor; it was, in fact, the People's Day."

The Brooklyn anchorage in the process of construction. Note the bundles of wire that compose each of the four central cables, yet to be wrapped in this image, and the footbridge to the left. The picture conveys the awesome power of the cables and the security of their attachment to the anchor plates (not themselves visible in the print). Note, too, the artist's rendering of the great height of the Brooklyn tower against the low skyline of 1870s Manhattan. (*Harper's New Monthly Magazine*, May 1883). (Library of Congress)

It was a day of great local pride, in Brooklyn especially. One store window displayed a sign that became a kind of motto of the day: "Babylon had her hanging gardens, Egypt her pyramid, Athens her Acropolis, Rome her Athenaeum; so Brooklyn has her Bridge." Crowds in the tens of thousands—crowds of local citizens swelled by visitors from nearby towns, cities, and countryside, arriving by train, boat, and wagon—thronged along the thoroughfares in both cities leading to the bridge.

Local as the immediate meanings were for the participants, the day was also national in significance, as the red, white, and blue flags and banners everywhere, including at the summits of each of the bridge's two towers, indicated. As Brooklyn Mayor Seth Low himself said, "it is distinctly an American triumph. American genius designed it, American skill built it, and American workshops made it." Thus the meaning of the presence of the chief of state himself, President Chester A. Arthur—a New Yorker, as it happened, the dapper former head of the New York Custom House and a great favorite among the crowds. The President played a role strictly symbolic—he had no speeches to make, no awards to present—only to be there in recognition of the national import of such a bridge. As the New York *Sun's* reporter quipped: "the climax of fourteen years' suspense seemed to have been reached, since the President of the United States of America had walked dry shod to Brooklyn from New York."

Above all else it was a festive day—happy crowds scouting the celebrities, buying souvenirs, and awaiting with mounting excitement the evening's promised climaxes of the day's public drama. At midnight the bridge was to be thrown open to pedestrians, and many positioned themselves for that unique experience: their first walk "dry shod" across the East River. But first, as darkness fell, came the moment that thrilled the crowd beyond all description—the contours of the bridge suddenly illuminated by strings of electric lights! And as the lights just as suddenly went out there followed the most spectacular display of fireworks (as it was described) ever witnessed on the continent—bursts of color which cast an eerie, many-hued glow on the bridge that was destined, even from its start 14 years earlier, to hold a special place in the life and the imagination of the wedded cities, of the nation, and of the world. The age of steel and electricity had begun.

AN INTERPRETATION

A week later, on Memorial Day, the entire roadway was thrown open to pedestrians. Someone shouted, "The bridge is falling!" and twelve people were trampled or crushed to death in the ensuing panic.

That event provides another reminder, bloodier than others, of the entire ambiguous history of this bridge, in which the idealism of visionary engineers collided with the sordid realities of everyday political life in American cities of the Gilded Age. The meaning of the building of the Brooklyn Bridge in just these years, 1869 to 1883, must include recognition of such ambiguities, the complexities of motive, the many-dimensioned facets of behavior that comprise the larger truths of all historical "stories." It must also include the implicit threat to life and limb of modern construction projects based on new technologies.

In the case of the Brooklyn Bridge one is tempted to celebrate the creative acts of the Roeblings, their staffs, and the nameless corps of skilled and unskilled workers responsible for the actual building of the bridge, and to push aside the parallel story of Tweed and Kingsley and Haigh. Yet the two stories are not simply parallel; they are intertwined as tightly as the wire strands of each of the main cables. To interpret the building of the bridge in historical perspective, all aspects of the related stories must be taken into account.

One lesson of the bridge lies in the contradictions within the age's definitions of private and public, between profit and the common good, which the story of its construction brings to the surface. The scandals themselves, whether substantiated or merely suspected, reveal a period of great uncertainty, of public distrust of the hierarchy of political and social figures above them, a deep suspicion of wealth and power. Writing in 1883 in the month before the opening of the bridge, the radical social critic and future opponent of Abram Hewitt in

Someone shouted, "The bridge is falling," and a
catastrophe followed. The rendering here emphasizes the
great crush of an urban crowd in panic, an image calling
to mind other mass scenes of the period, including those
of soldiers firing at fleeing strikers during the 1877 Great
Railroad Strike. Certainly such images helped plant the
thought that city crowds held the menace of turning into
fearsome mobs. (*Frank Leslie's Illustrated Newspaper*,
June 9, 1883). (The New York Public Library)

the mayoralty election in 1886, Henry George, described the bridge as an
emblem of the underlying contradiction in modern America between wealth
and poverty, private profit and public good:

> We have brought machinery to a pitch of perfection that, fifty years ago could
> not have been imagined; but in the presence of political corruption, we seem as
> helpless as idiots. The East River Bridge is a crowning triumph of mechanical
> skill; but to get it built a leading citizen of Brooklyn had to carry to New York
> sixty thousand dollars in a carpetbag to bribe a New York alderman. The
> human soul that thought out the great bridge is prisoned in a crazed and bro-
> ken body that lies bedfast, and could only watch it grow by peering through a
> telescope. Nevertheless, the weight of the immense mass is estimated and
> adjusted for every inch. But the skill of the engineer could not prevent con-
> demned wire from being smuggled into the cable.

The building of Brooklyn Bridge represented a historical transition, though what the future would hold was not at all clear at the time. John A. Roebling envisioned the bridge as a monument to the commercial and civic greatness of the cities. The story of corruption attending the making of the bridge certainly seems to sully that vision. But perhaps, in the face of the confused relations between private and public interest during this era, there was no other means of achieving Roebling's vision. The period of construction was dominated by the ruthless conviction on the part of the wealthy and powerful that they deserved whatever rewards they could achieve for themselves, whatever the social consequences. As it did for Henry George, the venality and mismanagement implied by the full story of the building of the Brooklyn Bridge would provide a useful lesson for progressive reformers in the following two decades, who proposed a more positive, direct, and responsible role by government in serving the collective interests of the public.

The bridge in 1883 represented an initiation into a significantly different way of life. Consider its contrast with the old ferry boats. With their tempo keyed to currents and weather, the ferries belonged to a relatively simple era ending throughout the United States; their replacement by Brooklyn Bridge in the 1880s would dramatically signal the arrival of modern metropolitan and industrial life. By its size and scale, Brooklyn Bridge stood for something radically new in scale— and in danger, as the Memorial Day disaster vividly proclaims. Yet the bridge also represents a transitional moment, one that still retains a connection with the craft traditions of earlier, preindustrial modes and systems of labor. The abilities of the workers at the site of construction represented highly skilled crafts in working with stone, wood, and metal, and also collective coordination, willingness to take risks for the sake of performing a job, feats of personal courage. The mechanics, masons, sand-hogs, carpenters, surveyors, and the unskilled as well, all remind us that the built world was made by the refined and intricate manual efforts of human labor. The human features of the story of the bridge bring that great structure to life as a lesson in the coordination of mental and physical abilities.

Finally, we can interpret the building of the Brooklyn Bridge as the manifestation of a conception, originally conceived by John A. Roebling and adapted by many others, of a harmonious metropolitan culture. Roebling thought of the bridge as a symbol of civic greatness, the towers standing as thresholds to the centers of each city. The elevated promenade was a special pride of the elder Roebling, signifying amenity; a respect for pauses in busy days, for the pleasures of open-air walks; and the unequaled visual excitement of the views of New York harbor. The least practical or profitable of the features of the bridge from the point of commercial utility, the promenade remains one of the bridge's most eloquent gifts to the cities it joins. To the future it offered an ideal of urban experience tied into, shaped and formed by, and yet not overwhelmed by modern technology. Brooklyn Bridge emerges from an age steeped in corruption and greed, as a hope for the possibility of community. It is for this that later generations have most valued Roebling's masterpiece. We can interpret the building of the bridge, then, as a story of a clash of values reshaping America as the nation entered the modern era.

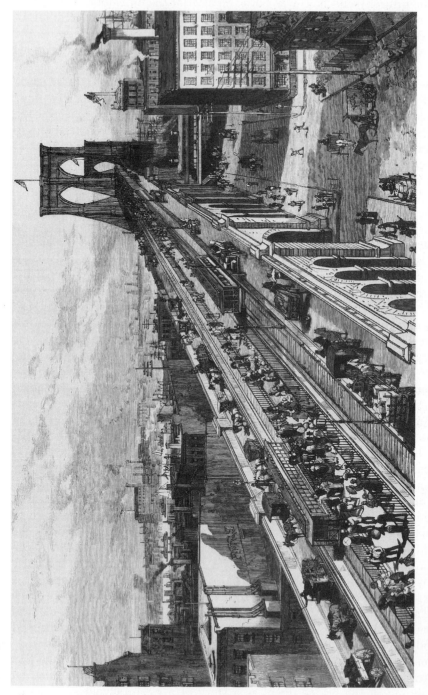

A panoramic view of the completed bridge, including its cable railroad trains, from the New York side. Note the variety of traffic: horse and wagon, electric-powered cable car, and pedestrian. (*Harper's Weekly*, June 2, 1883) (The New York Public Library)

Sources: The most convenient source of information about the building of the bridge, the personalities of the figures involved, the delays and scandals, is David McCullough, *The Great Bridge* (New York: Simon & Schuster, 1972). An interpretation of Brooklyn Bridge, including the art and literature it inspired, can be found in Alan Trachtenberg, *Brooklyn Bridge: Fact and Symbol* (New York: Oxford University Press, 1965). Most important among contemporary documents is John Roebling's initial plan, published as *Report of John A. Roebling, C. E., to the President and Directors of the New York Bridge Company, on the Proposed East River Bridge* (Brooklyn: Eagle Book and Job Printing Department, 1870). Other contemporary sources useful in reconstructing the story of Brooklyn Bridge include: William C. Conant, "The Brooklyn Bridge," *Harper's New Monthly Magazine* (May 1883); E. F. Farrington, *Concise Description of the East River Bridge* (New York: C. D. Wynkoop, 1881); and Montgomery Schuyler, "The Bridge as a Monument," *Harper's Weekly,* (May 24, 1883). The Roebling Collections at the Library of Rensselaer Polytechnic Institute include an indispensable collection of manuscripts and drawings by both John A. and Washington Roebling. The Special Collections of the Library at Rutgers University include a rich collection of personal manuscript materials and drawings by John A. Roebling, including his philosophical writings. Lewis Mumford sensitively places the Roeblings and the bridge in *The Brown Decades* (New York: Harcourt, Brace, & Company, 1931). Alan Trachtenberg's *The Incorporation of America: Culture and Society in the Gilded Age* (New York: Hill & Wang, 1982), provides an overview of the post–Civil War period.

3

THE HATFIELD–McCOY FEUD

Altina L. Waller

Most Americans first heard about the Hatfields and the McCoys in early 1888, while reading newspaper accounts of the New Year's Day midnight raid of eight Hatfields on the home of Old Ranel McCoy, deep in the Appalachian hills of Pike County, Kentucky. Old Ranel had escaped, but 2 of his 16 children were dead. When big-city reporters discovered that this was only the latest in a series of incidents dating back at least a decade, an interpretation of the feud emerged: Two almost barbaric backwoods families, remote from the institutions, restraints, and refinements of civilization, were locked in a petty, senseless, and deadly vendetta.

Altina Waller's story of the Hatfield–McCoy feud has a very different message. The events she describes take place in a region already undergoing economic modernization and laced with legal institutions that the Hatfields and the McCoys often used to resolve their differences. Neither were the principals in the struggle—whether Old Ranel McCoy, Devil Anse Hatfield, or Perry Cline—the rustic hillbillies depicted in the popular press of the day. Even the families involved were not the monolithic blocs inscribed in the legend of the Hatfields and the McCoys.

The Hatfields and the McCoys were feuding, then, not because they were too isolated, but because they were not isolated enough. Rendered in these terms, the tale seems less like a rural curiosity and more like other stories that might be told of the same period: the story of the Sioux Indians on the Great Plains "reservations," fleeing before the new railroads, the mining companies, and the white man's unquenchable thirst for land; the story of the central Illinois farmer, selling his wheat in world markets and in competition with the newly opened granaries of the Dakotas; or the story of the proprietor of the general store in Kearney, Nebraska, who in 1890 is about to find out that his customers have direct access to the goods he sells through the Sears & Roebuck mail-order catalog. These stories are all stories of penetration: the penetration of railroads onto the Plains; the penetration of the Sears company into rural homes; and—in the case of the Hatfields and the McCoys—the penetration, first of timbering companies and then of railroads and coal-mining operations, into the Tug River Valley. The story of the Hatfields and the McCoys is very much a part of the central phenomenon of the age: the rise of big business.

But simply because we have a new way of understanding the feud does not mean that the old way has nothing to teach us. Indeed, the mythic perspective on the conflict, embodied in the photograph on p. 56, must have been especially compelling to have lasted so long and to have been fashioned in apparent defiance of the evidence. What, then, might account for the origin and persistence of the older view? One possibility is that the myth was fashioned by sophisticated eastern city dwellers, for whom the primitives of rural Kentucky and West Virginia functioned as an "Other"—defining what they were not and did not want to be. But it is also possible that a nation engaged in a headlong rush toward the urban, industrialized, and bureaucratic world of the twentieth century relished the image of the gun-toting mountaineer as a sign that something still remained of the unfettered, intuitive freedom of the American frontiersman. Like Bonnie and Clyde in the 1930s, and Butch Cassidy and the Sundance Kid in the cinematic myth of the 1960s, the Hatfields and the McCoys were the objects of our collective desire.

In the 1870s Randolph and Sally McCoy lived on the Blackberry Fork of Pond Creek in Pike County, Kentucky. Randolph and Sally were in their 50s and presided over a family of 16 children. Their log home was typical of this mountainous region; called a "dog-trot" house, it consisted of two log houses connected by a kind of passageway or breezeway. In other external circumstances as well the McCoys were not very different from other families living in this remote region. Their log house was built on the side of a mountain with beautiful vistas on every side but little land that was level enough for cultivation. However, by supplementing farming with hunting and fishing, they managed to support themselves well enough.

Randolph and his wife Sally were the third generation of white settlers in this little community nestled along the tributaries of the Tug River. Despite the fact that the Tug River was the boundary between the states of West Virginia and Kentucky, Randolph and Sally, like most residents, considered *both* sides of the river their "neighborhood." Randolph—or "Old Ranel," as he was commonly known—had grown up just across the Tug in Logan County, Virginia (which became Logan County, West Virginia, when the new state was created in 1863). Only after he married Sally did the two move to the Kentucky side, so many family members and friends still lived on the West Virginia side. The river was not an obstacle to this sense of community; it was shallow and could be forded easily on horseback and often on foot as well.

On a fall day in 1878, Old Ranel McCoy made his way down the steep mountain trail that traversed the ridge between the headwaters of Blackberry Creek and then followed the road down Pond Creek. Near the banks of the Tug River the road passed the home of Floyd Hatfield. Despite the Hatfield name, Floyd was also related to the McCoys—he was married to Old Ranel's niece. Passing by Hatfield's barnyard, McCoy noticed to his chagrin that the hog pen contained a sow and her pigs that Old Ranel was sure belonged to him—they had been missing for weeks. Enraged, Old Ranel hurried off to the nearest Justice of the Peace where he lodged an official complaint. Despite the fact that the Justice of the Peace was also a Hatfield—a common name (as common as Smith in other parts of the country) on both sides of the Tug River—Old Ranel did not worry about getting fair treatment. The judge, William Anderson

Hatfield or "Anse," was also the minister of the local church, universally liked and trusted by everyone in the community. Even in his judicial capacity he was respectfully referred to as "Preacher" Anse.

Having listened to Old Ranel's tirade against Floyd Hatfield, Preacher Anse now faced a dilemma. He had known Old Ranel McCoy all his life so he was well aware that the old man had developed quite a reputation for malicious gossip. In one instance many years before, Old Ranel's own cousin had filed a suit against him for a slander; apparently Old Ranel had spread rumors about this cousin's sodomy with a cow. However, this official complaint was unusual; over the years, most Valley residents simply tried to avoid or ignore Old Ranel as his loose tongue rarely caused any real harm. The name by which he was familiarly known, "Old Ranel," conveyed something of the affectionate tolerance with which he was regarded. But now, Old Ranel's accusation of theft could not be easily dismissed. Hog theft, or indeed, any kind of theft in this small, isolated, closely knit community was a very rare and thus a very serious crime.

Worse, by accusing Floyd Hatfield of hog theft, Old Ranel was also indirectly challenging not only Floyd himself but the powerful figure of yet another Hatfield who lived across the Tug River in West Virginia. This Hatfield was, in fact, a second cousin of Preacher Anse who bore exactly the same name, William Anderson Hatfield. Although this repetition of names may sound confusing to outsiders, people who lived in the Tug Valley never had any problem distinguishing between the two. Although both were about the same age, tall and commanding in appearance with prominent noses, piercing dark eyes, and black beards, they had distinct personalities and played entirely different roles in the community. If "Preacher" conveyed the strong yet essentially gentle nature of the William Anderson Hatfield who lived on the Kentucky side, then his namesake who resided in West Virginia had a sobriquet that encapsulated *his* history and reputation. The West Virginia Hatfield was known as "Devil" Anse. Some in the community claimed he earned the sobriquet as a precocious child; others insisted it was a result of his brave, if sometimes foolhardy behavior as the leader of a guerrilla band during the Civil War; still others pointed to his accomplishments as the best marksman and horseman in the Valley or even his open contempt for religion in a community that took religious values very seriously. But wherever he got the name, he acquired it long before the feud began.

Old Ranel McCoy must have been just as conscious as was Preacher Anse that his tale of hog stealing would be considered not just an accusation of Floyd Hatfield but of Devil Anse Hatfield as well. This was not so much because Floyd shared the same surname (remember that Hatfield was as common a name as Smith or Jones) but because he was known as a loyal employee in Devil Anse's logging business. Because Old Ranel talked so much, everyone in the community was aware of his long simmering animosity toward Devil Anse and his timbering business. And, given Old Ranel's record of slander and gossip, local residents could be expected to be skeptical about the accusation. Yet local judicial traditions were strong and could not be easily ignored; Preacher Anse would not, indeed could not, dismiss Old Ranel without a hearing.

THE TUG VALLEY

Tug River

Pond Creek

Blackberry Fork

Home of
Daniel McCoy

McCoy
boys killed

Schoolhouse

Mates Creek

First home of
Anse Hatfield

Thacker Creek

Grapevine Creek

Devil Anse's
second home

Val
Hatfield
home

Home of
Ranel McCoy

Election Day
fight

Hatfield Creek

Blackberry Creek

Peter Creek

Home of
Asa Harmon
McCoy

KEY

Tug River

Creeks

Creeks that dry up part of the year

Mountain Ridges

N

The Tug Valley. (Reprinted, by permission of the publisher, from *Feud: Hatfields, McCoys, and Social Change in Appalachia,* by Altina L. Waller. Copyright © 1988 by The University of North Carolina Press.)

True to his reputation for fairness, Preacher Anse came up with a diplomatic solution. Calling for an immediate trial, he chose an evenly balanced jury; six Hatfields and six McCoys. In a clever maneuver on his part, one of the McCoys he chose to serve on the jury—Selkirk McCoy—was a nephew of Old Ranel's but, like Floyd Hatfield, was a member of Devil Anse's timber crew. With such divided loyalties, Preacher Anse hoped, Selkirk would vote on the side of truth and who could complain? And Selkirk did, indeed, vote with the Hatfields; Old Ranel lost the case and Floyd kept the sow and pigs.

Although Preacher Anse's strategy was initially successful, in the long term it was this court case that began the escalation of a long simmering animosity between Devil Anse Hatfield and Old Ranel McCoy from the realm of neighborhood name calling into a bizarre series of murders, ambushes, and pitched battles. These events not only shocked the community but gripped the attention of a nationwide audience, contributing in no small way to stereotypes of mountaineer lawlessness and violence that persist even to the present. Yet there was more to it than petty family grievances. America's most famous feud occurred at the very moment that economic modernization was about to destroy forever the rural isolation of the southern mountains.

This photograph of Devil Anse Hatfield probably was taken about the time of the feud. The jacket, tie, and Confederate medals indicate Devil Anse's pride in his role in the Civil War and his respected status in the community. (West Virginia and Regional History Collection, West Virginia University Libraries)

The history of the feud also reveals something of the capitalist transformation of Appalachia.

In the 1870s the Tug River community was still completely rural; it had no towns, no market center, no newspaper, not even a county seat. This meant that whenever a land transaction needed to be registered, a marriage license applied for, or taxes paid, a long and arduous journey was required. It was approximately a 30-mile trip by foot or horseback over rough mountain trails, either south to Pikeville, the county seat of Pike County, Kentucky, or north to Logan, the county seat of Logan County, West Virginia. The trip was physically exhausting and time-consuming and most people avoided it; they raised most of their own food—corn, potatoes, vegetables, cows, and pigs, voted in their own election districts within the valley, took their boundary disputes or other legal problems to the local Justice of the Peace and attended church only once a month when the circuit preacher made his rounds. For help in times of distress or sickness and for entertainment they depended on each other. It was a community more normally characterized by the stability of cooperation than by the divisiveness of conflict.

For the Tug Valley, even the Civil War—so divisive in many communities—reinforced community solidarity. During that conflict, despite its location straddling the boundary of two Union states, the people inhabiting the Tug Valley were almost unanimously loyal to the Confederacy. Ruled by state governments loyal to the Union and surrounded by Yankees (especially to the south in Kentucky, where the county seat of Pikeville was Yankee dominated) the Tug River was not spared the violence of war. A Union force under James Garfield (later President of the United States) invaded the Valley and burned the county courthouse in Logan, not because of any hostile actions taken by the residents, but simply because they were known Confederate sympathizers. When Devil Anse Hatfield formed a guerrilla band known as the "Logan Wildcats" as a defense against the Union Army and Yankee guerrillas who raided the Valley from places like Pikeville, almost every young man in the community served. Randolph McCoy, later Hatfield's nemesis in the feud, collaborated with the Logan Wildcats. Even when Randolph's brother, Asa Harmon McCoy, one of the very few Union sympathizers in the Valley, was killed, presumably by the Logan Wildcats, there was no legal action taken nor is there any legendary evidence that Old Ranel attempted any retaliation. The absence of conflict over this incident suggests community solidarity against Yankee traitors. Devil Anse and all those who served in the Logan Wildcats, were universally regarded as heroes.

If the Tug River community weathered the Civil War without serious internal conflict, it was not so harmonious in the postwar era when a very different set of problems emerged. One was the land itself. The terrain was so rugged that only one-third could be cultivated. This fixed supply of land severely limited economic opportunity for the younger generation. Tug Valley families were large, six to eight children on average. Devil Anse Hatfield, for example, had 13 children, while Old Ranel McCoy had 16. When these children grew to adulthood and required land, farms became smaller and located in more remote hollows. Indeed, the census schedules indicate that many young people could never hope to acquire farms. Between 1850 and 1880 the percentage of landless families rose dramatically from 35 to 50 percent. In a traditional culture in which land was essential not only for economic survival but for self-esteem and social status, this change had profound implications. But despite this declining economic opportunity, family ties remained strong, so much so that they constituted the second problem. Children expected to settle down near their families and were extremely reluctant to move out of the region. Changing economic circumstances had transformed a cultural asset—strong family bonds—into an economic liability.

In the 1870s and 1880s the hardship created by this demographic crisis had the potential of being partially offset by a new economic opportunity—one that did not require leaving home and family—the demand of industrialized America for timber. Although large-scale timbering was not feasible because of a lack of efficient transportation, the farmers of the Tug Valley, soon after the Civil War, had begun to supplement family farming by cutting small amounts of timber and floating it to market in the nearest urban centers of Cincinnati and Cattlettsburg.

Both Old Ranel McCoy and Devil Anse Hatfield engaged in the timbering business, with very different consequences. McCoy's involvement in marketing timber was to cause such serious family conflict that his parents lost their farm and were eventually divorced. In a court deposition, Old Ranel's mother explained how this came about:

> ... about eleven years ago [1867] as near as she recollects, said plaintiff [Daniel McCoy, Randolph's father] went into what is generally termed the timber business, that is cutting and hauling saw-logs for market, and . . . cut a huge quantity of timber upon lands . . . other than his own, and when remonstrated with by this respondent [Margaret McCoy, Randolph's mother] for doing so great a wrong and one that would involve him in a law-suit and eventually break him up, he became very angry with said respondent and has ever since acted towards her with a coolness and indifference that he never manifested before that time.

Unfortunately for Margaret McCoy's family, her prediction about the lawsuit and the "breakup" came true. Paying off the court ordered damages led to loss of the farm and the destruction of the family; Old Ranel's parents were divorced in 1871. Old Ranel himself escaped relatively unscathed economically because his wife had inherited a farm from her father. Yet he did not fare so well socially or psychologically. Old Ranel became notorious as a gossip and a complainer.

Devil Anse Hatfield, on the other hand, thrived on timbering. Undaunted by his lack of resources, Devil Anse, in a bold move, borrowed money and organized a company—a company rooted in family and neighborhood relationships. Of the approximately 30 men he hired, about half were kin, including his brothers Valentine, Ellison, and Elias; his brothers-in-law, John, Moses, and Tom Chafin; his sons, William Anderson (or "Cap") and Johnson (or Johnse); and assorted nephews and cousins (like Floyd Hatfield). Not all Devil Anse's relatives approved of Devil Anse or the timbering business; his youngest brother, Pat, refused to become involved in timbering or the later feud. Needing more men than the family could or would provide, Devil Anse hired more than half of the timber crew from neighboring families, not necessarily related, men such as Selkirk McCoy and his two sons, Lorenzo and Albert; the Whitt brothers, Dan and Jeff; the Christian brothers, Dan and Moses; and the Staton brothers, Bill and John.

However, despite Hatfield's enterprising spirit, he still lacked the large amounts of forested land required for success. That obstacle was overcome when, as the result of a lawsuit against his nearest neighbor Perry Cline, Hatfield gained possession of a large tract of prime timber land. Although some aspects of the case remain puzzling because of incomplete court records, the broad outlines are clear. In 1872, Devil Anse sued Perry Cline, claiming that Cline and others had cut timber from Hatfield's land. Settling out of court 5 years later, Cline turned over to Devil Anse 5,000 acres of land—his sole inheritance from his father. In a startling reversal of social roles, Cline had been impoverished while Devil Anse became one of the wealthiest men in the Tug Valley. Cline, now without farmland to sustain himself or his family, moved south across the mountain ridge to the town of Pikeville, Kentucky.

Devil Anse, entrenched with an unusually large parcel of land and a prosperous timber company, embraced the role of entrepreneur. He made contracts with local merchants, boldly sued them when disagreements arose, and instituted numerous lawsuits against his own neighbors when they dared trespass on his land. In an environment in which freedom to hunt, walk, or ride wherever one wished had been assumed, residents were shocked to discover that cutting one tree or trespassing on Hatfield land could land them in court where they stood to lose their own farms or animals. Although Hatfield certainly did not win most of these cases, the 5,000 acres of the "Cline tract" kept his timber crew busy. Hatfield had succeeded where Old Ranel McCoy had failed. But what Devil Anse won in profits and economic power he lost in friendship and good will. Worse, he angered his neighbors by demonstrating contempt for community values— values that associated such worldly pursuits as self-interest and profit with the Devil. "You can say," Devil Anse once declared, "that I belong to no church except the church of the world. You can say . . . I belong to the Devil's church."

Paradoxically, the opportunities provided by the timber market had accomplished what even the Civil War had not done: set neighbor against neighbor and seriously disrupted community and family harmony. In this newly competitive context, Devil Anse with his entrepreneurial maneuvering and flaunting of his success towered like a lightning rod, attracting the ill feelings of his neighbors. He seemed to be the most obvious example of just what happened when selfish competition replaced cooperation. Ironically, it was Old Ranel McCoy, whose family had been so severely scarred by greed and dishonesty in the timber business, who was the first to openly challenge the Hatfields. Old Ranel's accusation of Floyd Hatfield for theft was that challenge. The hog trial, then, was more than simply an argument over the possession of a sow and pigs. It threatened to expose community fault lines of such depth that most residents instinctively recoiled from the prospect.

Before the railroads and the mechanization of timbering, oxen, horses, or mules were used by family-based logging crews to cut timber in the mountains. (West Virginia and Regional History Collection, West Virginia University Libraries)

At first, Preacher Anse's strategy worked; although Old Ranel vociferously complained and attempted to persuade some of his kinsmen (there were many who lived nearby) to take some action against Devil Anse and his family, none would. When even his wife urged acceptance of the verdict, Old Ranel, grumbling, agreed. But in the long term the matter was far from settled. The younger generation—a few of Old Ranel's nephews and sons and some of Devil Anse's timber employees—continued to insult and harass each other, sometimes engaging in out-and-out brawls. Finally, two of Old Ranel's nephews killed a Hatfield timber employee. Arrested and tried in a West Virginia court, where Devil Anse Hatfield's older brother was the judge, the two McCoys were acquitted on grounds of self-defense. It was an unexpected verdict favorable to the McCoys but it did not cool the feud.

In the summer of 1880, McCoy hostility was refueled when Roseanna McCoy, the dark-eyed, 21-year-old daughter of Old Ranel McCoy, and Johnse Hatfield, Devil Anse's son, fell in love. Disowned by her father, Roseanna moved in with the Hatfield family and was soon pregnant. However, Johnse was not a faithful lover; he spent most of his time away, flirting openly with other women. Hurt and angry, Roseanna fled to the household of her Aunt Betty. Although Old Ranel was furious and, despite tearful appeals from his wife, would not allow his daughter to return home, he did not instigate any violence against the Hatfields.

It was Old Ranel's son, 26-year-old Tolbert, who seized the leadership in pursuing a vendetta against the Hatfields. Tolbert had spent most of his life subjected to Old Ranel's repeated tirades on the subject of Hatfield knavery. He had watched as his cousin Perry Cline lost his land to Devil Anse. He harbored vivid memories of the family humiliation at the hog trial. Now his sister had been "stolen" and then abandoned by Johnse Hatfield. Yet the Hatfields' arrogance seemed to bring them prosperity, admiration, and respect, while Tolbert himself faced a bleak future. Although he was 26 years old, a husband, and soon to be a father, Tolbert McCoy was hired out as a farm laborer with negligible prospects of obtaining his own farm.

Tolbert formulated a plot to have himself deputized by the Pike County sheriff so that he could arrest Johnse for some trumped up charge like carrying a concealed weapon or violating the liquor tax law. He ambushed Johnse on the Kentucky side of the river and would have hauled him off to the Pikeville jail had not Roseanna, still in love with Johnse, discovered the plan and informed Devil Anse. Devil Anse surprised Tolbert escorting Johnse, at gunpoint, toward Pikeville and retrieved his son without violence. In the process, however, Devil Anse treated Tolbert like a bad boy who needed spanking—taking away his gun and administering a tongue lashing that was profoundly humiliating. Tolbert never forgot it.

On election day in August of 1882, Tolbert McCoy, according to his friends, was drunk and "looking for trouble." At first his hostility seemed unfocused. Badgering a neighbor for repayment of an old debt, he disregarded repeated warnings from the local constable and Preacher Anse to cease his belligerent behavior. Finally, Ellison Hatfield, a brother of Devil Anse and partner in the timber business, intervened. Ellison Hatfield was a big man, a Confederate war hero much admired by the young women of the Tug Valley and full of his own importance. Challenging Tolbert's drunken antics, he is reputed to have shouted, "I'm the best goddammed man on earth!" Electioneering festivities came to a sudden halt in stunned silence. Enraged, Tolbert seized a knife and lunged at Ellison even while screaming at his brothers for help. Two of them rushed to his side and the three McCoys attacked the powerful, massively built, but unarmed, Ellison Hatfield. Before the bystanders could untangle the feudists, the McCoys had stabbed Ellison Hatfield more than two dozen times as well as fired several shots into him. And although he was not dead, it was difficult to imagine that Ellison would survive for very long.

A strange drama followed. Devil Anse Hatfield had not been present that day so a shocked community seemed to hold its breath until Ellison's brothers were notified. What would they do—especially if Ellison died, as he was likely to do, of his severe wounds? Once again, as in the hog dispute, Preacher Anse Hatfield took charge of the situation. He began by urging Tolbert McCoy and his brothers to submit to arrest and go quietly to jail in Pikeville. When Tolbert protested, saying they would rather fight, Preacher Anse painted such a graphic picture of what was likely to happen when Devil Anse arrived on the scene that the three McCoys meekly submitted.

But it was not Devil Anse who came after the McCoys. It was his older brother, Valentine, who took the initiative. Valentine Hatfield was a Justice of the Peace in West Virginia and, like Preacher Anse, his counterpart in Kentucky, he was a respected elder statesman. The next morning it was the venerable Judge Valentine Hatfield who crossed the river into Kentucky in pursuit of the three McCoy sons and the constables. He finally caught up with the party only a few miles down the rugged trail to Pikeville. At the trial, one of the constables described the scene that ensued:

> I was one of the guards, guarding the McCoy boys when Wall [Valentine's nickname] came to us he said that all he wanted was that the boys should stand the civil law. That he had not slept any the night before and was tired and worn out and that he wanted them to go down to the mouth of the creek to have a trial. That he wanted to be near his brother [Devil Anse] and wanted to get the evidence of Dr. Rutherford and old Uncle Wall Hatfield. [Dr. Rutherford was the local physician and Uncle Wall was one of the oldest, most respected members of the community.]

Without apparent resistence the constables capitulated and agreed to return to the Tug Valley with their charges. Once there Preacher Anse made another effort to mediate the explosive situation. He invited Valentine and Devil Anse (who had finally appeared on the Kentucky side of the Tug River) along with the McCoys and the constables to have dinner with him. Apparently he tried to persuade the Hatfields to allow the McCoys to face trial in Pikeville, that justice would indeed be accomplished there. Needless to say, both Hatfield brothers were skeptical, for Pikeville was not part of their world; they had long memories going back to Civil War days when Pikeville was the center of Union loyalty, a headquarters for the Union Army and the place where Union guerrillas were outfitted to raid the Tug Valley. Moreover, Devil Anse's old enemy, Perry Cline, had become a powerful figure in Pikeville politics; he certainly could not be counted on to see that the McCoys faced justice for their crime. Still, Valentine seemed more inclined to consider this alternative than Devil Anse who, growing impatient, stomped out into the front yard and ordered "all Hatfields to line up." It was his way of announcing that the argument was over; he intended to take the McCoys back to West Virginia and find out whether his brother was still alive before any decisions would be made.

Once in West Virginia, Devil Anse converted an abandoned schoolhouse (near the present Matewan, West Virginia) into a makeshift jail. Here he stationed some of his followers as guards while sending others off to inquire about Ellison's condition. When he learned that Ellison was still alive Devil Anse informed Tolbert and his brothers that if Ellison died, so would they; if Ellison survived, they would be returned to the constables for trial in Pikeville. In the all-night vigil that followed, Devil Anse allowed Tolbert's wife and mother to visit the prisoners while Devil Anse and Valentine questioned witnesses about the fight and debated their next step.

Forty-eight hours after the fight, Ellison Hatfield died. Despite some disagreement in the family about killing the McCoys, Devil Anse could not be dissuaded from his ultimatum. He and about 20 of his followers (including Valentine) took the McCoys back to the Kentucky side of the Tug River, tied them to some pawpaw bushes on the banks of the river, blindfolded them and in an execution ritual, shot all three. It was the first time that Devil Anse Hatfield had engaged in feud violence. By the next day, a horrified community became aware of the gruesome retribution.

In spite of this unusual violence, however, most people in the community seemed unwilling to take any action against Devil Anse. Once again Old Ranel attempted but could not persuade any of his relatives or neighbors to take up arms against the Hatfields. Although Tug Valley residents may not have approved of Devil Anse, many of them had actually seen the three McCoys kill Ellison Hatfield in an unfair fight before dozens of witnesses. Thus, although indictments were issued in Pike County for the 20 Hatfields who had killed the McCoys, no attempt was made to serve the warrants or make arrests. The Sheriff of Pike County made a terse note on the back of the warrant issued for the arrest of Devil Anse and his supporters: "Not found," and no further action was taken for fully 5 years.

Indeed, it is likely that the feud would have ended in 1882, and the world would never have heard of the Hatfields and McCoys, had it not been for the actions, 5 years later, of Devil Anse Hatfield's old nemesis, Perry Cline. Cline's career in Pikeville, after the loss of his inheritance to Devil Anse and his flight from the Tug Valley, had been a successful one. By 1887 he was a lawyer and sheriff of the county and belonged to the small circle of businessmen and politicians who wielded power in Pikeville. Rumor had it that as a friend and political supporter of Kentucky's newly elected Governor, Simon Buckner, Cline's power extended beyond Pikeville to the state capital.

Not only was Cline now in a position of power, but in the intervening 14 years since he had left the Tug Valley, his resentment toward Devil Anse for the loss of his property had grown more acute. In 1886 and 1887 it was obvious that the value of his lost property was about to skyrocket. First, in 1886, the Norfolk and Western Railroad announced its intention to build the "Ohio Extension" from Virginia to the Ohio River. But the building of the railroad was only the beginning; the very next year, 1887, the Kentucky legislature published the results of a geological survey that confirmed discovery of extensive seams of high quality coal in the Tug Valley. The geological survey was more than a routine report; it was also a public relations document through which the legislature signaled its plans to actively recruit investment by Eastern capitalists. Cline was only beginning to understand the extent of the economic boom about to engulf the entire region.

It was in this frame of mind, then, that Perry Cline listened to his old Uncle Ranel one cold winter day in the year 1886. Old Ranel had ridden over the mountain ridge to relate, once again, the tale of Hatfield crimes. In the 4 years since the election day fight and the killing of his three sons, Old Ranel had many times brought his complaints to Cline, who listened sympathetically but took no action. This time, however, Cline was more attentive. Although the most recent incident described by Old Ranel was not clearly part of the old feud, Cline perceived his opportunity to strike back at Devil Anse Hatfield. Yes, Perry Cline said to old Uncle Ranel, he would approach his friend the Governor about reinstating the arrest warrants against Devil Anse and the 20 men who had taken part in the execution of the McCoys. For the first time in 4 years Old Ranel rode back across the mountain ridge a happy man, while Cline began to marshal support from his influential friends.

By the following summer, Perry Cline had succeeded in persuading the Governor to revive the 5-year-old indictments against the Hatfields and actively prosecute the case. Just how he accomplished this, what arguments he used, it is impossible to know as no one involved kept any records or directly stated their reasons. All we can do is surmise from the circumstances surrounding the meetings. If the Governor did feel indebted to Cline, his inclination to go along with the request was probably strengthened by a desire to make Kentucky appear to be a law and order state, especially as recent national publicity about several other Kentucky feuds had created a violent image for the state. Newspapers in the state were already lamenting the inhibiting effect that feud violence might have on potential capitalist investment in the rich coal mining region, and the Hatfield–McCoy feud, although not active at the moment, was located in the most highly visible region for attracting coal investors. Whatever his reasons, the Governor issued official rewards for the capture of the Hatfields and began legal proceedings to extradite them from West Virginia.

The Governor's action had the effect of reactivating the feud, this time pitting the power of the state of Kentucky against Devil Anse Hatfield and his supporters. Back in Pikeville, armed with the authority of the Governor, Cline recruited a posse to cross the state boundary into West Virginia and, ignoring the extradition process, captured his first Hatfield supporter. Ironically, this first "Hatfield" captive was none other than Selkirk McCoy, who had served on the hog trial jury and voted with the Hatfields. This intervention by the state government was a shocking departure from the local autonomy of county government. The first response of Devil Anse Hatfield, however, was not violence, but bribery. He tried to buy off Perry Cline by offering him $250 to stop the posse raids and rescind the rewards. Cline initially agreed and accepted the bribe but then continued to send his posse across the border.

Next Devil Anse attempted a political solution. He approached the Governor of West Virginia, E. Willis Wilson, through a friend and political crony, John B. Floyd. Floyd had grown up in the Tug Valley and knew Hatfield and his family well. Both Floyd and Wilson were sympathetic to the Hatfields' dilemma because of their politics. Both men belonged to a faction of the Democratic Party that defended the interests of farmers and working people against wealthy businessmen and capitalists. They perceived the mountain farmers of the Appalachian region as victims who were losing their land to railroad and coal companies and rapidly being reduced from independent yeomen to wage laborers. Wilson spent his entire political career fighting big corporations and trying to protect his constituents from such exploitation. He advocated state control of the railroads and reasonable levels of taxation for absentee corporations which controlled West Virginia's valuable mineral resources. An idealist, he was the last of a vanishing breed in late-nineteenth-century politics. In fact, he was the last Governor of West Virginia to actively oppose corporate domination of West Virginia's politics and economy. When Wilson heard from John Floyd of the Hatfields' history of legal and economic difficulties with Perry Cline, and Cline's influence with the Governor of Kentucky, he was willing to consider the possibility that the Hatfields, too, were victims. He delayed signing the extradition papers by requesting further information from Governor Buckner of Kentucky.

But for some of Devil Anse's supporters, including his sons Cap and Johnse, none of this was enough. Cap came up with a plan to get rid of the people who had caused their problems—the family of Old Ranel McCoy. He proposed burning down the McCoy home in a midnight raid that would destroy all potential witnesses against them. It was a desperate solution, so shocking to most Hatfield supporters that they refused to be involved.

But Cap Hatfield was so infuriated (and probably frightened) that he ignored all advice to the contrary, even his father's. Just past midnight on January 1, 1888, accompanied by only eight of the Hatfield group (Devil Anse not among them), he led the attack on Old Ranel's home on the Blackberry Fork of Pond Creek. This was the infamous New Year's Day raid in which two of Old Ranel's children were killed—both shot as they attempted to run from the burning house—and his wife Aunt Sally McCoy was beaten when she tried to reach her dying daughter in the snow. Old Ranel and the other children escaped and made their way to Pikeville where Perry Cline took them in. Meanwhile, the Hatfields realized with horror that the whole idea had been a tragic blunder, one that far from resolving anything, would only exacerbate the trouble.

It was this incident that catapulted the feud into national attention as Perry Cline and his friends seized the public relations offensive by circulating press releases to Kentucky newspapers, which were then picked up by papers all over the country. The first newspaper item that focused national attention on the feud was headlined, "A MURDEROUS GANG—A TERRIBLE TRAGEDY PERPETRATED BY DESPERADOES—MOTHER AND SON MURDERED WHILE FATHER AND DAUGHTER ESCAPE A FIERY GRAVE." During the next 6 months, the names Hatfield and McCoy became household words all over America, as newspapers from Maine to California sensationalized every detail and reported every rumor as though it were fact. Reporters from Pittsburgh and New York City arrived on the scene and attempted to interview anyone remotely connected with the two families but received most of their information from Perry Cline. *New York World* reporter T. C. Crawford rushed into print a book on the feud entitled *An American Vendetta: A Story of Barbarism in the United States*. It was only the first of many sensationalized accounts.

Cline was not content with a journalistic war, however. He stepped up his raids into West Virginia during the month of January and managed to capture eight more Hatfield supporters, including Justice of the Peace Valentine

Hatfield. In the process, two Hatfield supporters were shot and killed. The final violent confrontation came at the end of January when a Hatfield posse met a Cline posse and engaged in a quasi-military skirmish. It became legendary as the Battle of Grapevine Creek.

Now alarmed by violence in the Tug Valley, Governor E. Willis Wilson of West Virginia was willing to admit that he could have misjudged the situation. If so he was ready to take drastic action by sending in the militia to keep the peace. He even urged Governor Buckner to do the same. Before giving the order, however, Governor Wilson sent a personal emissary to the Tug Valley to investigate. The report returned by the special investigator assured the Governor that the violence was not as severe as had been rumored. It also, however, substantiated his earlier belief that the Hatfields were victims. "I visited all the Hatfields," stated the investigator, "and found them to be good, law-abiding citizens who have the respect and confidence of everyone in the neighborhood."

This information confirmed that of Wilson's trusted political ally, John Floyd, who argued that the trouble had only arisen because Perry Cline had decided "he would stir up the thing again and make some money out of it, knowing that the Hatfields owned some good property." Convinced of Cline's culpability in the affair and infuriated that the state of Kentucky was violating extradition procedures by kidnapping and jailing West Virginia citizens, Governor Wilson went on the offensive. Refusing to sign the extradition request, he issued formal rewards for the arrest and capture of members of Cline's posse who had killed the two Hatfield supporters.

But Governor Wilson was still not satisfied. There were important moral and legal principles involved, he thought, and he intended to pursue them at the highest possible level. Convinced that Governor Buckner and the state of Kentucky had illegally "invaded" West Virginia to capture its citizens, Wilson filed writs of habeas corpus for the Hatfields in the federal district court in Louisville. This meant that the Sheriff of Pikeville had to produce the eight Hatfields in the Louisville court for a determination as to whether they were being illegally held in the Pikeville jail. When the appointed day arrived for the hearing, Governor Wilson himself, accompanied by John B. Floyd, appeared to argue West Virginia's case.

Although the district judges ruled against West Virginia and sent the Hatfields back to Pikeville to stand trial, the case was appealed to the United States Supreme Court where it was heard in May of 1888. However, the Supreme Court also decided in favor of Kentucky, arguing that states possessed only "limited sovereignty" and therefore could not seek redress with habeas corpus to reclaim citizens who had been kidnapped. In effect the Court ruled that it did not matter *how* the accused Hatfield supporters came to be in Kentucky—once there, the authorities could legally arrest them.

While these legal proceedings were in process, actual violence between the Hatfields, McCoys, and Cline had ended with the Battle of Grapevine Creek, but the rewards offered by both states brought into the Valley a number of bounty hunters, usually members of private detective agencies such as Eureka and Baldwin–Felts, intent on scouring the mountains for anyone remotely resembling a feudist. Fear and suspicion of strangers mounted as local residents, who were, after all, most of them related to the Hatfields and McCoys, could expect to be accosted, beaten, or even killed in the manhunt. Newspapers, employing sensational rhetoric, played up the violence and attributed every encounter between a Tug Valley resident and a detective as a feud incident directly caused, not by outside bounty hunters, but by the violent and lawless nature of mountain culture itself.

Ironically, Perry Cline had contributed to this growing national perception that *all* Appalachians were, as he said of the Hatfields in a letter to Governor Wilson, "outlaws" and desperadoes who had been "in arms" since the Civil War, the worst "merauders" [sic] ever who would not live "as citizens ought." Further reinforcing the stereotype, Cline spread the rumor that Valentine Hatfield, Devil Anse's older brother and long time respected county judge, had "five wives and thirty-three . . . children" and had "peculiar ideas of polygamy." Without any evidence other than Cline's word, the *New York Times* repeated this false story, reporting that the "fact" of Hatfield's five wives made it "evident that a strong course of common schools, churches, soap and water . . . is required before these simple children of nature will forbear to kill a man whenever they take a dislike to him." This latest "vendetta," declared the *Times*, ". . . shows the purely savage character of the population." In a strange twist of events, the hillbilly stereotype produced by the feud was to obscure to history the role played by Devil Anse as an ambitious, and typically American, entrepreneur.

As the Hatfields became the target for every private detective in the East, Devil Anse Hatfield decided that enough was enough and retreated. With nine of his supporters lodged in the Pikeville jail, and private detectives waiting to ambush him at every turn, Devil Anse concluded that life on the banks of the Tug had become too dangerous. He sold the hard won 5,000 acres for half what it was worth to an agent for a group of Philadelphia capitalists. All through the 1880s this agent had been buying up the lands of local farmers in anticipation of the railroad and coal mines that would soon open up. Most farmers were completely unaware of the plans then being made that would soon make their forested slopes much more valuable. But he had not been able to persuade Devil Anse, who was far too independent and stubborn to sell. Now, however, with the threat of arrest by detectives, Devil Anse sold the land for half its value and moved his family back away from the Tug boundary to Main Island Creek near the town of Logan, where he built a virtual fortress on the side of a mountain.

Within a year of his move, at about the same time as Devil Anse's brother Valentine and other supporters were being tried in Pikeville, the railroad was built right through his former land and the town of Matewan sprang up where the three McCoys had been killed in 1882. Although the Pikeville trials led to the deaths of two (Valentine Hatfield died in prison, while Ellison Mounts was hanged in February of 1890) and the life imprisonment of the others, Devil Anse was never captured or extradited. Safe on his mountain, Devil Anse

Ellison Mounts was a Hatfield feudist and the only one to be executed by the state of Kentucky. His hanging on February 18, 1890, was the last such public spectacle in Pike County. (Altina Waller)

outlived Old Ranel McCoy, who died in a fire in 1914 and Perry Cline, who had a heart attack in 1891 at the age of 42. In 1921 Devil Anse's death of old age was overshadowed in the press by the outbreak of a series of bloody wars between mine workers and private police employed by the coal companies. Progress, it seems, had not brought peace to Appalachia.

AN INTERPRETATION

The Hatfield–McCoy feud traditionally has invoked images and stereotypes of ignorance, violence, and family loyalty gone berserk. Derogatory stories and jokes about Appalachian mountaineers continue to be acceptable today, at a time in which there is sensitivity to insults directed toward blacks, women, Indians, and other minority groups. Even middle-class Americans whose roots are in the Southern mountains frequently accept these negative assumptions and feel ashamed of their background.

Yet in many ways the world of the Hatfields and McCoys was not at all unusual. The feuding families were part of a traditional farming community, like farming communities located in New England, upstate New York, Pennsylvania, and small farm areas of the South in the antebellum era. Extensive kin networks defined individual identity and status in the community as well as economic activity and local government. Community self-sufficiency and autonomy predominated, but there was never a complete absence of commerce with surrounding regions or isolation from larger political issues at the state and national levels. The complex family relations manifested in the story of the feud could apply to almost any region before the Civil War. Appalachians, then, initially were not so different from most Americans; why then did the violence of the late-nineteenth-century erupt and why did it become so well known?

The initial stage of the feud was brought about because of a demographic and economic crisis within the Tug Valley community itself. Not enough land and too many people with strong family bonds led to declining opportunity, which in turn produced anxiety, tension, and increased competition for scarce resources. To this increased competition for traditional farm occupations was added the "opportunity" to supply industrialized America with timber. Rising land values, competition for trees, and the cash that could be gotten from selling them led to disruption of a traditional subsistence economy based on community cooperation and sharing. More significantly, it led to a breakdown in a spirit of cooperation in the community. The animosity that polarized around those committed to a market economy (timber) versus those still primarily engaged in semisubsistence farming became apparent in the initial stage of the feud when only members of the timber operation were singled out as enemies by the McCoys. Preacher Anse Hatfield as well as many of Devil Anse Hatfield's brothers, uncles, and cousins were not attacked by the McCoys, nor did they rush to the defense of Devil Anse. The feud story also reveals that many of Old Ranel McCoy's relatives refused to become involved or, like Selkirk McCoy, took the Hatfield side. Family bonds were strong in the Tug Valley but apparently not strong enough to overcome emerging economic conflict and the emotional response that went with it.

The story of the feud also reveals that mountain communities were neither chronically lawless nor violent. The local judicial system was strong and functioned effectively. Devil Anse, for example, apparently won his case against Perry Cline on solid legal grounds and when he did not win in court, Devil Anse did not use force or violence or ignore judicial authority. Violence emerged from the threat or the reality of outside infringement on the local system of authority. The first example apparent in the feud was the problem caused because the Tug Valley community was arbitrarily divided by the boundary between West Virginia and Kentucky. When Devil Anse's brother Ellison was killed on the Kentucky side of the river, the Hatfields, who had always before been willing to rely on the courts, could not allow Ellison Hatfield's killers to be taken to Pikeville for trial. Valentine and Devil Anse were reluctant to engage in vigilantism—to take the law into their own hands— but were convinced they had no choice. Significantly, they did not simply kill the three McCoys on the West Virginia side of the river; fearful that West Virginia authorities might take legal action against them, they took the McCoys back to the Kentucky side before executing them. It was a way of keeping themselves law abiding in West Virginia and, at the same time, administering justice. Still, it was not until Perry Cline took his case to the Governor of Kentucky

This photograph of the Hatfield family was taken in 1897 by an itinerant photographer well after the feud had made the Hatfields famous. Attempting to exploit that notoriety, the photographer posed the family with guns prominently displayed. This picture has become one of the most famous images associated with the feud. (West Virginia State Archives)

that the local judicial system broke down entirely. When Cline and his Kentucky posse raided West Virginia and the Hatfields retaliated with the New Year's Day raid on the McCoy home, it was obvious that state intervention had completely shattered the local system of authority.

At this point the feud took on much broader political and economic dimensions. Governor Buckner allied Kentucky with capitalists and modernizers both inside and outside the region; he perceived the mountaineers as obstructing the economic development of the region and hoped to make an example of the Hatfields. Governor Wilson of West Virginia represented that strain of late-nineteenth-century political thought identified as "agrarian" or "populist," which sought to resist the overweening political and economic power of the Eastern industrialists. Wilson's earnestness in defending the Hatfields was part and parcel of his entire career as a defender of small farmers in his state. Thus, when the case went to the Supreme Court at Wilson's instigation, it could be interpreted as a national level dispute over the rights of weaker, powerless people in opposition to the economic and political power of the modernizers. Although this issue was not overt in the arguments before the Supreme Court, put in the larger context of the changes in the federal judiciary toward protecting corporations at the expense of individuals and ruling against minority groups such as blacks and Indians, this case can be interpreted as part of a larger pattern.

Finally, if the worst violence of the feud was brought about by the industrialization process, why was that process so much more violent than in the rest of the country? For the most part, antebellum communities in the North or even other parts of the South did not experience the level of violence during industrialization that Appalachia did. Part of the answer may be that the process was more gradual in other areas, allowing people time to adjust, but the key factor for Appalachians may have been that it was largely imposed on them from outside. Although local boosters collaborated with outside industrialists, local capital was not sufficient to make the process indigenous and thus most mountaineers were exploited in much the same way as the people of Latin America or the Philippines as the United States took on more and more foreign ventures. Thus, the relationship became adversarial and violent as many Appalachians, like the Hatfields after Kentucky's posse raids, realized that they would no longer be allowed to control their own future or benefit from the process of economic development.

Sources: This story is based on extensive research in the County Court Records of Logan County, West Virginia, and Pike County, Kentucky; the Kentucky State Archives in Frankfort, Kentucky, and the West Virginia State Archives in Charleston, West Virginia; newspapers such as the *Louisville Courier–Journal,* the *Logan Banner,* the *Wheeling Intelligencer,* the *New York World,* and the *New York Times;* and books written with firsthand information such as T. C. Crawford's *An American Vendetta: A Story of Barbarism in the United States* (New York: Bedford, Clarke & Co., 1889), and Truda McCoy's *The McCoys: Their Story as Told to the Author by Eyewitnesses and Descendents,* edited by Leonard Roberts (Pikeville, KY: Pikeville College Press, 1976) which is based on interviews with many women involved in the feud. The best short narrative treatment of the feud is Otis Rice, *The Hatfields and the McCoys* (Lexington: University Press of Kentucky, (1978). For the most detailed examination of the feud and its economic and social implications see Altina L. Waller, *Feud: Hatfields, McCoys, and Social Change in Appalachia 1860–1900* (Chapel Hill: University of North Carolina Press, 1988).

4

COXEY'S ARMY: DRAMATIZING THE MALAISE OF THE 1890S

Carlos A. Schwantes

The "army" of about 400 men that massed in the nation's capital in late April 1894 did not in most ways resemble an army at all. In their dark suits, vests, and bowler hats, the unarmed "recruits" seemed more prepared for a dinner party than battle. One of its commanders resembled Buffalo Bill Cody, and the other, "General" Jacob Coxey (who was not a general), could have been mistaken for an accountant. The group referred to itself as the "J. S. Coxey Good Roads Association" or the "Commonweal of Christ," names whose evocations of social reformism and spiritual crusading must have aroused more curiosity than fear. But the press had called it "Coxey's Army," and that was that.

Coxey's legions were from Ohio and West Virginia, Los Angeles and Seattle, Montana and Illinois, Portland and Denver, and dozens of other places. As Carlos A. Schwantes's story reveals, the movement was remarkably strong in the trans-Mississippi West, where a diminishing supply of free land had shed doubt on the ability of the nation's economy to absorb the unemployed. Some supporters had dodged railroad police to hitch a ride on a freight train, others had rafted down the Missouri, and still others—the largest contingent, as it turned out—had followed Coxey's route, traveling by foot from Northeastern Ohio and across the Appalachian Mountains to Washington, D.C., where they hoped to convince the national government to mount a federal jobs program.

Surely something had to be done. Serious economic depressions, of the sort that created widespread unemployment and threatened the social order, had become a regular feature of the American scene. In 1877, a series of strikes that had begun on the railroads produced general strikes and violence in many cities and towns. The economic downturn of the mid-1880s was less severe, but was marked nonetheless by violent confrontations over the 8-hour day, culminating in the 1886 "riot" in Chicago's Haymarket Square and the hanging of the "anarchists" who supposedly were responsible for the tumult. Then, in 1893, a financial panic sent the economy into a tailspin and left millions of workers without jobs and millions more with reduced wages. This depression lasted 4 years and produced several memorable events: the great Pullman strike of 1894; a last, failed effort by William Jennings Bryan to rally

*workers and farmers under the banner of monetary reform; and Coxey's Army of the
unemployed.*

*Nearly 40 years later, another "army," this one composed of unemployed veterans
of the Great War, would call on the federal government to help its constituents through
yet another depression—the Great Depression of the 1930s—and by mid-decade
Franklin D. Roosevelt's New Deal had produced just the sort of public works programs
that had once seemed so radical. By 1963, when Rev. Martin Luther King, Jr., spoke of
freedom—and jobs—to hundreds of thousands from the steps of the Lincoln
Memorial, the "march on Washington" had become almost an American tradition.*

*To the congressmen and senators peering from their office windows at the strange
aggregation that moved on Capitol Hill on the morning of May 1, 1894, Coxey's ideas
were outrageous, and his army as unpredictably dangerous as the Haymarket
troublemakers. There was a price to be paid for pioneering.*

By noon an estimated thirty thousand spectators—men, women, and children—
waited elbow to elbow under the canvas awnings and shade trees that lined
Pennsylvania Avenue. The crowd nearly covered Capitol Hill. Normally only
the inauguration of a President attracted so many onlookers, but this was no
inauguration: Grover Cleveland occupied the White House, his term not yet
half completed. This Tuesday—May 1, 1894—belonged to Jacob Sechler Coxey
and his army, a protest as unprecedented in the history of the United States as
the massive unemployment that gave it life and purpose.

Coxey's name was on everyone's lips, first as a murmur and then as a shout
as his carriage pulled into view. Behind him marched the 400 tatterdemalion
veterans of the Commonweal of Christ, the advance guard of America's first
national crusade against unemployment, a "petition in boots" that hoped to
pressure Congress into financing a program of public works to employ the jobless until the economy could regain its health.

Some called Coxey a revolutionary; others dismissed him as a crank. Slight
of build, clean-shaven except for a light brown mustache, wearing wire-
rimmed glasses and a dark gray business suit, he looked more like a harmless
middle-aged professor than the wild man that newspaper cartoonists typically
sketched to represent cranks. Occasionally he rose and bowed to the crowd. His
flashing blue eyes suggested a sense of humor.

For the past 6 weeks Americans had read numerous accounts of Coxey, his
ragtag army of the unemployed, and the several imitators he inspired. The
daily press often carried the story on page 1, and rare was the 4-page country
weekly that did not print at least some news of the Commonweal. In fact, since
the end of the Civil War in 1865, perhaps only the disputed election of 1876 had
generated more intense newspaper coverage.

Readers had pondered, laughed at, or worried about the Coxey movement
a great deal. Some regarded it as a national joke, only slightly less humorous
than Congress and certainly less expensive. They wondered whether it drew its
inspiration from the showman Phineas T. Barnum or from the radical
Communards who gained control of Paris in 1871. There were always many
questions and few answers.

"General" Coxey's name became a household word, although he personally shunned the military terminology that journalists used to describe the movement. He preferred to style himself simply as president of the J. S. Coxey Good Roads Association of the United States and ex-officio of the Commonweal of Christ, the formal name that organizers gave their protest movement. Like the odd name itself, much about the Coxey movement defied conventional logic; and that, together with the hard times that began in mid-1893, helped to account for the seemingly insatiable popular interest in its progress.

Coxey was a wealthy man, the owner of a quarry in northern Ohio that produced a special type of white sand needed by the steel, glass, and pottery industries that until recently had enjoyed boom times. By the early 1890s he had expanded his holdings to include a stock farm located outside his hometown of Massillon (south of Cleveland) and ranches near Lexington, Kentucky, and Guthrie, Oklahoma, where he raised several dozen blooded race horses. Most horses in the march down Pennsylvania Avenue were his: For a single stallion he reportedly paid $40,000, enough money in the 1890s to hire 80 laborers for a year.

When in late March Coxey's thinly clad Commonwealers tramped out of Massillon in a snowstorm, it seemed impossible that they would survive to parade through the streets of Washington. Could they live off the land for more than 400 miles? Not since William Tecumseh Sherman and his Union soldiers marched 300 miles through Georgia 30 years before had anything like it been attempted. But when Coxey's marchers crossed the Appalachian Mountains and descended into the valley of the Potomac, disbelief and derision turned to amazement and alarm. No one knew how large or dangerous the Commonweal might become by the time it reached Capitol Hill.

A portrait of Jacob Coxey at the age of 40 at the time of his famous march. Afterward, he often campaigned for public office—primarily as a monetary reformer—and lost, the sole exception being his election as mayor of Massillon in 1931. Coxey died on May 18, 1951, his life having spanned the administrations of 19 presidents—from Franklin Pierce to Harry S. Truman. [Henry Vincent, *The Story of the Commonweal* (Chicago: W. B. Conkey Company, 1894)] (Library of Congress)

Turning from Fourteenth Street onto Pennsylvania Avenue, marchers glimpsed the White House off to their right. Except for the extra guards, life there appeared normal. A routine cabinet meeting was reportedly in progress. Outwardly the President was calm, stolid as the Rock of Gibraltar, to which the heavyset chief executive bore a slight resemblance. But those around him were clearly nervous. They scanned the minute-by-minute dispatches forwarded by special agents who shadowed the procession. Guarding the President was the largest detail of Secret Service agents, District of Columbia police, and watchdogs assembled since Civil War days. Special telephone lines had been strung to call in police reserves if necessary. Throughout the city 200 extra policemen were on duty, and detectives from several large cities of the Northeast quietly mingled with the spectators.

Many of the President's men feared that Coxey's army would attract violent individuals, possibly not as marchers but certainly as sympathizers. Within living memory, men of this description had assassinated two Presidents; and just 6 months ago another had gunned down the popular Mayor of Chicago. During the past winter a "Jack the Ripper" had slipped unnoticed into the White House, slashed the curtains in the Green Room, and stabbed his knife through several elegant sofas and chairs. All this, combined with the many threatening letters the President had received of late, lay behind the effort to "crank-proof" the White House. "The air seems to breed cranks and the demon of destruction is abroad in the land," fretted the *Chicago Herald*.

As Commonwealers continued slowly down Pennsylvania Avenue, spectators who had waited peaceably for hours rushed out to greet Coxey. Some seemed so determined to climb into his carriage that journalists formed a cordon of special guards to keep off intruders. At several locations sympathizers nearly blocked the broad thoroughfare until a vanguard of 25 mounted policemen pushed them aside.

The procession took nearly an hour to pass. Coxey's troops, mostly veterans of the long march from Massillon, stepped along smartly in dilapidated shoes yellow with the dust of country roads, threadbare shirts and jackets, and battered but functional hats that shielded their well-tanned faces from the noonday sun. Each man carried a long oaken stave of peace bearing a white flag with the slogan "Peace on earth, good will toward men, but death to interest on bonds." A Commonweal band of six pieces, mostly bass drums and cymbals, pounded out a rendition of "Marching through Georgia."

Two black trotters pulled a carriage bearing Coxey, his wife, and their 2-month-old son, Legal Tender—"Leeg" for short. The baby's odd name was a reflection of his father's lifelong obsession with monetary reform. As a young man Coxey had spent countless hours reading and thinking about the money question that so agitated post–Civil War America, arguing endlessly about interest rates, paper money, and bank credit with fellow workers in the iron-rolling mill where he was once employed. A Good Roads Bill, which combined Coxey's highway-building proposal, fiat-money ideas, and desire to help the unemployed, had been introduced in Congress in 1892 but got nowhere. Two years later Coxey added a proposal for non-interest-bearing bonds, a complicated

Members of Coxey's Army encamped on the outskirts of Washington to pre-
pare for their historic rendezvous on Capitol Hill. "The money lenders tremble
now," their leader Jacob Coxey asserted. "Congress takes two years to vote on
anything if left to itself. Twenty-millions of people are hungry and cannot wait
two years to eat." (Library of Congress)

plan that would provide federal loans to enable local governments to construct
schools, courthouses, libraries, museums, and other public buildings in addition
to streets and highways, all of which would provide jobs for the unemployed.

"Coxey! Coxey!" The roar continued along the length of Pennsylvania
Avenue. Although Coxey gave his name to the movement and used it to publicize his public works program, the man who actually conceived the march on
Capitol Hill was Carl Browne, a Californian who served as the Commonweal's
chief marshal. Riding astride a magnificent gray stallion at the head of the procession, he sported a large white sombrero tilted rakishly over his right eye and
long hair that cascaded over his shoulders. Buttons fashioned from silver dollars
decorated his fringed buckskin jacket and caused Browne to resemble Buffalo Bill
Cody, the popular showman of the Wild West. An eccentric, energetic, and flamboyant man with a genius for self-promotion that anticipated Hollywood, he originated the marchers' many bizarre banners and catch phrases.

Road-weary wagons decorated with Browne's cartoon-like artwork and slogans creaked along at intervals. One banner read "Co-Operation, the cerebellum of the Commonweal," and another, "The medulla oblongata and all other parts of the reincarnated Christ in the whole people." The juxtaposition of mysticism with a call for jobs made sense to Browne and certainly helped to attract the eye of the press, but it also brought forth guffaws and derisive words from skeptics who refused to accept the Commonweal as a legitimate reform movement. For Browne the money question was both personal and visceral: His slogans, lurid artwork, and speeches denounced Wall Street bankers as heartless and blasted the gold standard as an "old vampire."

On Capitol Hill the Senate convened at noon and remained in session for 12 minutes; members adjourned as custom dictated when they received news of the unexpected death of a colleague, Francis Stockbridge of Michigan. Members of the House spent the morning discussing bills pertaining to the accounting offices of the Treasury Department and protection of birds and game in Yellowstone Park. Congressmen wanted to remain in session until after the Commonweal arrived to avoid creating the unseemly impression that they had adjourned early out of fear. Even so, extra guards were on duty in the building, and heavy pine gates, such as were used to control inauguration crowds, were in place on each side of the main rotunda.

At the other end of Pennsylvania Avenue more dispatches reached the White House. "House reports there is large crowd all about the Capitol but everything quiet." "Coxey army just reached Peace Monument and going up hill to B Street and Delaware." After weeks of protest and posturing, Coxey's Army halted in the shadow of the Capitol. Lawmen nearly surrounded the building, and more were hidden inside. If the Ohioan still expected to deliver his speech from the Capitol steps, he needed somehow to push through the sea of blue-jacketed officers. But would he? Would club-wielding policemen beat back Coxey and his followers in an effort to discourage others still on the road? The nation held its collective breath and waited.

An important question that no one could answer that May Day was how many troops Coxey actually commanded. Not even Coxey knew. His crusade had produced such a sudden and spontaneous outpouring of support across the United States that he had no way to keep track of every local division and regiment that claimed to be part of "Coxey's Army." The ranks filled most rapidly in cities of the Far West, where the daily drumbeat of newspaper publicity inspired unemployed workmen to form a dozen additional contingents. To Coxey's jobs program they added a peculiarly regional demand that Uncle Sam hire the unemployed to dig irrigation ditches to bring water to the nation's vast arid domain: "When the ditches are dug and the lands reclaimed we can register homestead claims and be self-supporting ever after." Motivated both by desperation and dreams of a bright future through irrigation, Western armies pledged to conquer both distance and desert terrain to rendezvous with Coxey on Capitol Hill.

Underscoring the challenges they faced was an incident at the crest of the Cascade Mountains in remote Washington, the state which contributed more recruits per capita than any other. At the 2-mile-long Stampede Pass tunnel, where driving winter winds piled snow nearly 30 feet high, marchers found federal marshals blocking the west portal. Lawmen gave Commonwealers the cruel choice of scaling the pass high above the railway line or returning home. There were no alternatives. Though ill-fed, lightly clad, and without snowshoes, most crusaders defied the odds and struggled over the mountains, courting pneumonia all the way. Driving them on was a passionate desire to join the great protest on Capitol Hill. Ahead lay an uncertain future, but one of hope; behind lay the assured misery of joblessness and a hand-to-mouth existence.

At times the Coxey protest was so varied and complex that it resembled a 20-ring circus with half a dozen sideshows. In addition to Coxey's own band, which captured the most national and international attention, large armies converged on the nation's capital from the urban West, and not just one contingent from each major city but two or three from Los Angeles and Denver. A Polish Coxey's Army organized in Chicago and marched across America's industrial heartland.

One newspaper counted 13 contingents numbering more than 5,000 troops on the road, and that guess was probably as good as any. Of equal worry to opponents of the movement were the unknown thousands who joined Coxey in spirit. These included supporters who fed and sheltered marchers along the way, as well as those who turned out with brass bands and banners to cheer them on or to intimidate the federal marshals and other lawmen who attempted to halt their progress.

Especially for crusaders from the Far West, the aid of sympathizers was vital. Those Commonwealers, too poor to charter passenger coaches to take them to Capitol Hill, stole rides east on railway cars and walked only when unsympathetic lawmen barred them from the trains. When this happened they sometimes stole the trains themselves. That happened on at least 50 separate occasions, with the most celebrated incident occurring in Montana, where a trainload of federal marshals raced after Coxeyites in the most dramatic locomotive chase since the Civil War. The Westerners' struggles across high mountain passes and seemingly endless miles of empty desert made Coxey's journey from Massillon seem almost like a Sunday School picnic by comparison.

This was a war—a curious one to be sure—but a war nonetheless. Newspapermen who covered the protest called themselves "war correspondents" and addressed Coxey as "general." Federal authorities dispatched regular Army troops on several occasions and confined captured Coxeyites in hastily constructed prisoner-of-war camps. The battle line ran nowhere in particular, sometimes through the rolling hills of western Pennsylvania and sometimes through the plains of Kansas or Montana.

From the beginning most newspapers tended to belittle the Commonweal as nothing more than a collection of tramps; but the sheer volume of press coverage contradicted that simplistic view. Americans would not walk around the corner to see tramps. They preferred to "vag" them—that is, to sentence vagrants to the local workhouse, where they could spend 30 days breaking stones, chopping wood, and learning the value of the American work ethic. Before the advent of the Commonweal, armies of tramps rode freight trains to seasonal jobs across the West and seldom received any attention.

On one level the Coxey movement was engaging melodrama, complete with heroes like the swashbuckling John Sherman Sanders and his men, who stole a train in Colorado and dashed east across the prairies in a locomotive chase that appealed to anyone who had ever read a dime novel. Many of the Montana Coxeyites, thwarted in their efforts to run a stolen train all the way to Capitol Hill, built rafts instead and sailed down the Missouri River in a great American adventure straight from the pages of *Huckleberry Finn*. Perhaps even Jack London's tales of struggle for survival owed something to the Coxey crusade: Well before he achieved fame for *White Fang* and other best-selling novels, London accompanied a California contingent of Coxey's Army halfway across the continent.

No one did more to foster the press's melodramatic treatment of the movement than the outrageous Carl Browne. In many ways Browne was a parody of the Gilded Age promoter, forever dabbling in patent medicine, panoramic art,

Commonwealers on the Chesapeake and Ohio Canal west of Washington. After the long hike overland from Massillon to Cumberland, Maryland, weary marchers welcomed the chance to ride in two boats. A third boat, a coal barge christened the *Flying Demon,* was commandeered by the accompanying journalists. The name was a response to Commonweal marshal Carl Browne, who had once berated the press as "lying demons." Browne himself stands by the flag. (Library of Congress)

journalism, and political nostrums. But it would be a mistake to treat him as a simple-minded charlatan. A sometimes journalist himself, Browne recognized that the movement's bizarre trappings attracted the attention of a jaded press and excited more publicity than any reformer could ever dream of purchasing. Even Samuel Gompers, the founder and longtime head of the American Federation of Labor, who had only harsh words for "reformers" who treated American workers as pawns, called Browne "a big-hearted lover of men, a dreamer and an idealist."

Often obscured by the emphasis on melodrama was the fact that Browne, Coxey, and other guiding spirits of the movement managed to illuminate the economic ills besetting America in the late nineteenth century as few had done before. During those years the nation experienced a disturbing and poorly understood transformation from a rural-agrarian to an urban-industrial economy. One

"Peace on Earth, Good Will Toward Men! He Hath Risen!!! But Death to Interest on Bonds."
This legend appeared on a popular Commonweal banner prepared by Carl Browne, a religious mystic who believed in reincarnation and used the language of religious mysticism in his reform manifestos. Some cynics noted a striking similarity between the images of Christ on the banners and Browne himself. (Ohio Historical Society and Massillon Museum)

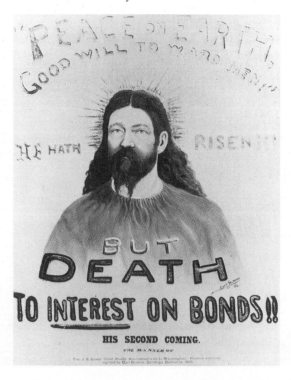

result was a roller-coaster business cycle. Hard times in the 1870s had been accompanied by a series of major railway strikes and urban disturbances. During a less severe slump in the mid-1880s, white workingmen on the West Coast rioted against Chinese who they feared would displace them by working for less money. In 1893, with the coming of the worst downturn yet, normally confident and optimistic Americans shuddered at the thought of what the future might bring. Already during the winter of 1893–1894 the ominous cry "Bread or Blood" had been heard in several of the nation's cities, and the rise of Coxeyism suggested that worse was yet to come.

The season of economic despair began in mid-1893, when panic on Wall Street signaled the start of a depression that would last 4 years. Within 6 months nearly 500 banks and 16,000 businesses failed. No matter what the industry, people fortunate enough to retain jobs frequently saw their wages slashed by one-fifth—or even by one-half. Every month thousands more involuntarily joined the ranks of the unemployed, although no one could be certain of the exact number. The federal government did not keep such statistics then, and neither did most states. Any estimate of the number of jobless Americans was crude and not always meaningful. One report claimed that as of January 1, 1894, 25 percent of the breadwinners of Montana and Utah were without work. Fifty thousand were jobless in California and 100,000 in Chicago, while in New York City the number fell somewhere between 100,000 and 200,000, depending on who was guessing.

Newspapers added a human face to the unemployment statistics when they told of hopeless, penniless old men wandering the streets of St. Paul, or men in the prime of life without jobs in the timber country of Wisconsin and Oregon. The annual convention of casket manufacturers reported that business was off because of the depression, and one member tried to make light of the situation by quipping that times were so bad that the sick could not afford to call a doctor and thus improve their chances for recovery. But unemployment was no joke. The blow was psychological as well as economic.

The main alternative to joblessness and starvation was private charity, which took a bewildering variety of forms. The *New York World* gave away more than a million loaves of bread, and the rival *New York Herald* distributed thousands of dollars worth of clothing. A cheap and efficient method of relief favored by both private and municipal charities was the soup kitchen. Great caldrons filled with donated meat and vegetables provided mulligan stew to all comers, though in some locales an able-bodied man might first be required to earn his meal by chopping firewood, which was then distributed to heat the homes of the poor. Destitute women were occasionally assigned jobs in a municipal laundry in exchange for a meal. In some places the poverty was so overwhelming and the confusion so great that city officials were reduced to throwing loaves of bread at crowds of the unemployed.

In cities of the East the jobless congregated outside newspaper offices every morning, scrambling to be first to scan the help-wanted ads. Occasionally they also participated in public protest demonstrations and signed petitions that were forwarded to Congress. That was probably the most ineffective thing an unemployed person could have done in 1893.

It was not that congressmen were insensitive to the plight of the jobless. Most were charitable men, but in their politics they nonetheless reflected the survival-of-the-fittest ethic that then prevailed in America. When asked what the government could do to help, the nation's leaders typically answered, "Nothing." They argued that "economic laws are a part of the machinery of the universe as much as the laws of gravitation." Unemployment was a natural phenomenon like an earthquake or cyclone, a product of forces beyond human control. Each bout of economic depression in the nineteenth century yielded its crop of platitudes about the need for the jobless to bear their suffering and privation with patience.

That advice was not without irony. In Chicago in 1893 the World's Columbian Exposition opened in May to celebrate four centuries of American achievement. Until the exposition closed in October, Chicago was the meeting place of America's past and future, where replicas of Christopher Columbus's three caravels competed for attention with the transformers and dynamos of General Electric and Westinghouse. It was also where the accomplishments of industrial civilization stood in greatest contrast to its failures. Surrounding the White City of the exposition were filth and squalor, disease-ridden slums, and air heavy with stench. Who could give meaning to such vivid examples of the contradiction haunting late-nineteenth-century America? Why was progress so clearly juxtaposed with poverty?

Not all the excitement of the great Chicago fair was confined to the exhibition halls, where visitors could view a map of the United States in pickles or a Krupp cannon weighing 130 tons, or to the Midway Plaisance, where the sinuous and much-talked-about Little Egypt danced the hootchy-kootchy. Chicago was equally alive with ideas. Churchmen and academics gathered for international congresses. One such gathering attracted monetary reformers who in speech after impassioned speech suggested how to resolve the contradiction between poverty and progress. Here the odd friendship between Coxey and Browne had its chance origin.

After a heated dispute between Browne and another delegate over a section of the platform, Coxey walked over to congratulate the Californian. Browne was grateful for any support. "I felt immediately drawn toward Mr. Coxey and among all the men I had met he impressed me the most." Coxey was similarly impressed by Browne and invited him home to Massillon to discuss further his good roads program. However, except for their common interest in monetary reform, the two men were studies in contrast. The shy and retiring Coxey scarcely uttered a word publicly during the Chicago money congress. The tall and powerfully built Browne reveled in the sensation he created when he appeared on the floor of the gathering sporting his Buffalo Bill garb. The Californian was only too glad to speak at length to anyone willing to listen.

The march, as distinct from Coxey's message, was largely a product of Browne's frontier activism. His cartoons lampooning wealthy San Francisco citizens first attracted notice in the late 1870s when they appeared in a radical newspaper called *The Open Letter.* Browne's lurid caricatures so amused Denis Kearney, leader of a white workingmen's movement to rid California of competing Chinese laborers, that he made the artist his personal secretary. The two crossed the continent together in 1878 to take the cause of Chinese exclusion to Boston's workingmen in historic Faneuil Hall, and they even claimed to have instructed President Rutherford B. Hayes during an interview at the White House. Some contemporaries suggested that Browne was the real brains behind the Kearney movement, but that claim was surely an exaggeration. It is true that during the Kearney agitation Browne toyed with the idea of organizing a march of the unemployed to demand jobs from California lawmakers. He also polished his skills as a stump orator for a variety of West Coast causes before discovering Coxey's crusade.

It was during the 1893 Christmas season in Massillon that Browne formally proposed to organize a march on Washington to publicize Coxey's reforms. The Ohioan was appalled at first—fearful that thousands of destitute people would descend on his farm—and warned Browne that "he could not afford to feed all the hungry men in the country." Coxey soon changed his mind, but left most of the organizing work to Browne.

The Californian devoted every waking hour to the "petition in boots." Browne was a prolific writer and promulgated so many manifestos that Coxey worried about the cost of having them all printed. One bulletin in late March contained Browne's order to the troops and several anthems composed especially for the crusade. When the weather warmed enough to permit Browne to work outside, he turned his attention to painting slogans on the panorama wagon that he insisted must accompany the march. He fashioned dozens of Commonweal banners to be carried in the procession. At its head was a huge oil painting of Christ, which bore a suspiciously close likeness to Browne, or "Humble Carl" as he preferred to style himself.

Popular interest in the Commonweal remained almost nonexistent until early March 1894 when suddenly it attracted the attention of the nation's press. It was Coxey's good fortune that a local newspaper, the *Massillon Independent,* had an energetic young reporter who saw in the bizarre crusade an opportunity to grab plenty of space and recognition for himself in the big city dailies. This young man's dispatches over the wires of the Associated Press began to familiarize newspaper readers everywhere with the name of Coxey. By mid-March many of the country's best-known daily papers had sent reporters of their own to investigate the developing curiosity.

The more news the press carried about the Commonweal, the more people and mail poured into Massillon. Many people sent poetry and checks. A Chicago man requested permission to join the march with 150 baseball players and raise money for it by offering an ongoing tournament in towns along the way. Each day the freight trains passing through Massillon dropped off new recruits; and each day the telegraph wires leading out of town pulsed with millions of dots and dashes that when translated into newspaper stories, introduced a nation to the unemployed barbers, cooks, miners, and laborers who were the main actors in the unfolding drama.

All the excitement and publicity did not please Coxey's neighbors. Many only shook their heads in wonder. They could not understand why one of the wealthiest and shrewdest men in the county wanted to head such a dubious enterprise. "Browne is a deep dyed villain, and he is working for Coxey's money and nothing more," fumed the leader's divorced first wife, who held a second mortgage on his sandstone quarry. "The idea of bringing the name of the Savior into this movement and displaying banners inscribed with His name and decorated with His picture is an outrage. Browne is to blame for all this, and he is a wretch, but Coxey is sincere."

For all the excitement, only 122 crusaders marched with Coxey out of Massillon on Easter Sunday in late March, and of those an unknown number were undercover officers sent by the chief of police of Pittsburgh to join the ranks, watch the movement, and get acquainted with the marchers. Most significant for the future of the Commonweal was its unofficial honor guard of 44 journalists, a number greater than covered many major party presidential conventions. Whenever Browne appeared in public he was immediately surrounded by eager reporters. "Carl is a friend to the reporter. He gives them all the news," gushed one.

People who dismissed the Commonweal as a bubble that had burst because so few recruits set out from Massillon missed its true significance. What Coxey and Browne essentially did was to create an unemployment adventure story that the press found irresistible. With characters sufficiently colorful and the perils of the journey sufficiently great, curiosity alone drew to the drama readers who cared little or nothing about complex economic issues or what it all portended. Whether by accident or design, the originator of the Commonweal march applied to social protest a few of the lessons he had learned in art. Browne knew from having exhibited his gargantuan panoramas in California that no matter how bad a work of art might be, it would elicit comment and attract wide attention if it were sufficiently outrageous.

For some newspaper commentators, particularly those from the Far West, anything the Coxey phenomenon revealed about unemployment was less significant than what it portended for the region and the nation. The *Seattle Telegraph*, which worried a great deal about the supposed closing of the frontier in 1890 and the end of an era of free Western lands, observed, "The Anglo-Saxon race has hitherto gained its triumphs through individual self-reliance. It is something new that from all points along the Pacific Coast between Canada and Mexico, organized troops of men have set their faces toward the East to seek from the government what their fathers would have scorned from the hands of the state."

Scarcely 9 months before Coxey launched his crusade, a young history professor from the University of Wisconsin, Frederick Jackson Turner, spoke to one of the learned gatherings at the same Chicago fair that introduced Coxey and Browne. He called attention to the "democracy born of free land" and wondered what problems would result from the apparent end of the frontier. No longer would a series of frontiers "furnish a new field of opportunity, a gate of escape from the bondage of the past." From the assertions of Turner and others a person might easily conclude that America was used up.

A Seattle newspaper succinctly expressed the popular concern when it editorialized in early 1894, "All social problems solve themselves in the presence of a boundless expanse of vacant fertile land." Free land in the West was perceived by many Americans as their God-given inheritance, distinguishing them from the less richly endowed inhabitants of Old World nations. Especially during periods of hard times, the West had long been seen as having a special quality, its free land mythologized into a kind of safety valve relieving the discontent that arose among dwellers in the nation's densely populated industrial neighborhoods.

Thus Americans had a right to wonder whether the numerous episodes of train stealing by unemployed westerners heralded the end of the free-land era. Certainly the rise of Coxeyism made Turner's pronouncements seem almost prophetic. The fact that Canada, with millions of acres of fertile land still available almost for the asking, was spared the trauma of roving armies of indigents seemingly confirmed the correctness of the popular and long-standing environmental approach to America's unemployment problem.

Regardless of their regional or philosophical perspectives, American newspapers made the most of the inherent ambiguity of the Coxey drama. Part of the suspense lay in speculating whether the Commonwealers would make it to Capitol

Coxey's Army marches through a small town in eastern Ohio or western Pennsylvania. Local coal miners offered food and moral support to Commonwealers. (Library of Congress)

Hill or what they would do once they got there, but readers also wondered whether a clear meaning for America would finally emerge from all the discordant elements. Each day's press coverage was similar to peeling off one layer of an onion only to find another. What would removal of the final layer reveal?

That was what thousands of spectators on Capitol Hill on May Day had come to learn. "We do not regard the invasion of Coxey's Army as a joke," fretted one Treasury Department official. He worried that if the marchers failed to achieve their objectives on Capitol Hill, someone would cry, "Here is the United States Treasury filled with money, while our families are starving." Every clerk was supposed to render military duty if necessary, and rifles and carbines rushed from the Springfield arsenal were cached all over the building. The vaults were temporarily closed to the public, and police allowed entrance to the building through one door only.

A few days before the rendezvous on Capitol Hill, Coxey went to the office of the police commissioner to obtain permission to speak from the Capitol steps. The chief lawman looked Coxey in the eye. "Then it is your idea to make a speech from the east front of the Capitol?"

"Yes."

"You can't do that," the commissioner responded. "The law prohibits it."

"Is there any law against making a speech on the streets?"

"Yes, the law prohibits that, too."

"Well," responded Coxey, becoming annoyed, "that's what we propose to attempt. It's a Constitutional right." The commissioner snapped that he would not grant Coxey a permit to speak in public because Coxey intended to violate the law.

"I claim it under the Constitution." The words burst from the Ohioan's lips like rifle shots.

When told that only the presiding officer of the Senate or the Speaker of the House could suspend the law, Coxey set out to find them, but here he again met with frustration. Finally, when Coxey learned that an 1882 act of Congress prohibited demonstrations on the Capitol grounds, he turned to a reporter for the *Washington Star* and said, "We will keep off the grass around the Capitol. Of course, I appreciate as well as anyone else the fact that the preservation of the grass around the Capitol is of more importance than saving thousands from starvation." Coxey was determined to march and speak from the Capitol steps without a permit.

The saber rattling reminded many people of Civil War days. The parallel was inescapable, and it heightened fears in Washington. On the eve of the confrontation at the Capitol, newsboys on downtown streets shouted out, "Extra! Extra! Bloodshed expected tomorrow! U.S. Troops may be called out to prevent the Coxey army from marching to the Capitol."

As clocks struck one, Coxey's troops made their way up the gentle rise of Capitol Hill and halted just beyond the B Street entrance to the House of Representatives. Waiting for them were an estimated 20,000 spectators. Three to four hundred policemen blocked access to the building—one for nearly every Coxeyite on the march.

Among the many promotional items prepared by Carl Browne was this hand-drawn map showing the proposed route of the march. It contains numerous exhortations for people living along the way to support the Commonwealers. (Ohio Historical Society)

"Attention, Commonweal, Halt!" Browne's booming voice rose above the noise of the restless onlookers. Dismounting, he pushed through the throng to Coxey. "This is the east front," he murmured low. "Are you ready?" Coxey nodded. Rising in his carriage, he stooped low to kiss his wife in a display of affection that brought cheer after cheer from the onlookers. Browne handed his sombrero to Mrs. Coxey. Her husband looked pale as he jumped to the ground.

A mounted policeman blocked Browne's way. "You can't pass here with that flag."

"Why can't I pass?" questioned Browne, who was holding one of the staves of peace. Before the officer could answer, an onlooker cried, "Jump over the wall!" In a moment both Coxey and Browne had cleared the low stone wall and disappeared into the crowd. Small trees, bushes, and flower beds were flattened by the onslaught of mounted officers in pursuit. Browne in his Buffalo Bill suit made an easy target. And that was his plan: to decoy the officers while Coxey made his way unseen through the crowd to the steps where every President since James Monroe had been inaugurated. On this site of new beginnings Coxey planned to deliver his long-promised speech offering a cure for unemployment.

Browne led officers on a wild chase through the shrubbery before a dozen of them finally tackled him at the southeast corner of the building. "I am an American citizen. I stand on my Constitutional rights," he bellowed. Browne spun around suddenly and sent surprised policemen whirling off into the crowd. As officers wrestled Browne into a nearby patrol wagon, bystanders attempted to come to his rescue. Grabbing the bridles of the lawmen's horses, they forced the animals into the low wall and spilled their riders violently to the ground. At this, the police lost their heads. They charged into the crowd, beating everyone within range; people dropped to their knees, dazed by repeated blows from billy clubs.

While this commotion was going on, Coxey slipped unnoticed halfway up the Capitol steps. Then the onlookers spotted him and sent up a great shout. Coxey paused for a moment to catch his breath, turned toward the sea of upturned faces, and tipped his hat. He turned to continue his climb but two officers blocked his way.

"What do you want to do here?" one asked, posing the question on everyone's mind.

"I wish to make an address," Coxey responded in an emotion-choked voice.

"But you can't do that."

"Then can I read a protest?" The Ohioan drew a typewritten manuscript from his pocket and proceeded to unfold it. But before he could open his mouth, officers pushed him firmly backwards down the steps. Coxey tossed the document to a nearby reporter, saying, "That is for the press." His message—an appeal for better treatment of the "poor and oppressed"—was published in several newspapers and in the *Congressional Record.*

Bystanders watched as officers escorted Coxey to his carriage. Someone in the crowd shouted his name, and others joined in, louder and louder until everyone was shouting "Coxey!" Police charged into the crowd to disperse it, causing people to fall over one another in a desperate effort to get out of range. The tatterdemalion army remained quiet and orderly at the center of the tempest.

Police cited Coxey for walking on the grass and displaying banners on the Capitol grounds, although Coxey's only "banner" was the small American flag pinned to his lapel. For this crime a judge sentenced Coxey, Browne, and another associate to 20 days in jail. When the leaders emerged from prison they found that the Coxey movement had faded away, having lost both its popular momentum and its ability to interest the press.

If Coxey ever had cause to regret his association with Browne, it was not because the Californian spent too much of his money or caused him to be denounced as a "crank," but because the 47-year-old Browne secretly courted his teenage daughter Mamie. When reporters announced that the couple had been quietly wed in mid-1895, Coxey disowned Mamie and disavowed Browne. That was probably the main reason Coxey did not lead another march to Washington that year as he had earlier planned to do.

At the turn of the century, the couple was living at Browne's "Commonweal Castle," a modest retreat near Calistoga, California, where Mamie bore a son. They split up a short time thereafter. Browne occasionally mounted a soapbox on the streets of San Francisco during the early years of the twentieth century to champion radical causes, primarily those of the Industrial

Workers of the World and the Socialist Party. He could be counted on to attend every radical gathering open to the public. Once during a 24-hour anti-capital-punishment rally in San Francisco in 1912, Browne turned up to issue hourly "extras" throughout the day and evening. He reported the speeches, illustrated them with his cartoons, and sold the finished products on the spot. Browne proudly summed up his life by quoting a San Francisco journalist who wrote of him, "Carl Browne has spent his life championing the cause of the underdog."

After his 1894 march, Coxey returned to Ohio where he campaigned often for public office—distinguishing himself primarily as an indefatigable monetary reformer—and lost, with the one exception of being elected Mayor of Massillon in 1931 as a Republican. The following year he ran for President as the Farmer-Labor party candidate and received 7,309 votes. Party labels meant little to Coxey, who also ran for office as a Democrat, Greenbacker, and Populist.

Coxey returned to Washington in 1914 and this time spoke legally from the Capitol steps. On May 1, 1944, on the occasion of the fiftieth anniversary of the great march and in the ninetieth year of Coxey's long life, the elder statesman of American reform once again mounted the Capitol steps and with the permission of Speaker Sam Rayburn and Vice President Henry A. Wallace completed the protest speech he had attempted to deliver there in 1894. Two hundred curious listeners, mostly federal employees and servicemen, heard Coxey repeat his original address, which included this indictment: "Up these steps the lobbyists of trusts and corporations have passed unchallenged on their way to the committee rooms, access to which we, the representatives of the toiling wealth producers, have been denied. We stand here today in behalf of millions of toilers whose petitions have been buried in committee rooms, whose prayers have been unresponded to, and whose opportunities for honest, remunerative, productive labor have been taken away from them by unjust legislation, which protects idlers, speculators, and gamblers."

There was no way to measure accurately the educational impact of the Coxey crusade, yet even hostile observers believed it had one: "These men, after their own fashion are building more wisely than they know of," asserted the *Press-Times* of Seattle. They had made an impression on Americans, "and once the national mind agrees upon the fact that a new direction must be given to affairs, there is no telling to what great and good ends it may lead." The *Rocky Mountain News* of Denver, a supporter of the movement, added that the Commonweal would move the country at the polls. "Better, wiser and more humane laws in the near future must be the outcome." In short, a variety of contemporaries perceived Coxeyism as having chipped away at the popular belief that poverty and unemployment were mainly the result of individual weakness and laziness and promoted the idea that the federal government was responsible for the economic well-being of its citizens.

Although Coxey's jobs and money proposals were never enacted into law, the public-works principle of his crusade was embodied in the New Deal's relief and recovery programs that put the nation's unemployed to work building dams and a host of other projects during the Great Depression of the 1930s. By 1944 his basic ideas were no longer considered radical, and Coxey had attained the status of historical curiosity. Coxey died in Massillon at age 97. Two generations of Americans after 1894 used the epithet "Coxey's Army" to describe any disorganized undertaking, although, in fact, Coxey's followers had generally been well-organized and well-disciplined.

AN INTERPRETATION

The Coxey crusade represented a double-barreled challenge to the economic beliefs cherished by most Americans. It raised troubling questions about the nation's prevailing commitment to laissez-faire, especially when the Commonweal's prominence in the hinterland West undermined the popular conviction that fertile agricultural lands of the frontier represented America's most practical form of social security and offered a wise alternative to governmental paternalism.

In the popular mythology of the West, pioneer residents were self-reliant, rugged individualists, or at least they publicly aspired to that status. But in reality Westerners had been quick to turn to the federal government for help. That should not seem so strange, for Uncle Sam's presence was more visible in the West than in any other region. The federal government was (and still is) the most prominent custodian of the region's natural resources. Legislators on Capitol Hill voted to create homesteads on lands most would never see, to encourage private development of remote timber and mineral resources, and to grant the land and loans that helped to finance most of the western transcontinental railroads. Uncle Sam's Army occasionally protected Western settlers from Indians (or vice versa).

Why, then, Western Coxeyites asked, should not the federal government put the unemployed to work making the desert bloom through irrigation? The jobless of 1894 only wanted Uncle Sam to lend them a helping hand as he had done earlier for the entrepreneurs who built the Pacific railroads or the homesteaders eager to tackle the problems of farming 160 acres of prairie land. Thus for unemployed Westerners the call for federal sponsorship of irrigation projects to put the jobless to work building canals in the ultimate hope of resettling them in the new garden marked no real break with the past.

The irrigation scheme was only a way of buying time, however, and finally the mythology of the free-land safety valve proved to be a poor tool to deal with massive unemployment in an urban-industrial society. But it took the hard times of the 1890s and disorders such as the Coxey crusade to hasten the process of exploding the myth. Only when people discarded the environmental approach to unemployment were they able to recognize that the state might deal with the problem without using free land as an intermediary.

Eventually the idea voiced by the Coxey crusaders—that the federal government should provide them with public-works jobs—found its way onto the national political agenda and was finally accepted by the President and Congress during the hard times of the 1930s. In a 1935 radio speech, President Franklin D. Roosevelt observed: "Today we can no longer escape into virgin territory. . . . We have been compelled by stark necessity to unlearn the too comfortable superstition that the American soil was mystically blessed with every kind of immunity to grave economic maladjustments." In sum, the modern welfare state was a response by government to some of the social and economic problems that the supposed free land of the West reputedly solved. If nothing else the Coxey crusade of 1894 vividly revealed that the sparsely populated West's role as a free-land safety valve for the nation's unemployed was a myth.

Sources: This story is drawn primarily from my book *Coxey's Army: An American Odyssey* (Lincoln: University of Nebraska Press, 1985). There is also Donald L. McMurry, *Coxey's Army: A Study of the Industrial Army Movement of 1894* (Seattle: University of Washington Press, 1968 reprint of 1929 edition). Newspapers devoted thousands of column-inches of space to Coxey and his protest crusade in 1894. Probably the best dispatches were filed by Ray Stannard Baker for the *Chicago Record* and are available on microfilm. Henry Vincent, a reform journalist, authored *The Story of the Commonweal* (New York: Arno, 1969 reprint of 1894 edition), a tract sold to raise money for the marchers. A collection of Coxey memorabilia is preserved at the Massillon Museum and also on microfilm at the Ohio Historical Society in Columbus.

5

EMPIRE IN THE PHILIPPINES: AMERICA'S FORGOTTEN WAR OF COLONIAL CONQUEST

Stuart Creighton Miller

The conquest of the Philippines was only one of a series of overseas actions that collectively forged a new American empire and redefined the United States as a formidable world power. Between 1898 and 1917, when the Congress approved Woodrow Wilson's call for a Declaration of War against Germany, the nation took Cuba, Puerto Rico, Guam, and the Philippines from Spain; promoted a rebellion in Panama that paved the way for the canal; dispatched troops to protect American commercial interests in Santo Domingo, Haiti, and Nicaragua; and—under the same General Frederick Funston who appears in the following account—occupied the city of Vera Cruz during the Mexican revolution.

In terms of square miles of territory taken, the American empire was hardly an empire at all—nothing at all like the vast African and Asian colonial empires of Great Britain, France, and Germany. Despite this difference, V. I. Lenin, the Communist leader of the Russian Revolution, lumped the American empire with the European ones, treating them all as an outgrowth of what he called in 1916 "the highest stage of capitalism"—that is, "monopoly" capitalism. The timing of America's imperial escapades roughly fits Lenin's model; a massive merger movement, beginning in 1897 and concluding in 1902, virtually completed the transformation of the economy into a system of oligopolies, with many industries dominated by a few massive corporations. According to this controversial theory, the new American empire reflected the needs of the new, giant corporations and the desires of the men who ran them. American "New Left" historians of the 1960s and 1970s also emphasized the economic origins of empire.

In contrast, not a single businessman appears in Stuart Creighton Miller's account of the American intervention in the Philippine archipelago. Instead, Miller's analysis relies on the behavior and rhetoric of ordinary soldiers and their commanding officers to give us some sense of what Americans were doing in the jungles of the Pacific. It will take some courage to see ourselves in this story, for Miller's portrait is unflaggingly critical, with each character establishing an impressive—and depressing—new standard for racism, bigotry, and truculent nationalism. (In understanding these soldiers, it might help to realize that President Theodore Roosevelt, who after September 1901 managed the nation's imperial adventures, shared their racist and nationalist sentiments.)

Nonetheless, this story of how Americans fought the Filipinos and talked about their exploits can help reveal the lines of influence that came together to yield an American empire. One of them, surely, was the frontier—officially declared "closed" in the 1890 census when the supply of unsettled land seemed to have been exhausted— yet remarkably alive in the American mind. Another was the exuberant self-confidence of the United States, refracted in the words of thousands of soldiers who went overseas absolutely convinced that they had only to show up to win great victories (Americans would export their products with the same assurance). Racism was another line of influence, running from the Philippines back and forth through turn-of-the-century laws that segregated blacks from whites and disfranchised black voters in the Southern states. American empire was the product, too, of just the sort of confusion over ideals and purposes that made it difficult for even Filipino leader Emilio Aguinaldo to be certain what American troops were doing in his homeland. Was the United States the standard-bearer of civilization and democracy? Or an elitist nation with unfulfilled imperial ambitions? As Americans and Filipinos eyed each other warily in the wake of the siege of Manila, no one—least of all the Americans—knew for sure.

The evening of February 4, 1899, was an ideal moment to begin the war with the fledgling Republic of the Philippines, as most of its leaders were off at a celebration in Malolos, some 30 miles north of Manila. The United States Army had taken Manila the preceding August during the war with Spain, only to be bottled up in the city when the Filipino army, America's erstwhile, de facto ally against the Spanish, re-formed its line of siege around the land side of the city on August 11, 1898. The nationalist leader, General Emilio Aguinaldo y Famy, justified this aggressive action, reasoning that the city could be returned to Spain in the peace negotiations underway in Paris from which his government was excluded. Once the Treaty of Paris was made public in December, converting the Spanish colony into an American one, Aguinaldo continued his siege, insisting that two thirds of the Senate would never consent to a treaty that so violated cherished American principles. That august body heatedly debated an imperial future for America, and finally scheduled a vote on the treaty for February 6, 1899, one that was predicted to be extremely close.

Meanwhile, the two armies facing each other on the outskirts of Manila were ostensibly at peace, but tensions between them escalated daily. Finally, just 2 days before the Senate's scheduled vote, around 8 o'clock that evening, some unarmed, probably drunk, Filipino soldiers refused to heed commands by a sentry of the Nebraska volunteer regiment, and mocked him with their own shouts of "Halto! Halto!" They were quickly gunned down, and a crescendo of gunfire erupted from both the American and Filipino lines facing each other on the outskirts of Manila. Heavy firing continued until 2 o'clock the next morning, most of it pretty wild in the ensuing darkness, and largely coming from the state volunteer regiments manning the northern sector of Manila's defense perimeter. One regular officer assumed that they must be repulsing a Filipino attack and sent his aide to see if they needed help. He returned to report with disgust that there was no attack, just "green Dakotans wasting ammunition firing away at no discernible targets."

Neither side made a serious effort to advance on the other, and no significant casualties had occurred by the time the firing ceased at 2 A.M. So the skirmish could have easily been dismissed in the sobering light of the next morning as an unfortunate incident caused by the growing tension between the two armies. Instead, land batteries, along with the heavy guns of Admiral George Dewey's warships, began to hammer Filipino positions once the first rays of light had put them in silhouette. At 8 A.M., after several hours of this devastating barrage, the bugles sounded, and the "boys in blue" charged out of Manila with "Montana screams, Tennessee howls, Jayhawk cheers" and fixed bayonets. As Private William Christner described it to his parents: "With a good old Pennsylvania yell we charged up the hill through a hail of bullets," reassuring them that "I hardly think I was born to be killed by a nigger." Actually, the "Pennsy vols" were among the few regiments that received significant fire that day. Most found only dead or wounded in the opposing trenches and continued on for miles past their assigned objectives. Colonel Frederick Funston led his Kansas regiment up the coast so fast that it came under fire from the *U.S.S. Charleston*. Officers of the California regiment even threatened to shoot their own men if they did not halt, but only fatigue ended that charge miles later. Once the Washington and Idaho regiments trapped some retreating Filipinos at midstream in the Pasig River, the slaughter began with a murderous cross fire. "From then on the fun was fast and furious," as the dead "piled up thicker than buffalo chips," one soldier wrote home. Another informed his father that "picking off niggers in the water is more fun than a turkey shoot."

The wild scramble for glory left Filipino stragglers behind American lines to snipe from the rear. The American commander, General Elwell Otis, ordered a scorched earth tactic to deny cover for them, although he later attributed all the burning to the retreating enemy. The incident also created the widespread belief among American soldiers that wounded Filipinos left on the field were shooting at them. "Because a Filipino is so treacherous even when badly wounded, he has to be killed. When we find one that is not dead, we have our bayonets," one soldier explained to his parents. About 3,000 Filipino soldiers— but only 60 Americans—died that first day.

The American presence in Manila had begun with Admiral George Dewey's stunning victory on May 1, 1898, over Spain's Pacific Squadron anchored in Manila Bay, only days after Congress had declared war. Many Americans were surprised by the action, because the propaganda against Spain leading up to the war had focused on Spanish cruelty in suppressing a rebellion in Cuba, ignoring other Spanish colonies. Indeed, most Americans had never heard of the Philippines. As the character "Mr. Dooley" confessed, in a humorous newspaper column, he "didn't know if they were islands or canned

The island of Luzon is the largest and most populous within the Philippine archipelago. Much of the fighting between Americans and Filipinos occurred in the immediate vicinity of Manila and in the provinces of Pampanga (just north) and Batangas (to the south). The hideout of Filipino leader Emilio Aguinaldo was in the town of Palanan, on the northeast coast.

goods." According to legend, the news of Dewey's victory even sent President William McKinley scurrying to a globe to discover the location of "these darned islands."

A small group of dedicated imperialists in government, led by Theodore Roosevelt and Massachusetts Senator Henry Cabot Lodge, knew their precise location, as they had their eyes on the Philippines for potential coaling stations and a naval base to protect America's trade routes to China. As assistant secretary of the navy, Roosevelt was instrumental in stationing a fleet under Dewey's command in Hong Kong to lie in wait for the war to begin. While waiting, the admiral and two American diplomats stationed in Hong Kong and Singapore began negotiations with exiled Filipino leaders of an earlier failed rebellion against Spanish rule in 1896. They would be potential allies against Spain should a war begin. Rebellion in the Philippines had flared anew, and Dewey urged this junta to join him when he sailed for Manila. The Filipinos were in Singapore, however, when America declared war, so Dewey left without them. Following his victory, he dispatched a ship to bring them to Manila. Before

Filipino dead in their trenches on the first day of combat, victims of deadly American naval and land bombardment that began without warning at dawn of February 5, 1899, after a 3-hour lull in the extensive, but ineffective, exchange of rifle fire that had erupted between the two lines the preceding evening. (National Archives)

departing, Aguinaldo left money with an American diplomat to purchase arms for his cause.

Once back on Luzon, the largest, most populated island in the archipelago, Aguinaldo took charge of the rebellion and began to attack Spanish garrisons throughout the Philippines. He laid siege to Manila on its land side, bottling up the Spanish commanders. He also wrote a formal Declaration of Independence modeled after that of his "ally, the Great North American Nation, the cradle of liberty, and therefore friend to our people." The Declaration was "witnessed by the Supreme Judge of the Universe," and was "under the protection of the Mighty and Humane North American Nation." Lieutenant Colonel L. M. Johnson, commanding a small American advance party, signed this document for Aguinaldo as a witness. The nationalist leader then created a government at Malolos, designed a national flag, and ordered his legislative branch to write a constitution, again using the American one as a model. Most of this was accomplished before the American army arrived in significant force, and through it all, Aguinaldo received encouragement from his "good friend," Admiral Dewey.

By mid-June, the steady flow of American soldiers arriving aroused Aguinaldo's suspicions, but he reasoned with his own subordinates that the war in common against Spain, the apparent alliance, plus America's anti-colonial tradition and the fact that the U.S. Constitution made no provision for colonies, would ensure that America would not replace Spain as a new colonial master. Dewey was even able to persuade Aguinaldo to make room for the newly arrived American troops on his line of siege around Manila.

Aguinaldo discovered the extent of America's duplicity on August 11, 1898, when American troops took Manila after a prearranged sham battle with the Spanish that excluded the Filipinos. Aguinaldo's immediate resumption of his line of siege, bottling up the Americans in Manila, enraged American commanders, but Washington refused to give them a green light to attack him.

By December, when the Treaty of Paris officially confirmed Aguinaldo's worst suspicions, the relations between the two armies had already deteriorated to the breaking point. Insults, hostile gestures, and occasional bullets flew in both directions. American soldiers addressed Filipinos of whatever rank as "nigger," and, as one officer warned, "the natives are beginning to understand what 'nigger' means." American sentries took their frustrations out on unarmed Filipino soldiers passing through their lines to visit Manila. Some were knocked down with the butt of a Springfield rifle merely for "looking surly" or "seeming disrespectful." A few were shot for "looking suspicious." Such acts were generally committed by volunteers in the state regiments, already notorious among the regulars for their lack of discipline.

General Otis launched his own diplomatic offensive designed to humiliate the nationalists, ranging from petty refusals to return salutes from an "armed mob," lest it constitute recognition of Aguinaldo's "so-called government," to extraordinarily worded threats if Aguinaldo did not relinquish positions that Otis had quite arbitrarily decreed to be within Manila's municipal boundaries. Otis appears to have undertaken this entirely on his own. Indeed, on September 5

Filipino officers posing for a photographer before the Philippine-
American War began. Most of these soldiers were shoeless and
poorly equipped and trained, however proud and courageous.
(Library of Congress)

Otis informed Washington that "relations friendly, but require delicate manipula-
tion." Three days later, he ordered Aguinaldo out of one position by September
15, or he would be "obliged to resort to forcible action." So outrageous was the
language of this ultimatum that Aguinaldo asked Otis to withdraw it in favor
of a simple request with which he would comply. Otis refused even this face-
saving plea. Aguinaldo withdrew, which evoked disgust from Otis's aide that
the Filipinos would not fight in the face of such "humiliation." Otis also started a provocative surveillance of Filipino positions under the guise of "recreational activities," and he expressed outraged innocence when Aguinaldo
banished back to Manila Americans caught photographing and measuring
Filipino fortifications.

When the Spanish garrison at Iloilo on the island of Panay, some 300 miles south of Manila, offered to surrender to the Americans in December, Otis readied a task force under General Marcus Miller to occupy that city, but Dewey refused to transport it without specific orders from Washington. The orders came, but stipulated that the transfer of power must be peaceful. By the time Miller arrived at Iloilo at the end of December, the Spanish had already departed, and he was greeted by the mayor, who informed him that he may "not land foreign troops without express orders from the central government" at Malolos. In spite of Washington's orders, both Miller and Otis wanted to take the city by force, but Dewey vetoed this. Otis ordered Miller to hang on at anchor "until something happened."

Over the next few weeks, Otis made sure that "something" did. In the meantime, he carefully prepared himself for that event, ordering his officers out of dress whites and into "fighting khaki." He moved the Utah Battery up to a more favorable offensive position and coaxed Dewey into maneuvering his warships closer to shore on the flanks of Aguinaldo's semicircular line. On February 2, 1899, he discharged all Filipino civilians in his employ, placed his army on full alert, and tested the waters by ordering sentries posted at a hotly disputed position from which he had earlier forced the Filipinos to retreat. The colonel commanding the Nebraska regiment was personally on hand to post them, and a Filipino lieutenant called him a son of a bitch, whereupon the colonel ordered him arrested. The next day, Otis posted no sentries there, but on February 4, he did so again, this time with instructions to shoot intruders. It paid off, creating the incident that justified Otis's full scale offensive the following dawn.

America had experienced only easy victories in the war against Spain. It lasted 100 days, leading Roosevelt to complain that "there wasn't war enough to go around." Dewey needed less than 6 hours to destroy the Spanish fleet caught napping at anchor, and the phony Battle of Manila lasted 3 hours. It was easy to assume that Aguinaldo's army had now been shattered in less than 12 hours. As evening approached on February 5, Otis refused to meet with Aguinaldo's emissary carrying a peace proposal, who was curtly informed by an aide that he "lacked proper credentials," and that an audience with Otis might be construed as "recognition of [his] so-called political organization." Headlines proclaimed a total victory over a thoroughly demoralized enemy:

AGUINALDO WEEPS FOR HIS BLUNDER
SITS CRYING IN HIS QUARTERS
AFRAID TO SURRENDER TO THE AMERICANS

In reality, the war had just begun, and it would last another 41 months, claiming the lives of 4,200 American soldiers, while up to 20,000 Filipino troops would perish, along with about 200,000 civilians, most of whom would die of war-related starvation and disease. Nevertheless, to this day Washington maintains the official fiction that it was not a war, but merely an "insurrection."

General Arthur MacArthur, the father of Douglas (then a plebe at West Point), commanded the northern division that continued in pursuit of Aguinaldo. The Filipino commander was much too wise to risk battle with the Americans, who had superior firepower and marksmanship. He settled for delaying actions as he continued his steady retreat northward to a mountain refuge. He abandoned Malolos in flames, and narrowly missed entrapment several times by an American amphibious landing to his rear and "flying columns" of hard riding U.S. cavalry. Meanwhile, Otis, back in Manila, fired off salvos of press releases describing "smashing victories," or "crushing blows" and "final moments," which were dutifully parroted in the nation's press. Editors favored an analogy with former Indian wars, labeling the enemy "Filipino Braves," or even "Apaches" in their headlines.

Actually, the more heavily equipped Americans, prepared for more conventional battle, rarely caught up with their lightly clad adversaries, who moved swiftly on bare feet over familiar terrain. As one soldier complained to his parents, "you have niggers you can't see shoot at you until you get close enough to shoot at them and then Mr. Nigger tears off to another good place and shoots again." One wife in Kansas City sent hometown clippings to her husband, Lieutenant Samuel Lyon, a regular officer, who had fought in the "battles" ballyhooed in the local press. He wrote back: "I hope the idiotic newspapers haven't had you worried to death about those heavy engagements. 'Battles' out here are greatly exaggerated. This rebel is like a flea you can't see."

The war was fought as much in the headlines as it was on the field. It was not just a question of Otis's misleading dispatches, but also of some senior officers engaging in histrionics that had little military value in order to impress correspondents on hand and garner some personal media attention. Colonel Funston, one of the most feted heroes of this war, led a company-size charge into an already abandoned Malolos in flames. He joined three men to swim across a river to take an abandoned fortification when MacArthur had already forded that river elsewhere much closer to the retreating foe. Another publicity hound, General J. Franklin Bell, leapt from a rowboat to reconnoiter enemy defenses while swimming. Lyon pointed out to his wife that "the newspapers featured this, ignoring the fact that from the level of the water his view wasn't nearly as good as it would have been with a good glass on one of the ships or even in the rowboat."

Funston's heroism at Calumpit, however, was quite genuine in carrying out a very daring maneuver to outflank General Antonio Luna's well fortified position on the Rio Grande de Pampanga. Funston had two Kansans swim a line across the river and secure it to the opposite bank. He joined eight men on the first raft propelled across by that line. More trips augmented his force to 41, with which he surprised the enemy, who quickly retreated before discovering how small Funston's contingent was, and before dismantling the railroad bridge so coveted by MacArthur to haul supplies and artillery across the river. Funston was awarded the Congressional Medal of Honor and promoted to brigadier general of volunteers for this brilliant feat.

By May, the rainy season arrived, with the U.S. Army controlling little territory outside Manila. When towns were taken, they were soon abandoned rather than permanently garrisoned, allowing the nationalists to return and murder any inhabitants suspected of cooperating with Americans during their brief occupation. Otis protected his ludicrously optimistic view of the war by imposing a rigid censorship on the correspondents. It became clear that the censorship was designed less to keep information from the enemy than to cover up Otis's ineptness as a commander. Reporters could bypass the censor by mailing dispatches to Hong Kong for transmission on its cable terminal, but that took time and also risked the general's wrath and possible deportation for "sedition." Finally, these correspondents, including those who were Otis's "favorites," rebelled, mailing a collective protest to their editors. Headlines in response blared that "Situation in the Philippines Is Not 'Well In Hand'," reversing one of Otis's pet phrases. The entire nation had been "snookered" by the "foolish pollyanna" of General Otis, lamented many editors. Oblivious to this reaction, Otis denied that there was any censorship, then announced the appointment of a new censor. He continued to release reports of "final blows" and "crushing victories," until one editor declared that Otis did not "even have enough sense to come in out of the rain."

Under the terms of their enlistment, the state volunteer regiments returned in the summer of 1899 and disbanded. As civilians, these veterans were free to impugn the official view of the war with no reprisal from Otis. They also corroborated the rumors of American atrocities that originated in private letters from soldiers, which were not subjected to censorship. As long as these letters were confined to small, local audiences, they were of little concern to Otis or the government. But sometimes one would fall into the hands of an editor opposed to the war, who would promptly publish it, and it would soon make the rounds of the anti-imperialist press. Then citizens would open their morning paper over coffee to discover a private "report on this nigger fighting business" in the Philippines:

> Last night one of our boys was found shot and his stomach cut open. Immediately orders were received from General [Lloyd] Wheaton to burn the town and kill every native in sight which was done to a finish. About 1,000 men, women and children were reported killed. I am probably growing hard-hearted, for I am in my glory when I can sight my gun on some dark skin and pull the trigger.

Other letters described widespread looting and senseless destruction of property. Captain Albert Otis (no relation to the general) boasted that he "had enough plunder for a family of six. The house I had in Santa Ana had five pianos. I couldn't take them, so I put a big grand piano out of a second story window. You can guess its finish." An Iowa volunteer expressed amazement over such conduct: "You have no idea what a mania for destruction the average man has when the fear of the law is removed. I have seen them . . . knock chandeliers and plate glass mirrors to pieces just because they could not carry them. It is such a pity."

Captain Matthew Batson wisely warned his wife not to let "outsiders" see his complaints to her about the conduct of American soldiers, "as it reflects on the discipline of our Army, and if published would cause me trouble." Batson described barbaric destruction, looting, and the slaughter of innocents. Americans "ransacked churches, private homes, and wantonly destroyed furniture, and not satisfied with this they enter cemeteries, break open the vaults and search the corpses for jewelry." He worried that "these people seem to be devout Catholics, and it will do no good to take their images of Christ and their saints and dress them up in ridiculous garb and generally insult their religion." Some soldiers, he added, "make no distinction between property belonging to insurgents, or the innocent, they simply loot everything they come to." Batson described the total destruction of a pretty village in Pampanga and the slaughter of its inhabitants for no apparent reason, before writing in anguish: "We come here as a Christian people to relieve them from the Spanish yoke and bear ourselves like barbarians."

Once such a letter found its way into print, it could not be ignored, and the War Department would order Otis to investigate. His idea of an investigation was to send a copy of the offending letter to the writer's commanding officer, who had little trouble wringing a retraction from him. It was just "a tall tale to thrill some maiden aunt in Wichita," or some such explanation was proffered. The imperialist press dutifully crowed that "the truth is now made clear," and "another atrocity fable failed the test of time."

On one occasion, however, Private Charles Benner refused to recant his report that Colonel Funston had ordered the Kansas regiment to take no prisoners. This forced Otis to order MacArthur to investigate. Benner confronted that general's advocate general with Private William Putnam, who confessed to shooting two prisoners under orders. Major John Mallory collected a number of corroborative affidavits, including two from officers, suggesting that Benner's original charge was accurate. Private Harris Huskey swore under oath that he had witnessed Major Wilder Metcalf shoot a prisoner on his knees begging for mercy. MacArthur forwarded Mallory's report to Otis, who, amazingly, ordered Benner court-martialed "for writing and conniving at the publication of the article which brought about this investigation," and also Putnam "for assisting by shooting, in the execution of two prisoners." When the judge advocate wisely warned Otis that "if put on trial, it is probable that facts would develop implicating many others," the matter was dropped.

As a civilian, however, Funston was not so easily protected. Charges that he had "commanded, condoned, and rewarded rapine and murder" came from his former officers and seeped into the press. One editor published a letter from a former civilian teamster with the Kansas regiment describing Funston leading a mock mass in a church while wearing stolen ecclesiastical garb to amuse his soldiers from the "Bible belt." A nurse accused him of looting two silver chalices and a lavishly embroidered robe he had removed from a statue of the Madonna to give to his wife.

Under clouds of suspicion, Funston accepted an offer to command a brigade of three new national volunteer regiments. He arrived in Luzon at the end of 1899, when the Filipino nationalists began guerrilla tactics, a mode of warfare not entirely suited to Funston's impetuous personality. He was not back long when he called a press conference to announce that he had just summarily executed two prisoners in retaliation for a successful ambush of his Macabebe scouts. This confirmed the worst rumors that he had left behind, and a headline in the San Francisco *Call* announced that he would be court-martialed. Funston then claimed that he had been misquoted: The prisoners had been killed "while attempting to escape."

A year later, having survived yet another Army inquiry into his past conduct that was more of a cover-up, Funston again became the hero of the hour in the spring of 1901 when he masterminded and led a daring maneuver to capture Aguinaldo in his remote hideaway in Palanan, just off the rugged northeastern coast of Luzon. Soldiers in Funston's command captured a courier from Aguinaldo to his cousin, Baldomero, with a coded message requesting more troops. Once Funston deciphered it and persuaded the courier to reveal Aguinaldo's location, he assembled 80 Tagalog-speaking Macabebe volunteers to pose as the requested reinforcements. Four renegade "insurgent" officers and a former Spanish officer were recruited to play the roles of officers. Naturally, Funston had to get in on the act, so he and four American officers went along as "prisoners" captured en route to Palanan. The Navy dropped them off on the coast far enough away to avoid any detection, and the group trekked over 100 miles to grab Aguinaldo in the midst of a birthday celebration for him. The ruse was carried off so cleverly that the astonished Aguinaldo first thought it was a joke. Funston brought his prize back to the coast for a prearranged rendezvous with the *U.S.S. Vicksburg* on March 25, 1901.

Once again, Funston dominated the headlines. Editors compared his latest feat to Roosevelt's charge up San Juan Hill in Cuba, and even to Dewey's victory on Manila Bay. A year earlier, Republican leaders had thought his heroism at Calumpit would take Funston to Topeka as Governor of Kansas, but now they began to think in terms of a Roosevelt-Funston ticket in 1904. Vice President Roosevelt, long an admirer of Funston, whom he classified as "a perfect corker," pushed the president to reward him with a regular commission at his present rank, the youngest in the Army at age 41. Only weeks earlier McKinley had declared that Funston was "not a man of proper temperament for any rank higher than that of a lieutenant in the regulars." But now that Funston had become a national idol, McKinley, once dubbed "The Emperor of Expediency," capitulated.

As he often did following one of his escapades, Funston rushed into print his own version of this spectacular coup for a popular magazine in order to milk more publicity from it. By entitling the article "The Exploit Which Ended the War," he reinforced the popular view that he had singlehandedly ended this vexatious conflict. In reality, Aguinaldo was little more than figurehead for the nationalist forces during the guerrilla phase of the war. Indeed, the complete autonomy afforded local commanders by Aguinaldo's isolation made the guerrillas much more effective, as quick decisions could be made in response to immediate conditions. Thus the war continued for another 15 months officially,

General Frederick Funston, aboard the *U.S.S. Vicksburg.*
(National Archives)

and on September 27, 1901, the Army suffered its worst setback in the war when bolomen, disguised as mourning women, charged out of a church in Balangiga on the island of Samar to massacre the American garrison there.

General Adna Chaffee, a celebrated Indian fighter with hard-line views on how to deal with "savages," had recently relieved MacArthur in command. He was encouraged "to take the most stern measures to pacify Samar" by his new commander-in-chief, Roosevelt, who had succeeded the assassinated McKinley shortly before the Balangiga disaster. Roosevelt made it clear that he did not intend "to repeat [in the Philippines] the folly of which our people were sometimes guilty when they petted hostile Indians." For the "pacification" effort, Chaffee handpicked another famous Indian fighter, General "Hell Roaring" Jacob Smith, already infamous in the anti-imperialist press for violating flags of truce and for having proudly posed for photographs in front of his "tiger cages," in which he crammed Filipino suspects for months with no toilet facilities. Smith's orders to Marine Major Littleton Waller, commanding a brigade on loan to the Army for the Samar campaign, were not subtle: "Kill and Burn! The more you kill and burn the more you will please me." He ordered Waller to make the island "a howling wilderness," and to kill all males 10 years and older found outside the coastal towns. Actually, Waller had more respect than Smith for the rules of civilized warfare, and informed his men that under no circumstances were they to make war on women and children.

Chaffee had already unleashed General J. Franklin Bell in the province of Batangas in Southern Luzon. Bell, too, was a well known veteran of Indian wars, and like Chaffee, a cavalry hero. While his orders were not as bizarre as Smith's, they were in some ways more sinister. In writing, he gave his officers the "right of retaliation," and directed them "to execute a prisoner of war" for each guerrilla assassination, "one selected by lot from among officers and prominent citizens held [prisoner] . . . chosen when practicable from those who belong to the town where the murder or assassination occurred." Bell also created concentration camps. The Army euphemistically labeled these facilities "models of sanitation" and worried that their inhabitants might not want to leave them following pacification, but an estimated 11,000 Filipinos perished in them, although Bell's tactics merely exacerbated smallpox and cholera epidemics that had preceded him to Batangas.

The year 1902 opened with an investigation into the conduct of the war by Senator Henry Cabot Lodge's Committee on the Philippines, largely due to pressure from the senior senator from Massachusetts, George Frisbee Hoar, a rare anti-imperialist Republican. The first 2 months were spent listening to "safe" witnesses, such as Generals Otis, MacArthur, and Robert Hughes, Admiral Dewey, and Governor of the Philippines William Howard Taft. Even they made some damaging concessions. Hughes, for example, conceded that civilized warfare was not being waged by America, and then tried to justify this by insisting that it was impossible to do otherwise because the enemy was not "civilized." Taft admitted that the "water cure" had been used "on some occasions to extract information." He was referring to a rather mild form of torture in which the victim on his back was forced to swallow huge quantities of water, sometimes salted, until he talked. None died, or was rendered permanently disabled from it, but anti-imperialist propaganda had made it much more draconian in the public mind. As though sensing the enormity of his error, Taft tried to make light of it, recounting that some Filipino suspects actually demanded that they be first subjected to this torture to have an excuse for divulging information. But the damage was done.

Critics on Lodge's committee soon forced the chairman to subpoena more critical witnesses, and by March, the public was being exposed to daily litanies of American atrocities. Ex-Corporal Richard O'Brien, for example, described the senseless destruction of a peaceful village ordered by ex-Captain Fred MacDonald, who spared only the life of a beautiful mestizo mother, whom he and the other officers repeatedly raped before turning her over to the men for their pleasure. Lodge desperately sought more "reliable" veterans, subpoenaing MacDonald to deny O'Brien's charges, which the chair then decreed to be "hearsay." Sometimes this backfired when a carefully selected witness, such as ex-Sergeant Mark Evans, testified that extermination of the natives was the only solution to the problem in the Philippines, and had to be quickly hustled off the stand. To end his investigation on a better note for the administration, Lodge recalled Dewey, Otis, MacArthur, and Taft before abruptly terminating the hearings in June, over anti-imperialist protests.

By then, however, new developments embarrassed the administration. Secretary of War Elihu Root rushed into print a document designed to demonstrate to the public that in those allegedly "rare instances" in which an American atrocity was committed, the perpetrators were swiftly and severely punished. Forty-four specific crimes committed by Americans were listed along with the punishments meted out. Despite Root's good intentions, the punishments were so ludicrously light that they quickly evoked editorial chortles in the opposition press. Six officers drew nothing more than reprimands for such crimes as rape, murder, and torture. But it was the case of Lieutenant Preston Brown that became the cause célèbre among anti-imperialists. Brown had been appropriately dismissed from the service and sentenced to 5 years at hard labor for

The *Evening Journal* in New York infuriated apologists for this war of conquest with this cartoon, inspired by General Smith's infamous orders to Marine Major Waller. "Of all the sins of 'yellow journalism,' this is by far the worst," the *New York Times* declared of it. There is some truth to this charge as Waller was much too professional to follow Smith's orders literally. (New York Public Library, Newspaper Collection, Astor, Lenox and Tilden Foundations)

murdering a prisoner, only to have President Roosevelt commute that sentence to forfeiture of half his pay for 9 months and a loss of 35 places on the promotion list!

Added to this was a series of devastating leaks to the press of very damaging documents thought to have been safely closeted under lock and key in the War Department. Investigations of Funston and of the rapine of Macabebe scouts against the hated Tagalogs, along with whistle blowing reports on Bell's Batangas campaign suddenly appeared in print. General Wheaton even agreed that "all native troops when they can escape the immediate control of their officers, are liable to commit murders, and they will rob and ravish whenever they have the opportunity." However, the private letters of their commanding officer, Major Batson, the same officer who once complained about similar conduct by American soldiers, reveal that he had encouraged such tactics:

> I am king of the Macabebes and they are terrors. . . . Word reaches a place that the Macabebes are coming and every Tagalog hunts his hole. . . . The time has come when it is necessary to conduct this warfare with the utmost rigor. "With fire and sword" as it were. But the numerous, so styled humane societies, and the poisonous press makes it difficult to follow this policy if reported to the world. . . . At present we are destroying, in this district, everything before us. I have three columns out, and their course is easily traced from the church tower by the smoke of burning houses. . . . Of course no official report will be made of everything.

The individual responsible for these leaks was unquestionably the Army's top commander, General Nelson Miles, who had presidential aspirations. To this end, he had pestered Roosevelt to place him in personal command of the Army in the Philippines. When this was denied, Miles went on an inspection tour of the islands, and returned in complete agreement with the anti-imperialists that his Army had routinely committed atrocities, hoping that this issue might open a path for him to the Democratic nomination later that year. The *New York Times* called Miles "one of those birds which fouls its own nest," but Roosevelt refused to make him a martyr for the anti-imperialists, and he served until he reached mandatory retirement age in 1903.

In March, Root got word that Waller had executed 11 prisoners on Samar without benefit of trial. He must have seemed an ideal scapegoat to Root, coming from the rival Navy Department. To Root's chagrin, however, Waller was acquitted by a court-martial in Manila when he revealed the bizarre orders that he had received from Smith. Editors committed entire front pages to bits and pieces of these orders in extraordinarily large type such as, "KILL ALL!" and "MAKE SAMAR A HOWLING WILDERNESS." One political cartoon depicted little Filipino boys lined up before a firing squad over the caption: "Criminals Because They Were Born Ten Years Before We Took the Philippines." In it, the American eagle was portrayed as a vulture in the national shield. Root simply had no choice but to court-martial Smith. He insisted, however, that Smith's orders were never meant to be taken literally, whereupon Smith declared to reporters that they were, and that this was the only way to fight "savages." Smith was found guilty in May and forced to retire.

As though the administration needed any more embarrassments, the war's greatest hero, "Fighting Fred" Funston, returned to the states early in 1902 to recover from a botched appendectomy. Over the next few months, Root might have wished that Army doctors had sewn up the general's mouth by mistake. Funston soon embarked on a cross country speaking marathon at various banquets in his honor. He was idolized by adoring crowds that blocked his train at whistle stops until he emerged to say a few words. Headlines greeted "Aguinaldo's Brave Captor" in each city while hordes of reporters dogged him everywhere he went. He rarely disappointed them. Funston scorned the veterans testifying before the Lodge committee as "prattlers" feeding "tall tales" to a few "scoundrelly politicians"—that is, Democratic war critics. Such veterans had "ornamented the inside of a grog house longer than they distinguished themselves in the field," he declared. Funston also mocked Governor Taft's "misguided attempt to establish democracy" in pacified areas: "We believe everything and everybody should have a vote, down to cattle and horses." Instead, "bayonet rule" was needed, as "the only thing a Filipino respects is force." His greatest contempt was aimed at war critics, who "prolonged the war by giving the Filipinos false hopes." The "blood of fallen American boys was on their hands." Such speeches won congratulatory headlines and fawning editorials in the imperialist press: One front page declared:

> BRAVO! GENERAL FUNSTON
> GREAT SPEECH BY LITTLE KANSAN
> SILENCE WHILE BULLETS FLY
> IGNORANT TALK AT HOME HAS SLAIN OUR SOLDIERS
> GOT TREMENDOUS APPLAUSE
> AND PROLONGED APPLAUSE
> AND CRIES OF "THAT'S RIGHT!"

Either such headlines went to the general's head, or gin rickeys affected his judgment, as he would later claim, but Funston also bragged about an escalating number of prisoners that he had summarily executed to deter guerrilla activity. At the posh Lotus Club in New York City, this braggadocio took an even more ominous turn when Funston told of hanging two black American deserters, and suggested that it would have been better to string up war critics at home. For starters, he even suggested hanging those who had recently signed a peace petition to Congress. While imperialist editors remained silent, their anti-imperialist counterparts first expressed shock and then rage. "Funston Advises Hanging. Gallows Would Suit Some Americans," announced the *Call's* front page, while its editor explained how prominent were Funston's proposed victims: "the presidents of nearly all American universities and the leading clergymen of all denominations in the union." The paper advised Funston "to repair his inflated condition and sheath his unruly mouth."

In the middle of his "gallows speech," Funston periodically shouted: "Bully for Waller!" All the way back to San Francisco, he would emerge from his train to shout this and "Hooray for Smith!" at adoring crowds. When he arrived, he insisted to the waiting reporters that he "stood by everything" he had said, although he did claim that his suggestion of hanging Americans was "merely an abstract comparison." He also informed astonished reporters that the President was in complete agreement with his views. That was too much for Roosevelt, who sent a private warning to Funston via their mutual friend, William Allen White, the eminent Kansas journalist, confidant of Presidents and Republican leaders, and Funston's fraternity brother at the University of Kansas. Apparently Funston was unable to control self-destructive impulses. At his next duty station in Denver after his long "recuperation" furlough, he mocked "the overheated conscience" of Senator Hoar at a local banquet. This was the proverbial straw that broke the camel's back, and Root ordered him to give no more speeches or press interviews. An official presidential reprimand followed.

Not everybody was satisfied with front-page headlines announcing that "Roosevelt Muzzles Funston." Over the next few weeks, Hoar and fellow war critics denounced Funston for hours on the floor of the Senate. Senator Edward Carmack of Tennessee called him "the mightiest Sampson who ever wielded the jawbone of an ass as a weapon of war." Congressman Samuel McCall informed the Harvard Republican Club that he would push for an indictment, and would not be intimidated "by the threats of some microscopic general [Funston was about 5 feet, 4 inches tall] who knows as much about the rules of civil government as he does about the rules of civilized warfare." But Funston led a charmed life, and he managed to escape relatively unscathed.

In the midst of all this political *sturm und drang,* Roosevelt pulled the rug from under his critics by simply declaring that the war was over in his Fourth of July speech in 1902. Describing it as the most glorious war in the nation's history, he commended "the bravery of American soldiers" fighting "for the triumph of civilization over the black chaos of savagery and barbarism." He did express regret over "the few acts of cruelty in retaliation [for] the hundreds committed by Filipinos against American soldiers."

AN INTERPRETATION

Roosevelt would have been on firmer ground arguing that atrocities on both sides are endemic to guerrilla warfare, enhanced in this case on the American side by the rapid expansion of the Army that spread experienced junior and noncommissioned officers too thin. Senior officers, such as Wheaton, Bell, and Smith, along with the commanders who protected them, Otis, MacArthur, and Chaffee, had spent most of their military careers fighting Indians, which probably hardened them to a certain amount of brutality. Funston did not have the luxury of this excuse. While most soldiers were too young to have fought in Indian wars, they were predominantly Western and Southern descendants of Indian fighters, often alluding to this in letters home. Add to this recipe, the intense nationalism of the era along with the vicious racism that permeated American society at the turn of the century, and one comes up with a formula that made it that much easier for many American soldiers to dehumanize the Filipinos, often ignoring the rules of civilized warfare. Even those who initially criticized such brutality, such as Batson and Lyon, soon capitulated to the view of the majority.

There has been considerable scholarly debate over the causes of an American empire. Some argue that empire was the product of monopoly capitalism. Yet most businessmen opposed the war with Spain; the country had just emerged from a serious depression, and they simply did not want to risk the recovery with new, unpredictable adventures. Other scholars have emphasized the roles of a few well-placed imperialists, including Roosevelt, Lodge, and Dewey. But their imperialistic appetites were severely limited. They wanted strategically located pinpoint colonies rather than large, heavily populated ones. Their interest was in coaling stations and naval bases to protect American interests in Asia. They specifically wanted to avoid "England's folly in India" and were initially interested in keeping Manila alone. Aggressive German naval maneuvers in the Philippines plus Japan's colonial interests enhanced the military's argument that Manila alone was indefensible.

Ultimately, the popular appeal of an empire was too strong to resist. The jingoistic fury of the people pushed McKinley into escalating his demands beyond Manila to Luzon and, by summer's end, to the entire archipelago. Having been patriotically aroused to fight Spain, emotional inertia alone made it easier for Americans to conquer the Philippines in the name of "civilization."

There is a related lesson to be learned in the attitudes toward the war that are revealed in the letters that servicemen sent home to family and friends. In our own day, the official ideology of war requires that war at least be talked about as if it were at best an unfortunate event, to be completed as quickly as possible and with as little blood and gore—hopefully, as in the Gulf War of 1990, in a series of "surgical" strikes.

The turn-of-the-century youth who fought in the jungles of the Philippines did not feel that way. They were full of passion for the action and excitement, the shooting and killing, that were part of the conflict. Youth enthusiastically embraced imperialism at the turn of the century, perceiving an empire as a new "frontier" that would both challenge them and provide new opportunities. Above all, the empire offered adventure. As a result, there were no problems getting young men to volunteer to serve in the war, and the morale of the soldiers was extraordinarily high, in spite of the inept and uninspiring leadership of General Otis. Young, swashbuckling, and bumptious leaders, such as Frederick Funston and Theodore Roosevelt, became national idols and spokesmen for the nation's warrior tradition.

American rule was also characterized by ambivalence and limits. As the story reveals, not all Americans approved of the nation's overseas adventures, and criticism in the press and Congress did not end with the war. While the United States was the last of the major powers to acquire an empire, it was also the first to become disillusioned with a formal empire, turning internal control over to Filipino *independistas* by 1907 and pledging future independence in the Jones Act of 1916, when Britain was still jailing Indians calling for independence. At bottom, neo-imperialism—those indirect informal controls over legally independent states—has always been more attractive to Americans. Not only is it more cost effective, but it also protects American innocence with the illusion that the nation can at once have an informal empire, and yet be true to its sacred principle of self-determination.

Sources: Most of the sources for this essay were primary ones, particularly the manuscript collection at the United States Army Military History Research Center at Carlisle Barracks in Pennsylvania. Letters, diaries, unpublished manuscripts, and unofficial army newspapers written by hundreds of soldiers from private to general are here. More such records are in the Library of Congress and the National Archives, particularly papers of important leaders, civilian and military, during the war. Other archives, at Harvard, the Boston Atheneum, and the Historical Societies of Massachusetts, Pennsylvania, and California were valuable for the papers of anti-imperialists. Senate and House documents, reports of commanding generals and the War Department were also used along with a carefully balanced, geographically and politically, sample of newspapers and periodicals. Such contemporary publications as *Public Opinion* and *Literary Digest* were valuable in tapping editorial opinion across the nation.

Related secondary works were also examined, including books written by Teodoro Agoncillo, Bonifacio Salamanca, Reynaldo Ileto, Theodore Friend, Glenn May, Peter Stanley, David Joel Steinberg, E. Berkeley Tomkins, and Richard Welch.

6

WILLIE BOY IN TWO WORLDS: AN EPISODE IN INDIAN– WHITE RELATIONS

James A. Sandos

Larry E. Burgess

The story of the hunt for Willie Boy unfolds in 1909, in the midst of the Progressive Era, a period of explosive change, when the United States was becoming the industrial and urban world power that it is today. Many of the economic and technological phenomena that we associate with that new American nation—the assembly line, motion pictures, the use of electricity to light the cities and run huge factories, rapid transit systems, automobiles, airplanes, turbines, enormous bureaucratic corporations, radio—were either new or recent achievements, or just around the corner.

The impact of these developments on the lives of working- and middle-class Americans did not go unnoticed. To protect industrial workers from abuse, and to limit discontent, Progressive Era reformers at the local, state, and national levels passed laws that regulated air and water pollution, required companies to install safety devices around dangerous machines, provided compensation for industrial accidents and pensions for widows with children, limited child labor, created boards to censor films, built school systems designed to train young people to work in the new vocations, and made efforts—the Sherman Act of 1890, the Federal Trade Commission Act of 1914—to regulate and restrict the big corporations in order to keep the economy reasonably competitive. Although most of these campaigns were supported by men and women and blacks and whites, the movement to break up the largest corporations—to "bust the trusts"—was something that only white men cared much about.

As told by James Sandos and Larry Burgess, the saga of Willie Boy contains only hints of that familiar story of Progressive Era "reform." Indeed, the account probably reveals more about the "dark" side of the Progressive Era, the side that disenfranchised blacks in the South, favored a program of eugenics to restrict the propagation of "inferior" peoples, made war against the Filipinos (see Chapter 5), or worked to limit severely the immigration of peoples from Asia and southern and eastern Europe (finally succeeding in 1924). In reading the story, look for evidence of both these aspects of the Progressive Era. Just as important, think about why Americans undergoing the changes described above might have found the tale of Willie Boy compelling.

While the other stories in this book tell one story, this account of Willie Boy consists of two or even three stories; in a sense, it is a story about stories, about the process of storytelling and the act of remembering. One story is the story (actually, stories) pieced together and told by whites; another story is the story told by Indians. And there is a third story—a mixture of narrative, analysis, and guesswork—which is the story that Sandos and Burgess believe to be true. Why so many stories? Is the story of Willie Boy a special story that has to be told this way? Or should every story receive this kind of treatment? As you read through the book, think about how some of the other stories might be told from different perspectives.

"'Love is hard.' Whenever my grandmother would tell this story," Alberta Van Fleet, a Chemehuevi Indian woman, told us, "she would begin by saying 'Love is hard.'" The story concerned Alberta's great-uncle Willie Boy and his beloved Carlota, but this story had been taken over by whites from its appearance on the deserts of southern California in 1909, and told from their perspective in the media more than 40 times. Eight decades later we sat in Alberta's living room asking for and listening to the story from a Chemehuevi viewpoint. What we learned contradicted almost the entire white-told tale.

THE "WHITE" STORY

The truth or truths of the matter are for you to decide. We must begin, however, with what had become the standard version. Willie Boy, a Paiute Indian to whites, got uncontrollably drunk, the alcohol inflamed his lust and he went to the temporary camp of William Mike on the Gilman Ranch in Banning, determined to take away Mike's 14-year old daughter. When the old man objected, Willie Boy murdered him with a stolen rifle, took the girl and ran away with her across the desert, into the Morongo Basin. A posse followed them, but although the pursuers got close enough to hear her sobbing, they could not capture the couple and finish the chase. En route the posse found signs that Willie Boy was "having his way with her," the euphemism for rape, and that she had run her shoes to shreds, leaving behind only bloody footprints in the sand. Although the posse men were mounted and Willie Boy and Carlota fled on foot, the couple nonetheless managed to elude their pursuers. When she began to slow his flight, risking his capture, however, Willie Boy ruthlessly murdered her, then ran further into the desert. Some days, with temperatures of nearly 100 degrees, Willie Boy covered 50 miles of desert terrain on foot—his tracks at times an astonishing 7 feet apart—demonstrating to his pursuers a remarkable level of physical conditioning and stamina. For unexplained reasons Willie Boy

One of several approximations of the route of Willie Boy's flight. (James L. Carling, "On the Trail of Willie Boy," *The Desert Magazine*, November 1941, p. 9.)

returned to the vicinity of his crime against her and encountered another posse. He ambushed them at the base of Bullion, later renamed Ruby Mountain and, during the ensuing exchange of gunfire, Willie Boy seriously wounded a posse man. As the wounded man was being taken out under cover of darkness, another gunshot rang out. A week later yet another posse discovered its effect: Willie Boy had killed himself with his last bullet.

Even though Willie Boy had eluded the posses sent after him by committing suicide, the white story became one of the triumph of law over disorder. Over time the episode became known as "the last great Western manhunt," one that brought a "bad Indian" to justice. Sixty years after the episode Abraham Lincoln Polonsky, a writer and director who had been blacklisted during the Hollywood Red Scare of the late 1940s, wrote and directed a film entitled *Tell*

Them Willie Boy Is Here (Universal, 1969). Polonsky cast Robert Redford as all the posses rolled into one man called Coop, and Robert Blake as Willie Boy. While providing some original plot twists, Polonsky told the standard story.

To sort out the complexities of the tale we must begin with how the story came to white attention and determine how it was created. "Kills Man, Steals Girl, Escapes Toward Desert," blared the headline of the *Los Angeles Daily Times* of September 28, 1909, a proclamation echoed by other papers. On the night of September 26, Willie Boy had come to Old Mike's camp to ask for his daughter, had been refused, and the tale began to unfold. Nothing had been reported to local authorities until the next day, because Willie Boy had threatened the family with death were anyone to follow. Nonetheless, Carlota's mother sought the aid of Indian police, and ultimately white men, to act as a posse to secure the return of her daughter. The Mike family, like Willie Boy, was Chemehuevi (whites had misidentified Willie Boy as Paiute) and Carlota's mother, Maria, did not want family members involved in the pursuit. Hence the two primary Indian trackers from the nearby Malki (now Morongo) reservation, were Segundo Chino, a forty-ish part-Chemehuevi man not related to the Mikes, and the much younger John Hyde, a Yaqui originally from northern Mexico and a noted runner. These two men provided non-Cahuilla allies from the predominantly Cahuilla reservation.

As much as the whites prided themselves on their tracking ability, it was the Indians who took the lead ahead of the main posse and reported back the signs. Yet newspaper coverage generally paid no attention to the Indians with the posse and focused instead upon the white men. Ben De Crevecoeur, on temporary duty as an Indian Constable to assist in the manhunt, and Charlie Reche, proved especially newsworthy. Chino and Hyde, however, found the "evidence" that Willie Boy was sexually violating Carlota: that her feet had become bloody. Such stories continued to fuel the posse's demand to find the couple, even though the arduous nature of the chase was beginning to wear down the pursuers. Later, Chino and Hyde found that Carlota had written an inscription in the sand (or in the mud or on a rockface, the story varies) that her "heart was almost gone" and that she would "be dead soon." This was a

This message, ostensibly scrawled in the sand by Isoleta Boniface as she was being forced to accompany Willie Boy in his flight, was translated by Indian Jim Pine as "My heart is almost gone . . . I will be dead soon." (James L. Carling, "On the Trail of Willie Boy," *The Desert Magazine*, November 1941, p. 6.)

remarkable accomplishment since no California Indian language had a written form, but whites chose to believe what Chino and Hyde told them.

Most of the press reported that Reche discovered the corpse of the girl on the morning of September 30. Only one local newspaper accurately noted that Indian tracker Hyde had been the first to come upon her body. When it was returned to Banning, the white townspeople became incensed and joined the press in branding Willie Boy a double murderer. Outrage spurred the formation of other posses to enter the desert, find Willie Boy, and bring him back "dead or alive."

White posse motivation to punish Willie Boy for his alleged rape and murder of a 14-year-old girl (she was actually 16), even though both were Indian, stemmed from the same racial anxieties that prompted an epidemic of white lynching of black men in the South in the late-nineteenth-century.

Ruby Mountain ambush site, from rock outcropping, behind which Willie Boy hid. The location of the vehicle approximates the approach of the posse. (Courtesy Tom Mohr)

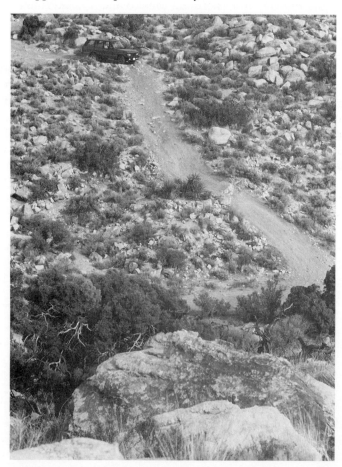

White fears of racially motivated sexual assault against the weakest element in their society—women, frequently young adolescents—came to be seen as an attack upon white power that demanded immediate vigilante "justice" to protect society and to terrorize men of color into submission. In southern California Willie Boy's supposed crimes of kidnap and rape, followed by murder, would have been of no interest to whites if they had taken place on a reservation, out of their sight. But the fact of publicity, that the crimes occurred off the reservation and in public view, even though they were "only" among Indians, demanded immediate retaliation to preserve the subordination of Indians to white societal norms.

On October 7, a week after finding Carlota's body and 10 miles from that spot, a posse approached Ruby Mountain. When the men dismounted to look for signs of his trail, Willie Boy, hidden on the slope above them, opened fire, killing three of their horses, wounding one, and driving off another. In the gunfire Willie Boy hit Reche; the bullet splintered on the handcuffs Reche carried on his hip and a fragment tore downward through hip and thigh, causing a deep wound. Reche lay sprawled on the ground in great pain, exposed to Willie Boy's field of fire 30 yards away and unable to move. Whites sent Hyde on a run of 35 miles back to their base camp and then on to Banning for a doctor. The rest waited for dark to haul Reche out. On their withdrawal they heard that final shot, unsure of its meaning.

When they brought Reche to Banning, enthusiasm for a return to the ambush site proved low. They had chased Willie Boy over nearly 600 miles of desert and were exhausted. Perhaps that last shot was the sound of suicide. If not, Willie Boy would simply run away. Why bother? At this point fate and deception intervened to offer new reasons to mobilize a posse. The reasons were: the visit of President William Howard Taft and the alleged threat to his security Willie Boy might pose, the prospect of an Indian uprising in support of Willie Boy or even led by him, and the previously unknown role that alcohol supposedly had played in initiating the story.

President Taft arrived in southern California while the manhunt was in progress, scheduled to travel from San Bernardino to Redlands and then to Riverside on his excursion inland. Taft traveled west that fall to mend political fences. He had fallen out with his mentor, former president Theodore Roosevelt, over what TR saw as Taft's softness on "trust busting." California Republicans were as divided as the national party and Taft sought to heal the division for the 1912 presidential election. Reporters for national newspapers accompanying the president, however, were bored by local news stories about teas and statue dedications, and so the Willie Boy chase provided fodder for their deadlines. "Taft in Willie Boy Land," declared the *New York Sun* on October 13, observing further that the "President Divides Attention with Bad Indian."

Could Willie Boy, a legendary marksman, pose a threat to the president? Taft's 300-pound size prompted making a special chair for him to sit in at Riverside's Mission Inn hotel; size also made him a large target. Eight years earlier a political dissident at Buffalo's Pan-American Exposition had gotten close enough to President William McKinley to shoot him twice in the stomach.

(*New York Sun*, October 13, 1909.)

TAFT IN WILLIE BOY LAND

PRESIDENT DIVIDES ATTEN-
TION WITH BAD INDIAN.

Four Posses After the Redskin, and Local
Committees After Taft—Long Trip
in Automobile Over Dusty Roads
Through Citrus Belt to a Banquet.

RIVERSIDE, Cal., Oct. 12.—President
Taft was in the Willie Boy country today.

What? Never heard of Willie Boy, the
Indian murderer, desperado and refugee? A score of crimes are laid at his
door and locally he is described as "the
craven slayer of an old man, the slaugh-
terer of a child whom he kidnapped for
love and the mutilator of three of his
trackers."

We', they are out after Willie and they
were just getting under way as the President of the United States whizzed by in
his automobile through Redlands this
afternoon.

They want Willie dead or alive, but
preferably dead.

Sheriff Ralphs of San Bernardino county
has offered $200 out of his own pocket to
the man who fires the bullet that brings
the desperado down, and the supervisors
have authorized him to spare no expense.

It was the fourth division of the posse
that was getting ready to move from Red-

McKinley died a week later of those wounds. Either fearing or feigning a possible replay—McKinley had visited this very part of southern California prior
to his assassination—the national press goaded locals into finishing the Willie
Boy chase. Added to this fear was word that Paiute Indians from other areas
were coming to Willie Boy's aid. With him or under his leadership, local papers
confidently reported they would rise up and oust all whites. The *Los Angeles
Times* announced on October 14 that: "Armed Piutes [sic] Come to Aid;
Redskins from Colorado to Help Willie Boy." Two days later the same newspaper declared that: "Piutes Are on Warpath; Indian Uprising Imminent Says
Sheriff Wilson; Willie Boy to Lead Natives against Whites; Washington
Apprised of the Grave Situation." Other newspapers echoed these sentiments,
arousing memories, and fears, of the Ghost Dance and of Wounded Knee.

The Wounded Knee massacre of December 1890 remained inscribed in
popular memory. On December 29, 1890, under the leadership of Big Foot,
Miniconjou Sioux, camped on Wounded Knee Creek on the Pine Ridge reservation in South Dakota, were coming in to be reconciled with federal authorities after having fled the reservation. Their flight had been the culmination of
a period of growing violence between Indians and whites surrounding a

movement known to whites as the Ghost Dance. While the Ghost Dance had originated in western Nevada in 1889 and spoke of a coming new world in which Indians would live in peace and whites would disappear, the message, when it reached the Great Plains, took a different turn. Sioux and other Plains Indians who had not reconciled themselves to reservation life, and who were starving from inadequate government rations, saw in the Ghost Dance a promise of the return of the buffalo and of the destruction of the whites. Sioux created "Ghost Shirts" made of muslin and painted with inscriptions that allegedly would render them impervious to the white man's bullets. Skirmishes between Indians and whites began to erupt and white fears of a resumption of the Indian Wars ensued. Big Foot's flight, followed by his decision to return and disarm his warriors, should have been seen as peaceful. But the Indians found themselves surrendering to the 7th Cavalry under the command of Colonel James Forsyth. The 7th Cavalry under George Armstrong Custer had been humiliatingly defeated, massacred, by Sioux and Cheyenne Indians 14 years earlier at a site Indians called "greasy grass" but that was known to whites as the Little Bighorn. Now, during the Indian disarming at Wounded Knee, someone began firing. Indians stopped laying down their arms and started shooting and hand-to-hand fighting followed. The army had Hotchkiss rapid-firing guns and in the ensuing slaughter more than 300 people were killed. To whites this was the victory that avenged Custer and finally ended the Indian Wars. Thus a possible new Indian uprising in 1909 raised again the specter of Wounded Knee and the need to end the threat posed by Indians and Willie Boy once and for all.

Ben De Crevecoeur, however, contributed perhaps the deciding element to the remount effort. He had been hired as a temporary Indian Constable with the Bureau of Indian Affairs (BIA) when the couple fled Banning. Fifteen days after the pursuit began, on October 11, he reported a startling confession made to him by an unidentified white youth who was vacationing in Banning from Los Angeles with his parents. To get a sense of rural life, the young man had stayed in the bunkhouse at the Gilman Ranch in a room adjacent to where Willie Boy slept. The boy had gone into the town of San Bernardino in "wet" San Bernardino County, purchased a large quantity of whiskey and beer, brought it back to Banning in "dry" Riverside County and hid the unconsumed portion in his part of the room. The following Monday the lad discovered the liquor gone and decided that Willie Boy must have found and drank it the previous Saturday night, before the killing and kidnap took place.

With this new information, the local press had fuel to immediately inflame local white fears. "Temperance Lesson in Blood," proclaimed the *San Bernardino Sun*, continuing "Drink Fest Is Cause of All Trouble Brought On by Fugitive Indian." The temperance movement had divided southern California, as it had much of the nation, between those who wanted to use the power of government to deny all access to alcohol because of its ill effects upon some, and those who opposed any such restriction. Social reformers knew that alcohol abuse had ruined homes and individual lives; reformers, especially Indian agents, were also certain that alcohol was a scourge among Indians introduced by unscrupulous whites. Providing alcohol to Indians, then, was a serious matter, but De

Crevecoeur believed that the lad was an ignorant outsider who had shown genuine remorse and so spared him any public humiliation or prosecution. But this final element had crystallized the need to return to Ruby Mountain. A drunken Indian's fate had to be known and punishment meted out if he still lived.

On October 15, Ben De Crevecoeur led the posse that discovered what that final shot had meant. Behind a boulder they found the badly decomposed body of Willie Boy. He had placed his rifle on the ground and propped it against his chest, under his heart, and after having removed his shoe squeezed the trigger with his toe. He had committed suicide. The posse might have been disappointed, since Willie Boy had denied them their victory over him. But no. Despite the fact that Willie Boy had held the high ground above them, the posse told the story that they had had Willie Boy surrounded (surrounded on one side as one wag put it); Willie Boy had been down to his last bullet and had killed himself in desperation, worn out by the many posses' pursuits. "Willie Boy is dead," read the account in the *Los Angeles Herald*,

> and with his death is ended the meteoric career of probably the most famous Indian renegade of late years, whose trail was blazed by two of the most cruel murders in the criminal annals of the two counties in which they occurred and by the most thrilling manhunt in the history of the great dreary desert, in the desolate midst of which, huddled in his lonely rock protected garrison, the desperate Piute [sic] murderer, broken in spirit by the hardship of the long chase and weak from the exposure and hunger, cheated his pursuers from their ambition of capture by using his last cartridge to end the life sought by a horde of officers whom, he thought would, in a few hours, close in on him.

Randolph Madison, a journalist from the *Los Angeles Record*, rode with this last posse, celebrated its exploits in his writings and photographed much of what he had seen. Because the body was in an advanced state of decay, the posse decided to burn it where it lay rather than to bring it back to Banning. Madison took photographs proving that they "got their man," but respecting the sensibilities of the day he did not take a close-up of Willie Boy's face.

Madison, a descendant both of James Madison and of the Randolphs of Virginia, brought his Southern "tidewater" sensibilities about the West with him when he came to Los Angeles to work as a newspaperman. To him the West was the last frontier, a place of excitement and danger where one could still see Indians; it was also a place where horseback riding, especially outside major cities, was common. Having been an avid horseman in Virginia, he could continue it in California. His visit to the desert and his ride with the last posse influenced his telling of the Willie Boy story.

Madison found his experience an exciting adventure. He described "the chase . . . [as] the most remarkable of any in the history of crime." It was an archetypal masculine experience, one in which men, pursuing a man, could behave as men. Free of the shackles of city life, these men rode hard, handled firearms skillfully, made a simple camp, and pursued their quarry relentlessly. Describing the close of the search, he observed Constable De Crevecoeur "riding ahead of the posse with the rest of us bunched behind."

Willie Boy's body, surrounded by posse members. (*Los Angeles Record,* October 16, 1909.)

Madison continued, "De Crevecoeur suddenly swung around in his saddle and shouted: `Look out boys!' Quick as lightning he [De Crevecoeur] whipped his long-range rifle from its scabbard, and, bringing it to his shoulder, fired. As quick as possible we rushed to the constable's aid, fully convinced that we would see the murderer running and dodging behind rocks, down the opposite slope. As we came to the ridge and looked over there lay the body" of Willie Boy.

Madison found some of the white men coarse, however, and so chose to lay his bedroll down next to the Indian trackers. He conversed with them and with De Crevecoeur about Indian customs. From the Indians he learned of Carlota's "written" message that they then recreated. He learned about the supposed Paiute custom of "bride kidnap," in which the suitor abducted his intended, stayed away overnight, and then forced the parents to concede their marriage.

To Madison, Willie Boy had tried to live like a white man but reverted to his Indian ways because of alcohol and lust. In a meditative piece that showed some sympathy with the Indian, Madison wrote "He Wanted Her—He Took Her—But He Couldn't Be a Piute [sic] in the White Man's World." To Madison, Willie Boy heard "the blood of his fathers calling him," those old Indian customs that would allow him to live his life "after the pattern of his fathers and his fathers' fathers" that proved incompatible with the higher goals of white civilization. In Madison's words, whites had branded Willie Boy "a bad Indian . . . until a 30-30 bullet made him a good Indian, which of course, is a dead Indian."

In the wake of the manhunt several white people benefited. The sheriffs of both Riverside and San Bernardino counties ran for reelection using their participation as a voter draw. Ben De Crevecoeur found his temporary position regularized by his superior as a result of his strong temperance stand and his posse riding. For Indians the results were mixed. Maria Mike had lost a husband, a daughter, and a potential son-in-law but had saved her remaining children from harm. Willie Boy's death meant that she need not fear future reprisals from him. And she later married Segundo Chino, whom she had gotten to know in his capacity as tracker for the posse.

Within 20 years the story began to appear in print, taking on a life of its own in frequent retellings. But what had been discovered last—the alcohol incident—became first in the retellings. In 1958 a journalist accompanied posse descendants, who rediscovered the site where Willie Boy had been cremated. Local law enforcement agencies then decided to erect a monument to themselves and to "The West's Last Famous Manhunt" on the spot of Willie Boy's suicide. In the meantime the burial site, for in Indian terms that is what it was, had been desecrated, bones and even the skull taken as souvenirs. Over time the Cahuilla Indians at the Morongo Reservation began to adopt the Willie Boy story as part of their own, since Hyde and Chino had come from that reservation. And interest in the story grew.

Abraham Lincoln Polonsky bought the film rights to a novel of the incident and then wrote and directed *Tell Them Willie Boy Is Here* (Universal, 1969). Polonsky reversed the posse praise of the traditional telling and portrayed Willie Boy as a violent young rebel, in the James Dean film tradition, who is pure in heart but nonetheless falls victim to white society's prejudices. Willie Boy's death is translated skillfully to the screen by having him confront the fictional Coop menacingly with his empty rifle, forcing the sheriff to kill him. In the end Coop washes Willie Boy's blood from his hands with the dirt of the West, playing Pontius Pilate to Willie Boy's Christ, while the gathering night signals the end of the frontier and the story. But Willie Boy remains a product of white imagination, a man who uses liquor and engages in bride capture. Although Willie Boy and Carlota, called Lola in the film, were real historical people and Polonsky used their historicity to sell his film, he did not treat them like historical subjects. Instead he used them as objects to comment on American society as he saw it.

To Polonsky's admirers the film is a Marxist comment on the consolidation of American Empire as seen in the lives and loves of four people. The Indians portrayed as Willie Boy and Lola are victims, the displaced original inhabitants removed by the relentless force of capitalism. She, however, wants to assimilate, to become a teacher like the Indian Agent Liz Arnold tells her, and she wants Willie Boy to become a farmer in Nevada. He will have none of it. He will resist to the end. Liz is from the East, representing the best schools and

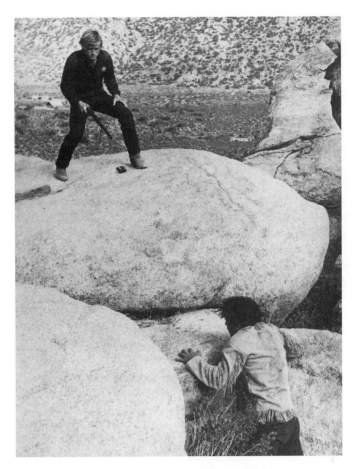

Showdown between Coop and Willie Boy, from *Tell Them Willie Boy is Here* (1969). (The Museum of Modern Art Film Stills Archive)

education for a woman of the time, a woman who both wants sex and yet is ashamed to see a man naked. Coop is the antithesis of Western film icon Gary Cooper, the model of manly decency. The son of a famous Indian-killer, Coop is a brutal man of the West, enforcing the law at the expense of the indigenous people.

Polonsky's story intercuts between the lovemaking of Indian and white couples, presenting the Indians as the Edenic ideal and the whites as degraded, conflicted between their desire for sex and love, for acceptance and respect. The American Empire oppresses them all but affects each one differently. And, while unremarkable at the time, Polonsky's treatment of women in the film would today be called misogynist. Yet it is his version of the story that is the best known today because it reached millions of Americans upon release and over the ensuing 30 years continues to touch countless millions more at home and abroad through film festivals, video and television replay.

AN INTERPRETATION OF THE "WHITE" STORY

For the general public this became a story of murder, kidnap, and rape instigated by a "savage" Indian, an offense against American law and society that demanded punishment. It was a morality play, a tale of savagery versus civilization with good and evil clearly defined. It also celebrated a spirit of masculinity and the new American empire while simultaneously raising anxieties about both empire and manliness. That was because the story touched upon an ancient fear; it raised the specter of an Indian uprising, of other native peoples joining Willie Boy to overthrow white rule at the very time that the President of the United States was visiting southern California. Willie Boy raised anew the dread that Indian resistance as embodied in the Ghost Dance had not died at the tragedy of Wounded Knee 20 years earlier. In 1907–1909, as Americans faced immigration in unprecedented numbers from areas of Europe considered inferior by many already here, Americans saw this outburst of insurgency as a serious threat from a group already considered conquered. By 1909, the Indian had become the "vanishing American," a people all but extinct except for this last irruption.

The story fascinated Americans over the years because it evoked images of the West both as a place where exotic things happened and as a process of "civilizing" a wilderness; and because of its location in a desert, a mysterious foreboding setting where the unimagined might occur. Randolph Madison's writings epitomized the attitudes of many whites toward the assimilation of native peoples. Civilization for Indians should involve assimilation, the idea that Indians should adopt white ways, and, when they fail to do so, when they cannot "stick with it," their tribalism triumphs over civilization.

Madison the Southerner brought his background of seeing and not seeing the "other" in his region, the African American, with him when he came to California. He apparently did not find it an odd custom that an Indian culture in the exotic West would initiate marriage and future family life by the groom's murdering his prospective father-in-law and then kidnapping and raping his intended bride. He believed the wild stories told him by posse members, especially De Crevecoeur, Chino, and Hyde.

Madison, supposedly sensitive to the Indian Willie Boy's story, did not ask troubling questions that the episode raised. If Willie Boy had been drunk, as De Crevecoeur first "established," then how did he manage to kill a man, kidnap his daughter, evade her family, and flee? Did he not need to sleep it off somewhere, sometime? Could not Carlota have used that opportunity to flee if she had been taken against her will? How could a man on foot outrun posses on horses? If Willie Boy loved Carlota then why would he kill her? Why would he return to the scene of his alleged crime if he already knew that she was dead? And why did Chino and Hyde incite the white posse to even greater anger against Willie Boy? Why did Chino and Hyde gamble that their fueling white hatred toward Willie Boy would not be directed at other Indians as well? Most of these questions went unraised at the time and continued to go unasked during the retellings.

THE INDIAN STORY

Because most local newspapers at the time called Willie Boy a Paiute, and since Randolph Madison claimed that Willie Boy had followed old Paiute Indian customs, all subsequent writers adopted the premise that Willie Boy's tribal affiliation was Paiute. The supervisor for Indian Schools in the region, however, described Willie Boy in 1909 as a mixed-blood Paiute and Chemehuevi man, meaning, in the language of the time, that Willie Boy's father had been Paiute and his mother Chemehuevi. When we began to do our ethnographic field

Willie Boy (*Los Angeles Record*, October 16, 1909.)

work, that is to visit Indians on their reservations to talk with them about this story, we learned that Willie Boy's father had left the nuclear family unit while his son was a small child. This meant that Willie Boy's tribal affiliation had been through his mother, making him culturally a Chemehuevi.

Therefore a Chemehuevi version of the story is in order. This is for them a simple story, but one containing important tribal information to be passed on to younger people, and to remind the mature and the elders of what they valued. "Love is hard," is the way the story always begins. Then Willie Boy is described as a young man living with his mother in the desert, able to provide for them by his remarkable skill as a hunter. His hunting prowess comes from his ability to run faster than many animals. He needs a wife but there are no young women around. "One day he saw his cousin Carlota," the story continues, "and he wanted her. She looked back at him openly, and they both ran away together." Members of both families pursued the couple, and found and separated them, admonishing them against further contact.

The Chemehuevi story recognizes Willie Boy's need for a wife but disapproves of his, and her, choice because they were "cousins." In Chemehuevi culture at that time, men were encouraged to marry outside the tribe in order to provide new blood and to prevent the physical debilitation caused by inbreeding. "Cousin" was an imprecise term used to indicate that the bloodlines were too close to permit marriage. When the couple defied tribal taboo to the point of running away, members from both families participated in the hunt to find, return, and separate them. There is no reference to "bride capture" because it was not practiced among the Chemehuevi. (In ethnographic fact, the Paiutes only rarely engaged in bride abduction, Paiutes in California did not use it at all, and firearms were never used.) This story then seems to convey a normally functioning Chemehuevi society, correcting deviance according to traditional standards.

But, as the story relates, "both their hearts were restless." One night Willie Boy got a rifle and went to talk with Carlota's father—a man of imposing physical stature—about marrying her. It is in the tension between Willie Boy and Carlota's father, Old Mike, however, that we can begin to see that all was not smooth in Chemehuevi society at the time. Old Mike is described as "a man of power," the Chemehuevi way to indicate that he was a shaman. Shamans in Indian societies and in the Chemehuevi tribe were people with special spiritual abilities derived by following dreams and developing a unique rapport with an animal helper to secure their goals. Some shamans could cure with their medicine; others could give advice that would help another get what she or he wanted. Shamans preserved traditional customs and ways.

Willie Boy, on the other hand, was a special type of runner, a member of an elite group that we think came under the spell of change promised by the Ghost Dance revival of 1890. None of this, of course, was known by whites. The revived Ghost Dance, taught by a Northern Paiute man named Wovoka, promised his followers that if they followed his dance they could bring back their ancestors, that the dead would rejoin them and all would live together in a peaceful world from which the whites would fade away. Wovoka taught a new message of hope to defeated peoples and his teachings spread. He advised his followers to watch white people carefully, to learn from them what was good, and to shun what was bad. Among the bad things whites did, according to Wovoka, was to drink alcohol. As a runner Willie Boy had been moved by the Ghost Dance with its promise of a new life. Prior to the episode in 1909 he had left the tribe to live near and observe white people by residing or working temporarily at Victorville, Redlands, and Banning. During that time he earned a reputation among whites as a hard working, sober Indian, a reputation that vanished after the alcohol story emerged.

"They argued," according to Chemehuevi tradition, "and Willie Boy got mad. Willie Boy killed her father, then he and Carlota ran away again." This time whites and Indians pursued them. After hiding Carlota in a wash, he went for food and this time "he ran in the old way, for he was like the wind, and no one could catch him then." After returning with supplies, he could not find Carlota. He began searching for her everywhere, not knowing that she had died. Encountering the posse, Willie Boy shot their horses, forcing them to follow him on foot—something they could not do. He ran away and in his running, according to the story, "he came again to his mother, but she now turned away. He ran further, far out into the desert, away from all his family . . . we later heard that he had died." To the Chemehuevi, and to other Indians, Willie Boy lived in Nevada for another 20 years following the episode. Whatever pictures the posse had produced they believe to be fakes: An animal, probably a bear dressed in old clothes, had been substituted for the supposed body of Willie Boy.

AN INTERPRETATION OF THE INDIAN STORY

This version, unlike the white tale, situates Willie Boy within a family and a tribe, describes cultural taboos that Willie Boy and Carlota violated and the consequences that violation had for them. To whites Willie Boy was a loner; to the Chemehuevi he, along with his mother, Old Mike, and Carlota, was part of them. The Chemehuevi do not mention alcohol in their telling. To understand the context of the Chemehuevi story we must delve into their ethnographic history.

There are aspects of Chemehuevi culture that are directly pertinent to this story. Willie Boy's proficiency as a hunter is attributed to his ability to outrun some animals. Later in the tale he is described as running "in the old way . . . like the wind." During the course of the manhunt Willie Boy ran the equivalent of two back-to-back marathons, over sixty miles, across hot desert with little or no water, carrying a rifle. His running impressed whites, although they attributed it to fear. Conditioning and training, however, not fear, makes for marathon endurance, and many Indian tribes had runners of remarkable power. In Chemehuevi culture, then, the source of that possible training had to be identified and considered.

We discovered in ethnographic writing about the Chemehuevi that they had a cult, in decline by the turn of the twentieth century, called "the runners."

This was a small band of young men with exceptional natural abilities as runners whose individual talents were cultivated by training so that they could act as couriers for chiefs. They also needed excellent memories because, in the absence of a written language, they were to carry a chief's message in their minds while they carried his staff of authority in their hands to the chief's intended recipient. To run with such speed required practice and intimate knowledge of the terrain, a knowledge that would reveal to them watering holes and resting places during the course of their journeys. Songs became the vehicle for learning game trails and watering spots, so the runners would sing as they ran. They literally articulated aloud what whites would call a map. We thought that Willie Boy's behavior suggested strongly that he had been a "runner"; when we conducted our interviews with the Chemehuevi, they confirmed it.

When he decided to seek Carlota for his wife and she accepted him, they challenged the traditional Chemehuevi tribal taboo. To do so Willie Boy must have drawn upon his self-confidence as a runner and his new Ghost Dance–influenced views. Old Mike, however, was not only a shaman but also a physically powerful man, larger than the slight and wiry Willie Boy. So Willie Boy brought with him the white man's rifle to offset the shaman's physical, and perhaps spiritual, power advantage. As the Chemehuevi story relates, Willie Boy got angry and killed Old Mike, then ran off again with Carlota. More than tribal marriage taboo had been broken now; he had killed a shaman. Even if it had been accidental, Old Mike lay dead by gunshot wound and Willie Boy fled.

In the course of his pursuit, according to the Chemehuevi, Willie Boy hid Carlota in a wash and left to find supplies, only to return and find her gone. While searching for her he encountered the posse at Ruby Mountain. We think that Willie Boy left his canteen and jacket with Carlota when he departed. While he was gone someone shot her. We think it was one of the Indian trackers riding ahead of the posse. She was found in the early morning and the bullet wound that felled her was consistent with a shot fired at a distance of at least 200 yards. Since Carlota was 2 inches shorter and 20 pounds lighter than Willie Boy, these differences would not have been noticeable had she been wearing his jacket to protect herself against the morning chill. Moving among the rocks she must have appeared to a tracker to be Willie Boy, and the anxious pursuer fired. The Indian trackers then identified Carlota's "written" message that contributed to the general public's sense that Willie Boy had killed her when she had become a drag on his flight. But the Chemehuevi, like all other California Indians, did not have a written language. Chino and Hyde therefore perpetrated a hoax on gullible whites that reinforced Willie Boy's guilt while deflecting attention from themselves as possible culprits.

When Willie Boy ambushed the posse there was a period from the initial exchange of gunfire until nightfall during which he and posse members exchanged taunts. We think it was during this exchange that he learned that Carlota was dead and that he had been blamed for it. According to the Chemehuevi, Willie Boy did not stay at Ruby Mountain. He ran away after the ambush because none of his pursuers could follow him. From the Chemehuevi perspective, moreover, he had alienated his tribe irreconcilably; hence when he returned to his mother she turned away from him. She had been forced to make the painful choice between reuniting with her son and living as an outcast with him, or staying with the remainder of her people. She chose to stay.

Alcohol is central to the white man's tale, but it does not appear in the Chemehuevi story. How can one reconcile these versions? When we discovered the timing of its appearance in the development of the tale, we were skeptical. Ben De Crevecoeur's story was self-contained, meaning it began and ended with him. There were no other witnesses he would identify. Craftily, he never said the boy gave or sold the alcohol to Willie Boy. In fact no one saw Willie Boy drink. In De Crevecoeur's story, alcohol had been placed near Willie Boy, and in white imagination he drank it. Because of Willie Boy's conditioning as a runner and his adherence to Wovoka's teachings, we concluded that getting drunk, especially before confronting a shaman, would not have been his behavior. We have only recently learned that Ben De Crevecoeur lied about the liquor incident so that his boss in the BIA and an archenemy of liquor, William Johnson, could add De Crevecoeur permanently to his force prosecuting bootleggers. Johnson did this even though by his own admission the Willie Boy chase "had no direct connection with whiskey." Removing the stigma of alcohol abuse helps to reframe what happened.

Another issue clouding understanding has been the theme begun by Madison and repeated by subsequent tellers: reversion to savagery. Such a view cannot admit that a supposedly lesser culture, in this case Indian, can pick and choose items of value both material and spiritual from white and Indian cultures and create something new. This is a trait today called cultural mixing and it was and is something many Indian cultures and the Chemehuevi practiced. As the encouragement for men to marry outside the tribe attests and as Wovoka's teaching further explain, these Indians practiced a cultural pluralism that foreshadowed the California of the twenty-first century. That cultural mixing or adaptation was not seen then or now as necessarily bad. The tension between the new and the old, however, was part of the core of this story for these native peoples.

In the Chemehuevi view this was a love story, and we historians must agree. Given his feelings for Carlota, we do not think that he killed her. We do think that upon learning of her death during the exchange with the posse at Ruby Mountain, Willie Boy confronted profound choices. Whites wanted him for two murders. He had alienated his own people and killed a shaman over the love of this young woman. Now she was dead. Surrender to the whites meant trial and undoubtedly death. Yet he could not return to his people. The Ghost Dance held out a promise. The dead would rejoin the living and the best time to see them would be at dawn. Under the cover of darkness the posse took Reche for treatment. Darkness gave Willie Boy the cover to join Carlota by killing himself.

In the story that the Indians tell, the Ghost Dance is not mentioned and traditional Chemehuevi values are upheld. To them the cremation site is a fake, not an Indian burial site. But to us it is. The clothes on the body could not have been put on a bear because the animal, if there were one, would have been too large for any human clothes. Moreover, the presence of a bear at that time is not credible. The grizzly bear, the California state animal, had been hunted to the point of virtual extinction by the turn of the twentieth century. The last one killed in the mountains adjacent to Ruby Mountain had been taken in the 1890s. The black bear, smaller than the grizzly bear, was not introduced to the San Bernardino area until 1933.

To us, then, Willie Boy's death at Ruby Mountain and his grave are real. This represents an impasse between the white and Indian worldviews. Nonetheless, we have come to respect and try to incorporate into our version of the story, the meaning of the Chemehuevi words, "love is hard."

Sources: The newspapers of the time, local, regional, and national, provide the basic outline of the story as it appeared to whites. Randolph Madison's stories and photographs generally appeared in the *Los Angeles Record,* but there are others in the archives of the Newspaper Enterprise Association in New York City. On masculinity in the era see Gail Bederman, *Manliness and Civilization: A Cultural History of Gender and Race in the United States, 1880–1917* (Chicago: University of Chicago Press, 1995). The quintessential study of the Ghost Dance and its consequences, especially for the Plains Indians, is James Mooney, *The Ghost-Dance Religion and the Sioux Outbreak of 1890,* Anthony F. C. Wallace, ed. (Chicago: University of Chicago Press, 1965, reprinted and abridged from *The Fourteenth Annual Report of the Bureau of Ethnology to the Secretary of the Smithsonian Institution, 1892–93,* part 2 [Washington: Government Printing Office, 1896]. For the best study of Wovoka and his teachings, see Michael Hittman, *Wovoka and the Ghost Dance* (Yerington, NV: Yerington Paiute Tribe, through a grant from the Grace Dangberg Foundation, 1990). Harry Lawton's fictional account *Willie Boy: A Desert Manhunt* (Balboa Island, CA: Paisano Press, 1959) provided the inspiration for Abraham Lincoln Polonsky's film *Tell Them Willie Boy Is Here* (Universal, 1969). For a treatment of Polonsky's career, including all his films, see Paul Buhle and Dave Wagner, *A Very Dangerous Citizen: Abraham Lincoln Polonsky and the Hollywood Left* (Berkeley: University of California Press, 2001). The subject of Indian runners in the Western Hemisphere over two centuries is treated in Peter Nabokov's *Indian Running: Native American History and Tradition* (Santa Fe: Ancient City Press, 1981). Nabokov did not mention the Chemehuevi. The best published ethnography of the Chemehuevi is Carobeth Laird's *The Chemehuevis* (Banning, CA: Malki Museum Press, 1976). For our interviews with the Chemehuevi descendants of the Willie Boy and Mike families, along with a Chemehuevi oral tradition of the story and our preliminary interpretation, differing from the one given here, see James A. Sandos and Larry E. Burgess, *The Hunt for Willie Boy: Indian-Hating and Popular Culture* (Norman: University of Oklahoma Press, 1994). We thank Joseph Herring of the National Endowment for the Humanities for sharing with us the letter of William Johnson to Commissioner R. G. Valentine regarding alcohol and the appointment of Ben De Crevecoeur as a regular officer. On bears in the San Bernardino area see Harold M. Hill, M.D., "An Historical Review of the Status of the Game and Fur Bearing Mammals of the San Bernardino Valley and Mountains," *Quarterly of the San Bernardino County Museum Association,* XXXII (Spring and Summer, 1985).

7

THE LEO FRANK MURDER CASE

Leonard Dinnerstein

Leonard Dinnerstein's story of the Leo Frank case has two victims: Mary Phagan, a working girl, brutally killed in an Atlanta, Georgia, pencil factory in 1913; and Leo Frank, the pencil factory's Northern, Jewish manager, wrongly accused of the murder, convicted and, in 1915, dragged from prison and lynched in the town of Marietta, where Phagan had grown up. The most important testimony was provided by Jim Conley, the plant's black janitor, whose portrayal of Frank as a pervert who took sexual advantage of his female employees—and then killed one of them—was somehow persuasive for the jury. Other protagonists in the drama included Hugh Dorsey, the prosecuting attorney; Frank's defense counsel, whose errors contributed to his plight; the United States Supreme Court, which heard the appeal; Georgia Governor John M. Slaton, whose efforts to secure something resembling justice may have caused Frank's death; and some portion of Georgia's citizens, who for a variety of reasons, some of them complex, wanted Leo Frank to die.

The Leo Frank case resonates with the tensions of the American South in the Progressive Era. As usual, the problem of race was central to Southern society. In Georgia, the Progressive Era produced a curious sort of progressive "reform": a literacy test and a "grandfather clause" that made it virtually impossible for blacks to exercise the right to vote. Given the intense racism of the period, it is all the more remarkable that an all-white jury found a black man's testimony credible—or was willing to act as if it had.

After the turn of the century the South had to deal with a problem, besides race, that would prove equally difficult: modernization. Led by "New South" advocates like Georgia's Henry Grady, the region encouraged industrialization and welcomed northern capital and northern managers—among them Leo Frank—to come south to participate in the area's transformation.

By 1910, the process was well under way, with results that were not to everyone's liking. Factories brought jobs, and that was good. But the jobs were often in faraway places like Atlanta, and small-town people found themselves worrying about people dear to them—friends, sons and, especially, daughters who had gone to the big city to find work. Parents were concerned that their adolescent children might be too young to deal successfully with all the challenges, including sexual ones, of an adult world.

To limit the exposure of youths to situations in which they were likely to be exploited, most Northern states had laws that prohibited children under the age of 14 from working in factories. Georgia's ordinance, typical of the less restrictive regulatory legislation of the Southern states, set the age limit at 12. Mary Phagan was 13. When her body was found, the search was on for a murderer who could be made to stand not only for what had happened to Mary, but also for what was happening in Atlanta, Marietta, and throughout the New South.

The Leo Frank case began with the discovery of a murdered girl in the basement of the National Pencil Factory in Atlanta, Georgia, at about 3:30 A.M. on Sunday, April 27, 1913. The night watchman had gone downstairs to use the "colored" toilet, and his flashlight shone on a human heap in the corner. It turned out to be a hefty girl with matted blood on her hair, bruises and lacerations about her face, swollen and blackened eyes, a strong cord and two strips of her underdrawers pulled tightly around her neck, a protruding tongue, distorted hands and fingers, and a filthy dress. Sawdust and grime covered both the garment and the human form to such an extent that it was difficult to see immediately whether she was white or black. The night watchman called the police, who arrived within 10 minutes. The sister-in-law of one of the officers worked in the factory, and she was summoned to identify the victim. "Oh, my God," she cried, "that's Mary Phagan."

Because the body was found in the basement of the factory, the police went to the home of Leo Frank, its manager, and brought him first to the mortuary to see it and then back to the scene of the crime. He did not recognize the dead girl, but after being given her name he checked his records and acknowledged that she had been paid the previous day, a Saturday. What would be revealed in the newspapers was that since it was Confederate Memorial Day, Mary had put on a fancy dress and silk stockings and had gone downtown to collect her wages. She planned to spend time afterward watching the Memorial Day parade and having fun with her friends. She reached the factory and was paid at about noon. Thereafter no one claimed to have seen her alive.

As the police searched the basement for clues, they discovered two notes purportedly written by the girl while being murdered! They read:

Mam that negro hire down here did this i went to make water and he push me down that hole a long tall negro black that hoo it wase long sleam tall negro i wright while play with me

he said he wood love me land down play like the night witch did it but that long trall black negro did buy his slef

That a person being attacked would have had time to pen such things was, of course, utterly preposterous. However, more plausibly, some police thought they had been written by the murderer to push suspicion onto someone else. That was just about the only correct assumption the police made.

In addition to these scraps of paper, which would thereafter be labeled the "murder notes," observers saw a path from a ladder to where the body was found; another trail from the body to the back door, which was open; blood-stained

Copy of notes found near Mary Phagan's body on the morning of April 27, 1913. Hugh Dorsey, the prosecuting attorney, would later argue that the note came from a pad in Frank's office. During the trial the prosecution made no comment about the location of the pad, but a later investigator suggested that the pieces of paper had to have come from the basement, where the old pads had been stored. (Courtesy, American Jewish Archives)

fingerprints on that door; and a girl's hat and parasol, a ball of twine, and formed human excrement at the bottom of the elevator shaft. When the elevator was later used, it crushed everything at the bottom of the shaft and led to the spread of a foul odor. At the time no one realized how important these clues were and how significant was the crushing of everything at the bottom of the elevator shaft. Police sawed off a board in the door and took the corpse's jacket with the intent of searching for fingerprints, but no report of such tests (if they were indeed done) was ever made. A couple of days later police arrested Jim Conley, the African-American janitor, after an informant observed him washing blood off a shirt; but the police lost the shirt before analyzing the blood.

The nature of the corpse, the circumstances under which the white "little girl" was found, and the kind of work that she had been forced into—laboring in a factory with male supervisors who probably "had their way" with their female employees—aroused a city that had not been so exercised since the 1906 riot in Atlanta.

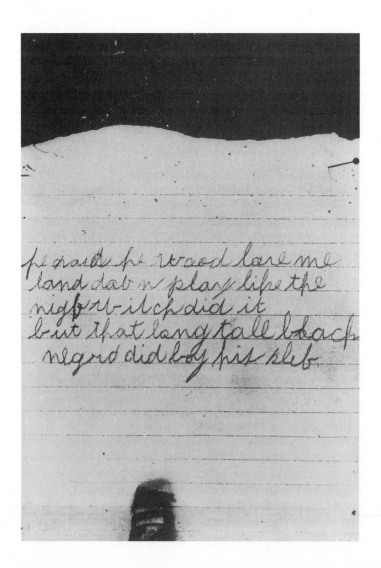

One of the reasons the populace reacted so violently to the child's death stemmed from changes caused by industrial exploitation. Mary Phagan's family was among those rural dwellers who moved to the city in search of a better life. But a "better life" meant that everyone would have to be gainfully employed; most of the opportunities for children were in the new industrial establishments. Both Baptist and Methodist preachers (an overwhelming majority of Southern workers were either Baptists or Methodists) had warned their parishioners that urbanization and industrialization would sap their strength and corrupt their morals. But the industrialists who denied labor a living wage had no qualms about undermining Christian teachings.

Since the 1880s Atlanta had transformed itself from a sleepy village into an industrial metropolis. As cotton textile mills and other newly formed manufacturing enterprises proliferated, the city's population mushroomed. Census takers counted fewer than 40,000 people in the city in 1880, but found 89,000 people there in 1900. By 1913 an estimated 173,000 persons lived in Atlanta. Despite the growth of the population there were not enough laborers, and the new entrepreneurs, many from the North, hired women and children to perform menial tasks. But wages were low (Mary Phagan had earned 10 cents an hour) and hours were long. Factory workers remained at their tasks from 6 A.M. to 6 P.M. except for Saturdays, when they finished at noon. Not only were the establishments in which they spent most of their days filthy, but safety and health regulations were almost nonexistent, and many a child caught a finger or hand while operating machinery.

Atlanta proved a particularly harsh environment for workers. Thirty-five thousand families had to make do with only 30,000 dwelling units in the city; recreational facilities were inadequate and health hazards abounded. From 1904 to 1911 the number of diphtheria cases in the city increased by 347 percent, typhoid fever increased by 307 percent, and tuberculosis increased by 602 percent. Not surprisingly, Atlanta had one of the nation's highest death rates. Of 388 American cities, only 12 recorded more deaths per 1,000 people than Atlanta. The city also had an appallingly high crime rate and an inadequate police force. More children were arrested in Atlanta in 1905 than in any other city in America; 2 years later, only New York, Chicago, and Baltimore—cities with much larger populations—arrested more children than did Atlanta. That same year, 1907, the city counted 102,000 people and 17,000 arrests. It is no wonder therefore, that the 1913 president pro tem of the Southern Sociological Congress, then meeting in the city, stated, "If social conditions in Atlanta were of the best—if conditions in factories were of the best; and lastly, if children of such tender years were not forced to work, little Mary Phagan would probably never have been murdered." No doubt such thoughts crossed the minds of mourners who were present while they laid the child's body to rest.

At Mary's funeral her mother's wailings interrupted the singing of "Rock of Ages" dozens of times. "The light of my life has been taken. Oh, God," her mother sobbed, "her soul was as pure and as white as her body." Newspapers reported that before the completion of "Rock of Ages," "there was scarcely a dry eye in the whole church." The presiding minister proclaimed that he believed "in the law of forgiveness. Yet I do not see how it can be applied in this case. I pray that this wretch, this devil, be caught and punished according to the man-made, God-sanctioned laws of Georgia."

"The assault and murder of 14-year-old Mary Phagan," the *Atlanta Constitution* reported, "comprise the most revolting crime in the history of Atlanta. Homocide is bad enough. Criminal assault upon [a] woman is worse. When a mere child, a little girl in knee dresses, is the victim of both there are added elements of horror and degeneracy that defy the written word." The editorial went on to denounce the "human beast with more than jungle cruelty and less than jungle mercy" who committed the crime. "The detective force and the entire police authority of Atlanta are on probation in the detection and arrest of this criminal," the editorial warned. "All Atlanta, shocked at a crime that has no local parallel in sheer horror and barbarity," the writer continued, "expects the machinery of the law to be sufficient to meet the call made upon it. If ever the men who ferret crime and uphold the law in Atlanta are to justify their function it must be in apprehending the assailant and murderer of Mary Phagan."

The police had been sloppy in the past and there had been 18 unsolved murders in the city during the previous 2 years; the prosecutor had lost his two previous cases. This time, incompetence would not be tolerated. Law officers felt the city breathing down their necks. One day after the body's discovery newspapers headlined the hiring of Pinkerton detectives. Leo Frank did that to protect the interests of the National Pencil Factory.

With the city in a state of extreme anxiety, the police arrested five alleged culprits on scanty evidence. One was the African-American night watchman who found the body and who was tortured and encouraged to "confess" to the crime. Others included stray men who had had some contact with Mary on Confederate Memorial Day or who were known to have been in the factory on that day.

Policemen even arrested Leo Frank, the factory superintendent. Frank had asked the night watchman to come in earlier than usual on the day of the murder and then asked him to leave and return at his normal time. After Frank left the plant he called the night watchman to find out how things were in the factory. He had never done either of those things before. Frank also appeared nervous and "out of sorts" after having been awakened Sunday morning, given the news of the murder, and asked to view the body in the morgue.

Other "clues" led police to focus on Frank. He had given Mary her pay on Saturday afternoon and had been, to the best of anyone's knowledge, the last person to have seen her alive. Another factory employee, Monteen Stover, came into Frank's office around noon on the day of the murder but did not see anyone. She said that she waited for about 5 minutes and then left when no one appeared. A couple of days later what appeared to be strands of hair and "blood stains" (which after microscopic examination turned out to be chips of paint) were found in a factory workroom near Frank's office.

At the coroner's inquest a 14-year-old boy stated that Mary had been afraid of Leo Frank, and that the factory superintendent had flirted with her and had made inappropriate advances. The statement could be neither proved nor dismissed,

GIRL SLAIN IN STRANGLING MYSTERY

These images of the victim, Mary Phagan, reveal something about what her
death meant to many southerners. On the left is an unretouched family photo; it
appeared in *Watson's Magazine* in March 1915. On the right is an idealized image
that appeared in the *Atlanta Georgian* on April 28, 1913, the day after her body
was found. (Courtesy, American Jewish Archives)

but it fit in with the prosecution's need, and the public's hunger, for a culprit
to be identified. And relationships of the sort described—or imagined—by the
boy, were not uncommon in the nation's mills and factories.

The arrest of Frank satisfied a number of inner cravings that many of
Atlanta's populace probably had but did not know how to articulate. These
yearnings were perhaps best expressed several decades later by the pastor of
Mary Phagan's church. "My feelings, upon the arrest of the old negro night-
watchman, were to the effect that this one old negro would be poor atonement
for the life of this innocent girl. But, when on the next day, the police arrested
a Jew, and a Yankee Jew at that, all of the inborn prejudice against Jews rose up
in a feeling of satisfaction, that here would be a victim worthy to pay for the
crime." Unbeknownst to himself, Leo Frank had become a symbol.

Although born in Paris, Texas, on April 17, 1884, raised in Brooklyn, New
York, and educated at Cornell University, Frank did not think of himself as an
unusual person. After graduating from college in 1906 and working in the
North for a time, he accepted a job offer from an uncle to come down to Atlanta,
buy a share in the uncle's pencil factory, and manage it. In his new city, he met,
and in 1910 married, Lucille Selig, daughter of a prominent Atlanta Jewish family; they had no children. In 1912 other lodge members elected him president of
the local B'nai B'rith organization.

Although he was highly regarded by those who knew him well, others viewed Frank from a different light. He was well educated in a city that did not regard education as egalitarian, he was Jewish in a stronghold of Protestant fundamentalism, and he managed a factory in a city where workers were generally ill treated. Once the police fingered him, therefore, every aspect of his being came under analysis by the press and the public. He was a "small, wiry man, wearing eyeglasses of high lens power. He is nervous and apparently high-strung," the *Atlanta Constitution* informed readers. He smoked cigars, dressed neatly, spoke fluently and had a "nervous, billious temperament which at first repels rather than attracts."

Those who knew Frank were appalled as the press continued to publish items and rumors too preposterous to believe but too salacious to ignore. Reading the newspapers in Atlanta during the month following Frank's arrest, one "learned" that Jewish men were allowed to "violate" gentiles but not members of their own faith, that Frank's wife had been about to divorce him, that he had another wife and children in Brooklyn, that he had another wife in Brooklyn whom he had killed, that his wife in Atlanta believed him guilty and therefore did not visit him in jail, that he had had children out of wedlock, that he was a pervert, that he pulled girls off trolleys while they tried to resist him, and that he "was a Mason and the Masons were all for him; that he was a Catholic and they were all for him; that he was a Jew and the Jews were all for him."

The charge of "perversion" probably hurt Frank the most, but no newspaper ever explained what was "perverse" about him. During his trial, prosecutor Hugh Dorsey, who used the Frank case as a steppingstone to the state governorship, alleged, but never stated, that Frank had had an abnormal relationship with one of the teenaged boys in his employ. Being a Jew, a Northerner, and an industrialist, Frank never was able to overcome the feeling in Atlanta that the police had fingered the murderer.

Contributing to this belief were the assertions of Hugh Dorsey, the solicitor general, that there was no doubt that the right person had been apprehended. Why Dorsey was so keen on this thesis has never been discovered, although speculators have suggested that he believed a conviction in the case would propel his political career, while a defeat would have ended it. Had the police and the solicitor general not made up their minds too early, they could have focused upon a much more likely suspect: Jim Conley, the African-American janitor at the pencil factory, who had been arrested for having been seen washing blood off one of his shirts.

On the day that Dorsey went to the grand jury seeking an indictment against Frank, Conley was being given the third degree in the police station. The janitor had been asked to write copies of the "murder notes," but claimed that he could not write. After hearing someone remark upon this in his presence, Frank told the police that Conley certainly could write, and then the officers had the janitor rewrite the "murder notes." Conley's handwriting matched the notes more closely than that of any of the other suspects, and finally the police, with their crude methods of interrogation, obtained a confession from him.

Leo Frank, the defendant, in the foreground. His wife and
other people are sitting behind him in the courtroom during
the trial. Do you think this picture would lead people to think
Frank was "perverse"? (Courtesy, American Jewish Archives)

According to Conley's tale he had been called into Frank's office the day
before the murder and Frank had asked him to pen the words found on the
papers. Frank allegedly mumbled something like, "Why should I hang." When
Conley's account was released to the press, journalists raised two important
questions. Why should Frank, or anyone else, have dictated the "murder notes"
the day before the event? And why would Frank, who absolutely refused to
speak with reporters during his incarceration, have made such a strange statement about hanging? The affidavit simply did not ring true.

Responding to these criticisms, the police requestioned Conley and got
another affidavit from him. In this second statement he acknowledged having
been in the factory on the day of the murder and claimed that he had stood
guard for Frank while the factory superintendent "entertained" a young woman

in his office. Then Frank allegedly whistled for Conley to come up, told the janitor he had just committed a murder, and instructed Conley to write the "murder notes." This affidavit did not satisfy the newspapers either, and so a third one had to be obtained, in which Conley claimed to have helped Frank remove the body to the elevator and take it to the basement. Subsequently there was a fourth affidavit, and thereafter the police kept Conley secluded from reporters until after the trial.

That any rational person would believe the bizarre and irreconcilable words of a person who had been brutalized by the police before giving sworn statements is difficult for modern readers to accept. But most people do not follow criminal accusations logically or put the pieces together themselves. A brutal murder had occurred, the police focused upon a Jewish, Northern factory owner as the culprit, and almost everyone in Atlanta seemed to think Frank was guilty. Several newspaper reporters had pointed out inconsistencies in the janitor's successive accounts. In response, the police reexamined Conley and encouraged him to assemble a tale that would meet public acceptability.

Frank's trial opened in Atlanta on July 28, 1913. Solicitor General Hugh Dorsey and members of the police assured the public that they had no doubts that they had found the murderer and asked everyone to give them the time necessary to prove their case in court. Frank reportedly had the best Southern attorneys money could buy: Luther Z. Rosser and Reuben R. Arnold. The state prosecutor, Hugh Dorsey, had at his side another well-known Georgia attorney, Frank Hooper. The prominence of these men led the *Atlanta Constitution* to speculate that observers would witness the "Greatest Legal Battle in the History of Dixie."

The prosecution began its case with familiar "facts" indicating that blood spots on the floor and strands of Mary Phagan's hair appeared in a workroom near Frank's office. Doctors had established the time of Mary Phagan's death at between 12:00 and 12:15 P.M. Frank claimed earlier that he had been in his office during that 15-minute period.

The prosecution also presented several teenaged female factory workers who swore under oath that the factory superintendent had often looked into the girls' dressing rooms, sometimes touched them, and often looked at them leeringly. Whether these things happened or not is impossible to say since many of the witnesses later changed and rechanged their testimonies. What was important, however, is that these accusations fueled public beliefs that Frank was a pervert and molested innocent females.

All of these witnesses, however, constituted a prelude to Jim Conley, upon whose shoulders rested practically all of the state's case. Conley's statements sounded "glib" and rehearsed to the reporter for the *Atlanta Journal*, but to the spectators in the courtroom and members of the jury, they rang true. The janitor recalled that he had come to the factory early on the day of the murder. Frank had allegedly then sent him on some errands and told Conley when to return because he was expecting a young lady with whom he planned to "chat," and he wanted the janitor to "watch out" for him as he had allegedly done in the past. Frank supposedly had a signal which would indicate to Conley when he should lock the downstairs door and when it should be reopened.

Conley then stated how Mary Phagan had come into the building and had gone up to the second floor office. Then he heard footsteps going back to the metal workroom and shortly thereafter a girl screamed. Right after that, Conley stated, Monteen Stover arrived and went up to Frank's office. "She stayed there a pretty good while," and then left. Soon afterward Frank allegedly stamped his feet, a signal for Conley to come up to the office. When he got there, the sweeper related,

> Mr. Frank was standing up there at the top of the steps and shivering and trembling and rubbing his hands. He had a little rope in his hands—a long wide piece of cord. His eyes were large and they looked right funny. He looked funny out of his eyes. His face was red. Yes, he had a cord in his hands just like this here cord. After I got up to the top of the steps, he asked me, "Did you see that little girl who passed here just a while ago?" and I told him I saw one come along there and she came back again, and then I saw another one come along there and she hasn't come down, and he says, "Well, that one you say didn't come back down, she came into my office a while ago and wanted to know something about her work in my office and I went back there to see if the little girl's work had come, and I wanted to be with the little girl, and she refused me, and I struck her and I guess I struck her too hard and she fell and hit her head against something, and I don't know how bad she got hurt. Of course you know I ain't built like other men." The reason he said that was, I had seen him in a position I haven't seen any other man that has got children. I have seen him in the office two or three times before Thanksgiving and a lady was in his office, and she was sitting down in a chair and she had her clothes up to here, and he was down on his knees, and she had her hands on Mr. Frank. I have seen him another time there in packing room with a young lady lying on the table, she was on the edge of the table when I saw her. He asked me if I wouldn't go back there and bring her up so that he could put her somewhere, and he said to hurry, that there would be money in it for me. When I came back, I found the lady lying flat on her back with a rope around her neck. The cloth was also tied around her neck and part of it was under her head like to catch blood. . . . She was dead when I went back there and I came back and told Mr. Frank the girl was dead and he said, "sh-sh!" He told me to go back there by the cotton box, get a piece of cloth, put it around her and bring her up.

Frank then allegedly asked Conley to remove the body to the basement via the elevator, which, Conley claimed, he did before returning the elevator to the second floor. After returning to Frank's office Conley was asked if he could write, and when he answered affirmatively, Frank allegedly dictated the murder notes.

Conley told his tale deliberately, and people in the courtroom hung onto his every word. He looked and sounded believable. What's more, Frank's attorneys could not break him. Nor did they comprehend the impact that allegations of Frank's alleged sexual improprieties would have upon jurors and the public. For 16 hours Rosser and Arnold questioned Conley. They were the ones who induced the janitor to talk about other occasions when he had supposedly "watched out" for Frank while the superintendent was alone with the girls and young women in his employ.

A montage of newspaper drawings during the trial. The man with the cord is Hugh Dorsey, the prosecuting attorney. The man in the chair is Jim Conley, the prosecution's main witness. The three women are sitting in the courtroom. What do their expressions suggest about their interest in the trial? (Courtesy, American Jewish Archives)

Conley made one mistake. During his testimony, he acknowledged that he had defecated at the bottom of the elevator shaft on the morning of the murder. Since police had seen formed stool (along with Mary Phagan's parasol and other personal items) at the bottom of the shaft on the day that Mary's body was found, this meant that the elevator had not been used from the morning before the murder until the next day. Inquiry along this line might have been profitable, but Frank's attorneys did not pursue it. Two years later Governor John M. Slaton would remark on this aspect of the testimony.

Frank's attorneys also erred when they tried to have Conley's testimony about other times that he had "watched out" for Frank stricken from the record. In doing so, they had not only initiated the topic, but encouraged the sweeper to tell what he knew. The prosecutors agreed that the material should not have been admitted, but they also acknowledged that once the defense attorneys had introduced the subject, encouraged Conley to make his remarks, and allowed the jurors to hear the story, it was too late to remove Conley's devastating tales.

Although prosecutors never argued that Mary Phagan had been sexually assaulted, it obviously helped their case to have the defense attorneys induce witnesses to talk about other times that the accused may have behaved improperly with his female employees. The presiding judge also recognized that the defense attorneys had miscalculated. He observed that while inappropriate testimony might be expunged from the record, "it is an impossibility to withdraw [it] from the jury's mind."

Conley proved to be an extraordinarily effective witness. Those who heard him speak found the testimony mesmerizing. Bigots, who had no respect for African Americans, concluded that if Frank's allegedly brilliant attorneys, who knew "the negro character thoroughly," could not get the janitor to change his story, then he must have been telling the truth. As one reporter who witnessed the trial later observed, "a man of his mental capacity could have been broken if he was lying."

In his own defense, Leo Frank took the stand on Monday, August 11, shortly after 2 P.M. His appearance had been eagerly awaited since he had refused to speak with newspaper reporters beforehand; this would be the first time he spoke publicly. As he approached the courthouse that afternoon the usually boisterous crowd hushed; as he took the stand to speak, and for the following 4 hours, spectators in the courtroom hung on his every word. Under 1913 Georgia law, a defendant charged in a capital case could not testify under oath or be cross-examined by the prosecutor. An individual could, however, make a statement on his own behalf. Frank chose to avail himself of this opportunity and presented his case strongly, articulately, and without emotion.

Frank claimed that he had been at the factory all morning, had gone home for lunch at about 1 P.M., and had returned to the factory shortly after 3 P.M. He explained that Monteen Stover might not have seen him when she came to the office because he might have been sitting at his desk where he could neither see anyone in the front of the office or be seen if the safe door was open. Alternatively, he suggested that he might have been out of the office for a few moments because of "a call of nature."

Frank's account of his time made it impossible for him to be telling the truth and for Conley also to have been accurate. Reporters had already tried to do what Conley said he had done for Frank: observing the girl entering the building and going up to the second floor, being called up to Frank's office, being asked to remove the body, and then being asked to write the "murder notes." It took them more than an hour to reenact the alleged activities. The Atlanta *Georgian* thought Frank had defended himself well, while the *Constitution* noted that Frank's comments "carried the ring of truth in every sentence."

The jurors, however, had to contend with more than the witnesses and the evidence. The trial took place on the first floor of a building with large, and open, windows. Spectators, both inside and outside of the courtroom, were vocal in their cheers when the prosecution scored a point, and Hugh Dorsey, the prosecutor, was lionized as he entered and left the courtroom each day. Shouts came from the outside, "Hang the Jew," and others claimed that jurors had been warned, "Hang the Jew or we'll hang you."

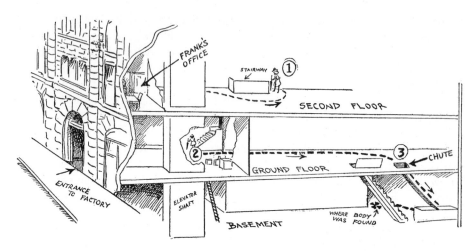

A cutaway drawing of the Atlanta, Georgia, pencil factory where Mary Phagan was murdered. The drawing was made from a model of the factory used by the defense at Leo Frank's trial. (The *Atlanta Journal,* August 10, 1913) (Courtesy, American Jewish Archives)

In summation Frank's attorneys argued that their client was victimized because he was a Jew, and they claimed that he would not even have been put on trial had he been a Christian. Dorsey, in rebuttal before the jury, denied that Frank's religion had entered into consideration, but he went on to state that while some Jews such as former Prime Minister Benjamin Disraeli of England and former Confederate Cabinet member Judah P. Benjamin had praiseworthy accomplishments, other Jews "sink to the lowest depths of degradation."

The trial lasted 4 weeks, yet it took the jurors less than 4 hours to find the defendant guilty. Presiding Judge Leonard Roan had anticipated a riot if Frank had been found innocent, and in the presence of the jury asked the sheriff how the crowds would be handled under such a circumstance. Georgia's governor made plans to call out the National Guard. Frank's attorneys were asked to keep their client away from the court when the jury rendered its verdict. They agreed. The judge had also decided not to sentence the convicted murderer at the time that the jury provided its decision.

After hearing the jury's finding and the judge's resolution to postpone sentencing, Hugh Dorsey left the courtroom. According to the *Atlanta Constitution,* "Three muscular men" immediately slung him "on their shoulders and passed him over the heads of the crowd across the street to his office. With hat raised and tears coursing down his cheeks, the victor in Georgia's most noted criminal battle was tumbled over a shrieking throng that wildly proclaimed its admiration. Few will live to see another such demonstration."

The next day Judge Roan secretly convened the principals in the case and sentenced Frank to hang. This had been done quietly and without fanfare because Roan feared the consequences if Frank's public appearance became known. A north Georgia newspaperman later wrote, "There is no use mincing words when a human life is at stake. If the jury in the Frank case had brought in a verdict of 'not guilty,' the defendant would have been lynched."

As soon as the trial ended, Frank's attorneys made plans for an appeal. They also sought assistance from Louis Marshall, president of the American Jewish Committee, an organization primarily dedicated to the preservation of civil rights for Jews. Marshall recognized that the matter would have to be dealt with quietly, behind the scenes, and with Southerners, rather than Jews, appearing in the forefront seeking justice. Behind the scenes, Marshall and other Jews were willing to help with money, legal assistance, and careful publicity. But they were adamant in stating that whatever assistance Frank received must come from individuals; they did not want it to appear that any Jewish organization was assisting a Jew who had been convicted of criminal activity.

Although Frank's Georgian attorneys sought Marshall's assistance, they did not take his advice. He argued that in their appeal to the state's Supreme Court, they should raise federal questions about whether there had been due process of law if the defendant was forced to absent himself from the court. His attorneys did not do this. They thought they would easily win a new trial because in their first appeal the trial judge, Leonard Roan, stated that he had thought about the case more than any other he had ever tried and was not certain whether Frank was guilty. "The jury was convinced," Roan concluded, and he felt it was his duty, therefore, to deny the motion for a new trial.

By a 4 to 2 vote, the Georgia Supreme Court denied the appeal. The majority did not think that Roan's personal opinion warranted a retrial or that the demonstrations favorable to the prosecution witnessed by the jury sufficed to reverse the original decision. Subsequently new evidence was found which indicated that some of the jurors might have been antisemitic, that the "murder notes" had been written on old note pads found only in the basement, and that many of the prosecution witnesses might have been coerced into giving false testimony. But these tidbits also failed to induce the Georgia Supreme Court to order a new trial. At that point Frank's attorneys sought redress from the United States Supreme Court in Washington.

Twice Frank's attorneys petitioned the Supreme Court. Once they did so on the ground that Frank's involuntary absence from the courtroom at the time the jury rendered its verdict constituted lack of due process of law; the Supreme Court rejected that position, arguing that his attorneys should have raised the issue earlier, when petitioning for a retrial in Georgia. The second time, however, it was brought to the Supreme Court's attention that Frank had involuntarily absented himself from the courtroom *because of the fear of mob violence,* and that this constituted lack of due process. This point appealed to the Supreme Court, and the justices voted to hold hearings and render a decision.

Ultimately the Supreme Court, by a vote of 7 to 2, rejected Frank's claims. Some of the bases for the decision were technical but one was quite clear: Frank's attorneys' failure to raise the issue of his absence from the court near its end should have been noted in the first appeal. "Because it was waived by his failure to raise the objection in due season when fully cognizant of the fact," the majority rejected that argument as relevant. The members of the majority claimed that Frank had received every opportunity to defend himself that the courts could provide.

The two best-known and most highly regarded members of the Supreme Court at that time, Oliver Wendell Holmes and Charles Evans Hughes, dissented. They focused on one issue: popular influence upon the jurors. "Mob law," they wrote, "does not become due process of law by securing the assent of a terrorized jury."

With all of the judicial appeals over, Frank's attorneys presented their evidence to the Georgia Prison Commission, which would take the petition, vote on it, and make a recommendation to the governor. The Prison Commission had not only the trial record, but the records of the judicial appeals and the new data that Frank's attorneys had unearthed. But they divided 2 to 1, with the majority opposed to clemency.

Frank's final hope lay with Governor John M. Slaton, who not only reviewed the records carefully but also took the unusual step of visiting the pencil factory where the murder had been committed to inspect the building's layout. Since the prosecution had asserted that the murder had been committed in the second-floor workroom near Frank's office, and the defense had argued that the crime had taken place in the basement, the Governor wanted to familiarize himself with these areas as well as the elevator.

The Governor devoted several days to this case and then, before announcing his decision, had Frank removed from the county jail in Atlanta to the state prison in Milledgeville. Slaton then announced that he was commuting Frank's sentence to life imprisonment. "Feeling as I do about this case," he wrote, "I would be a murderer if I allowed that man to hang."

The Governor then elaborated upon his decree. He focused upon the human excrement found in the basement the day after the murder. If Conley were telling the truth, he would have taken the girl's body to the basement in the elevator on Saturday. But items belonging to Mary Phagan and formed feces were seen in the shaft on Sunday morning. Because Conley had acknowledged defecating in the elevator shaft on Saturday morning, his tale about the use of the elevator on Saturday afternoon had to be false. If the elevator had not been used, the governor concluded, then Conley's entire account had to be discounted. And without Conley's testimony there was insufficient evidence to convict Frank.

The Governor also noted that Mary Phagan had been smashed in the head. But no blood appeared in the workroom, on the floor nearby, in the elevator, or on the steps leading from the second to the first floors. Blood had been found, however, along with sawdust and grime, in Mary's nostrils, which meant that she had met her doom in the basement, where those ingredients appeared in abundance. Slaton also accepted Frank's attorneys' argument that because the date listed at the top of the "murder notes" read "190—," the pages had to have been ripped from old records stored in the basement. The governor concluded that he could not allow Frank to hang on the basis of the evidence that he had seen. Elaborating upon his actions a few days later Governor Slaton observed:

Two thousand years ago another Governor washed his hands of a case and turned over a Jew to a mob. For two thousand years that Governor's name has been accursed. If today another Jew were lying in his grave because I had failed to do my duty I would all through life find his blood on my hands and would consider myself an assassin through cowardice.

Privately, Slaton confided to friends that he thought Frank innocent. He assumed that once tempers in Atlanta calmed down, one of his successors would be asked to review the case again, would recognize that Frank was innocent, and would probably give Frank a full pardon. Slaton thought that if he had pardoned Frank, there would have been a lynching. The Governor was probably right. What he did not realize at the time, however, was that his own life would also be in jeopardy.

The popular reaction to Slaton's decision was explosive. Mobs attacked Jewish homes and stores in several Georgia towns and cities. The Governor was hanged in effigy and denounced as "King of the Jews and Georgia's traitor forever." A lynching party tried to storm the Governor's mansion, but state guards held them back. Slaton's term ended 4 days after he announced his decision and during that entire time, until he was escorted to a train leaving from Atlanta on June 26, 1915, he was heavily guarded. People wondered if he would ever return to Georgia. He did—at the end of World War I—but he never again ran for public office.

Commutation and life on the prison farm may have given Frank a new sense of hope, but it was short lived. After only 1 month in Milledgeville, a fellow prisoner slit Frank's throat with a butcher knife. The culprit claimed he had been called "from on high" to slay the Jew. Frank was quickly taken to the prison hospital and was recovering nicely from the nearly fatal wound when, on August 15, 1915, some of the "best men" from Marietta, Georgia, Mary Phagan's hometown, drove across the state and took Frank from his bed. They drove him back the 175 miles to where they came from and hung him from a tree on the morning of August 16. The Dean of the Atlanta Theological Seminary described the lynch mob as "a sifted band of men, sober, intelligent, of established good name and character—good American citizens."

This "sifted band of . . . sober, intelligent" citizens had been planning the lynching since Governor Slaton had pardoned Frank in May. They included a clergyman, two former justices of the Georgia Supreme Court, and an ex-sheriff. These men believed that Frank had been given every legal opportunity to reverse the original sentence, and they were well aware that all of the courts had refused his appeals. They despised Slaton for commuting Frank's sentence and for allowing him to live, even though the Georgia state constitution gave the Governor the power of commutation and/or pardon. In the minds of the lynchers, justice had been undermined by the Governor, and they felt that they had to take the law into their own hands.

As Frank was driven back to Marietta, he convinced two of the men who rode in the same car with him that he was innocent. When all of the cars converged in Marietta, just before dawn, he convinced several others as well. But

**Men standing around the body of Leo
Frank** after lynching. They are from
Marietta, Georgia. Notice Frank's hands
and neck. (Courtesy, American Jewish
Archives)

four individuals wanted the execution to take place, day was breaking, and the
kidnappers felt the need to finish their task before other townspeople began
their daily chores. The lynchers feared being discovered. So they quickly tied
the knot around Frank's neck, flung the rope over the branch of a sturdy oak
tree, and secured it in place. They then lifted Frank onto a table, saw to it that
his feet barely touched the platform below, and then removed the table. As they
left, they saw Frank swaying in the wind.

The lynching met with the approval of most Georgians. The local newspaper editorialized, "We regard the hanging of Leo M. Frank . . . an act of law
abiding citizens." Two years later Lucian Lamar Knight, one of the most prominent of the state's historians, wrote, "There is something inherently fine in the
passionate desire of a people to keep inviolate the honor of womanhood and to
visit swift punishment upon a wretch who dares to stain the purity of a child's
life."

After the lynching the men who committed the evil deed lost their sense of
purpose. But soon Colonel William J. Simmons stepped into the vacuum as he
sought to revive what he regarded as a hallowed Southern institution dedicated to preserving women's honor, exalting Anglo-Saxon superiority, and reaf-
firming the Protestant fundamentalist faith. The nucleus for this new group
was Frank's lynching party, then known as the "Knights of Mary Phagan." One

night in the fall of 1915, they joined Simmons at Stone Mountain, just east of Atlanta, where together they proclaimed a revived Ku Klux Klan.

AN INTERPRETATION

In retrospect, what can we say about Leo Frank? That he was innocent there can be no doubt. He was in the wrong place at the wrong time and thus became a victim of circumstances, because someone "important" or "prominent" was needed to pay for the death of Mary Phagan. The few bits of evidence used to connect him to the crime were clearly insufficient to either arrest or convict him.

What motivated Hugh Dorsey and the police is impossible to say. They could have focused upon Jim Conley, for whom there were much better reasons to convict. Why they failed to do so is not clear. Perhaps they truly believed Frank guilty; perhaps Dorsey and the police were too committed to Frank's guilt to alter their original positions; perhaps a black janitor would not have sufficed as the perpetrator of such a vicious crime. Who knows?

Had Frank been a Protestant Southerner from a prominent family he would not have been a serious suspect. But as an alien Jew he emerged as a symbol of the exploitative industrialist who "ruined" the South and took unfair advantage of its workers. He could be made to pay for all the perceived crimes against Southern society. When Frank emerged as the prosecution's prime suspect, he had few defenders in Atlanta outside of his immediate circle of friends and family. People were too quick to believe rumors, police assertions, and Conley's frequently changed affidavits.

Once the community made up its mind about Frank's guilt, no jury could have rendered a verdict of not guilty. The jurors had to live with their neighbors long after the trial ended. Lawyers and others familiar with the judicial system know that juries almost never go against the sentiments of the communities with which they identify. Frank was convicted in the eyes of Atlantans long before the trial began. Conley's testimony, and the defense attorneys' inability to break his story, sealed Frank's fate. Evidence to the contrary of the will of the majority was simply not considered seriously by members of the jury.

In 1982 an elderly man came forward and told a Tennessee reporter that he had witnessed Conley carrying Mary Phagan's body to the cellar on the day of the murder. Conley allegedly told him, "If you tell anyone about this, I'll kill you." The 13-year-old boy ran home and told his mother of the incident. She advised him to keep his mouth shut and not to get involved. Coming as it did in his eighty-second year, the man's tale, although it reinforced the views of those who had always thought Frank to be innocent, failed to convince those who thought him guilty. This is not surprising because studies have shown that whereas there is a negative correlation between evidence and belief (−.03), there is a significant correlation between desire and belief (+.88). In other words, people believe what they want to believe and rarely allow factual evidence to disturb firmly held convictions. Therefore, we might safely conclude that no amount of new information suffices to change people's long-held views on an emotionally charged topic.

Leo Frank was murdered in 1915, more than three-quarters of a century ago. But his trial and lynching stand as a reminder that anyone, however honest and sincere, can be caught up and victimized by a swirl of events well beyond an individual's control. Frank was the culprit that the prosecution and the police needed. He was also a scapegoat for the ills that beset an emerging and troubled industrial society.

Sources: The Leo Frank case involved broader issues and greater complexities than could be dealt with in a short narrative. For more detail, and other interpretations, see Leonard Dinnerstein, *The Leo Frank Case* (Athens: University of Georgia Press, 1987), Harry Golden, *A Little Girl Is Dead* (Cleveland: World Publishing, 1967), C. Vann Woodward, *Tom Watson: Agrarian Rebel* (New York: Rinehart, 1938), Charles and Louise Samuels, *Night Fell on Georgia* (New York: Dell, 1956), and Albert S. Lindeman, *The Jew Accused* (Cambridge: Cambridge University Press, 1991). An essay focusing on the city of Atlanta and its problems at the turn of the century is Leonard Dinnerstein, "Atlanta in the Progressive Era: A Dreyfus Affair in Georgia," in Frederick Cople Jaher, ed., *The Age of Industrialism: Essays in Social Structure and Cultural Values* (New York: Free Press, 1968), pp. 127–157. Steve Oney wrote a brief article summarizing the Frank case, "The Lynching of Leo Frank," *Esquire* 104 (September, 1985): 90–104, whereas Nancy MacLean wrote a gender-based analysis of the case, "The Leo Frank Case Reconsidered: Gender and Sexual Politics in the Making of Reactionary Populism," *Journal of American History* 78 (December 1991): 917–948.

8

THE BLACK SOX SCANDAL

Ronald Story

In the fall of 1919, key members of the pennant-winning Chicago White Sox conspired with gamblers to throw the World Series to the Cincinnati Reds. Two years later, following a trial in which the players were found innocent, a stunned nation learned from baseball czar Kenesaw Mountain Landis that eight members of the team, including Shoeless Joe Jackson, one of the greatest natural hitters ever to play the game, were banned from organized baseball for life.

As harsh as the Commissioner's decision seemed, there were many who found it justified. After all, most of the eight were clearly guilty—in fact, several had signed confessions—and many Americans no doubt believed that the national pastime could be maintained in its pastoral purity only by expunging the offending players. That interpretation of the "Black Sox" scandal seems logical enough, and it certainly accords with professional baseball's current image as an impeccably "clean" game, played on artificial turf rather than grass, and under domes that shelter fans and players from the weather itself.

But, as Ronald Story's vivid narrative suggests, baseball wasn't like that at all— not in 1919, anyway. The sport had a pastoral quality, to be sure; but the men who played it—and the men who watched it—were an unruly bunch that drank, swore, and, fatefully, gambled. Against this background, Landis's ruling takes on a different meaning. Far from being an attempt to reclaim for baseball its own lost virtue, the ruling was part of a larger process through which the game was "modernized" and made compatible with the developing consumer society. Through advertising, public relations, lavish department stores, Hollywood movies, and sports spectacles, Americans were being encouraged to think of themselves less as employees, with bonds to their workplaces and other workers, and more as consumers, dependent for identity and happiness on the quality and quantity of their purchases.

While Landis presented his decision as if it were a neutral and moral one, the ruling was, in fact, highly political. It could not touch the gamblers who paid the athletes. Moreover, it did not acknowledge the responsibilities of White Sox owner Charles Comiskey, who, like other owners of baseball teams, dominated and controlled his players just as factory owners of the day dominated and controlled the lives of wage earners. In retrospect, Landis might be understood as sport's version of Woodrow Wilson, whose two-term presidency was ending just as the scandal was breaking: puritanical, moralistic, and convinced of his own rectitude, yet pursuing policies that were very much those of a particular economic class.

Conflicts between classes and ethnic groups are central to the American historical experience, and never more so than they were in the extraordinary year of 1919. A militant labor movement, emboldened by the Russian Revolution of 1917, launched dramatic strikes in the Seattle shipyards, among Boston policemen, and—only days before the World Series opened—in the steel mills. Apparently convinced that the nation was about to be overrun by Bolsheviks, Wilson's Attorney General arrested thousands of immigrant aliens and Communists in a series of dramatic raids undertaken in total disregard of elemental civil liberties. In late October, Congress passed the Volstead Act, providing the enforcement apparatus for the Eighteenth Amendment on prohibition—a measure that came down especially hard on the urban working class. When the baseball season opened the following April, fans had to go without their usual beer.

The Black Sox scandal took place in a climate broadly shaped by these events. Like the nation, the White Sox players were polarized by class and ethnicity. In the intensely political atmosphere of 1919, some of them decided that they had been victimized by an unfair employer, just like other workers. Landis would have none of this. His decision not only ignored the baseball player's claim to the status of worker, but also accelerated baseball's evolution from a rowdy representation of male, working-class culture to the respectable, middle-class, family game that modern Americans know so well. By the fall of 1921, Landis had put baseball back on the straight-and-narrow and Congress had passed an important law severely restricting immigration. Baseball, and the nation, were headed full speed into the homogenized world of the mid-twentieth century.

Cincinnati was astir on October 1, 1919, as seldom before. The Cincinnati Reds, champions of the National League, winners of their first pennant since joining the fledgling league back in 1876, were getting ready to play game one of the World Series. It would be their first Series ever, and therefore their first Series game at home, so that even though it was Wednesday and a workday, people began streaming toward Redland Park long before noon to cheer the boys on to victory that afternoon.

The Reds faced a formidable foe: the Chicago White Sox, winners of the American League flag 2 of the last 3 years. The White Sox sported a fearsome attack—left fielder Joe Jackson batted .351, Happy Felsch in center field slammed 52 extra-base hits, second baseman Eddie Collins hit .319 with 33 stolen bases; and a balanced attack—seven of the eight regulars hit .275 or better, seven stole 10 or more bases, five scored or drove in at least 80 runs. In the field the Sox featured the flashy Collins at second base; a strong-armed Felsch in the outfield; fiery catcher Ray Schalk; tough third baseman Buck Weaver; and the remarkable Chick Gandil, who led American League (AL) first basemen by making just three errors all season! As for pitching, future Hall-of-Famer Red Faber had a sore arm. But that still left Eddie Cicotte at 29 wins and 7 losses; Lefty Williams at 23–11; rookie Dickie Kerr, 13–7 in two-thirds of a season; and a manager in feisty Kid Gleason who knew (or thought he knew) how to use them.

But the Reds were plenty good. They had won the pennant by nine full games over John McGraw's tough New York Giants, and they considered themselves the probable winners of this Series. And so did the 31,000 ticketholders for game one and the tens of thousands of others who crammed every Cincinnati hotel lobby, cigar store, barbershop, and saloon to talk baseball and bet on the hometown favorites.

Cincinnati's backers, to be sure, were not getting the odds they might have expected, given Chicago's reputation. As of the morning of October 1, in fact, the odds were downright bad, only 5–6 on the Reds to take the nine-game Series, down from 2–1 a few days earlier and even money only yesterday. Lots of Reds backers bet anyway, despite the odds. More should have. Because what they did not know, and what underlay the shifting odds, was that eight Chicago players had agreed to "throw" the 1919 World Series.

It began in early September when Chick Gandil, the fancy-fielding White Sox first baseman, telephoned Joseph "Sport" Sullivan, a Boston bookie and gambler, to set up a meeting at the Hotel Buckminster, where the Chicago players were staying during their series with the Red Sox. A flashy operator with good connections, Sullivan earned a fair living making book on sports events, especially ball games. Gandil had fed him tips on how various games might go since Chick's Washington Senators days before 1916. He knew Chick was a rough customer who lived on the edge of honesty. But that hardly prepared him for Gandil's current proposition—that for $80,000, the White Sox would "bag" the upcoming World Series. Initially incredulous, then excited, Sullivan hastily closed the deal with Gandil in principle and started to scout around for the money.

Betting on baseball had been common enough since baseball became the most popular American spectator sport after the Civil War. One reason for the standardization of playing rules was to make games easier to handicap. With gambling, however, often went corruption. Gamblers sometimes paid players to lose particular games; sometimes promoters or saloonkeepers paid players to divide a series of games in order to keep interest, and therefore attendance, high. In 1877 four major league players were expelled for throwing games, but gambling accusations and investigations remained commonplace throughout the nineteenth century. Because baseball retained more than a few traces of the brawling, sensual, hard-drinking nineteenth-century male subculture from which it originally grew, there was undoubtedly much fire behind the smoke.

The actual fixing of games supposedly declined after 1900, but baseball betting pools thrived, particularly after the closing of the nation's racetracks during World War I, and players were still suspected of "lying down" in exchange for money, whiskey, or women, or under the threat of violence. "Prince" Hal Chase, a graceful first baseman with five big-league teams, was supposedly behind countless thrown games. But league investigations of Chase and others were little more than perfunctory whitewashes. After all, accusations against one player might lead to accusations—and penalties—against many others and to the wreckage of valuable big-league franchises. So reporters, players, and owners, whatever they might think, kept quiet in public.

Nevertheless, Gandil's proposition was startling. First, it involved the World Series. There would be big money around but also much publicity; and therefore, much risk of detection. And because sports fans, and Americans generally, were so passionate about the Series, if things went awry the penalties might involve more than whitewash. Also, here the players, not the gamblers, seemed to be taking the initiative—and not just players, but members of the best and most famous team in baseball.

There were reasons, to be sure. For one thing, the owner of the White Sox, Charles Comiskey—"Commy" himself, the famous "Old Roman"—paid his ballplayers poorly. A son of Irish Chicago, an outstanding player-manager with the fabled St. Louis Browns of the 1880s, the only ex-player to become sole owner of a big-league team, a popular hero of South Chicago where Comiskey Park was located, Comiskey had a substantial fortune that came entirely from his ownership of the White Sox club, which he had established in 1900 at the time he was helping found the American League. In the process of becoming rich Comiskey had gained two reputations: one for generosity with fans and reporters, many of whom touted him for mayor, and one for tight-fistedness with his players. After a war-shortened 1918 season, Comiskey had capped salaries unusually tightly, except for players like Eddie Collins who were on multiyear contracts. He then added insult to injury by distributing only $3 per day in meal money when the team was on the road, the lowest stipend in the league, and deducting the cost of laundering the players' uniforms from the players' paychecks. When attendance unexpectedly boomed in 1919, the White Sox players nearly struck in July to protest continued low pay in the midst of sky-high revenues.

There was also a festering factionalism on this ball club. One clique centered around Eddie Collins, a college graduate whose $14,500 salary was twice that of any other player, creating much resentment. Near Collins could usually be found catcher Ray Schalk, an intense competitor; pitchers Red Faber, a college man like Collins, and Dickie Kerr, the rookie; and a part-time outfielder and lead-off batter, Shano Collins. The chief antagonists of this Collins faction were Gandil, a rough ex–copper miner and boxer from California; Swede Risberg, the shortstop, another Californian and even tougher, reputedly, than Gandil; and Risberg's buddy, utility infielder Fred McMullin. Around this trio were ranged at various times the club's two Southerners, Jackson and Williams; plus Felsch and Weaver, good-time Charlies who enjoyed an occasional drink and roll of the dice; plus the team elder, Cicotte.

There may have been a class factor in this factionalism. The Collins group and others on the club came mostly from small-town America and had a secondary education or better. Jackson, by contrast, was an illiterate Carolina millhand, Felsch a Milwaukee carpenter, Weaver a mechanic from the Pennsylvania coal country, Cicotte a copper miner like Gandil. There may also have been an ethnic and regional factor. The Collins group included no one who was not of English, German, or Irish extraction or from the Northeast or Midwest; their adversaries included two French-Canadians and a Scandinavian as well as two Southerners. Perhaps reflecting this divergent background, several members of the Gandil clique had supported an unsuccessful effort in the early 1910s to organize a players union.

This gang of eight was probably less a tight clique than a coalition of "hard livers" shaped by grudges against Comiskey off the field and Eddie Collins on it. To be sure, the faction's hard living—drinking, gambling, fighting, flashy clothes—would have been less distinctive a generation earlier when baseball was closer to its roughhouse roots than it was in 1919, or at least less than the Collins group was. At any rate the factions existed—for one 2-week period Risberg actually refused to throw the ball to Collins even to start a double play! And Gandil knew it.

Chick Gandil's first recruit was Eddie Cicotte. Gandil had to have Cicotte, who would pitch game one and start at least two additional games in a long Series. Cicotte listened. He'd just had a great season, but at 35 years of age he

Charles Comiskey, owner and president of the Chicago White Sox, with his crosstown counterpart, William Veeck of the Chicago Cubs, 1920. A wealthy man who affected, like Veeck, the expensive hats and three-piece suits favored by tycoons of the day, Comiskey was never comfortable among Chicago's established families, preferring the rougher company of journalists, politicians, and baseball magnates such as Veeck, an ex-sportswriter as well as Cubs president. At one time the most powerful owner in the American League, Comiskey seemed to be on the verge of founding a baseball dynasty until the Black Sox scandal destroyed his team. (Chicago Historical Society, SDN 0062205)

was nearing the end of his career, and he faced stiff mortgage payments on a new Michigan farm with no financial cushion beneath him. Cicotte agreed, for $10,000 in advance. Next came Lefty Williams, certain to start game two and another likely three-game pitcher if the Series dragged on. Lefty hesitated, then agreed because Cicotte was in, again for the going rate of $10,000. There was also Swede Risberg, whose glove at short would be a Series key; Comiskey paid Risberg under $4,000, one of the lowest salaries of any starting American Leaguer. The Swede not only came in but insisted that his pal McMullin be included, too. Gandil agreed. Finally, with pitching and defense in tow, Gandil went after Buck Weaver, Joe Jackson, and Hap Felsch, the three-four-five hitters in the lineup. Jackson, nicknamed "Shoeless" from an incident early in his career when he removed his spikes during a game because they were new and hurt his feet, came in for the money and because his friend and fellow Southerner, Williams, was in. When Felsch and Weaver finally agreed, the scheme was complete. Chick had worked not only the grudges against Comiskey but the team factionalism—and in doing so had the players he needed to work the fix.

Because the players never discussed just who would do what to lose which Series games, this crucial part of the scheme remained murky to the last. Things were equally murky, for now, on the gamblers' end. Not only had Sport Sullivan failed as yet to line up the $80,000, another "operator"—a former big-league pitcher named Sleepy Bill Burns—had rolled into New York fresh from a successful speculation in Texas oil leases. When Burns heard rumors of a Series fix, he contacted Eddie Cicotte, an old baseball friend, who confirmed the rumor but said no money had changed hands. Burns now determined, with the help of a couple of cronies, to raise the money himself, only to discover that Gandil was now demanding $100,000 rather than $80,000.

In 1919, $100,000 was a considerable sum, especially for a small-time plunger like Sleepy Bill Burns. So for help Burns turned to the one man sure to have that kind of money on hand: Arnold Rothstein—known as "AR," the "Big Bankroll"—a New York sports gambler and hoodlum with intimate ties to New York City politicians and police and a luxurious gambling establishment in Saratoga, New York. AR discussed the fix with Burns, then, on reflection, informed Burns that he would not underwrite so risky a scheme. In actual fact, he had decided to do precisely that—except that he would work through Sport Sullivan, whom he knew and respected, rather than through Burns, whom he did not. Rothstein gave Sullivan $40,000 to give to the players prior to the Series opener, and had another $40,000 placed in a safe in Chicago for distribution when the Series was over. Sport found the $40,000 advance money (which was all he had access to) a grievous temptation—so much so that, thinking he had the players on a string anyway, he bet $30,000 of it, on the Reds to win, for himself. He then gave the remaining $10,000 to Chick Gandil, with a promise of "more later."

This was far less than Gandil expected or than he had promised the players, who were getting jittery. With the Series mere hours away, Cicotte still refused to throw game one without cash in hand; so Sullivan's $10,000 had to go to him. But Williams now told Gandil he wanted out, and so did Weaver. Jackson told him he wanted $20,000 instead of $10,000, then told Kid Gleason, the Sox manager, that he didn't feel like playing at all. Obviously no one was happy. Fortunately for Gandil (or so it seemed) Bill Burns had decided, even without Rothstein's participation, that he, too, would try to play the fix by promising to pay the players money after each game they lost from the profits he would make by betting on that game. With money coming from two directions, from Sullivan and from Burns, Gandil and the others believed they would still get something significant. In any case, several of them had placed bets of their own on the Cincinnati Reds. By now Cincinnati was alive with rumors of a Series fix, and a swarm of gamblers was now in evidence, including a St. Louis syndicate and a gaggle of Chicagoans that numbered the likes of Nick "The Greek" Dandalos, songster George M. Cohan, and Big Tim O'Leary, owner of the biggest speakeasy in the stockyards district. The odds had swung so far toward the Reds that gamblers were trying to "fix" the Reds, too! The Black Sox were in deep, maybe over their heads—maybe too deep to get out.

As for the Series, it was an insiders' game all the way. In the bottom of the first inning, Eddie Cicotte hit the Cincinnati leadoff man squarely in the back with his second pitch—a prearranged sign to Arnold Rothstein, who was watching the game's progress on an electric scoreboard in a New York hotel lobby, that the fix was on. Rothstein promptly added another $100,000 to the $200,000 he already had down on the Reds to win the Series. In the fourth inning, with the score tied 1–1, Cicotte booted a double play ball and started grooving his pitches, and by the time the inning was over the Reds had a 6–1 lead that would lengthen to 9–1 by game's end. Game two was tighter. Lefty Williams allowed just four hits while Chicago got ten. But the Reds combined two of their hits with three Williams bases on balls for a three-run fourth inning. Final score: 4–2. Arnold Rothstein by now had another $85,000 on the Reds.

The teams headed for Chicago and games three through five under thick clouds of suspicion, not only from the press corps—Ring Lardner of the *Chicago Tribune* strolled through the train singing "I'm Forever Blowing Ballgames"—but from Ray Schalk, who jumped Lefty Williams under the stands after game two; from Kid Gleason, who publicly tongue-lashed Cicotte and Risberg and swung at Chick Gandil; and from Charles Comiskey himself, who was tipped by a Chicago gambling acquaintance about what might be happening. Not that much money had materialized. Sleepy Bill Burns managed to come up with a measly $10,000, which he passed on to an enraged Gandil (who stuffed it in the lining of his suitcase) along with the brazen suggestion that maybe the Sox should win game three to improve the odds! Gandil, incensed, told Burns the fix was still in all the way. That afternoon he handled 15 chances without an error and drove in two runs while Swede Risberg made 10 flawless plays, stroked a long triple, and scored. Little Dickie Kerr tossed a three-hit shutout. Chicago won 3–0. Sleepy Bill lost his shirt betting on the Reds and bowed out of the Series doings.

This Chicago victory and the roles that Chick Gandil and Swede Risberg had played in it disturbed Sport Sullivan enough to prompt a call to Gandil, who told him that the group of eight was no longer bought. Sullivan panicked,

The most famous practitioner of the slash-and-run "inside baseball" favored by
the White Sox of 1919 was the great Ty Cobb, seen here hook-sliding into third
base. It was a game well-suited for old-fashioned rough-cut men such as Buck
Weaver and Chick Gandil (who fought Cobb twice on the field) and for old-
fashioned ballparks where fans sat close enough to the action to respond to its
nuances and intensity. (National Baseball Library, Cooperstown, New York)

quickly scraped together $20,000, which he wired to Gandil. Chick split it even-
ly among Risberg, Felsch, Williams, and Jackson. Gandil and Cicotte had their
$10,000 already. McMullin would have to wait. Weaver, who in Chick's view
was playing to win, was asking for, and would get, nothing.

Game four was a near-repeat of game two. Cicotte allowed only five hits, but
two came in the fifth inning along with two errors by Cicotte to allow two runs.
The White Sox collected a meager three hits. Final score: Cincinnati 2, Chicago 0.
And so with game five, the third straight before standing-room-only Comiskey
Park crowds. Lefty Williams gave up four hits, but three came in the sixth inning
along with errors by Felsch and Risberg, enabling the Reds to score four times.
The Sox again had just three hits. Final score: Cincinnati 5, Chicago 0.

Gandil expected another $20,000 from Sport Sullivan to be waiting when the
clubs arrived back in Cincinnati on October 7 for game six. When it wasn't, there
was more rage and yet another change of heart. Dickie Kerr did not sparkle the
way he had in game three, but Weaver, Jackson, and Felsch went 7-for-14 with
three doubles, and Gandil drove in a run in the ninth for a 5-4 victory. The next

day Jackson and Felsch drove in two runs each, and Cicotte held the Reds to a lone tally. Chicago pulled within a game of Cincinnati in the Series with two possible games remaining, both in Chicago where the White Sox, apparently back on track and with Lefty Williams up, would have a home field advantage.

Arnold Rothstein had seen enough. With nearly $400,000 riding on this Series, he was in no mood to take chances. AR summoned Sport Sullivan to New York and told him to make absolutely certain that Chicago lost game eight, preferably in the early innings. There could be no mistake; matters were critical. Sullivan, duly frightened, put a call into one "Harry F." of Chicago, a hired gunman. Sport told Harry F. to make sure Lefty Williams threw tomorrow's game in the first inning, even if it meant threatening to murder his wife, and sent him $500 advance money.

Harry F. did what he was paid to do. Kid Gleason sent Williams to the mound after delivering a clubhouse harangue in which he threatened all sellouts with "iron"—meaning a gun. But the Kid's words were just words; the gunman's iron was real. Buck Weaver singled and doubled, Shoeless Joe Jackson homered and doubled, Chick Gandil tripled, and Ray Schalk made the only error, all before another big Comiskey Park crowd. But Lefty had made his decision. Disregarding Schalk's signals, he threw batting-practice fastballs down the heart of the plate to the Reds batters, who feasted on them, then feasted some more on Gleason's parade of journeyman relievers. Final score: Cincinnati 10, Chicago 5. Arnold Rothstein's money was safe. So was Sport Sullivan's—along with Lefty Williams and his wife.

One bit of unfinished business remained. Sullivan went out to Chicago to give Chick Gandil the $40,000 that Rothstein had had sequestered in the safe. Of this amount, Gandil gave $10,000 to Risberg and $5,000 to McMullin. The remainder he kept, unbeknownst to his accomplices, for himself.

For Charles Comiskey, the Series had been a dismal affair. He strongly suspected seven players of throwing games; he even named them (omitting only Buck Weaver) to a friend. Understandably, Commy felt betrayed by his players and desperately wanted to punish the guilty parties. But there was much to consider, as talks with his lawyer, the urbane Alfred Austrian, made clear. If Comiskey acknowledged that there had been a fix and released the guilty players, he would weaken his team and damage his franchise, while the very players he released might sign with other clubs and play against him. On the other hand, if he did nothing, he ran the risk of exposure at some later date, with possibly the same consequences, except that he would look guilty along with the players. Austrian advised him to do nothing because there seemed to be more hearsay than hard evidence in the case. Comiskey could cover himself by announcing a "private" investigation with a reward for information on Series corruption.

Comiskey took Austrian's advice. Informants seeking reward money did emerge. One said Risberg bet on the Reds; another mentioned the St. Louis syndicate. Austrian considered both leads flimsy because neither described money changing hands. Joe Jackson wrote offering to discuss "crooked" plays; he received no answer. Comiskey hired a private detective to investigate the players, then not only shelved the report but urged the Illinois State's Attorney, a friend of his, not to inquire into Series corruption in view of the "insubstantial" nature of the evidence. Comiskey had initially withheld the World Series checks (losers' shares amounting to $3,254) of his seven suspects. Now, with talk of a fix smothered, he mailed them.

The 1920 season began on a sour note. Chick Gandil did not report for spring training. Swede Risberg reported just 2 days before the opening game. Jackson and Buck Weaver held out before signing 3-year contracts. Once set, however, the team played excellent baseball, settling into a summer-long three-way pennant race with the Cleveland Indians and the New York Yankees. With Jackson and Collins leading the way, the Sox topped the league in batting average, stolen bases, and runs scored, while Cicotte and Williams won 20 games again. So did Red Faber, back from arm trouble, and Dickie Kerr, who proved that 1919 was no fluke. Attendance at Comiskey Park—and revenues into Charles Comiskey's pocket—rose by 50 percent.

If the White Sox were so good, why didn't they run away with the pennant in 1920? Partly because the Indians and Yankees were also good. Tris Speaker hit .388 at Cleveland; Babe Ruth walloped an incredible 54 home runs for New York. But there was another, less visible reason: Midwestern gamblers were threatening the Series fixers with exposure if they did not throw additional games from time to time. And throw games they did, all through the summer—not many, but enough. Eddie Collins went to Comiskey about suspicious play in August, to no avail.

Ban Johnson, president of the American League, now quietly began an investigation of his own that turned up not only enticing, if circumstantial, evidence about suspicious activity during the 1920 season but leads to possible Series corruption the previous fall. Johnson, a respected baseball man, had cofounded the American League with Charles Comiskey, then his close friend. For obscure personal reasons, by 1920 Johnson had become Comiskey's mortal foe, eager to see the White Sox shattered. He therefore pressed his investigation hard. By midsummer, stories about possible crooked play were peppering the nation's sports pages.

The result was exactly what Charles Comiskey had feared and Ban Johnson had hoped for: the empaneling in early September of an Illinois Grand Jury to probe reports of corruption in major-league baseball. Comiskey loudly proclaimed his loyalty to the national pastime and his willingness to suspend any Chicago player proved to have thrown games and accused Ban Johnson of pursuing a personal vendetta against him. The Grand Jury, undeterred, began its work.

Initial testimony was more tantalizing than conclusive. Gamblers and baseball officials reported various, sometimes contradictory, rumors of payoffs to various players, including White Sox players. Rube Benton, a pitcher for the New York Giants, said he heard about a Series fix from none other than Hal Chase, recently retired as a player but long reputed to be on the take. Chase (said Benton) had heard from Sleepy Bill Burns that gamblers gave Chick

Gandil, Happy Felsch, Lefty Williams, and Eddie Cicotte $100,000 to throw Series games, and that they had done it. Much of this testimony leaked out to the newspapers, producing sensational headlines concerning baseball—and World Series—corruption and the need, as the Chicago Tribune put it, to "SAVE BASEBALL FROM GAMBLERS."

Then on September 27 a Philadelphia newspaper published a story, based on interviews with anonymous gamblers, entitled "THE MOST GIGANTIC SPORTING SWINDLE IN THE HISTORY OF AMERICA." The story described how a group of White Sox players headed by Eddie Cicotte had thrown games one, two, and eight of the Series for a promise of $100,000. The players, said the paper, saw only $10,000 of the promised payoff money because the gamblers who started the whole thing lost everything when Chicago won game three. The story was only partially accurate in its account of the Bill Burns initiative and mostly inaccurate in its omission, save for the game eight loss, of the far more significant Rothstein-Sullivan initiative. But it rang true enough to panic Eddie Cicotte, who went that morning to see Alfred Austrian, Comiskey's lawyer, who got him to sign a confession, together with a waiver of immunity that would show the confession to have been uncoerced. Austrian then took Cicotte to the Grand Jury. "Yeah," said Eddie, "we were crooked. Gandil was the mastermind. I did it for the wife and kids and a farm. I'm through with baseball."

The floodgates were open. Joe Jackson, hearing that Cicotte had talked, went to see Felsch and Risberg. Swede, recounted Jackson, threatened "to kill you if you squawk." Jackson went to the Grand Jury judge's chambers anyway. There he met Alfred Austrian, who had Jackson, like Cicotte, sign an immunity waiver and a confession and advised him that the authorities were after the gamblers, not the players, and that he should tell everything. What he told the Grand Jury that afternoon was that although he had gotten his $5,000 from Williams, the ringleaders were Gandil and Risberg. He then asked for bailiff protection because "the Swede is a hard guy." Lefty Williams also met with Austrian, to whom he gave a signed statement confirming the Series fix and his part in it and fingering Gandil as the organizer. Later that day Felsch said much the same thing to a Chicago reporter. Weaver spoke briefly to Austrian and the State's Attorney but refused to confess. When Charles Comiskey informed the suspected players of their "indefinite" suspension by cable that evening, he sent eight cables. One went to Weaver.

The White Sox lost their last season series, and therefore the pennant, to Cleveland. According to Chicago novelist James T. Farrell, when Shoeless Joe Jackson and Happy Felsch emerged from the locker room after the final Cleveland loss, a fan shouted "It ain't true, Joe!" The surrounding crowd (which included the young Jimmy Farrell) took up the call, "It ain't true, Joe!" Both men walked silently away through the crowd. In late October the Grand Jury, its work completed, announced 13 indictments. Five were from the gambling fraternity: Bill Burns, Hal Chase, Sport Sullivan, and two other minions of Arnold Rothstein. From the baseball fraternity came Gandil, Risberg, Jackson, Felsch, Williams, Cicotte, McMullin, and Weaver—thereafter to be known as "the Black Sox."

Arnold Rothstein did not like the looks of the indictment list because it included men whose testimony could drag him deeply into the proceedings. This he proposed to avoid, even if it cost him a significant amount of money to do so. First, he would ensure that Sullivan and his other gambling contacts could not be extradicted to Chicago for trial. He would—and did—pay Sullivan to go to Mexico until the trial ended; he would—and did—pay to ensure "errors" in the extradition proceedings against Hal Chase and the rest. Second, Rothstein himself went to Chicago in early October, where he testified that he was entirely innocent, that the Series tampering had all been the doing of Sport Sullivan (now safely in Canada) and the rest, and (most outrageously of all) that he personally had bet "not a cent" on the World Series. While in Chicago, AR also met with Alfred Austrian about the Grand Jury testimony and the players' confessions and immunity waivers. Was there a way to obtain these documents and thus avoid the possible incrimination of Rothstein and also, if Charles Comiskey was interested, the conviction and likely disbarment of these valuable ballplayers? Apparently there was. The documents turned up missing shortly thereafter. Austrian meanwhile declared, for the record, that he believed Arnold Rothstein to be "entirely innocent"—just as he claimed.

Amidst the storm of corruption charges sweeping the nation and the prospect of widespread public disaffection and anger with the "grand old game," organized baseball, too, was moving to shore up its interests. The high tribunal of baseball at this time was a three-man national commission comprised of the presidents of the National and American leagues plus a third member selected by the other two. But many people had no faith in this commission, including its most influential member, Ban Johnson himself. The commission had already proved ineffectual in dealing with baseball corruption, and given current circumstances this ineffectualness simply could not continue if the game were to remain financially and also morally healthy. Albert Lasker, an advertising executive and Chicago Cubs stockholder, proposed a simple solution: Abolish the national commission and replace it with a single commissioner of uncompromising rectitude from outside professional baseball, who would be paid enough to place him above temptation and have enough power to make decisions stick. All eight National League owners liked the Lasker Plan because it would undercut the influence of American Leaguer Ban Johnson; three American League clubs—the White Sox together with the New York Yankees and Boston Red Sox, both under new ownership—also supported it. Two meetings of the 16 major league clubs failed to reach consensus because five American League clubs remained loyal to Johnson, who naturally opposed the new plan. Only after the "reformers" threatened to establish a new 12-team major league did the Johnsonites relent. And so in November 1920, not long after the Grand Jury handed down its indictments, organized baseball got its new commissioner, a flamboyant federal judge named Kenesaw Mountain Landis. His salary: $50,000 a year—$42,500 more than he had made as a mere judge. No one knew quite what Landis would do. But everyone, Charles Comiskey included, hoped for the best.

Comiskey, after all, had big interests at stake, bigger perhaps than anyone (save possibly the ballplayers), and he was maneuvering hard to protect them. The Lasker Plan, which undercut Johnson, Comiskey's nemesis in this as in every other affair, was a part of that maneuvering. So was the pilfering from the State's Attorney's office of the ballplayers' signed confessions and immunity waivers. Copies existed, but the copies were unsigned and therefore might not be admitted as evidence, and without them neither guilty verdicts nor disbarment were likely. In addition, as the July 1921 trial date approached, the indicted players were approached by prosperous-looking lawyers offering to help with the players' defense. These lawyers were prominent in the Chicago bar—"fancy operators" and "lawyerin' birds," in the players' parlance, including one who started the case working for the prosecution only to switch, for no apparent reason, to the defense. Not only that, they were offering their services for little or no money. Charles Comiskey's telegram suspending the Black Sox had said that they would be reinstated if they were "innocent of any wrongdoing." Clearly, he was pulling out all stops to ensure that at least in the eyes of the law, innocent they would be.

As the long-awaited trial began in the summer of 1921, the prosecution sought to prove five charges of conspiracy against the defendants: conspiracy to defraud the public, to defraud Ray Schalk, to commit a confidence game, to injure the American League, and to injure Charles Comiskey. Because no gamblers ever materialized, thanks to Rothstein's machinations, the only defendants were the Black Sox. Bill Burns, whom Ban Johnson's agents had found hiding in the back country of Mexico, was the state's chief witness because Burns could testify that he attended meetings at which the defendants discussed throwing the Series and, more important, that he himself gave money to some of them. Burns also testified that, according to Cicotte, it was the players, not the gamblers, who instigated the scheme. The prosecution persuaded the judge to admit copies of the confessions and immunity waivers of Cicotte, Jackson, and Williams as evidence, even though they bore no signatures. The ballplayers themselves were never called to the witness stand, presumably because they would have denied having thrown any games. The prosecution concluded, in what was probably a tactical mistake, by demanding 5 years imprisonment and a $2,000 fine for each defendant.

The defense lawyers attempted to undermine Burns as a witness by showing that Ban Johnson had paid him to come to Chicago and that his testimony could not be corroborated. Because only the players could have corroborated it, the defense, too, avoided calling them to the stand. The defense also labored to prevent testimony as to whether the Black Sox had played beneath their abilities. When the prosecution questioned Kid Gleason and Ray Schalk on this point, the defense successfully objected on the grounds that the witnesses could not answer the question reliably.

The main defense strategy, however, was to portray the players not as perpetrators but as victims. The players had agreed to throw ball games, argued the defense, not to defraud anybody but for the money, which they needed because Charles Comiskey (who was hopping mad at this line of reasoning by lawyers that he was paying) paid them such miserable salaries. The real culprits, claimed the defense, were not these poor ballplayers but big-time gamblers who were not even on trial, especially the "Big Bankroll" himself, Arnold Rothstein. It was an argument designed to appeal to the jury, which consisted of blue-collar and clerical workers who might identify with players depicted in this light. It was also an argument designed to appeal to the judge, who might construe the charges literally by requiring the jury to find premeditated malice on the part of the players rather than simply injurious effect.

The defense strategy worked. On August 2, after a trial of almost 6 weeks, the judge instructed the jury that the state's charges required a finding of malicious intent to injure particular parties, not simply the throwing of games. Two hours later the jury returned a verdict of "not guilty," and the courtroom erupted in cheers and congratulations. The players retired to a nearby Italian restaurant to celebrate. When they found the jury doing likewise, the two

The Black Sox seated in court, summer 1921 (left to right, beginning second from left): Joe Jackson, Buck Weaver, Eddie Cicotte, Swede Risberg, Lefty Williams, Chick Gandil. Standing behind them (and seated to far left) are their attorneys. Normally gaudily attired with spats and diamond stickpins, the players are wearing subdued suits for their court appearances. Their relaxed good humor suggests that they knew the trial was going their way. Weaver and Jackson later sued Comiskey for the salary from the years remaining on their 3-year contracts. Comiskey eventually settled both cases out of court—although not before the missing confessions showed up in his lawyer's briefcase. (Photographer—Chicago Daily News) (Chicago Historical Society, 1921, SDN 0062959)

groups celebrated together. Charles Comiskey's gambit appeared to have succeeded. The players had been found "innocent," if not of "any wrongdoing," at
least of any legal crime, and would presumably not only avoid the penitentiary
but be reinstated—and in the nick of time, too, as the decimated White Sox
were mired deep in the second division.

The celebration was premature. Legal innocence was not the same as
moral innocence, at least to Kenesaw Mountain Landis, the new commissioner of baseball. The following morning Landis issued this statement:
"Regardless of the verdict of juries, no player who throws a ball game, no
player that undertakes or promises to throw a ballgame, no player that sits in
conference with a bunch of crooked players and gamblers where the ways
and means of throwing a game are discussed and does not promptly tell his
club about it, will ever play professional baseball!" The Black Sox might be
free from prison, but they were not reinstated, whatever Comiskey might
think. On the contrary, they were barred from all professional baseball everywhere—for life.

Not everyone accepted this decision. A group of Chicago citizens circulated
a petition urging reinstatement; Kid Gleason signed it. Some American League
owners expressed outrage, as did a few editorial writers. Landis, however, was
unyielding, and for the most part he was hailed in the national press as a hero
whose "reassuring dictum" earned him "the nation's confidence and respect"
for returning sports to "decent sporting circles." The Illinois State's Attorney
meanwhile declared the case closed—meaning that there would be no inquiry
into either the stolen Grand Jury documents or the role in the affair of one
Arnold Rothstein.

The Black Sox scandal ended the careers of the eight indicted players,
who tried to play semipro ball, then drifted into other work unconnected
with baseball. It also shattered Charles Comiskey, who increasingly withdrew from active club management or league participation and lived more
and more at his summer retreat in upstate Wisconsin. He did spend freely in
an effort to rebuild his shattered franchise and, like other owners of the
1920s, to expand Comiskey Park's seating capacity. But few of the gaudy
purchases worked out, and in any case the Old Roman reverted to form.
After Dickie Kerr won 19 games in 1921, Comiskey cut his pay because his
earned run average was too high. When Kerr returned the contract unsigned,
Comiskey refused to tender him another, and Kerr sat out the 1922 season in
protest. Then because he played for pocket money in a semipro game against
expelled players, Landis suspended him for 1923 as well. So Comiskey's
stinginess cost him a good pitcher for 2 years instead of one. The White Sox
finished in the second division every year from 1921 until Comiskey's death
in 1931 and in 16 of the next 20 years. The franchise was still valuable—
Comiskey left his son $3 million—but nothing like what it might have been
with no scandal.

Arnold Rothstein, the only big winner to emerge from the Black Sox scandal, was shot dead a few years later in a high-stakes New York poker game.
Sometimes you win, sometimes you don't.

The Black Sox episode had both less and more influence on the history of baseball than people expected. The public revulsion against money grubbing and corruption that many feared never really materialized. Attendance was as strong in early 1921, months after the fix had hit the newspapers, as in early 1920, and the fans, reassured perhaps by Commissioner Landis's hard line against the Black Sox, remained enthusiastic throughout the decade.

There was smaller, less obvious influence, however. When the story of the fix hit the papers in September of 1920, the Chicago White Sox were about to win their third pennant in 4 years, and as only Eddie Cicotte was close to retiring they looked good for more years of American League dominance during baseball's most lucrative decade to date. Kenesaw Mountain Landis's accession to power changed that. Landis not only ruined the White Sox franchise by barring its best players, he permitted practices that led to striking long-term imbalances within major-league baseball. He showed extraordinary leniency toward the New York ballclubs in particular, refusing, for example, to press inquiries into the widely known gambling affairs of John McGraw, manager of the Giants and, more important, failing to prevent the establishment, following the purchase of Babe Ruth, of a long-term sweetheart relationship whereby the New York Yankees acquired outstanding players from the Boston Red Sox for modest remuneration, including five 20-game winners who went a collective 541-346 while wearing New York uniforms. Baseball supremacy passed from the White Sox to the Yankees for the next 40 years in part because Landis tolerated this dubious relationship. By supporting the new commissioner system, Comiskey may have gotten rid of Ban Johnson, but it cost him and the rest of the league dearly. In this respect, they were perhaps the final victims of the Black Sox scandal of 1919.

AN INTERPRETATION

American baseball and American culture crossed a great divide with the advent of Babe Ruth and Kenesaw Mountain Landis. Baseball was, most notably, both effect and cause of the consumerism that was so defining a force in the culture of the 1920s. Even casual fans, after all—even men who had never played baseball or women and small children—could appreciate Babe Ruth's exploits and Yankee prowess and would buy tickets to see them. Seeing the money to be made, other clubs, too, cultivated powerful offenses; batting averages and power hitting jumped sharply everywhere. Baseball's potential audience, already large, thus became larger. And because a significant part of this new audience consisted of girlfriends and wives and families, management labored to make the game and the parks more decorous and respectable. Grandstands became better policed. There was less open gambling, rowdiness, swearing, and bottle throwing. Spittoons vanished, as did hard liquor. Umpires, backed by Commissioner Landis, reduced fighting among players and arguing among managers. Spitballs were banned because they were distasteful not only to power hitters but to fans. Landis and the great owners with their big, cleaned-up stadiums thus wrenched baseball farther from the drinking, brawling, gambling, ramshackle nineteenth-century subculture of sensuality where it was born, and planted it solidly at the center of twentieth-century consumer society, a fit companion to the great department stores on the one hand and the giant movie palaces on the other.

The comparison with the motion picture industry is instructive in another way, too. When the movie studios faced criticism of Hollywood immorality in the 1920s, they drew on the example of baseball to appoint an "outside commissioner," Will Hays, to review film content. Progressives had long urged the use of central administrators—city managers, a federal trade commissioner—to control unruly areas of life. The appointment of baseball and movie "czars" merely extended this control mechanism to the world of leisure and entertainment. Moreover, the illusion of control, of "somebody in charge," was nearly as important as the control itself. Image mattered. Albert Lasker, whose plan made Landis commissioner of baseball, had made his money in advertising. His most memorable slogan was for Ivory Soap: "99 and 44/100 percent pure—and it floats!" Banishing the Black Sox was a step toward a pure image for baseball. Not surprisingly, when other professional sports came looking for ways to deal with instability and image, they imitated baseball, too.

Landis's expulsion of the Black Sox also corresponded to major efforts—prohibition in 1919, the arrest and deportation of radicals in 1919 and 1920, restrictive immigration laws in 1921 and 1924—to impose greater homogeneity and conformity on American society. Until the Black Sox scandal, professional ballplayers had conducted themselves pretty much as they pleased while they were not playing. Many of them drank, fought, ran pool halls, played dominoes, chased fire engines, hung out at vaudeville houses, and patronized prostitutes the same way most young urban males did when they had the chance, and club owners paid little attention as long as they showed up to play ball the next day. Landis's ruling against the crooked players began to change that. The ruling sent a signal to professional ballplayers that from now on their behavior off the field and out of season would be subject to unprecedented scrutiny from the commissioner's office.

And this level of control involved more than homogenization. It also involved hard-nosed economics. The 1920s witnessed sweeping triumphs not only by consumer culture and commission politics, but also by industrial corporations over their labor adversaries, who lost three big strikes—by police in Boston, steelworkers in Illinois, and workers generally in Seattle—in 1919 alone, then virtually every big conflict for the next 15 years. As the defense attorneys claimed, the Black Sox scandal was in part a quarrel between a profit-maximizing capitalist, Charles Comiskey, and his underpaid workers, the players. Chick Gandil and the others threw ballgames, it is clear, in order to increase their income. In banishing them, Commissioner Landis announced, in effect, that the subversion of the integrity of the game by the players in this way was an unfair labor practice that would not be tolerated. What's more, Landis ruled repeatedly over the next decade that because players were bound by contract to play ball exclusively for their owners, they could not participate, except by

The most famous practitioner of the new "power game"
favored by the New York Yankees, who dominated the
American League after 1921, was Babe Ruth, pictured
here during batting practice at Yankee Stadium in the
mid-1920s. There was nothing subtle about Ruth, who
held his bat at the end and swung for the fences. When he
connected, the ball flew—much to the delight of fans
everywhere in the giant park. Comiskey expanded his
own park in the 1920s not so that Chicagoans could see
the White Sox, who by now were no good, but so they
could see the Yankees and Babe Ruth. (National Baseball
Hall of Fame Library, Cooperstown, New York)

permission, in unauthorized barnstorming or semiprofessional games during
the off-season. Landis defended this ruling on the grounds that appearances in
the off-season might dilute the value to the owners of regular-season play,
which may have been true in some cases. What he did not say, although it was
equally true, was that off-season income from playing ball might strengthen
the negotiating leverage of the players at contract time, thereby raising salaries
and reducing profits.

In other words, not only would the ballparks be well policed in the 1920s, so would the players, and not in the interests of public image and homogeneity alone. Indeed, one implication of Landis's stance was that if players wanted to improve their lot, they would have to do so not through gambling or organizing their own teams but through forming a real labor union. In the 1930s industrial workers finally stopped losing. A generation later, ballplayers did, too.

Sources: The standard account of the 1919 World Series and the Grand Jury investigation and trial that followed is Eliot Asinof's novelistic *Eight Men Out* (1963). Asinof should be supplemented by the summer 1920–1921 issues of the *Chicago Tribune* and *New York Times,* and by "Harry's Diary" in Bill Veeck and Ed Linn, *The Hustler's Handbook* (1965). Useful for leading personalities are G. W. Axelson, *"Commy": The Life Story of Charles A. Comiskey* (1919); Donald Gropman, *Say It Ain't So, Joe!: The Story of Shoeless Joe Jackson* (1979); Leo Katcher, *The Big Bankroll: The Life and Times of Arnold Rothstein* (1959); Marshall Smelser, *The Life That Ruth Built* (1975); and J. G. Taylor Spink, *Judge Landis and 25 Years of Baseball* (1947). The most helpful interpretative study of the American sporting scene is Benjamin G. Rader, *American Sports from the Age of Folk Games to the Age of Spectators* (1983).

9

DEADLY FUEL: AUTOS, LEADED GAS, AND THE POLITICS OF SCIENCE

David Rosner

Gerald Markowitz

When workers began dying at a Standard Oil of New Jersey plant in late October of 1924, the newspaper headlines were vague and frightening: "Another Man Dies from Insanity Gas"/"Gas Madness Stalks Plant." It was soon clear that the killer was tetraethyl lead, a recently discovered compound that was being manufactured as a gasoline additive. For the next two years, scientists, public health officials, government agencies, social reformers, the press, representatives of organized labor, and the nation's largest and most powerful corporations studied the potentially lethal substance, debated its merits and liabilities, and determined a course of action—one that allowed the unfettered use of tetraethyl lead for more than a half-century.

The almost hysterical response to the deaths at the Elizabeth, New Jersey, facility was unprecedented. Disasters of much greater magnitude had occurred during the Progressive Era—in December 1907 a single explosion killed 361 West Virginia coal miners—but aroused nothing like the level of public anxiety and even paranoia that followed the Standard Oil tragedy.

Two factors were responsible for the heightened response to tetraethyl lead. One was the nature of the hazard. Death in a coal mine was horrible, to be sure, but it was also understandable and statistically, at least, predictable; to work underground in the presence of methane gas was to take a certain obvious risk. In contrast, tetraethyl lead did its damage gradually and virtually imperceptibly, attacking the nervous system in ways that ordinary people found almost incomprehensible.

The second factor was even more important. While an earlier generation of reformers had been almost entirely concerned with occupational hazards, tetraethyl lead posed a potential environmental problem, as the substance in question was to be used in automobiles, and automobiles were everywhere. In general, occupational hazards affected only workers. Environmental hazards affected members of every economic and social class.

156

Had the crisis over tetraethyl lead occurred in the Progressive Era, it no doubt would have been resolved differently—probably with federal or state legislation. But it occurred in the 1920s, only a few days before the voters would enthusiastically elect a conservative Republican, Calvin Coolidge, to the presidency. Of course, Progressive Era reformers like Alice Hamilton were still around. But the imperatives of the 1920s were far removed from the moral concerns that had helped humanize the industrial and business system only a few years before. The climate of deregulation in the 1920s might be likened to that of the last decades of the twentieth century, when federal regulatory and welfare functions were turned back to relatively ineffectual state governments, or eliminated altogether.

The world described by David Rosner and Gerald Markowitz was driven by the imperatives of technology, consumerism, profit, and what was labeled "progress." At the Washington conference that determined the fate of tetraethyl lead—and that of millions of Americans who were condemned to inhale its fumes—the most powerful voice was not Hamilton's but that of the Ethyl Corporation's Frank Howard, trumpeting the virtues of growth and progress while glorifying tetraethyl lead as an "apparent 'gift of God.' " In a society given over to such values, science was inevitably corrupted and "regulatory" agencies proved incapable of regulating. Worst of all, the decision was made to sacrifice the future to the god of the present.

Ernest Oelgert of Elizabeth, New Jersey, a laboratory worker in the Standard Oil Company's plant in Elizabeth, New Jersey, died strangely on Sunday, October 26, 1924. Witnesses declared that he had been hallucinating on Thursday, had become severely paranoid and, by Friday, was running around the plant "in terror, shouting that there were 'three coming at me at once.'" On Saturday, he was forcibly restrained and taken to Reconstruction Hospital in New York City, where he died the next day. Although company officials at first denied any responsibility, claiming that Ernie "probably worked too hard," the workers at the plant were not surprised. They all knew that Ernie worked in what was called "the looney gas building," an experimental station secretly established the previous year. Only 45 workers were employed in the laboratory and their fellow laborers had already made them the object of "undertaker jokes and farewell greetings." Standard Oil spokesmen suggested that "nothing ought to be said about this matter in the public interest."

By Monday, another worker had died and 12 others were hospitalized from what everyone at the plant called "insanity gas." Terror-stricken workers were being carted away to New York City in straitjackets, hallucinating, convulsing, and screaming about the visions that were coming before their eyes. Yandell Henderson, professor of applied physiology at Yale University, said that the victims had been poisoned by a gasoline additive called tetraethyl lead, which he regarded as one of the "greatest menaces to life and health." At first, Standard Oil said that Henderson's charge was itself a paranoid fantasy, and, in fact, "bunk." But, as the workers continued to be hospitalized and as the New York newspapers began to pick up the story, it became more and more difficult to deny its significance. Without naming the gas, Standard Oil issued a statement that claimed that the company had done everything possible to "make the work safe." They maintained that every new product carried with it certain inherent risks, but that these risks were necessary for the nation's progress: "This newly invented gasoline combination made it possible for automobile engineers to produce a more powerful engine than any yet in use . . . plans for putting this new engine on the market have advanced simultaneously with the experiment on lead gasoline."

By Friday, as the fifth victim of "looney gas" died—and as three-quarters of the laboratory's workers lay sick—the New York City Board of Health, the City of Philadelphia, and various municipalities in New Jersey banned the sale of leaded gasoline. The *New York Times*, the *New York World*, and all the regional newspapers were by this time blaring out front-page headlines like, " 'Mania Gas' May Kill through a Dual Poison," "Odd Gas Kills One," "Tetraethyl Lead in Victim's Brain," and "Gas Madness Stalks Plant."

The story really begins with the emergence of the American auto industry in the early 1900s. Throughout the country, scores of local bicycle and buggy companies began to attach to their vehicles motors powered by steam, electricity, and gasoline. One producer, Henry Ford, broke away from the pack by revolutionizing the production system through the development of the assembly line to produce an affordable automobile. Suddenly the car was not a luxury and thousands upon thousands of Americans could think for the first time of owning their own cars. By 1919, there was one automobile for every 16 Americans.

This enormous expansion of the market for cars whetted the appetite of other industrialists eager to cash in on a potential bonanza. E. I. DuPont, for example, patriarch of the famous chemical conglomerate, invested heavily in the General Motors Corporation (GM). In contrast to Ford's famous Model T that looked the same year after year, GM offered powerful cars whose appearance and engineering changed constantly. No longer would a 6-month-old car look the same as one that was 4 years old. It was now possible to tell who had the latest, the most powerful, and most fashionable automobile. Built-in obsolescence and the consumer society were born. GM's fortunes took off and, by the end of the 1920s, it replaced Ford as the nation's leading car manufacturer, producing 40 percent of all the cars in the country. By 1929, there was one car for every six Americans and President Herbert Hoover predicted that there would soon be a "car in every garage."

But to provide the power required by the new generation of automobiles, the manufacturers needed a more efficient fuel than plain gasoline, which burned far too quickly and unevenly in larger engines. In 1922, Thomas Midgley and his co-workers at the General Motors Research Laboratory in Dayton, Ohio, discovered an answer. Gasoline mixed with tetraethyl lead—a viscous, dark-brown, foul smelling liquid composed of lead molecules embedded in a compound of hydrogen and carbon—would burn evenly in a car engine. That would eliminate engine "knock," enabling the car to get more power from every gallon of gas. GM, which had an interlocking directorship*

---

*DuPont owned more than 20 percent of General Motors' stock and had several members of its board of directors on GM's board.

with the DuPont Chemical Company, quickly contracted with DuPont and Standard Oil of New Jersey to produce leaded gasoline. It was placed on sale in several markets on February 1, 1923. The "no-knock" product was popular, and the following year DuPont and General Motors created the Ethyl Corporation to market the substance. A few years later, the new company took over the manufacture of tetraethyl lead, which it still makes today. (In 1985, its plant near New Orleans produced millions of barrels of the additive.)

In the very year that Midgley and his team made their find, however, several scientists warned that the use of tetraethyl lead could expose large numbers of people to the dangers already associated with simple lead—neurological problems, kidney damage, even madness—or to other hazards that could not be predicted. DuPont and GM recognized that they would have to respond to scientists' apprehension. They also knew that such fear would not be assuaged in a study conducted by a corporation with an interest in tetraethyl lead. So the companies struck an agreement, in September 1923, with the U.S. Bureau of Mines. The agreement called for the General Motors Research Corporation to provide funding for an investigation of the dangers of tetraethyl lead. The Bureau of Mines would provide the facilities and do the work. And the U.S. Government would certify the results. The Bureau, which had authority to regulate and stockpile fuels and other resources that would be needed in wartime, was considered to have the greatest familiarity with the occupational hazards posed by gasoline.

The contract was the first in a series of agreements that would develop between the Bureau of Mines and the corporations. It allowed the government agency considerable freedom to report its conclusions. But the contracts also indicated the subservience of government to the commercial interests of the corporations. S. C. Lind, the chief chemist of the Bureau of Mines, wrote to the superintendent of the Bureau's Pittsburgh field station where the investigation was being carried out, objecting to the government's use of the trade name "ethyl" when referring to tetraethyl lead: "of course, their [GM's] object in doing so [is] fairly clear, and among other things they are not particularly desirous of having the name 'lead' appear in this case. That is alright from the standpoint of the General Motors Company but it is quite a question in my mind as to whether the Bureau of Mines would be justified in adopting this name so early in the game before it has the support of popular usage." The superintendent replied that the avoidance of "the use of 'lead' in the interbureau correspondence" was intentional because of fears of leaks to the newspapers. As the Bureau had agreed to a blackout of information, he asserted that "if it should happen to get some publicity accidentally, it would not be so bad if the word 'lead' were omitted as this term is apt to prejudice somewhat against its use." The willingness of the Bureau of Mines to avoid publicity and even the use of accurate scientific terminology reflected the Bureau's weak position vis-à-vis the giant corporations, GM and DuPont.

By June 1924, GM wanted much more control over the results of the research. It rewrote the contract to require that the popular press not be informed of the research results and added a new stipulation that "all manuscripts, before publication, will be submitted to the Company for comment and criticism." Two months after the Bureau acquiesced to this new stipulation, the newly created Ethyl Corporation took over the contract from GM and asked for an important change. A new clause providing for corporate review of findings read, "before publication of any papers or articles by your Bureau, they should be submitted to [Ethyl] for comment, criticism, and approval."

The Bureau of Mines, which had always been sympathetic to the industries it regulated, agreed. Not surprisingly, its decision was widely interpreted as a sign of apparent collusion with GM, DuPont, Standard Oil, and Ethyl to certify the safety of tetraethyl lead. On September 27, 1924, Yale Professor Henderson, who was to become an important opponent of tetraethyl lead's manufacture, wrote an angry letter to R. R. Sayers, the Public Health Service researcher who was conducting the studies for the Bureau of Mines. "It seems to me," Henderson wrote, "extremely unfortunate that the experts of the United States government should be carrying out this investigation on a grant from General Motors." He called for "an absolutely unbiased investigation." C. W. Deppe, the owner of a competing motor car company, was much blunter in his criticism of the government's relationship to GM: "May I be pardoned if I ask you frankly now, does the Bureau of Mines exist for the benefit of Ford and the GM Corporation and the Standard Oil Company of New Jersey, and other oil companies parties to the distribution of Ethyl Lead Dopes, or is the Bureau supposed to be for the public benefit and in protection of life and health?"

Soon, however, tetraethyl lead's opponents found that they had much of the public on their side—thanks to the disaster in late October, in Elizabeth, New Jersey (the site of Standard Oil's Bayway chemical plant), and to the growing skepticism of government and industry fostered by the exposure of massive corruption during the administration of President Warren G. Harding. After Harding died in August 1923, the public gradually learned that major industries had bribed high government officials. It became apparent that there was a pattern of officials being manipulated by private industries in violation of the law and the public's trust. Significantly, the most famous scandal—called "Teapot Dome"—involved the oil industry and the Department of Interior, home of the Bureau of Mines. In 1924, a congressional investigation revealed that Secretary of the Interior Albert Fall had leased vast oil reserves owned by the government to a private oil company in exchange for hundreds of thousands of dollars delivered to him as cash in "little black bags." Fall was the first member of any presidential cabinet to go to jail.

In the midst of these revelations, and on the day after the fifth victim from Standard Oil's Elizabeth plant disaster died, the Bureau of Mines released its preliminary findings. Not surprisingly, its report exonerated tetraethyl lead. Also, not surprisingly, public officials did not trust the integrity of its conclusions. New York City banned the sale of leaded gasoline and New Jersey quickly followed suit.

While public health officials largely ignored the report, many labor activists and scientists agreed with Dr. Alice Hamilton, the Harvard professor and reformer who was a noted expert on the hazards of lead poisoning, when she called for "an investigation by a public body which will be beyond suspicion."

Perhaps the strongest criticism of the Bureau of Mines' report came from the Workers' Health Bureau, an organization of labor activists who investigated hazards to workers' safety and health. The group's advisor, Professor Henderson, voiced the concern of the public health profession—a loose fellowship of sanitarians, toxicologists, health educators, and bench scientists—over the fact that "the investigators in the Bureau of Mines have used experimental conditions which are fundamentally unsuited to afford information on the real issues." The Bureau's researchers had examined gas-station attendants and truck drivers. But they looked neither for the subtle motor problems that signal organic lead poisoning nor even for gross coordination trouble; the only sign of poisoning that their studies were designed to detect was raving lunacy or death. Further, the research on humans focused on workers in plants and gas stations—there was no inquiry into the effects of exposure on those who did not work with the substance, but simply lived in a city where it was used. Henderson was the most persistent critic of the Bureau's report and his critique went farther than mere criticism of its technique. Charging that the introduction of tetraethyl lead into the environment was "probably the greatest single question in the field of public health that has ever faced the American public," Henderson warned that the use of lead in gasoline "would cause vast numbers of the population to suffer from slow lead poisoning with hardening of the arteries, rapidly decaying teeth, weakening of certain muscles and other symptoms."

Not all public health professionals sided with the opponents of lead, however. In the months after the Bureau of Mines report, as the corporations involved sought to win back a skeptical public, a leading figure in their efforts was Emery Hayhurst, a respected and ostensibly independent industrial hygienist who worked for the Ohio Department of Health. Even before the Bureau of Mines issued its report, Hayhurst had decided that tetraethyl lead was not an environmental toxin. He had advised the Bureau of Mines to include a statement that "the finished product, Ethyl Gasoline, as marketed and used both pure or diluted in gasoline retains none of the poisonous characteristics of the ingredients concerned in its manufacture and blending." No one knew that throughout the months of public controversy over tetraethyl lead, while Hayhurst was advising the Workers' Health Bureau and other labor groups about industrial hygiene, he was also working for the Ethyl Corporation as a consultant. In fact, Hayhurst was supplying advocates of tetraethyl lead with information regarding the tactics to be used by their opponents. After the Bureau of Mines report had been released, Hayhurst secretly sent to the Public Health Service a copy of the criticisms developed by the Workers' Health Bureau (which that group had decided not to send to the government) so that the Public Health Service and Bureau of Mines could frame a detailed reply.

Hayhurst and Sayers also worked together to build public and professional support for the Bureau of Mines' and the Ethyl Corporation's position that tetraethyl lead was not a public health danger. After the Bureau of Mines report had been criticized, Sayers urged Hayhurst to use his position as an editor of the prestigious and ostensibly neutral *American Journal of Public Health* to lend "scientific" credence to industry's position. Hayhurst obliged, and his statement ran as an unsigned editorial that proclaimed, "Observational evidence and reports to various health officials over the country . . . so far as we have been able to find out, corroborated the statement of 'complete safety' so far as the public has been concerned."

While Hayhurst and the public health officials sought to quell professional doubts about the safety of tetraethyl lead, Midgley, now vice president of General Motors and known as "the father of ethyl gas," called a press conference to quiet popular fears. In an effort to show the harmlessness of tetraethyl lead, he asserted that workers could have it spilled on them without ill effect. To prove his point, Midgley called for an attendant to bring a container of tetraethyl lead to him and he "washed his hands thoroughly in the fluid and dried them on his handkerchief." He told the reporters, "I'm not taking any chance whatever. Nor would I take any chance doing that every day." What he did not reveal was that only a year before he had taken a prolonged vacation in Florida to cure himself of lead poisoning.

This public relations effort was incapable of quashing the doubts about the safety of leaded gasoline or the integrity of the Bureau of Mines report. After the incident at Standard Oil's Elizabeth facility, newspapers around the country began printing accounts of death, illnesses, and cover-ups occurring at other tetraethyl plants, including the DuPont facility in Deepwater, New Jersey, and the General Motors Research Division site in Dayton, Ohio. The *New York Times* revealed that there had been over 300 cases of lead poisoning among workers at the Deepwater plant during the past two years. Workers at the DuPont facility dubbed the plant "the house of the butterflies" because so many of their colleagues had hallucinations of insects hovering around their heads during bouts of lead poisoning: "The victim pauses, perhaps while at work or in a rational conversation, gazes intently at space, and snatches at something not there." The *Times* reported that "about 80 percent of all who worked in 'the house of the butterflies' or who went into it to make repairs, were poisoned, some repeatedly."

The local papers, on the other hand, printed very little news about what was happening at the plants. They said nothing about the death of Frank W. (Happy) Durr, who had worked in Deepwater for DuPont for 25 years. Durr had literally given his life to the company. He had begun working for DuPont as a 12-year-old child and died from exposure to tetraethyl lead at the age of 37 years. The editor of the local paper told the *Times*, "I guess the reason we didn't print anything about Durr's death was because we couldn't get it. They [DuPont] suppress things about the lead plant at Deepwater. Whatever we print, we pick up from the workers." DuPont's control even extended to the local hospital, where it was almost impossible to get information about the source of workers' illnesses.

Throughout April and May of 1925, the *New York World* ran nearly daily front-page headlines. The *World* proclaimed leaded gasoline a "menace." It warned that even "Columbia [University] Experts Assert[ed] Ethyl Gas Is Public Menace." The *Times* tried to get in on the action by asserting that leaded gasoline was a "Deadly Peril in the Streets." The *World*, known nationally as a leading muckraking paper, sought to use the Bureau of Mines, Report against the industry by asserting that "Tetraethyl Peril to All Motorists Indicated in Tests by Mines Bureau." These and other three-column front-page headlines dwarfed other stories on the fall of the German economy and "red scares" throughout the world. As a result of this publicity and the continuing public disquiet over the Bureau of Mines Report, the head of the Public Health Service, the Surgeon General, called a national conference to assess the tetraethyl lead situation.

On May 20, 1925, the conference convened in Washington, D.C., with every major party to the controversy in attendance. Each corporation and organization had prepared a statement, which its representative read to the assembly and then defended during a question and answer session. In the words of one participant, the conference gathered together in one room "two diametrically opposed conceptions. The men engaged in industry, chemists, and engineers, take it as a matter of course that a little thing like industrial poisoning should not be allowed to stand in the way of a great industrial advance. On the other hand, the sanitary experts take it as a matter of course that the first consideration is the health of the people."

The companies—General Motors, DuPont, Standard Oil, and the Ethyl Corporation—went first. Their speakers outlined the history of leaded gasoline and the reasons its continued production was essential to the nation. The Chairman of GM, Charles F. Kettering, and a lead researcher from GM's Kettering Laboratories, Robert Kehoe, both invoked one of the industry's most common arguments—that oil supplies were limited, and that tetraethyl lead would help stretch them out. (Industry spokesmen claimed that the world's petroleum supplies would run out in the 1940s if lead was not added to gasoline. With leaded gas, studies said, supplies might last until the 1950s.) Frank Howard, the Ethyl Corporation representative, stressed the broader point that, whatever the health risks, the entire controversy had to be seen from the economic and political perspective, as well as the environmental one. "You have but one problem," he remarked rhetorically, "Is this a public health hazard?" He answered that "unfortunately, our problem is not that simple." Rather he posited that automobiles and oil were central to the industrial progress of the nation, if not the world. "Our continued development of motor fuels is essential in our civilization," he proclaimed. Noting that at least a decade of research had preceded the discovery of tetraethyl lead, he called it an "apparent 'gift of God.' . . . Because some animals died and some do not die in some experiments, shall we give this thing up entirely?"

These remarks proved to be the recurrent themes for the industry: The nation's progress depended on gasoline, and the risks involved were worth it. Dr. H. C. Parmelee, editor of the industry trade magazine *Chemical and Metallurgical Engineering* stated, "The research and development that produced tetraethyl lead were conceived in a fine spirit of industrial progress looking toward the conservation of gasoline and increased efficiency of internal combustion motors." Parmelee believed that the companies did their best to safeguard the workers. In the end, he said, "its casualties were negligible compared to human sacrifice in the development of many other industrial enterprises." The company representatives blamed workers' carelessness for the deaths and illnesses in tetraethyl lead plants.

For their part, the labor activists and public health specialists who were fighting leaded gas pointed out that lead compounds were already known to be slow, cumulative poisons. They believed that the federal government had to assume responsibility for protecting the health of the nation, and they rejected the notion that the workers were the ones responsible for their own poisoning. Finally, they asked the conferees to consider not just lead's potential for causing occupational diseases, but also its effects on the environment as a whole. As the country's foremost authority on lead, Alice Hamilton, put it, "You may control conditions within a factory, but how are you going to control the whole country?"

Henderson, the Yale physiologist, compared tetraethyl lead to a serious infectious disease like the influenza and diphtheria that periodically swept the country. He was horrified at the thought that hundreds of thousands of pounds of lead were going to be deposited in the streets of every major city of America. The problem was not that more people would die like those in the laboratory in New Jersey, but that "the conditions would grow worse so gradually and the development of lead poisoning will come on so insidiously . . . that leaded gasoline will be in nearly universal use and large numbers of cars will have been sold . . . before the public and the government awaken to the situation." In a private letter to R. R. Sayers of the Bureau of Mines, Henderson wrote: "In the past, the position taken by the authorities has been that nothing could be prohibited until it was proved to have killed a number of people. I trust that in the future, especially in a matter of this sort, the position will be that substances like tetraethyl lead can not be introduced for general use until it is proved harmless."

Opponents were most concerned, however, about the industry propaganda that equated the use of lead with industrial progress and the survival of civilization itself. Reacting to the Ethyl Corporation representative's statement that tetraethyl lead was a "gift of God," Grace Burnham of the Workers' Health Bureau said it "was not a gift of God when those 11 men were killed or those 149 were poisoned." She denounced the priorities of "this age of speed and rush and efficiency and mechanics" and said, "the thing we are interested in [in] the long run is not mechanics or machinery, but men." A. L. Berres, secretary of the metal trades department of the American Federation of Labor, also rejected the prevalent conception of the 1920s that "the business of America is business." He told the conference that the American Federation of Labor opposed the use of tetraethyl lead, saying, "We feel that where the health and general welfare of humanity is concerned, we ought to step slowly."

Of course, the public health experts listening to the two camps hoped that scientific research would prove one position correct and the other wrong. Yet a final, scientific answer was impossible for two reasons. In the first place, scientists at that time did not adequately understand what they were studying. All

By 1929, Sunoco was appealing to the public rather than to the experts, who had by then deemed tetraethyl lead "safe." Here, Sunoco asked consumers to "be the judge and jury" and "render your own verdict." In another advertisement that same year, Sunoco claimed that "the verdict of the jury" was in and that unleaded Sunoco had triumphed. (Courtesy of Hagley Museum and Library)

previous experience with lead poisoning had involved inorganic molecules, which do not create symptoms until large amounts have been absorbed in the bones. Tetraethyl lead is what we would now call an organic compound, which creates symptoms very soon after entering the body. So while inorganic lead in the body tends to appear in blood or excretions before symptoms appear, traces of organic lead compounds may not be found until after severe symptoms have occurred. Naturally, the first cases of poisoning by organic lead compounds did not fit well into models created to explain the action of inorganic lead compounds, and so evidence of poisonings by tetraethyl lead was regarded as perplexing and ambiguous. Even the medical director of Reconstruction Hospital in New York, probably the only facility devoted exclusively to the study and treatment of occupational disease and accidents, could not explain the strange manifestations of chronic tetraethyl lead poisoning. Of the 39 patients he treated after the Elizabeth disaster, he said, "some . . . gave no physical evidence and no symptoms or any evidence that could be found by a physical examination that would indicate that they were ill, but at the same time showed lead in the stools."

The second reason that public health officials could not look to science was political. Pressured by industry's desire to market ethyl gasoline and the public's desire for speedy, definitive answers, scientists were designing studies that could be finished in a few months—simple research on worker health records, or a few tests on humans or animals with no follow-up after the initial work was done. These were not sufficient to provide the definitive proof of harm that the public wanted and the companies said did not exist. Many public health officials agreed with the industry that it would be unfair to ban the new gasoline additive until there was proof it was dangerous. Suggestive studies and possible problems were not enough to keep the product off the market, because of vigorous industry opposition. Pure science would not provide the answer. In the face of industry arguments that oil supplies were limited, and that there was an extraordinary need to conserve fuel by making combustion more efficient, most public health workers believed that there should be overwhelming evidence that leaded gasoline actually harmed people before it was banned.

In private, even the advocates of tetraethyl lead were ambivalent about the scientific issues. Hayhurst, for example, wrote Sayers that he accepted the argument that "lead has no business in the human body . . . everyone agrees lead is an undesirable hazard and the only way to control it is to stop its use by the general public." But, he went on, "I am afraid human progress cannot go on under such restrictions. Where things can be handled safely by proper supervision and regulation they must be allowed to proceed if we are to survive among the nations." Another investigator, Frederick Flinn of Columbia University, voiced similar reservations in private: "The more I work with the material [TEL], the more I am confused as to whether it is a real public health hazard." In the end, however, he was "convinced that there is some hazard—the extent of which must be studied around garages and filling stations over a period of time and by unprejudiced persons." As Flinn was a consultant for the Ethyl Corporation, it is not surprising that he ended his letter by saying, "Of course, you must understand that my remarks are confidential."

The public was not so philosophical. People were still alarmed by the previous year's accident and continuing reports of other deaths caused by tetraethyl lead. The *New York Times,* for example, continued reports of poisonings and deaths from tetraethyl lead: "Tetraethyl Lead Fatal to Makers," one headline announced in an article that claimed that eight had died and 300 were poisoned in one DuPont plant in Deepwater, New Jersey.

At the end of the Surgeon General's conference, the Ethyl Corporation announced that it was suspending the production and distribution of leaded gasoline until the scientific and public health issues involved in its manufacture could be resolved. Furthermore, the conference called on the Surgeon General to organize a Blue Ribbon Committee of the nation's foremost public health scientists to conduct the unbiased study of leaded gas that the Bureau of Mines had failed to produce.

But this apparent triumph for scientific inquiry over economic interests was ephemeral. The conference decided that the new committee had to report definitive findings by the end of the year—only seven months away. To meet the deadline, the committee members designed a short-term, and in retrospect, very limited, study of garagemen, filling station attendants, and chauffeurs in two cities in which lab equipment was available, Dayton and Cincinnati. The brief inquiry naturally missed the most significant aspects of possible lead poisoning from car fumes—the slow accumulation of the compound in the body over many years of exposure.

After its seven months were up, the committee duly found that "in its opinion there are at present no good grounds for prohibiting the use of ethyl gasoline . . . provided that its distribution and use are controlled by proper regulations." The report suggested the Surgeon General formulate specific regulations for the product's use, to be enforced by the states. Although it appears that the committee rushed to judgment, it must be pointed out that this group saw their study as only interim, to be followed by longer range follow-up studies in the coming years. Indeed, the committee had warned that

> Longer experience may show that even such slight storage of lead as was observed in these studies may lead eventually in susceptible individuals to recognizable or to chronic degenerative diseases of a less obvious character.

Recognizing that their short-term retrospective investigation was incapable of detecting such danger, the committee concluded that further study by the government was essential. Noting a "vast increase in the number of automobiles throughout the country," the committee remarked that this was "a matter of real importance from the standpoint of public health." It strongly suggested that studies be continued and that Congress appropriate funds for long-term investigations to be carried out by the Surgeon General.

These suggestions were never carried out. Instead, the Public Health Service dropped the issue and allowed all following studies on tetraethyl lead to be conducted by the Ethyl Corporation and scientists employed by it. The man who conducted those studies was Kehoe, who, in direct contradiction of the committee, interpreted its report to mean that there was no need to waste public money studying tetraethyl lead: "as it appeared from their investigation that there was no evidence of immediate danger to the public health, it was thought that these necessarily extensive studies should not be repeated at present, at public expense, but that they should be continued at the expense of the industry

The Organic Chemicals Department, DuPont Deepwater Chambers Work, Deepwater Point, New Jersey, 1951: the site of the Deepwater disaster, where tetraethyl lead production workers were poisoned in 1924. (Courtesy of Hagley Museum and Library)

most concerned, subject, however, to the supervision of the Public Health Service." It should not be surprising that Kehoe concluded that his research "fails to show any evidence for the existence of such hazards." Over the next 40 years, other studies came to the same conclusion. That too is not surprising, because between 1927 and 1967, there was no research conducted on tetraethyl lead that was not funded by either the Kettering Laboratories or by General Motors.

AN INTERPRETATION

The history of public policy regarding leaded gasoline must be understood as part of the history of the American chemical and auto industries. During the 1920s these industries emerged as the corporate backbone of the United States. Because leaded gasoline was critical to the development of these industries, a heated controversy arose regarding its possibly unhealthful effects. Public health professionals found themselves under intense pressure to sanction and minimize the hazards associated with the manufacture and use of this new potentially toxic substance.

Yet this controversy arose at a very particular moment in American history. The 1920s were marked by the almost unrestrained growth of corporate power and an ideology in government that, in Coolidge's words, the "Business

An advertisement from the British journal *Punch,* October 19, 1932, shows one way in which producers of leaded fuel overcame doubts about the safety of the tetraethyl lead additive. (Courtesy of Hagley Museum and Library)

of America is business." In the 1920s the federal government was small and weak in comparison with such giant corporations as General Motors and DuPont. Unlike the first two decades of the 1900s, when many groups were pressuring the federal government to expand its powers and assume responsibility for regulating big business, the 1920s saw unrestrained corporate aggrandizement as a part of the "Age of Normalcy." Hence, the protests that led to the initial ban of tetraethyl lead represented, in part, the older Progressive Era vision of government's role as regulator of business. During the 1920s, however, the country abandoned its older faith in public regulation and allowed voluntary agreements to replace legislative action.

The questions and issues raised in the 1920s continue to haunt us in the 1990s. How should society regulate private interests that threaten the public health and safety? Should public officials or private organizations have responsibility for establishing standards? How does one study potentially toxic substances while protecting the right to health of human subjects? Does industry have to prove a new substance safe or do public health experts have to prove it dangerous? In the face of scientific uncertainty concerning the safety or dangers posed by leaded gasoline, and the perceived need for this substance by the auto industry, the broader question became, What was the level of acceptable risk that society should be willing to assume for industrial progress? At every stage of the debate, the political, economic, and scientific issues were inextricably intertwined.

Every year thousands of new chemical agents are developed by industry and introduced into the workplace and environment. All too often, the threat these agents pose to the health and well-being of the community is only discovered after an environmental or occupational disaster. Bhopal, Three Mile Island, and Love Canal* have all come to symbolize the hazards of our modern industrial and chemical society. Although most people assume that toxic chemicals are introduced into the environment through ignorance or error, the actual history is usually more complicated. Lead's presence in our air, lungs, and bones was a product of political, economic, and public policy decisions, not simply a scientific mistake.

Forty years after the Surgeon General's conference, in the late 1960s, doctors in inner-city hospitals began reporting instances of lead poisoning among children living in tenements—coats of leaded paint, which had been applied to buildings before it was banned in the 1940s, and sometimes after, were peeling and being eaten by the children. By the early 1970s, studies of children's exposure were turning up the fact that people on lower floors had more of the metal in their systems than their upstairs neighbors. This led a new generation of researchers to look into automobile emissions. They found what their predecessors could not: evidence of lead's insidious and pervasive effects on the development of children. Thanks to the research, and the burgeoning environmental movement of the era, the federal government ordered the phasing out of leaded gasoline. The amount of lead permitted in gasoline is steadily shrinking. In the meantime, the political and scientific battles focus on how much lead can be put into "unleaded" gas. The issue of tetraethyl lead is still with us but no one now thinks of tetraethyl lead as "a gift of God."

As we look back on the controversy today from the era of nitrites, PCBs, and asbestos, we may be tempted to disapprove of a public health profession that failed to stop the introduction of ethyl gasoline. After all, prominent experts such as Alice Hamilton and Yandell Henderson warned about the dangers and strongly advocated an impartial government-sponsored scientific study, and opponents did manage to win a temporary moratorium on the manufacture of the substance until the scientists' results became available. What

---

*Bhopal, India, was the site of a massive disaster in which thousands of people were poisoned by the release of highly toxic gas from a Union Carbide Chemical plant. Three Mile Island was the site of the nation's worst nuclear reactor accident, and Love Canal is a community in upper New York State that was found to be contaminated by chemicals dumped by the Hooker Chemical Company.

went wrong? Why is tetraethyl lead still a prime source of lead in the environment? Of course, there were those who had such an ideological commitment to industrial progress that they were willing to put their science aside to meet the demands of corporate greed. But more important, we should look at those who considered themselves honorable scientific investigators for, ultimately, they could not distinguish their "science" from the demands of an economy and society that was being built around the automobile. Any boundaries between science and society, if they ever really existed, broke down as they agreed to conduct a short-term study that would provide quick answers—answers guaranteed, in retrospect, not to disrupt this vital industry. The symptoms of lead accumulation due to exhaust emissions would be unlike anything they had previously encountered in industrial populations. But because of compromises in their experimental design they could not possibly understand what we now know today: that those most affected would not be adults, but children, slowly accumulating lead. Their suffering is all the more tragic because of the amorphous and still poorly understood effects of lead on the nervous system of children. The best of the public health scientists of the 1920s were working from an inadequate model of disease causation. But their inability to draw conclusions valid from modern standards speaks more to the interlocking relationships between science and society than to the absence of a link between lead and disease.

Sources: A wide variety of different types of material was used to unravel the complex history of leaded gasoline. We began by looking at the newspapers and magazines of the period. This material gave us a good sense of the controversies that accompanied the introduction of lead into gasoline in the 1920s. The *New York World,* the *New York Times,* the *American Journal of Public Health, The Survey,* and various industry journals provided a sense of how the public, professionals, and industry viewed the issue. But this public literature provided only part of the story. Private correspondence and memos between industry spokesmen, government officials in the U.S. Bureau of Mines, and the Public Health Service were invaluable for understanding the interlocking relationships between government and industry during the period. The National Archives in Washington preserved this material, but other material in the hands of the industry is unavailable to scholars.

10

THE TOWNSEND MOVEMENT AND SOCIAL SECURITY

William Graebner

He was an old man and not much of a public speaker. He held no political office and, like millions of older Americans, he had no money. Despite these handicaps, in the midst of the Great Depression of the 1930s Francis Townsend became one of the most popular and influential men in America. The source of his strength was a plan— indeed, a very simple plan—for providing federal pensions to all retired people over the age of 60 years. In less than 2 years, Townsend parlayed his idea for old-age pensions into hundreds of Townsend Clubs and millions of devoted followers—the Townsend movement—with the strength to bully Franklin D. Roosevelt's New Deal into the landmark Social Security Act of 1935.

When Townsend first made his proposal in the fall of 1933, a small number of Americans already had some kind of claim to an old-age pension. Federal civil service employees were minimally covered under a law passed in 1920. Some military veterans and state and municipal employees could look forward to future benefits. And about 10 percent of employees in the private sector had some kind of coverage. But otherwise, most people had to depend on personal savings in their old age or count on their children to take care of them. If these sources of security proved inadequate, older people had only two options: In some states, the indigent aged could apply for public assistance; or they could seek room and board in the county almshouse. Although Germany, Great Britain, and most of the other industrialized nations of the world had had comprehensive national programs of old-age pensions and assistance in place for many years, the United States had nothing of the kind.

Even in ordinary times, the worsening condition of the nation's elderly would probably have brought forth an advocate such as Townsend. But these were no ordinary times. Across the country, young and old struggled to make ends meet, even to survive, in the most severe depression in the nation's history. The trauma was symbolized by Detroit, a city whose automobile assembly lines had represented the boom of the 1920s and that now found itself devastated by the Great Depression: By 1933, more than half of the city's workers were unemployed, and once-proud citizens dug homes in the ground, rummaged for food in alley garbage cans, or stole dog biscuits from the city pound. Conditions in other American cities, and in the small towns and countryside, were only marginally better.

Into this chaos stepped Townsend, full of hopes and high expectations, tempting the nation's aged with the promise of a better life. To Roosevelt, an economic conservative whose primary goal was to save the capitalist system, Townsend's spectacular promises made him a dangerous radical, a demagogue whose politics threatened the comfortable two-party system and whose economics endangered the fragile and partial recovery from the trough of the Great Depression that the New Deal had begun to piece together in 1934 and 1935.

There was, to be sure, a core of truth in this assessment of Townsend and his movement. But if Townsend was a radical, his was an odd sort of radicalism that came packaged as the American dream. To proud older people who valued their independence, Townsend stood for the prospect of a dignified retirement. To younger people, he offered the jobs that had been vacated by the recently retired. To young and old, he proposed a new kind of national economy, driven not by production but by consumer purchases. This mixture of security and social engineering was hardly revolutionary. In its own, more oblique way, Roosevelt's New Deal was moving in similar directions. And a half century later, Townsend's ideas—if not his plan—were national policy.

It was 1936. For 6 years, all years of the Great Depression that had begun with the crash of the stock market in the fall of 1929, Charles Lewis had struggled to make ends meet while working a 260-acre, rented dairy farm in the foothills of Chautauqua County, New York, not far from Lake Erie and only a few miles from the Pennsylvania line. Since 1898, Lewis had kept a daybook—a brief daily record—of weather and work. For the most part, the entries chronicle the year-round drudgery of cutting "poles" for fencing and drawing manure. But they also reveal Lewis's interest in the major spectacles of the day. During the year 1936, Lewis noted the death of the King of England; the electrocution of Bruno Richard Hauptmann, kidnapper and murderer of Charles Lindbergh's infant son; and Joe Louis's victory in a prize fight ("nigger Lewis & dakota farmer only one blow/struck and the nigger did it"). For June 28, Lewis wrote:

> Cold wind clowdy [sic] I picked some berries P.M.
> We all went over to Lily Dale to a big
> Townsen [sic] meeting awful crowd

Lily Dale was an established spiritualist community—the sort of place where one could find help in contacting the soul of a dead relative. But on this particular Sunday, the grounds had been given over to an all-day political rally. According to the *Jamestown Evening Journal*, an estimated 8,000 people, most of them representing Townsend clubs in Buffalo, Niagara Falls, Lockport, and other western New York communities, showed up for the day's events, which included a morning concert by the Falconer Townsend Club band, a noon "picnic basket," and an evening softball game.

Although Franklin D. Roosevelt had only the day before accepted the nomination of the Democratic Party for a second term as president, most of those who attended the Lily Dale rally had little interest in Roosevelt or, for that matter, in the more conservative Republican candidate, Kansas governor Alfred M. Landon. Many were considering voting for William Lemke, a North Dakota Republican who was running for president on the new Union Party ticket. But even Lemke's candidacy was suspect. As the day wore on, the Lily Dale delegates passed a resolution urging fellow Townsend followers to withhold support from the Union Party until Lemke had pledged his unequivocal support for the single-issue platform of the Townsend movement: the old-age revolving pension (OARP), otherwise known as the Townsend Plan.

At its core, the Townsend Plan was simple: Give every retired person over 60 years of age a "pension" of $200 per month, provided only that the pensioner agree to retire from the workplace and spend the money before the next check arrived. With the presidential election only months away, it seemed possible that millions of Americans would forsake the major parties to cast their ballots for nothing more than an old-age pension plan.

The cause of this bizarre situation was Francis E. Townsend, a gaunt, energetic, white-haired man 69 years of age. Born in a log cabin near Fairbury, Illinois, in 1867, Townsend was one of seven children reared in a poor, religious, and hard-working farm family. "We knew poverty in those days," he recalled in *New Horizons,* his 1943 autobiography,

> but it seems to have been a different sort of poverty. There were many years of my childhood when I am sure my father handled less than $100 a year in actual cash, but I have no recollection of ever being hungry after I was grown up. . . . As neighborhoods and as families, we were self-sufficient. We made our things or did without.

Participating in the same sort of unending round of labor that would characterize Charles Lewis's life in the 1930s, Townsend acquired a "distaste" for what he described as "this toilsome existence in which men were conscripted by life into an endless battle with nature and in which women grew old before their time." In contrast, Townsend fondly recalled the entrepreneurial energy of his brother-in-law, who in the serious depression of the 1890s had bought up Kansas lands that had been seeded and then, under conditions of drought, abandoned:

> The snows melted and soaked the good ground and the volunteer wheat came on from the dormant seed. . . . Crops grew and matured amazingly and these far-seeing men were ready with their great machinery [the enormous harvesting "combines" of the day] when the harvest time came on. They reaped and they reaped until all bins and granaries and barns that could be rented were full and overflowing. Such a harvest! At such an insignificant cost!

Following the family's move to Nebraska in the mid-1880s, Townsend spent more than a decade as a virtual transient. In 1887, he tried—and failed—to make his fortune during an early California land boom. A series of odd jobs in Spokane and Seattle were no more productive. Returning to Nebraska, Townsend taught school, worked a tract of land in northwestern Kansas, and completed a college preparatory course at Franklin (Nebraska) Academy. In 1899, having lost his farm, he enrolled at Omaha Medical College. Graduating in 1903, he practiced medicine among the miners and cowhands of Belle Fourche, South Dakota, and, in 1906, married "Minnie" Brogue.

After the Great War (World War I), when health problems made life in the Black Hills intolerable, Townsend took his family to Long Beach, California. Despite the city's rapidly growing population of older people, Townsend's medical practice remained a marginal one. Perhaps for this reason, in 1927 he put his ever scarcer resources into Midway City, a southern California real estate venture—again without success. Most of his remaining savings were lost in the first year or two of the Great Depression.

Townsend's luck seemed to have turned in 1930, when a former medical school classmate hired him for the staff of the county hospital to provide in-home care for the "needy ill" of Long Beach. "We were besieged incessantly with calls for help," Townsend wrote. But in the summer of 1933, in the depths of the Great Depression, the county program under which Townsend was employed was discontinued, and the job was gone. The stage was set for the Townsend Plan.

Just how Townsend emerged from the despondency of unemployment to advocate a celebrated "plan" is a matter of some dispute. One analysis, written in 1936, emphasized that Townsend's rise to "the position of national political dictator" was undeserved, the product of a "series of fortuitous incidents"—the last one a Long Beach election that had resulted in a political decision to discontinue the county's health programs. In *New Horizons,* Townsend preferred to represent his personal experience—indeed, the plan itself—as a typical product of twentieth-century life. "Here were mother and I," he wrote, referring to his wife,

> both past 60, both intelligent and experienced but not active enough to compete in the world of commerce and economics. Or was that true? Economics in America is something controlled by politics—and politics is votes. We might be too old to work, but we were not too old to vote. And there were millions of others like us. . . . An idea came to me which might alleviate the hopelessness of the aged people of our community.

According to the most frequently repeated explanation of Townsend's politicization—and, curiously, one that is not repeated in his autobiography—Townsend conceived of the plan one day in 1933, when he happened to observe three old women rummaging in garbage cans for something to eat. As Townsend later told the story: "A torrent of invectives tore out of me, the big blast of all the bitterness that had been building in me for years." Minnie's efforts to calm her husband were to no avail. "I want all the neighbors to hear me!" Townsend purportedly said. "I want God Almighty to hear me! I'm going to shout until the whole country hears!"

On September 30, 1933, the first version of the Townsend Plan appeared in the Long Beach *Press-Telegram* as a letter to the editor:

The Townsend Plan logo. The letters OARP stand for Old Age Revolving Pension, the plan's formal name, while LTD (for limited liability) was perhaps intended to emphasize that the plan was as solidly grounded as any other business organization. The slogan highlighted the plan's goal of redistributing by age a finite amount of work.

> Because of man's inventiveness less and less productive effort is going to be required to supply the needs of the race. This being the case, it is just as necessary to make some disposal of our surplus workers, as it is to dispose of our surplus wheat or corn or cotton.

Referring to an infamous New Deal program that had resulted in the slaughtering of six million little pigs to head off a glut in the hog market, Townsend wrote:

> But we cannot kill off the surplus workers as we are doing with our hogs. . . . We must retire them from business activities and eliminate them from the field of competitive effort.

Estimating the population of Americans over 60 years of age at between 9 and 12 million, Townsend proceeded to the heart of his plan:

> I suggest that the national government retire all who reach that age on a monthly pension of $150 a month or more, on condition that they spend the money as they get it. This will insure an even distribution throughout the nation of two or three billions of fresh money each month. Thereby insuring a healthy and brisk state of business, comparable to that we enjoyed during war times.

Townsend was just as frank about financing the plan. New taxes—substantial taxes—would be necessary. The proper tax, he argued, was a sales tax—"sufficiently high to insure the pensions at a figure adequate to maintain the business of the country in a healthy condition." Finally, Townsend called on readers to understand the growing role that the national government must take in stimulating economic activity when private businesses were too cautious. "This function of the Government," he concluded, "could be easily established and maintained through the pension system for the aged."

In the years that followed, there were changes in certain details and emphases of the Townsend Plan. The $150 would soon become $200—a lot of money at a time when only about 10 percent of all American families earned more than $2,500 in a year—and in legislation introduced in Congress in April 1935, the $200 would become a maximum rather than a guaranteed sum. It was not long, either, before Townsend dumped the sales tax for a "transaction" tax of 2 percent on all commercial and business transactions. "A sales tax would hit the little man," he told a Senate committee. "A transactions tax will make the rich fellow pay. The Townsend tax is in no way a sales tax." In addition, the movement's most widely used slogan—"Youth for Work/Age for Leisure"— reflected Townsend's growing inclination to present his pension movement as a boon to workers in their 20s and 30s, who in the absence of his pensions might have trouble finding employment. Referring to the Civilian Conservation Corps, a New Deal program that employed some 500,000 young men in forestry projects, a Townsend Plan ready-reference book said, "[Youth] do not want a mountain camp, segregated from society, under military dictatorship and martial law. THEY WANT A HOME and a place in the civil life of the nation." By and large, the Townsend Plan that soon became familiar to Americans closely resembled Townsend's first letter to the editor.

Within months, Townsend's simple idea was transformed into a social movement. By the end of October, the *Press-Telegram* carried a regular page of reader reactions to Townsend's proposal. By early November, in response to a 1-inch newspaper ad, a platoon of Long Beach elderly were accumulating thousands of signatures on the first of many Townsend petitions. From an 8- by 10-foot room in the rear of a real estate office, the Townsend organization moved

How the Townsend Plan was supposed to work: a closed system, with the government at its center, helping things along. The cartoon also reflects the plan's reliance on theories of the circulation of money as well as the confidence that American economic recovery could be achieved independent of the rest of the world. This illustration appeared in a Townsend publication in 1936.

to larger quarters. On New Year's Day, 1934, Townsend and his new partner, 40-year-old real estate promoter Robert "Earl" Clements, hung a large sign: "Old-Age Revolving Pension Headquarters." A few days later, the organization was incorporated as a nonprofit corporation; Clements, Townsend, and Townsend's brother, a Los Angeles hotel porter, were the organization's only directors.

Using direct-mail techniques, voluntary and paid organizers, and a newspaper, *The Modern Crusader* (later renamed *The Townsend National Weekly*), Townsend and Clements rapidly expanded the organization beyond Long Beach. San Diego, a city of 180,000 people with the nation's largest percentage of older people, was an obvious target. By early 1935, the city had some 30,000 dues-paying members and was able to produce 105,000 signatures on a petition endorsing the Townsend Plan. Stimulated by "Townsend budgets" that showed precisely how $200 per month might be spent (monthly payments on a refrigerator, an electric washer, a radio, and a vacuum cleaner totaled $30), many residents of San Diego and other cities acted as if payment of the pension were imminent. One San Diego couple, convinced that the November 1934 congressional elections would lead immediately to passage of a Townsend measure in Congress, insisted that a furniture dealer allow payments to be deferred until January, when the first Townsend Plan checks would arrive.

The movement registered similar successes in cities and towns throughout the Far West and the Midwest; among other communities, Los Angeles, Seattle,

A sign in Saw Pit, Colorado, September 1940. Although the sign describes what it means to be a "Townsendite," the heading—"Townsend"—reflects the continued importance of Townsend's personal leadership within the movement. Russell Lee, who took the photograph for the Farm Security Administration, probably also intended to emphasize that Townsend was no less a "product" of advertising than Bubble Up and Chesterfields. (Library of Congress)

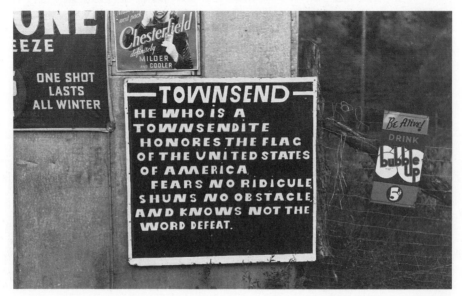

Portland, Chicago, Toledo, and Cleveland were bastions of Townsendism. By 1936, Townsend was claiming 3,500,000 supporters and a circulation for *The Townsend National Weekly* of some 2,000,000. The Northeast, and especially the South, where employers feared that the movement would threaten the supply of black labor, proved more resistant to the Townsend message.

As the movement grew, it was sustained by a network of locally organized but nationally administered Townsend Clubs. The first club was chartered in Huntington Park, California, in August 1934; by January of 1935, there were 3,000 clubs, each with from 100 to 1,000 dues-paying members. Reporting on the Townsend movement in the election year of 1936 for the *Twentieth-Century Fund*, a committee of prominent citizens expressed concern over the growth and power of the clubs. "If there are 7,000 Townsend Clubs with a membership of 3,500,000 organized by congressional districts, as Dr. Townsend claims, the organizations give him the balance of power between the two parties. That is, if one candidate of either party endorses the Plan and his opponent does not, the Townsend sentiment may decide the election."

The typical Townsend Club gathering of the mid-1930s drew a middle-class membership of farmers, clerks, clergymen, skilled workers, insurance agents, and small businessmen, many of them already retired and others thinking about retirement, to a small-town church or public school building. On the walls of the auditorium are the slogan "The Townsend Plan is religion in action" and cardboard pictures of the founder. Following the salute to the flag, a patriotic song or two, and a prayer led by a minister (amens echo through the hall), the local president reads a message "direct from Dr. Townsend and Mr. Clements in Washington" and exhorts the faithful to pay their dues—no doubt emphasizing, as a Townsend pamphlet did, that the plan was "an organization of the masses, the common people, supported by their nickels, dimes, and quarters." Addressing the throng as "You dear old folks," the evening's speaker —perhaps a candidate for Congress in the district—lavishes praise on the plan, lauds Townsend as a David slaying the Goliaths of "Wall Street" and "Moscow," and enjoins those assembled to "take up the cross of this crusade." The speech over, plans are made for selling official literature, collecting signatures on petitions, and securing new members—all with the goal of electing congressmen and senators pledged to vote for the Townsend Plan. The meeting closes with the audience on its feet, repeating after its leader: "The Townsend Plan must succeed. I therefore pledge my allegiance to its principles, its founders, its leaders, and to all loyal co-workers; and re-dedicate myself to maintain the democratic spirit and form of government in America."

In the first six months of 1934, as Townsend was building the strength of his organization in southern California, the President of the United States was laying the groundwork for his own program of old-age insurance (i.e., pensions), putting his administration on a collision course with the Townsend movement. In early March, Roosevelt discussed the problem over lunch with General Electric president Gerard Swope, a reform-minded businessman whose company had a "contributory" pension plan to which employees contributed a portion of their earnings. Like many executives of the nation's largest

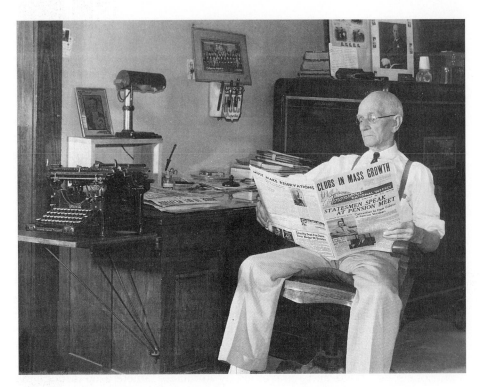

Real estate and insurance salesman and Townsend Club member John W. Dillard, reading the *Townsend National Weekly* in his Washington, Indiana, office, June 1941. Like Dillard, many Townsendites were thoughtful, respected—and elderly—members of their communities. Photo by John Vachon for the Farm Security Administration. (Library of Congress)

corporations, Swope believed that only contributory plans would allow employees the freedom to leave one job, and one geographical location, for another. He also favored a pension system run by the federal government rather than individual states, as only then would the costs of doing business be equalized across state lines and industries.

On June 8, Roosevelt outlined for Congress a comprehensive program of federal-state cooperation "to provide at once security against several of the great disturbing factors in life—especially those which relate to unemployment and old age." And he made clear that unlike Townsend, he favored a system funded by contributions, not by "an increase in general taxation." To produce the administration's package of legislation, Roosevelt appointed a special cabinet-level committee—the Committee on Economic Security (CES). The CES was headed by executive director Edwin Witte, a University of Wisconsin professor of economics. At Roosevelt's urging, Witte left Washington to consult with Swope, Walter Teagle of Standard Oil, and John Raskob of General Motors. Witte also met with Henry Harriman, president of the United States

Chamber of Commerce, whose "general attitude," Witte reported, "was that some legislation on social security was inevitable and that business should not put itself in the position of attempting to block this legislation, but should concentrate its efforts upon getting it into acceptable form."

Although the Raskobs and Harrimans had their say, the administration's old-age legislation was actually conceptualized and written by four people who were not exactly household names: Barbara Armstrong, professor of law at the University of California at Berkeley and author of a book, *Insuring the Essentials*, that advocated contributory old-age pensions; Murray Latimer, for years an employee of Industrial Relations Counselors, a private firm involved in pension consulting for Standard Oil of New Jersey and other large corporations; J. Douglas Brown, a young economist from the Industrial Relations Section at Princeton University; and Otto Richter, a pension actuary employed by American Telephone and Telegraph.

Armstrong and her colleagues in the old-age section of the CES did their important work—and wrote one of the most important bills in American history—under a variety of constraints and pressures. Although Roosevelt had given them a great task to do, his instructions—the June 8 address—were remarkably vague. Indeed, for a time even his commitment to old-age security legislation was in doubt. In her 1946 memoir, Secretary of Labor Frances Perkins presents the President as an early and firm advocate of a "cradle to the grave" system of social insurance. "There is no reason why just the industrial workers should get the benefit of this," Roosevelt told his cabinet. "Everybody ought to be in on it—the farmer and his wife and his family." But Roosevelt was giving the CES other, more negative signals. In fact, in a November 14 public statement, Roosevelt appeared to set aside a good portion of the CES agenda: "I do not know whether this is the time for any federal legislation on old age security." According to Douglas Brown, a deeply distressed CES staff now took "desperate measures." Armstrong used her contacts at the Scripps–Howard chain of newspapers to generate an editorial questioning Roosevelt's commitment to old-age legislation. Upset and exasperated, the President got on the phone to Perkins, who in turn sounded out Witte. As Brown tells the story, a "much excited" Witte rushed to the office that he and Armstrong shared. "He asked us if we knew how and why the speech had received such a bad press. From then on, the President seemed to take a greater interest in old age insurance."

Throughout the fall of 1934, the CES functioned under the shadow of the growing Townsend movement. As Perkins recalled, "The pressure from its [the Townsend Plan's] advocates was intense. The President began telling people he was in favor of adding old-age insurance clauses to the bill and putting it through as one package." Within weeks of his arrival in Washington, D.C., in late July, Witte had asked the Postmaster General to investigate the Townsend movement to determine if funds sent through the U.S. mails were being used for illegitimate purposes. (By late September he had his answer: the Townsend Plan was clean.) The heat was turned up a notch in November, when the election of a number of pro-Townsend representatives, including the eloquent and personable poet laureate of California, John S. McGroarty, made the introduction of a Townsend measure imminent. By December, when Townsend opened an office in the nation's capital to begin the lobbying process and sought a meeting with the President, Roosevelt refused to grant him an audience—an act described by the *Townsend Weekly* as "an insult that the masses of the people should resent."

At the Committee on Economic Security, an anxious Witte wrote a colleague of the growing danger:

> In the last three months I have become more concerned than ever with the Townsend Plan. There is no doubt that this movement has made tremendous headway. The battle against the Townsend movement has been lost, I think, in pretty nearly every state west of the Mississippi, and the entire Middle Western area is likewise badly infected. At this time the Republican party organization is at least flirting with the Townsendites. . . . The Townsend movement has become a terrific menace which is likely to engulf our entire economic system.

When the 74th Congress convened in January, the two sides were prepared for combat. The comprehensive administration package included a plan for unemployment insurance and two old-age measures. One of the old-age bills was a welfare measure, designed to provide joint state and federal relief for the elderly poor and for those who were too old to make sufficient contributions to an insurance plan. The other—in its essentials the future program of Social Security—provided for a national system of old-age insurance, to be funded by contributions from employers and employees. The Townsend bill, introduced by Rep. McGroarty, sought to do everything the administration measure did, but through the mechanism of the Old Age Revolving Pension Plan.

The issue was joined in the House Committee on Ways and Means, where the administration bill was the only one being formally considered, and where advocates of the administration measure—Democrats, all—were in control. Labor Secretary Perkins offered lengthy testimony. In language that sounded very much like Townsend's, she emphasized that "new and labor-saving machinery" and "new methods of work" on the one hand raised the standard of living "of the whole community" and, on the other hand, produced "transition periods" that were "extremely difficult for the individuals put out of work."

When asked about the Townsend Plan, however, Perkins was brutally critical. It was not "insurance," but a "dole," and an expensive dole at that. According to her estimates, payments under the plan would amount to "something considerably more than half of the total national income of the U.S.A." Perkins also challenged the claim that appropriations under the Townsend Plan would immediately and dramatically increase purchasing power and create a market for consumer goods. The plan, she concluded, was "in the realm of fancy rather than in the realm of practical statesmanship."

The next to testify was Murray Latimer. As head of the agency charged with administering the recently passed Railroad Retirement Act, Latimer could explain to the committee how that law had been openly designed to relieve crowded labor markets and increase efficiency by forcing the retirement of railroad workers over age 65. Latimer believed that the administration's proposal for old-age insurance could provide a similar service for the larger economy. If payments were large enough, they would induce considerable numbers of people to "withdraw from the labor market." "Nor," he added, "should the advantages of the maintenance of a large and continuing stream of purchasing power directed almost entirely to consumers' goods be overlooked."

Still another administration spokesperson, J. Douglas Brown, offered a rationale for the joint worker–employer contributions called for under the old-age insurance proposal. He emphasized that by contributing, workers would establish an "earned contractual right" to their annuities. And because employee contributions would result in larger payments in old age, they would "encourage the displacement of superannuated workers and of minor children and women supporting dependent old persons from the labor market."

Although the Committee on Ways and Means was not officially considering the McGroarty bill, it agreed to allow Townsend to testify; to have done otherwise would have been politically unwise. Townsend appeared on a Friday morning, February 1, 1935, as the Committee was concluding its second week of testimony. In a prepared statement, he set the stage for the presentation of his plan. "For the past five years," Townsend said,

> the people of the United States . . . have been starving in the midst of plenty. They have seen experiment after experiment tried out; experiments which bore the recommendation and hearty approval of men we call "economists." Experiment after experiment has failed. . . . The rich are growing richer and the poor are growing poorer.

Townsend called for a "new experiment," one that had not had "the blessing of the so-called 'economists.' " Describing his plan as "only incidentally a pension plan," he claimed it would solve the unemployment problem and, by restoring purchasing power to the people, bring back prosperity. "The old people," he added, "are simply to be used as a means by which prosperity will be restored to all of us."

As much as Townsend disliked economists, he knew the politicians would want evidence of how his plan would work economically. He told the committee that because he was "simply a country practitioner of medicine," he had arranged for Glen Hudson, an actuary, to appear before the committee. On the following Monday, Townsend and Hudson testified together.

Almost immediately, the committee's inquiries became pointed and aggressive. Representative Samuel Hill, a Washington state Democrat, questioned Townsend about who was eligible under his plan:

DR. TOWNSEND: We agree that the plan shall be nondiscriminatory and applied to all citizens equally.

MR. HILL: In other words, it would apply to John D. Rockefeller, Sr., to Henry Ford, to J. P. Morgan, as well as to a man who has no means of income at all?

DR. TOWNSEND: If they wish to acquire the pension under the provisions of the act.

When Hill inquired about the "revolving" concept claimed for the plan, Townsend appeared unsure and even confused. He could not clearly explain just how his plan "revolved," or how its revolving feature differed from any other dispersement of tax monies by the government. Townsend also had trouble fielding simple questions about the inner workings of the Townsend movement. Concerned about the size and strength of the Townsend organization, committee Chairman Robert Doughton (D-NC) asked Townsend to describe the plan's salaried sales force and explain the commission system used to compensate other employees.

DR. TOWNSEND: Mr. R. E. Clements is vice president and secretary, and he has all of that data.

THE CHAIRMAN: You ought to know. You are the head of the organization, and you should have such data before you.

Fortunately for Townsend, Hudson held forth through most of Monday afternoon, defending the plan with intelligence and enthusiasm. One congressman charged that the transaction tax would dramatically inflate the economy by adding 9 percent to consumer prices; another attacked the McGroarty bill for its failure to meet the needs of workers between ages 45 and 60, many of whom had trouble getting or holding jobs; and another claimed that at best, the Townsend Plan would retire only three million persons, far fewer than the 10 million retirements needed to eliminate unemployment altogether. Time and again, Hudson answered the critics by emphasizing that the plan depended for its success on the velocity of money. Because, he claimed, the average dollar turned over 34 times in 1 year, the economic stimulus provided by the Townsend pensions would be many times that of the money taken in through the transaction tax. Yet even Hudson was not thoroughly committed to every aspect of the McGroarty bill. Sensing Hudson's distance from the very measure he was there to support, Representative Jere Cooper, a Tennessee Democrat, asked a revealing question:

MR. COOPER: Suppose you sat in the seats that we occupy at this table. As the [Townsend] bill now stands in its present form, do you think you would be safe in voting to report it and support it, as a representative of the people?

MR. HUDSON: No; I do not.

Not long after the hearings concluded, an amended version of the administration bill passed the House on April 19 by a vote of 371 to 33. Most of the opposition came from Republicans. An earlier effort to substitute the McGroarty bill—the Townsend measure—received only about 50 votes. Nonetheless, the Senate Finance Committee seemed ready to reject compulsory old-age insurance—that is, until Witte told committee members in closed session that "the probable alternative was a modified Townsend plan." In mid-June, the Senate passed the bill, 77 to 6. When Roosevelt signed the measure on August 14, 1935, the Social Security Act became law.

Francis Townsend, addressing a newly organized club in Washington, D.C.,
March 6, 1937. The original caption for this photo noted that Townsend had
been recently found guilty of contempt of the House of Representatives yet was
"not the least apprehensive" that he might be sent to jail. (Library of Congress)

Even then, the Townsend movement would not go away. Indeed, it
gained strength as the provisions of the Social Security Act became known.
Over nine million Americans—domestic servants, government employees,
farm workers like Charles Lewis, and everyone over age 65—were not eligible for old-age insurance benefits—what Americans today refer to as "social
security." In contrast, even the very rich were entitled to benefits. Those who
qualified were to begin paying into the system immediately, but they would
not see their first check until 1942. Until then, those over age 65 could apply
to their respective states for old-age assistance payments that averaged $19.21
per month ($3.92 in Mississippi). Eleanor Roosevelt, who continued to speak
out against the Townsend Plan even when her husband would not, received
thousands of letters from irate Townsendites, many of them women. "Security
Bill is a joke so far as assisting the old people is concerned," wrote one woman.
Another described the "so-called 'social security' act" as "niggardly and inadequate."

In October 1935, less than three months after the passage of the Social
Security Act, some 7,000 inspired Townsendites assembled in Chicago for the
organization's first annual convention. They seemed ready to launch a movement rather than end it. A delegate from Texas took the floor to explain his
hope

to see erected in Washington, D.C., a statue with arms and legs made of strongest steel . . . adorned with a crown and priceless pearl . . . on his brow the word "Liberator," and under it all the name TOWNSEND. [applause, amens]

Although not a powerful speaker, Townsend rose to the occasion. To thunderous applause he described his movement as "an avalanche of political power that no derision, no ridicule, no conspiracy of silence can stem." Reaching for an analogy, he found one:

Where Christianity numbered in hundreds in its beginning years, our cause numbers in millions. And without sacrilege we can say that we believe that the effects of our movement will make as deep and mighty changes in civilization as Christianity itself.

Later, when some delegates asked for clarification during the reading of the financial report, the convention burst into song:

Onward Townsend soldiers
Marching as to war,
With the Townsend banner
Going on before.

Flushed with the triumphal meeting at Chicago, Townsend increasingly attacked the major parties. Looking ahead to the fall 1936 congressional elections, he predicted that politicians of both parties would have to renounce their Republican and Democratic affiliations and support the Townsend Plan in order to get elected. Against Clements's advice, he pressed for a third party. In doing so, he may have attracted some additional followers—among them, perhaps, Charles Lewis—but he had also threatened the existing distribution of political power. In mid-February 1936, the House of Representatives voted to initiate a bipartisan investigation of the Townsend movement. In late May, after three days of grueling testimony before a hostile committee, Townsend denounced the inquiry and walked out. A contempt citation was not issued until late in the year. In the meantime, Roosevelt had been elected to a second term in office with 27,751,612 votes; the Republican Landon, who had denounced the Social Security Act, received 16,681,913; running on the Union Party ticket and carrying the banner of the Townsend Plan, Lemke received only 891,858.

AN INTERPRETATION

The story of Francis Townsend and the Townsend movement is in part the story of how a significant and organized minority was kept on the margins of American political life. Roosevelt played a major role in this process of marginalization by refusing to meet with Townsend or to comment publicly on the Townsend Plan. At the Committee on Economic Security, Witte tried to use the U.S. Post Office to sabotage the movement. The Congress did its part, denying to the Townsend bill the primary status that was granted to the administration measure. The major parties, fearful that an attack launched by either the Republicans or the Democrats would injure the party taking the initiative, joined forces to investigate the Townsend movement, then, when Townsend walked away from what he rightly called an "inquisition," made sure that the 1936 elections were over before issuing a citation for contempt of Congress.

One could argue that this effort to purge Townsend and his movement from American political life was justifiable, in that Townsend was a demagogue— that is, he made irrational and irresponsible appeals to a mass audience incapable of separating truth from falsehood. As events at the 1935 national convention reveal, there is no doubt that he had a devoted and even fanatical following; that he was enamored of his own movement and perhaps, even, eventually attracted to his movement as a sort of modern-day Christianity. In addition, the movement utilized a variety of up-to-date promotional techniques that contributed to Townsend's personal success and to the movement's rapid growth. Charles Lewis, whose diary reveals an attraction to spectacle, might be interpreted as a typical Townsend victim. On the other hand, Townsend makes an unlikely demagogue: an old man, a boring speaker, incapable of controlling critical information. Hardly a man driven by the desire for adulation, Townsend emerged as a prominent political figure almost by accident. The most disturbing aspect of the Townsend movement's appeal was its reliance on religion, probably because this gave the cause a foundation exterior to traditional politics.

What makes Townsend's marginalization so remarkable is that many aspects of the man and his movement seem quite conservative. Although Townsend often couched his appeals in a familiar populist rhetoric of rich and poor, the Townsend Plan itself promised no significant distribution of income from one social class to another. As opponents pointed out, the sales tax, and the transaction tax that replaced it, were both harshly regressive. Furthermore, Townsend's desire to make his plan "nondiscriminatory" meant that even extremely rich people would be receiving checks for $200 per month that they did not need and probably would not spend. As Townsend's account of his life experiences reveals, the founder embraced and applied many aspects of capitalism, including speculation, promotion, entrepreneurship, and mechanical efficiency. His sharp criticism of the Civilian Conservation Corps confirms that Townsend did not wish to ameliorate suffering by creating agencies and bureaucracies; on the contrary, the thrust of the Townsend Plan was toward decentralization; it was a way of distributing money downward, in order to reinforce home and family. If anything, Townsend valued individual independence too highly. Overall, Townsend's conservatism explains his appeal to the rural middle class. But it may also account for the movement's failure—and it was a critical one—to attract significant support from industrial workers.

His radical-sounding rhetoric aside, perhaps Townsend was just another of those "economists" he regularly denounced. Indeed, Townsend's ideas about the economy and economic recovery resembled those of his New Deal adversaries. During the hearings before the House Committee on Ways and Means, Perkins expressed Townsend-like anxieties about the long-term impact of technology.

She and Latimer echoed the Townsend Plan's position on the importance of stimulating consumer spending; Latimer and Brown shared Townsend's enthusiasm for reducing unemployment by using old-age insurance to encourage the retirement of older workers from the labor force. While Perkins lambasted the Townsend Plan as a "dole," the Social Security Act was not strictly an insurance plan, as payments to the elderly were funded largely by the current contributions of those still working. The Townsend Plan probably was more than the nation could afford in 1935; its scope may even have been fanciful, as Perkins claimed. But its assumptions and mechanisms were in many respects part of the mainstream. In fact, Townsend's idea of turning the elderly into what historian Abraham Holtzman has called "distributor custodians" foreshadows the prominent role of consumerism in the post–World War II economy of affluence, and Townsend's emphasis on retirement anticipates the rising social security rates and private pension plans that would fuel the postwar retirement boom. Although the plan might well have damaged the economy had the McGroarty bill become law, Townsend's point—that the economy had been severely harmed while being managed by the same economic establishment that now attacked his plan as unworthy—was not unreasonable.

One could argue, in fact, that Townsend was anathema to politics not because his ideas were unfamiliar, but because he so blatantly articulated and presented the assumptions on which mainstream policy was based. When Roosevelt spoke about social insurance, he used the language of altruism, talking about a "cradle-to-the-grave" system of "security." Townsend, in contrast, spoke the language of the hard-nosed realists at the Committee on Economic Security. Although he was not without an altruistic side, he could also be very frank in explaining his goal of using the elderly to redistribute available work and to revive the economy.

By being so open, Townsend succeeded for a time in revealing the sources of the welfare state. One view of the origins of the welfare state, suggested by Roosevelt's rhetoric, locates the origins of measures like the Social Security Act in a benign response to the long-term insecurities produced by industrialization and urbanization. Even Townsend's life—a mobile life that began in the security of a large farm family and ended in the isolation of a city on the edge of the continent—supports this interpretation. Townsend's claim that the idea for the Townsend Plan came to him as he observed elderly women searching the garbage for food also sustains this view, although the fact that the story is not repeated in Townsend's autobiography suggests that the event may never have happened, and that Townsend concocted the incident only because he knew it coincided with what people expected to hear. Another interpretation of the emergence of the national welfare state emphasizes the growing power of organized labor. But as the story implies, organized labor did not play much of a role in the events leading to the passage of the Social Security Act.

The Townsend movement came under attack in part because it put in bold relief two other important explanations of the welfare state. Roosevelt's flacid leadership and lack of commitment to old-age insurance, as well as the Senate Finance Committee's rapid turnaround on the issue, are evidence that the

New Deal was moved to create a national welfare state partly by the ongoing challenge of a movement that lay beyond the regular party system. Once goaded into action by Townsend, Roosevelt, Perkins, Witte, and other New Deal liberals turned to the big business community—to Swope and Teagle, and to Latimer, Richter, and other experts who had advised the nation's largest corporations. Townsend's forthrightness in describing the operations of the welfare state stripped the welfare state of its ideological protections, revealing the prominent role played by big business in its evolution. In the process, Townsend became a marked man.

Sources: Francis E. Townsend's autobiographical *New Horizons* (Chicago: J.L. Stewart, 1943) remains an important source on the pension advocate's personal background. On the Townsend movement, see Richard L. Neuberger and Kelley Loe, *An Army of the Aged: A History and Analysis of the Townsend Old Age Pension Plan* (1936; New York: Da Capo Press, 1973); Abraham Holtzman, *The Townsend Movement: A Political Study* (New York: Bookman Associates, 1963); and David H. Bennetts, *Demagogues in the Depression: American Radicals and the Union Party, 1932–1936* (New Brunswick, NJ: Rutgers University Press, 1969); and the Twentieth Century Fund's indictment, *The Townsend Crusade* (New York: Twentieth Century Fund, 1936). Differing perspectives on the Social Security Act of 1935 can be found in W. Andrew Achenbaum, *Social Security* (Cambridge, MA: Cambridge University Press, 1986); Edwin E. Witte, *The Development of the Social Security Act* (Madison: University of Wisconsin Press, 1963); William Graebner, *A History of Retirement* (New Haven: Yale University Press, 1980); and Jill Quadagno, *The Transformation of Old Age Security: Class and Politics in the American Welfare State* (Chicago: University of Chicago Press, 1988). Frances Perkins's memoir, *The Roosevelt I Knew* (New York: Viking, 1946), is an important source, and there is much to be learned from congressional hearings on old-age measures (see U.S. Congress, House Committee on Ways and Means, *Economic Security Act: Hearings on H.R. 4120. . . . 1935* (Washington, DC: Government Printing Office, 1935).

11

HARLEM HELLFIGHTERS: THE 369TH IN WORLD WAR II HAWAII

Beth Bailey

David Farber

In the summer of 1942, members of the 369th Coast Artillery Regiment—skilled, proud, well-led, committed to its duty, and African American to a man—arrived in the territory of Hawaii, prepared to man the antiaircraft guns that would protect the islands from another Japanese attack. Expecting a mythic paradise of sand and sunshine, they found uniformed rednecks who wanted them off the sidewalks, brothels that refused their business, and a local population that was at once fearful, curious, and accepting. As Beth Bailey and David Farber explain, they also found in World War II Hawaii a set of conditions and circumstances that would change their lives: a mixture of peoples and colors that defied the rigid racial categories of the mainland; a national commitment to victory in war; a code of military rules and regulations to which everyone had to conform; and their own burgeoning self-confidence, rooted in the community of Harlem and nurtured in the palpable meritocracy of war.

If Hawaii seemed to open up possibilities for racial change, it was partly because conditions on the mainland were so unsatisfactory. On the eve of American entry into World War II, the United States was in most respects a segregated and racist society. Conditions were worst in the South, where at least six lynchings took place in the first 6 months of 1940, and where a great majority of African Americans could not or dared not vote. North and South, blacks and whites existed in separate worlds. Supported by decisions of state and federal courts, they went to separate schools, lived in separate neighborhoods, and went to the movies at separate theaters. As laughable as it now seems, in 1940 President Franklin D. Roosevelt helped celebrate a Chicago exposition that was described as "the first real Negro World's Fair in history." When Roosevelt's New Deal built some of the first public housing projects, they were intentionally segregated.

Conditions did not change overnight. Indeed, African Americans in many Southern states did not vote in significant numbers until the mid-1960s, and most schools remained segregated—in fact, if not by law—decades after the historic decision in Brown v. Board of Education *(1954). Even so, the war was responsible for a near revolution in American economic and social relations. Using the leverage of wartime, A. Philip Randolph and his all-black union, the Brotherhood of Sleeping Car Porters, forced the Roosevelt administration to commit itself to opposing racial discrimination in employment, initiating a process that would turn that commitment into the law of the land. Drawn from the Deep South to Northern cities by the demand for labor, hundreds of thousands of African Americans found industrial work at high wages, developed skills, and joined unions. The armed forces remained segregated, but military exigencies and black anger created a field of opportunity that made possible the 99th (Negro) Pursuit Squadron of Tuskegee, Alabama, and brought the 369th to Hawaii. Of more symbolic importance was a change in the tone of certain public gatherings, as Americans tried to live up to the democratic creed that sanctioned their participation in the war. Having been refused the right to sing in Constitution Hall in 1939 by the Daughters of the American Revolution, Marian Anderson performed there in 1943 before an integrated audience.*

Wartime changes in the racial status quo were inevitably accompanied by tension, conflict, and violence. In the South, the Ku Klux Klan added thousands of new members, and the number of lynchings and beatings of blacks rose alarmingly. Race riots or riots with racial overtones rocked Detroit; El Paso; Los Angeles; Springfield, Massachusetts—and Harlem. The 369th had missed the riot in their hometown, but the Harlem Hellfighters had surely lived some version of it—on the streets of Honolulu.

Every year on Veterans Day, dozens of African-American men gather at the Regimental Armory in Harlem. These men, who served with the 369th Coast Artillery (AA) Regiment during World War II, have been meeting every year since 1953, when one-time Chief Warrant Officer William De Fossett (by then a detective in the New York City Police Department) and some of his friends founded the 369th Veterans Association. The strong young men in the World War II Regimental photos are old now, retired from their jobs, ever fewer in number. But on Veteran's Day they meet, pass around family photos, plan community activities, laugh at each other's jokes, and remember the history of the 369th.

During these gatherings, the Armory echoes with the voices of young soldiers. There are uniformed Americans of all races and both sexes: the current members of the 369th. But during World War II, when these men served, the United States fought its battles for freedom and liberty with a segregated armed forces. Every member of the 369th Regiment—known as the "Harlem Hellfighters"—was black.

William De Fossett, president of the 369th Veterans Association for 26 years, joined the regiment when he was 16, almost 5 years before the Japanese bombed Pearl Harbor on December 7, 1941. He was supposed to be 18 to join, but he was big for his age and already playing as a fill-in for the professional Negro Baseball League during the summer. His parents had no objections, so Bill found a sponsor in the regiment and, along with several of his ball-playing buddies, became a private in the 369th Regiment of the New York National Guard.

For De Fossett, like many of the young men who lived in Harlem, becoming a member of the 369th was a rite of passage, a statement that he was somebody special in the neighborhood, a young man with a future. For in the years preceding World War II, the 369th was a symbol of black pride throughout the nation and a badge of honor for New York City.

The 369th's fame had been won during the waning days of World War I when the regiment, attached to the French Army, had fought in the Meuse-Argone offensive in the siege of Sechault. They fought under the French flag, as the United States government refused to have white and black Americans, even in segregated units, fighting alongside one another. The courage of the 369th had been exemplary under fire, and the French government awarded the Croix de Guerre to the 369th regimental colors and individually to more than 150 of the men. When they returned from "over there" at war's end, all of New York, white and black, had turned out to pay their respects as the regiment marched down Fifth Avenue.

The demonstrated courage of the 369th was highly publicized in the independent black press and in progressive northern magazines and newspapers, and stood in contrast to much being written and said about the performance of black troops in World War I. An article in *The Outlook* argued that the performance of the 369th Infantry, "characterized by some as 'possessing black skins, white souls and red blood,' ought to silence for all time the slanderous charge that Negroes are cowards and will not fight. . . ." In an era in which the President of the United States, Woodrow Wilson, could publicly celebrate a movie, *Birth of a Nation*, which depicted the Ku Klux Klan as heroic and the lynching of a black man as justice, the honors and accolades earned by the African-American men of the 369th stood in sharp contrast to the treatment usually accorded black Americans by white America.

William De Fossett was a natural for the highly selective and demanding 369th Regiment. At 16, he was best known in his Harlem neighborhood (just uptown from the Armory) for his athletic prowess. He could hit the long ball, and people had begun to call him "Babe," as in the great Babe Ruth. While still in his teens, he would play for the New York Black Yankees, the Pittsburgh Crawfords, the Baltimore Elite Giants, and with Alex Pompez's Cuban Stars. But De Fossett was more than just a standout ballplayer.

Bill De Fossett's parents had raised him and his older brother, Joe, to be hard-working, responsible, and studious. His mother was a college graduate, and though her skin color barred her from a job commensurate with her education (like most black working women in the North, she worked as a domestic for a white family), she emphasized the importance of education. William's father, too, set his boys an example. At night, home from his job at the Southern Pacific Steamship Company, he'd take out the *New York Times* crossword puzzle, begin inking in the answers, and ask his sons what new word they had learned that day. "Not a day should go by," their father told William and Joe more than once, "without learning a new word."

William and Joe De Fossett of the 369th Coast Artillery. Over a million service-men and war workers came to Hawaii during the conflict. (Courtesy William K. De Fossett)

De Fossett also had the advantage of growing up in one of the must cultur-ally rich neighborhoods of Harlem. His immediate neighbors in Harlem's Paul Dunbar Apartments included the singer and actor Paul Robeson, the dancer Bill "Bojangles" Robinson, the intellectual and civil rights activist W. E. B. DuBois, the labor leader and civil rights organizer A. Philip Randolph, and the explorer Mat Henson. As a kid, De Fossett and his friends played in Henson's apartment, trying on the Eskimo garb Henson had worn when he—and not Commander Perry, Henson told them—had become the first American to reach the North Pole. Paul Robeson, who was just "the singer on the third floor" to young Bill, taught him how to throw a football. Though Harlem had been disproportionally hard hit by the Great Depression of the 1930s, with black unemployment in New York City approaching 50 percent during the worst times, De Fossett came of age in one of the most vibrant communities in the nation.

As a child and then young man, William De Fossett was well aware of the illustrious history of the 369th, but at 16 his main reasons for joining were more in keeping with his age. On weekends the men of the 369th, in sharp uniforms, drilled outside the armory. They were often accompanied by what was gener-ally acknowledged as the best regimental band in the United States, and the neighborhood turned out to watch. Every summer the 369th spent two weeks in the mountains, training—or as De Fossett and his friends saw it, "playing soldier." They loved the idea that the state of New York would pay them for this "duty."

But in January 1941, in an early phase of the war buildup, the 369th was federalized. Hardly any of the men knew it, but the question of what duty to assign this black regiment in the segregated U.S. armed forces was an extremely controversial and much debated question in the higher circles of Washington, D.C.

The issue of what to do with black troops emerged directly from World War I and the heightened antiblack racism of the early twentieth century. Despite the superb records of the 369th and some other black troops during World War I, they were overshadowed by powerful criticisms. These criticisms had some basis in reality. In general, black troops had not performed especially well. They had been insufficiently trained and often badly led by unsympathetic or hostile white officers (one Southern white officer thought it appropriate to introduce himself to his men with the information that he had "suckled black mammies' breasts"). They lacked basic equipment, and morale suffered from discriminatory policies (unlike the white troops, for example, they were prohibited from most contact with French civilians). Due to widespread school discrimination in both the North and the South, a higher percentage of black soldiers than white were uneducated or illiterate. The explanations for failures abound; in that light the successes are more remarkable.

Many white army officers were, however, perfectly willing to attribute the failures to racial inferiority: Negroes would never make good combat soldiers, they argued, for blacks lacked both the necessary intelligence and the discipline. Major General Robert Bullard, the World War I commander of the Second Army (in which blacks had served as the 92nd Division), wrote in his memoirs, which he published in 1925: "Poor Negroes! They are hopelessly inferior." There was, however, an even more challenging message for those who sought equality. Drawing on diary entries from the war, Bullard mused: "If you need combat soldiers, especially if you need them in a hurry, don't put your time upon Negroes. . . . If racial uplift or racial equality is your purpose, that is another matter."

Going into World War II, the Army's policy toward the employment of black troops was predicated on the "lessons" learned in World War I. The goal of the Army, or of any other branch of the armed forces, was not racial uplift— it was mounting a successful fighting force as quickly and efficiently as possible. And coming into World War II, using black troops clearly presented problems. Racial tensions tended to flare when blacks and whites were in close proximity. Moreover, Army intelligence, G-2, argued against sending black troops just about anywhere beyond the U.S. mainland, for fear that the presence of blacks might create or exacerbate local racial tensions. The United States was not the only Allied nation with a race problem. Throughout the colonized world of America's allies, black troops might create political trouble.

Perhaps most important, the Army found blacks ill-prepared for military life. Black men, in aggregate, scored very badly on the Army General Classification

Test (AGCT) and the Mechanical Aptitude Test, which were devised to use in assigning men to units; the AGCT was intended to measure the level of skill and ability the inductee already possessed and to evaluate "how ready [he is] to pick up soldiering—how likely [he is] to learn easily the facts, skills and techniques necessary for carrying out Army duties." Scores were closely related to educational and cultural background, so it is perhaps not surprising that 49.2 percent of black inductees fell into the lowest quintile of the AGCT (compared to 8.5 percent of whites), and that 83.9 percent of blacks scored in the bottom two quintiles. (Test scores were meant to form a bell curve, and they did for white troops.) The vast majority of blacks inducted into the Army were unskilled, many illiterate. Officers found that it generally took two times as long to train a "black unit" as a "white unit."

Proponents of black combat forces during the World War II mobilization had a hard argument to make. Given the potential for disruptive racial tensions, even violence, given the poor promise indicated by AGCT scores—what evidence could they offer? Here, the 369th's actions in World War I were compelling evidence against charges that blacks were *constitutionally*, inherently, racially, poor soldiers.

One of the most outspoken champions of black soldiers during the World War II mobilization was Hamilton Fish, Jr., the fiercely anti–New Deal conservative white Republican congressman from New York, who had been a company commander with the 369th during the Great War. Fish had stood shoulder to shoulder with his black troops while under enemy fire and shell; he had seen his men bleed and die. In honor of their courage and as sign of his own, he tenaciously lobbied the indifferent and even hostile Secretary of War, Henry Stimson, to give black Americans a fair chance and an honorable role in the armed forces.

Other powerful voices, too, spoke up on behalf of blacks in the armed forces. Eleanor Roosevelt, Walter White of the National Association for the Advancement of Colored People (NAACP), A. Philip Randolph (leader of the Brotherhood of Sleeping Car Porters and William De Fossett's neighbor), the editors of black-run newspapers such as the *Pittsburgh Courier*, and many others argued that the United States must not go to war against the Axis powers blighted by the shame of officially mandated racism and discrimination.

As a sign of his concern, and in recognition of the pressures mounted by and on behalf of black Americans, Franklin Roosevelt did appoint a black civil rights activist as a special civilian aide to the Secretary of War. But Roosevelt knew this appointment was more sop than solution. Because racism was so ingrained in American life, President Roosevelt decided that the free and democratic country he led, notwithstanding its claims to equality and world leadership, would fight its enemies with segregated armed forces. And it would not be a "separate but equal" military force but one in which African Americans would be overwhelmingly restricted to a lowly caste of mess boys, stevedores, and common laborers.

The Secretary of War's office clearly stated the rationale for such segregation: "The War Department administers the laws affecting the military establishment; it cannot act outside the law, nor contrary to the will of the majority of the citizens of the Nation." Secretary of War Stimson and President Roosevelt were in accord with political reality; in overwhelming numbers, white Americans opposed integrating the armed forces. A wartime survey of five major American cities, north and south, showed that nine out of 10 white Americans supported a segregated army. Not surprisingly, most black Americans felt differently; the same survey showed that eight out of 10 African Americans opposed segregation in the armed forces.

In Harlem, the decision to continue government-sponsored segregation of the armed forces added fuel to the fire for those who opposed black participation in the American war effort. The black playwright Loften Mitchell reported: "Irritated black people argued that when colored Ethiopia was attacked [by fascist Italy], Uncle Sam hadn't raced to her defense, but when white Europe was in trouble Uncle was right there. . . . Others declared openly they were not going to fight for colonial England, colonial France, and Jim Crow America." But those openly opposed to black participation in the war were a tiny minority. Many more Harlemites subscribed to the position advocated by the editors of the *Pittsburgh Courier*, the largest circulation black-oriented newspaper in the country during the World War II era.

The *Courier* called for a "Double V" campaign: "Victory over our enemies at home and victory over our enemies on the battlefields abroad." The editor and publisher of the paper, Robert Vann, wrote: "We call upon the President and Congress to declare war on Japan and against racial prejudice in our country. Certainly we should be strong enough to whip both." Even though President Roosevelt made it clear that only one of those wars would be fought, most African Americans in Harlem and throughout the United States chose to support the national effort and to do what they could in ways small and large, private and public, to win that second "V" against racial prejudice.

William De Fossett, early in 1941 when the 369th was federalized, like most of the young men of the regiment, thought little about the larger political questions raging around Army racial policies that would so affect his life. Twenty-year-old De Fossett was much more concerned with practical and immediate questions: Where was the unit going? How long would it be gone? Would the United States get involved in the war spreading across the globe?

At first all De Fossett and the troops were told was that they had been called up to serve a one-year tour of duty and that they were to be trained for antiaircraft artillery (AA) duty. Some of the men, including those in the regiment's all-black officer corps, understood that the call-up of the 369th meant that the United States was beginning to seriously mobilize for the war that had already been raging in Europe for three years and in Asia for more than ten. Federalizing National Guard units like the 369th represented a major step in preparing the undermanned, poorly equipped and trained American Army for the looming war.

A few of the more politically sophisticated men recognized that the training for which the 369th was slotted represented a complex compromise between opponents and proponents of African Americans in the armed forces. The highly visible and well-championed 369th, along with the four other black regiments that had been assigned to antiaircraft artillery training, had done far better than most of the segregated African-American units. In the segregated American military, black troops were given low-status duties, regardless of the specific abilities or experiences of the men. In the Army, they served most often as cargo loaders, truck drivers, and common laborers. In the Navy it was worse: at best, black men could become messmen or bandsmen.

Antiaircraft duty, in contrast, was genuinely high-status and required arduous and demanding training. Army command was showing good faith in the "Negro" units selected. But as William Hastie, the special civilian aide in the War Department, wrote in protest to his boss, Secretary of War Stimson, AA units were "in a special category" of combat units:

> Such a unit could be given a separate and more or less permanent defensive station in the theater of operations. It need not be integrated with other combat forces. So the utilization of Negro antiaircraft units in the theater of operations was adopted as a device best calculated to confound the critics of any policy as to Negro combat troops without basically changing that policy.

As Hastie protested to no avail, Army command had cunningly slotted the 369th for the kind of combat training that would satisfy all but its most zealous champions, but which would minimize its integration into combat operations with white soldiers.

The War Department's racial motivations in assigning the 369th to AA duty were not publicized or publicly debated, and were not considered by most men in the 369th. In general, while most of the men had mixed feelings about being called up for active duty in early 1941, they were pleased about their duty assignment and particularly pleased when they found out where their training was to take place. The 369th were being sent to Camp Ontario in upstate New York. They would not have to endure the racist hell of a training camp in the Jim Crow South.

Racism was common throughout the United States, and none of the black men in the 369th escaped its reach. De Fossett, remember, was playing in the Negro Baseball League; blacks were not accepted in the National or American leagues until 1947, when Jackie Robinson broke the color barrier. The armed forces in which they served was segregated—by federal mandate. But conditions were much worse for blacks in the rural South, and Northern blacks sent to the South for military training confronted a more aggressive and demeaning racism than was commonly practiced in Northern cities.

When a reporter for one of the black newspapers visited the 369th at their training camp in Oswego, New York, he told stories about the camp at Fort Bragg, North Carolina, that shocked the young men from Harlem. The day they were sent south, some of them told the reporter, they would go "prepared for any and all emergencies." In fact, a few months later cadres from the 369th were sent to Camp Stewart in Georgia for special duty. After constant racist provocations and command indifference to their protests of on-base discrimination, they loaded their rifles and proceeded to level the Jim Crow facilities. The "Harlem Hellfighters," as one of the men later told William De Fossett, "do not go by this stuff."

369th Coast Artillery, 1943. (George Strock/Timepix)

Over the next year in Oswego the men worked hard. The snow was so deep at Camp Ontario that first winter that they had to form human snowplows, pushing through the waist-high snow eight men abreast. But they became expert in handling the antiaircraft weaponry they had been assigned, and Lieutenant Woodruff was able to tell the white press: "They're dead eyes . . . and I don't mean with the galloping dominoes." In less than a year's time the 369th, under black officers' command (with two white artillery officers serving as advisors in weapons training), had been transformed from young men playing soldier on the weekends to professional, highly trained soldiers.

Outside Harlem, in an area one of the men called "lily white," race became a more immediate issue for the men. They were dependent upon the town of Oswego for all their nonmilitary needs, and some of Oswego's white citizens were concerned about the presence of so many black men. But relations between the military and civilian populations were smooth overall until, in that first winter, a white woman brought charges of rape against one of the 369th.

The whole unit was lined up; each man was inspected for "evidence." The men believed the charges unfounded—the desperate act of a white woman

369th in training, Oswego, New York, 1943. (George Strock/Timepix)

caught breaking the taboo against interracial sex. But in any case, they believed their rights had been violated in the blanket lineup. These men read the *Amsterdam News* and knew about the treatment of other black troops. They were highly conscious that they were a special combat unit, and they meant to be treated with respect.

Angry and outraged at what they saw as racial politics, the 369th staged a boycott of Oswego. Many of the men remembered the "don't shop where you can't work" campaigns that Reverend Adam Clayton Powell had led in Harlem in the mid-thirties, and resolved to try similar tactics. The officers supported the men, and provided vehicles so they could take their business to other towns. Eventually Governor Lehman, partly in response to concerns of the Oswego business community, mediated the conflict. The charges were dropped. The 369th had won.

The remainder of the time at Camp Ontario was spent without incident, and the men were looking forward to completing their year's training and returning home in January 1942. But on December 7, 1941, their plans were changed.

Their first wartime assignment was to guard Cape Cod from air attack. A few months later, they were sent to defend the southern California coast, near the big Lockheed defense plant. Here, American race relations took another odd turn.

The military command worked out the coordinates and issued the orders, and the 369th did as they were told. But someone in the command hierarchy must have realized that they were sending the 369th into the backyards—literally—of some of the wealthiest white people in America, including a few major Hollywood stars. Each landscaped lawn hosted 12 men and their anti-aircraft guns.

Bill De Fossett, by then a regimental sergeant major, heard some complaints: "We've never had Negroes living here and now they're in our backyards with those horrible guns." But most of the residents welcomed their defenders. Humphrey Bogart told the men on his lawn they were welcome to use his house, and gave them keys to show he meant it. And black celebrities like Lena Horne, Hattie McDaniel, Eddie "Rochester" Anderson, and Leigh Whipper came out to visit the troops.

The southern California assignment lasted only a few weeks. The 369th had trained in Oswego for cold-weather duty. They had been issued cold-weather gear, including snow boots and heavy woolen union suits. So, as Army logic would have it, after a few weeks in sunny southern California, the men boarded a troop ship and set out for . . . Hawaii.

None of the men in the 369th had been to Hawaii. Back in the days before affordable air travel, Hawaii was the vacation spot of the rich. The only other men from the mainland likely to have spent time there were regular army—"the pineapple army," they called themselves. But like most Americans with any access to popular culture, these men had images of Hawaii. Some had heard the popular radio program, "Hawaii Calls," with live music broadcast from the terrace of the Royal Hawaiian hotel. Others had seen some of the movies that played up exotic Hawaiian locales—so many were produced in the 1930s that a *New York Times* film review referred sarcastically to "the well-known Hollywood suburb of Wacky-ki." The hula had even enjoyed a brief popularity in Harlem clubs and cabarets in the late 1920s.

But the soldiers who traveled to Hawaii from the mainland during World War II had quite a different experience from the wealthy tourists who made the 4-day trip on the Matson cruise ships. Troop ships were crowded. The men slept on canvas bunks that were laced to steel frames and stacked five high. The tables in the mess hall were at waist level; men stood to eat their two meals a day. Many of the men, of course, did not eat. They were much too seasick. Because it took two to three minutes for a submarine to sight and fire a torpedo with any degree of accuracy, the ships changed course every two or three minutes. They zigzagged all the way from San Diego to Honolulu, exacerbating whatever seasickness was normal for men who had never been on the open sea before.

The 369th came to Hawaii with a strong sense of purpose and good morale. They were well prepared for their assignment to defend the islands from air attack.

Ironically, however, as the troops of the 369th were transported on the small sugar-cane railroad from the harbor to their initial base camp, people reacted to them as if *they* were the invading force. Grown men and women ran away, frightened of the trainload of black men.

It did not take long to find out what had happened. Hawaii had almost no black residents before the war, and white Southerners—soldiers, sailors, and war workers—had spread rumors among the local people. They said blacks were dangerous, not fully human. They said blacks were animal-like. Some said that black men had tails, and if a local woman and a black man had a baby, the baby would have a tail like a monkey.

By the time the men of the 369th arrived in Hawaii in the summer of 1942, the tail story had gained great credibility. One story, perhaps apocryphal but widely circulated among the black men on Oahu, shows the power of the rumor. A small group of men were invited to a social gathering with a group of local people. It was very pleasant, but some of the men thought it odd that they were consistently steered to chairs with pillows on them. When one of the men began to sit down on a chair without a pillow, the host ran over and flung a pillow under the soldier's descending posterior. The punch line, of course, was that the hosts believed black men had tails. The chairs were hard. They were trying to be nice.

All over the island, in those first few weeks, men of the 369th explained that the tail business was a racist lie. How could it be true, they asked, that black men made monkey babies? But too often their explanations left a residue of uncertainty, and the men "dropped drawers" all over the island to prove, as Bill De Fossett (drawing on his father's passion for vocabulary) put it, that they "were an anurous biological species."

The Hawaii to which the 369th came was a complicated place. The terror of the Japanese attack hung over the islands for a long time, and Hawaii felt the presence of war more than any other part of the United States. The territory was under martial law until late 1944. Every night there was a total blackout; absolutely no light could show anywhere on the islands. The newspapers were censored and so was civilian correspondence. The beaches were strung with barbed wire. There were curfews and shortages, and at first gas masks were carried everywhere, even to weddings.

Over a million men came to Hawaii with the war. These were men from all walks of life, from all regions of the states. In most ways, though all Americans, they saw themselves as quite different from one another: the Italian kid from Brooklyn, the farm boy from Iowa, the one from Mississippi who called them both Yankees, the soldier with the "Harlem Hellfighters," and the sharecropper's son. Men from very different cultures were jammed together with little regard for the differences that loomed so large to them. There were tensions. And the tensions were made more complicated because of the nature of the society to which they came.

Unlike most of the places these men came from, Hawaii was not racially or culturally homogenous, nor was it organized as a bipolar racial society. A minority of wealthy whites exerted much disproportionate economic and political power in the islands, but the majority of the population were drawn from Asia and the Pacific. Fully a third of the islands' population were of Japanese descent. What that meant, for the men who came to Hawaii from the mainland (white or black), was that their notions of racial normality were upset. One could not be in wartime Hawaii and not confront the issue of race.

Some whites were angry and appalled; others saw possibilities for a new, better society. Some blacks wrote home of living "in a part of the world where one can be respected and live as a free man should"; others wrote of the suspicion evidenced by local people, especially the women, and of the rising racial tensions in overcrowded Honolulu. But because of the juxtaposition of so many different sorts of men from the mainland, in a context of unfamiliar racial composition and relations, the issue of race was explosive.

The men of the 369th had excellent relations with local residents. Bill De Fossett and his brother Joe hooked up with a semipro baseball team that played in the small town of Aiea. The manager was Hawaiian, the owner haole (the Hawaiian word used for whites), the coach of Japanese-American descent, and the players all of the above plus the De Fossett brothers. This integrated ball club was, to De Fossett, a symbol of hope for better days to come.

But on the streets of Honolulu, with other men in uniform, the old racial struggles persisted. The American armed forces understood, quite clearly, that racist practices were incompatible with military procedures, and that is one reason that African-American troops were either kept separate from white troops or confined completely to the lowest ranks of the service. Once black men became officers in an integrated armed forces, they would have command over white men. Military hierarchy would—must—take precedence over racial hierarchy. That inversion, most believed, would cause problems. And it did. On the overcrowded streets of Honolulu, most especially in the charged atmosphere of the vice district, known throughout the Pacific theater simply as "Hotel Street," white and black men clashed over issues of race.

From their first days of liberty in Honolulu, the men of the 369th faced racial harassment from white men in uniform, mostly Southerners. The setting was usually the densely packed streets of the Hotel Street district, where thousands of men in uniform, many of them drunk, wandered past the lines for bars and brothels, avoiding the street hustlers and shoeshine boys and sidewalk concessionaires. The black men would see, from a distance, a group of white soldiers or sailors coming down the street toward them. And then, right in their faces, there would be the words, the same words every time. "Nigger, get off the street!" And when the black men did not move, again: "Nigger, don't you know you're supposed to get off the street!" In the first few months in Hawaii, the men from Harlem faced this set piece again and again—Southern street protocol played out in the middle of the Pacific Ocean. But there were some very important differences.

The first difference was the 369th. These men claimed equality and respect, and meant to see that they got it. De Fossett saw it happen over and over. The white soldier or sailor would say those words: "Nigger, get off the street," and the black soldier would punch him. Hard. "We were raised in New York," De Fossett says. "We were not strangers to street fighting."

While the armed forces remained segregated in Hawaii, the semiprofessional Aiea baseball team had a Hawaiian manager, a Japanese-American coach, and players from across the racial spectrum, including the De Fossett brothers of the 369th. (Courtesy William K. De Fossett)

At least two white servicemen died in these confrontations. One struck his head as he dropped from the punch; another collapsed during a fist fight from an aneurism or other natural cause. Here, though, was the second difference between the Deep South and wartime Hawaii. In the Deep South in the 1940s, a black man who killed a white man over issues of racial protocol would be lucky to see the inside of a jail cell. But in these cases, both Preston Daniels and Wentworth Morris, the black servicemen involved, were cleared of all charges. The decisions sent a message as powerful as the individual street fights. A black man's right to self-defense was formally endorsed by the standards of military justice. The 369th made sure the word got around.

Street incidents were never completely banished, but the 369th had made a point. And the military police supported the men, acknowledging that they "did not seek trouble but . . . never backed up from trouble." Some of the other black troops on the island, members of the quartermaster's corps, for example, tried to borrow some of the 369th's respect. On pass, they'd replace their blue-trimmed caps with the red-trimmed caps worn by the 369th AA Regiment.

The Southern servicemen in Hawaii who had tried to enforce their racial hierarchy had lost. They could try to save face by ignoring the black men in uniform. But there was a problem with that tactic. Rank had to be observed. In the United States Army, enlisted men saluted officers; lower-ranking officers saluted their superiors. It wasn't simply custom; it was required.

Many of the white servicemen did not intend for their version of racial hierarchy to be overruled by the hierarchy of rank. As one young white private in a southern training camp told a black lieutenant: "If you would take your clothes off and lay them on the ground I would salute them but I won't salute anything that looks like you."

The solution adopted in Hawaii was equally novel, if a bit more practicable. No one knew whether it was a plan, or just a spontaneous act that inspired a group of white junior-grade officers, but the scene was repeated many times.

A lower-ranking white officer saw a black officer of superior rank. He began running—not away from the black officer, but toward him. He'd run right up to the man and begin shaking the officer's hand, "Hello, hello, how are you," as if the men were old acquaintances, even friends. Then he'd walk smartly away.

The white men were mocking the system. Perhaps they assumed that the black men would be pleased by the friendliness and would forget the breach of regulation. The white men were willing to feign intimacy, even to make physical contact, rather than to salute black men as their superiors. The tactic was so bizarre that it did, briefly, work.

It worked until a junior-grade lieutenant tried the routine on Major Edward I. Marshall, the Battalion Adjutant of the 369th. Major Marshall was a stern, commanding, even intimidating presence. He was not amused. He certainly was not flattered.

Military style, in full fury, he called upon the authority of rank and the force of the U.S. Army: "Do not shake my hand. I don't like you and you don't like me. But I am a Major!!! You are a lieutenant!!! Salute me!!!" The lieutenant complied in silence, and scuttled off, shaken. Regimental Sergeant Major De Fossett watched the whole thing with barely suppressed laughter. There were no more such incidents.

Major Marshall had commanded respect and he got it. Military protocol had been enforced by a black man answering to his own confident sense of twinned duty. But in Hawaii, Marshall and the men of the 369th were not operating in isolation. In these confrontations, the men of the 369th drew on their upbringing in Harlem and on their identity as elite combat troops. They had sources of strength that many other black troops in Hawaii and elsewhere lacked. But without the willingness of the military to enforce its own rules (a willingness markedly absent in many training camps and bases, especially in the South), these struggles might have turned out very differently.

To this end, their location in Hawaii was very important. In Hawaii race was defined and managed differently than anywhere on the mainland. Local customs were different, and somewhat more flexible. And—crucially—Hawaii was America's border of war.

The military governor of Hawaii, Lt. General Emmons, was an ally in their struggles. Emmons believed that racism was, in Hawaii, an inefficient system for maintaining the order he saw as critical to the war effort. Significantly, civilian government officials and the local elite raised no objections to Emmon's antiracist efforts.

On November 6, 1942, a few months after the 369th arrived in Hawaii, Emmons issued a confidential memo to each commanding general and to all commanding officers of every post, camp, station, depot, district, and service command in the Hawaiian Islands. Emmons was angry over the increasing number of "instances of interracial conflict in the city of Honolulu." He wanted the incidents stopped, and he laid the blame squarely on white shoulders.

"The fact that such incidents have occurred indicates a lack of proper training, instruction, and discipline on the part of the personnel involved, and of the officers under whom they are serving," Emmons wrote. He ordered all commissioned officers to "adopt every possible means to eliminate the causes for any racial discord" and, by example, to "inculcate a spirit of harmony and unity" among the men under their command. "It is of the utmost importance that our ranks present a united front in the present emergency and that racial prejudice, jealousies, and discord be not permitted to create or foster internal friction. The reasons for the total elimination of such friction are so apparent and so compelling that they require no reiteration."

Emmons's "compelling" reasons were not principles of equality or visions of social reform. They were the practical matter of winning the war. America's Pacific war was not going well; Hawaii was key to the Pacific campaign. There was no room for racial strife that, in any way, compromised the war effort.

In 1944 the 369th Coast Artillery Regiment was ordered to join the forces invading Okinawa, and these men, like so many who'd passed through Hawaii during the war, moved forward to war. The struggles over race would continue in Hawaii, for they were not the only black men in the islands, and the black-white dimension of racial struggle was only one in a complex panoply of racial difference. But the presence of the 369th on Oahu set an example of resolve and courage, and the men of the regiment took away lessons that would serve them well for the rest of their lives.

William De Fossett had, by the time the 369th departed for Okinawa, been reassigned to Task Force 58, an interservice unit that would fight in Saipan. He was battalion supply officer in an all-black unit. Here, De Fossett would confront the kind of direct and degrading racism that he had so far avoided in the armed forces.

Almost all the other men in his unit were Southerners, and this, unlike the 369th, was not a highly trained combat unit. De Fossett found the differences disturbing. The other men in the unit observed the protocol of racial hierarchy that he and his comrades had battled on the streets of Honolulu. When a white officer came into their area, the men would take off their hats. De Fossett argued with them. Salute an officer, he said, but your hat stays on. The other men said that was just how they'd been raised, and the white men expected it. De Fossett said he didn't care; they had to stop. The men did not like the order.

De Fossett was upset by their submissiveness. But he also understood the practical implications. If the other men took off their hats to whites and he did not, there was going to be trouble. De Fossett, however, did not intend to play that game.

Some of the men complained to a white officer about De Fossett's order. The battalion colonel called on De Fossett and, in a strong Southern accent, asked him what was going on. De Fossett replied: "Sir, I am following Army regulations." The colonel called him an "uppity nigger"—but he did not tell De Fossett to rescind his order. Henceforth, De Fossett's men kept their hats on. It was a small victory, but a sweet one.

After the war ended, some of the black men who had been stationed in Hawaii chose to stay. At least two men from the 369th demobilized there and married local women. While in 1940 the census of Hawaii recorded only 255 Negro residents, in 1950 there were 2,651 black men and women living in the islands.

De Fossett, however, chose to return to his native New York. Back in Harlem, he, like so many other returning servicemen, used the bonus points all veterans received on civil service exams to secure a good government job. Within a couple of years he was working for the New York City Police Department, and in 1963 he became the first black State Department Security Officer in the United States. William De Fossett raised his family in Harlem, and worked hard for the good of his community and its youth. He and the other men who returned from war became part of the force that transformed American race relations in the postwar era.

Like many of his comrades-in-arms from the 369th, William De Fossett saw the seeds of social change in his wartime experience. He was proud to have been part of the 369th, proud of his regiment and its war record. He was proud of how the men stood up to racism, and believed it significant that, if not always, at least *sometimes* the U.S. government had backed them up. But of all his memories of the war, and of Hawaii, he treasures the memory of playing ball in Aiea, he and his brother Joe, and their Japanese-American, Hawaiian, and white teammates. It still seems to him a hopeful vision.

AN INTERPRETATION

By the mid-1950s, African Americans and their white allies, openly and in large numbers, had begun to fight the racist system of injustice and inequality that had governed American race relations throughout the twentieth century. In the 1950s and 1960s, the civil rights movement, led by people like Martin Luther King, Jr., Thurgood Marshall, Ella Baker, Diane Nash, Medgar Evers, Stokely Carmichael, John Lewis, and Robert Moses, would defeat *legal* racial segregation and discrimination. The successes of the civil rights movement depended on the heroic efforts of hundreds of thousands of grassroots protesters and demonstrators. But large-scale changes begun earlier in the twentieth century set the stage for the civil rights movement of the 1950s and 1960s, and were critically important in making it possible.

One of the most significant changes affecting race relations was the growing power and authority of the federal government. In both the Great Depression of the 1930s and World War II, the federal government dramatically increased its role in the lives of the American people. New Deal policies implemented during the Roosevelt presidency created a national system of social provision and economic regulation. And while African Americans were greatly frustrated by the New Dealers' failure to confront racism and racial inequality, increasingly, many Americans looked to the federal government to tackle the nation's most vexing problems.

During World War II, the federal government (partly in the guise of the War Department) greatly expanded its power. In practice, this meant that the federal government exercised control over all matters deemed pertinent to winning the war, reaching into individual lives and into local communities in an unprecedented manner. The possibility for uniform national policy was greater than before.

But government agents, military or civilian, did not enforce laws and policies in a completely standard fashion. On particular issues, they often bowed to the weight of local or regional custom and tradition. Race was one of those issues. During World War II the policies affecting black Americans were shaped by competing, overlapping, and uncertain lines of political power and social authority. As a result, America fought World War II with a segregated and racially discriminatory armed forces.

Still, as the men of the 369th learned, the federal government had an agenda quite different than, say, the state of Mississippi. Sometimes, if pushed hard enough, the federal government would support limited racial progress. If African-American soldiers took the rights and freedoms that rank, regulation, and law seemed to guarantee, federal authorities might well support them. And the support of the federal government, because of its power and authority, meant victory over local racist practices.

While the story of the 369th during World War II is a complicated one, it pointedly reveals the changing nature of racial struggle in the United States. The 369th received combat unit designation because the federal government, in wartime, needed to show its African-American citizens that the United States was not an unremittingly racist nation. The men of the 369th received justice in New York, California, Hawaii, and overseas because the federal government— specifically, the War Department—had a set of rules and regulations that put military needs and protocol ahead of traditional racist practices. Though it was not easy, during World War II African Americans were learning to use the federal government to challenge and change racist policies and practices.

In the immediate postwar years, under pressure from African Americans and because of Cold War politics that made legal racism an international embarrassment, President Harry Truman would desegregate the armed forces. And by 1954, the Supreme Court would side with the legal arguments of the NAACP in *Brown v. Board of Education* and declare that state laws mandating racially "separate but equal" schools were inherently discriminatory and unconstitutional. While national politicians and federal officials would rarely take the initiative in confronting racial discrimination, African-American activists, building on World War II experiences such as those of the 369th Regiment, learned that if pushed hard enough the federal government could be made an ally in the fight for racial justice and equality for all Americans.

Sources: This story is adapted from Beth Bailey and David Farber, "The 'Double-V' Campaign in World War II Hawaii: African Americans, Racial Ideology, and Federal Power," *Journal of Social History* 26:4, 817–843. Interviews with members of the 369th were an important source for this account. For more on Hawaii during World War II, see Beth Bailey and David Farber, *The First Strange Place: Race and Sex in World War II Hawaii* (Baltimore: Johns Hopkins University Press, 1994). The most comprehensive book on African-American soldiers during World War II is Ulysses Lee, *The Employment of Negro Troops*, Vol. 8, *The United States Army in World War II* (Washington, DC: Government Printing Office, 1966). Other excellent sources on African-Americans and World War II include Merl Reed, *Seedtime for the Modern Civil Rights Movement* (Baton Rouge: Louisiana State University Press, 1991); Graham Smith, *When Jim Crow Met John Bull* (New York: St. Martin's Press, 1987); Jervis Anderson, *This Was Harlem* (New York: Farrar, Straus, Giroux, 1988); and Morris J. MacGregor, Jr., *Integration of the Armed Forces, 1940–1965*, Defense Studies Series (Washington, DC: Government Printing Office, 1981).

12

THE MAKING OF DISNEYLAND

George Lipsitz

The decade of the 1950s has a special place in Americans' collective memory. It is fondly recalled as the last "good" decade: an innocent, affluent, peaceful, and secure time, before the riots and protests of the 1960s set Americans against one another, and before the defeat in Vietnam, the Arab oil boycott, Watergate, and other events of the 1970s forced the American people to begin the painful process of reevaluating the nation's position and role in the world. God's country. Hula Hoops and Pat Boone. A two-bedroom ranch house in the suburbs. Television. Disneyland.

 Many Americans actually lived this idealized version of the fifties—enough so that it could be fashioned into a believable myth. After the Korean War ended in early 1953, the nation was at peace. Beginning in 1946, an unanticipated baby boom helped sustain high rates of economic growth while fostering a new family-based domesticity in the rapidly expanding suburbs. By mid-decade, living standards were at an all-time high, and Americans were buying consumer goods in unprecedented quantities. In a story entitled "Everybody Rich in the U.S.?" U.S. News and World Report claimed that poverty had virtually disappeared, and that it was an "unusual family that does not own a home, a car, a TV, many luxuries. Nothing like it has ever been seen before." Holding this "new economic order" together was the intrepid consumer, whose purchases would presumably prevent the economy from reverting to the depression conditions of the 1930s. There were, to be sure, anxieties about the "affluent society," even in the 1950s: Consumers were heavily in debt; automation was threatening to eliminate skilled work; and to some social critics the homogeneity of the suburbs seemed boring and even threatening. But by and large, Americans wanted to believe that their worries were over—and they did.

 When it opened in 1955, Disneyland represented this collective dream. As George Lipsitz's account reveals, all of Disneyland was fantasyland, an imaginary world of universal experience where poverty didn't exist, where slavery had never happened, and where no real work was ever done. Like the postwar suburbs, which generally excluded blacks and other minorities, Disneyland was designed not for all families, but for those—mostly white and middle-class—who could afford the admission charge and desired the isolating experience that the park provided. And in the shops on Main Street, park patrons lined Walt Disney's pockets and did what in the fifties seemed very much an act of social benevolence: They consumed.

If at times Disney's perspective seems narrow and provincial, it is well to consider that Disneyland was the success it was in part because the founder's fantasy so closely resembled the shared desires of millions of Americans. To what extent, then, does the Disneyland experience merely reflect American values? Were the white, middle-class Americans who patronized Disneyland in search of uniformity, homogeneity, and passivity? Were Americans responsible for Disney's pioneering multimedia promotions, or for the ugly heritage they have yielded: hour-long commercials that masquerade as entertainment; news "documentaries" that dramatically recreate past events; and feature films that relentlessly promote particular products? Did Americans seek to be constituted as consumers rather than producers? When youngsters bought Davy Crockett coonskin caps and spent their weekly allowances on Mickey Mouse ears, were they exercising free choice, or were they being prepared—like millions of visitors to Disneyland—for advanced consumer capitalism?

On July 17, 1955, a nationwide television audience watched the opening of the Disneyland amusement park on that evening's broadcast of the Disneyland television program. Before what was then the largest concentration of television equipment and personnel assembled for any one event (63 engineers and 24 live cameras), hosts Bob Cummings, Art Linkletter, and Ronald Reagan presided over ceremonies that one critic likened to "the dedication of a national shrine."

Despite three months of rehearsal for the program and an $11 million investment in the park, all did not go smoothly on opening day. Audio and video portions of the program went dead intermittently, and the hosts had considerable difficulty synchronizing their reporting with the pictures on the screen. The park's drinking fountains did not work, leading to long lines at the concession stands. Hot weather melted the freshly laid asphalt on streets and walkways, causing women in high-heeled shoes to sink into the pavement and providing small children with the opportunity to track footprints and leave rude messages on the sidewalks. In an emblematic indignity, the dramatic appearance of actor Fess Parker (dressed as his television character Davy Crockett) riding on horseback through Frontierland lost some of its intended drama when someone accidentally turned on lawn sprinklers, soaking Parker and his horse. One disappointed critic described Disneyland as being "like a giant cash register, clicking and clanging, as creatures of Disney magic came tumbling down from their lofty places in my daydreams to peddle and perish their charms with the aggressiveness of so many curbside barkers."

If everything seemed to go wrong for Disneyland on opening day, everything seems to have gone right for it ever since. By 1958, the annual attendance at Disneyland surpassed the number of patrons at Yellowstone, Yosemite, and the Grand Canyon combined. After 10 years of operation, one-quarter of the U.S. population had visited the park and Disneyland had earned $273 million for the Disney Corporation. In the early 1970s Disney Enterprises joined the list of the 500 largest corporations in America, and by the late 1980s California's Disneyland and Walt Disney World in Florida accounted for 62 percent of the sales and 70 percent of the operating earnings for a corporation the annual revenues of which approached $3 billion each year.

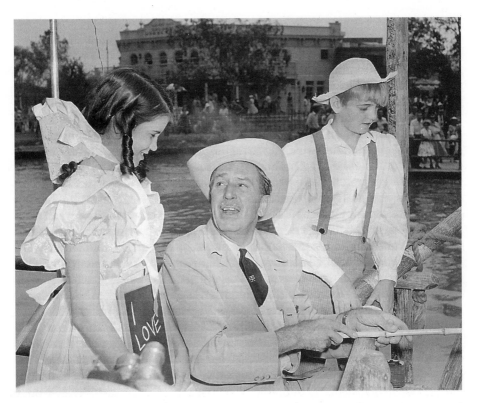

Walt Disney dons a straw hat and picks up a fishing pole as he poses for a photograph designed to provide publicity for the opening of Disneyland. Child actors pose as Mark Twain's characters Tom Sawyer and Becky Thatcher in a picture that presents Disney at the center of America's storytelling traditions. [Department of Special Collections, University Research Library, UCLA. Photos are in: Collection 1429, L.A. Times Negatives. (Neg. no. 99520)]

Disneyland has been more than just a financial success story. It has exercised an influence on American culture that can scarcely be measured in dollars. Film maker George Lucas (the producer of *Star Wars*) says that Disneyland was his favorite playground when he was growing up. The pop singer Michael Jackson visits Disneyland frequently, and astronaut Sally Ride borrowed from the park's terminology when she described her first trip into space as "a real E ticket ride." Harry S. Truman ceremonially received the Disneyland flag bearing the image of Mickey Mouse when the former president visited the park in 1957, and every U.S. President since has put in a personal appearance at the park, as have numerous visiting heads of foreign countries. Security concerns prevented the Soviet Union's Nikita Khrushchev from visiting Disneyland in 1959, but newspaper photographs over the years have captured Egypt's Anwar Sadat shaking hands with Goofy and India's Jawaharlal Nehru piloting the jungle boat in Adventureland. "Oh, this is so much fun, father is having such a good time," enthused Indira Gandhi, Nehru's daughter and herself a future Prime Minister of India. "We looked forward to Disneyland as much as anything on our trip."

As the creator of Mickey Mouse and numerous other popular cartoon characters, Walt Disney Studios had become an American institution by the 1930s. But Disney's personal wealth never equaled his enormous prestige, and by the late 1940s both he and the studio he headed faced serious financial problems. These financial pressures encouraged Disney to diversify into the amusement park business. At that time, amusement parks were not doing well financially, and few investors thought of them as places with a potential for profit making. He borrowed as much as he could from the Bank of America in California and the Bankers Trust Company in New York, but their skepticism about his chances of building a financially successful amusement park limited the amount of money they would make available to him. When Disney exhausted his credit with the bankers, he sold his second home at Smoke Tree Ranch in Palm Springs, California, and cashed in his life insurance policy in order to finance the amusement park. He took on a personal debt of over $100,000, confounding the bankers who expressed understandable skepticism about the likelihood of an amusement park repaying that kind of investment. Even Disney's brother Roy limited the financial investment of the studio in Disneyland to $10,000 because he considered the park to be just another of "Walt's screwy ideas."

Disney wanted to build a new kind of amusement park, one that broke with the traditions of the past. While planning his own park he inspected fairs and amusement parks all across the country to see what worked and what didn't. He was particularly depressed by the conditions at New York's Coney Island, which had been the first successful amusement park in the 1890s. One journalist reports that Disney found Coney Island "so battered and tawdry and the ride operators were so hostile that Walt felt a momentary urge to abandon the idea of an amusement park. But when he visited Copenhagen [Denmark] and saw that city's Tivoli Gardens, he proclaimed 'Now *this* is what an amusement park should be.' " He felt that most amusement parks had become unsavory places, that they placed too much emphasis on risk taking, danger, "thrill rides," games of chance, barkers, and concession stands.

Disney vowed to establish a park that replaced those sensations with "educational and patriotic values" transmitted through wholesome family fun. As a publicity brochure for Disneyland explains, "As a pioneer in the motion picture industry, Walt developed an intuitive ability to know what was universally entertaining. When his daughters were very young, Walt would take them on what he later called "very unsatisfying visits" to local amusement parks. He felt he could build a park at which parents and children could have fun together. He wanted Disneyland to be a place where "people can experience some of the wonders of life, of adventure, and feel better because of it."

Walt Disney wanted his amusement park to operate by the same principles as his motion pictures. "I hate to see a down-beat picture," he once explained, "so that when I come out [of the theater], it makes me feel that everything's dirty around me. I know it isn't that way, and I don't want anybody telling me that it is." That commitment to a wholesome and upbeat view of the world led Disney to take great pains with his creations. In the case of Disneyland, he wanted a park that would physically block out any view of the outside world, so that visitors could concentrate on the pleasant fantasies within its walls. He wanted to create a forum for fun, a public space free of danger, dirt, and depravity. To millions of Americans he succeeded magnificently, and they have repaid Disney and his heirs many times over with their patronage. But in order to accomplish all this he needed to raise large sums of money in a fairly short time.

It was Walt Disney's understanding of television that not only won him the financing necessary to build Disneyland, but also the resources to make it a

Vice President Richard M. Nixon, his wife Pat Nixon, and their daughters Tricia and Julie visit Disneyland in 1955. This staged photo displays one function of the park—its role as a site for adult celebrities to show their "personal" sides. The smiles and postures of Mr. and Mrs. Nixon in this photo indicate that they understand this role very well, but their identically dressed daughters seem less at ease with their day at Disneyland turning into an opportunity for publicizing their father's career. [Department of Special Collections, University Research Library, UCLA. Photos are in: Collection 1429, L.A. Times Negatives. (Neg. no. 94433)]

success after it opened. Disney had produced a successful Christmas special in
1950, and he knew that the new medium of television was hungry for the sort
of product that he could provide. He offered to produce a weekly series for television, but only if one of the networks would help finance Disneyland. ABC
network officials agreed to invest $500,000 directly and to guarantee loans of
up to $4.5 million for the amusement park in return for one-third ownership in
the park and a weekly series titled "Disneyland."

Armed with this new infusion of funds, Disney commenced construction of
the park. He commissioned the Stanford Research Institute (SRI) to identify a cen-
trally located tract of land available at a reasonable price. Harrison "Buzz" Price,
director of the Los Angeles branch of the Institute, recommended building the

During the construction of the park, Disney Corporation engineers
transformed fields of orange groves and palm trees into an environment
with many identities including the terrain along the Mississippi River.
This photograph shows what Disney tried so hard to hide about the
park—people doing actual labor in a real workplace. [Department of
Special Collections, University Research Library, UCLA. Photos are in:
Collection 1429, L.A. Times Negatives. (Neg. no. 93738)]

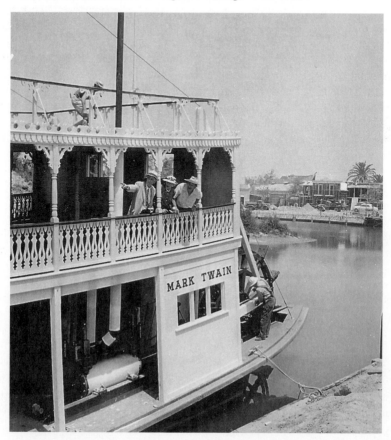

park in the vicinity of the main railroad station in downtown Los Angeles, but the cost of land in that location proved too high for Disney's budget. Disney rejected a proposed ocean-front location because he felt that the beach attracted unsavory individuals. Price and his fellow researchers noticed that residential growth in the Los Angeles area tended to follow the paths of new freeways heading east and south from the central city. They recommended several sites in suburban areas, but eventually settled on an Anaheim location because it received 5 fewer inches of rain per year than alternate locations in San Gabriel and in the San Fernando Valley. The SRI advised Disney to buy 65 acres of orange groves in Anaheim for $4,500 an acre; 10 years later the land was worth $80,000 an acre.

Disney cleared the orange groves and relandscaped them, sending his staff on scouting missions throughout southern California to find "interesting" trees and shrubs for the park. He deliberately reshaped the terrain so that once inside Disneyland, visitors would lose visual contact with the surrounding area. "I don't want the public to see the world they live in while they're in the park," he explained to his design staff. "I want them to feel they are in another world." Yet financial considerations led Disney to include at least one part of the outside world in the park: advertising. As part of his efforts to raise money, Disney got 32 major corporations to lease concessions in the park, in effect paying him for the opportunity to sell their products and advertise their brands. The Bank of America opened up a small branch in the "Main Street" section of the park, and the Continental Baking Corporation paid for the privilege of having "Wonder Bread" designated as the "official white bread" of Disneyland.

Financial rather than aesthetic considerations dictated the connection between television and Disneyland. In his heart, Disney felt that television (then largely a black and white medium) was actually a poor vehicle for displaying the vivid colors and high production values of his cartoons and nature films. But he needed money for the amusement park, and he thought that the new medium could be very important as a marketing device, not just for Disneyland, but for all of his studio's other ventures. "We wanted to start off running," Disney later told *Business Week* magazine in regard to his decision to tie the amusement park to a television series. "The investment was going to be too big to wait for a slow buildup. We needed terrific initial impact and television seemed the answer." The Disneyland television program went on the air on October 27, 1954, with a full hour program previewing the opening of the Disneyland amusement park the following summer. Two other programs later in the season gave progress reports on the park.

The success of the Disneyland television series, and consequently the success of Disneyland itself, stemmed in large measure from a three-part episode broadcast during the 1954 to 1955 season about the frontiersman Davy Crockett. At first glance, the likelihood for success of such a series seemed slight. Popular tastes at the time in film and television had been moving away from Western and frontier stories. Furthermore, Crockett himself was, at best, an ambiguous historical figure—a man celebrated as a hero for his part in clearing the wilderness, fighting Indians, serving in Congress, and dying in battle at the Alamo, but one equally reviled as a villain for his destructive hunting practices (killing 105 bears in one season, shooting six deer in a day and leaving five of them to hang in the woods), the betrayal of his political supporters when he turned against Andrew Jackson and joined the Whig Party, and his crude antisocial behavior. To further complicate matters for Disney, the actor selected to play Crockett, Fess Parker, was allergic to horses and hated the costumes his role required him to wear. According to one account, Disney personnel had to teach Parker how to ride a horse, and he disliked the leather breeches that he had to wear so much that when out of camera range "he shied away from them as if they were a bunch of poison ivy, swearing they would give him 'crotch rot.' "

Whatever shortcomings the story of Davy Crockett presented for purposes of history or drama, it nonetheless offered an ideal marketing opportunity for Disney executives. While the show was still in the planning stages, Disney merchandisers explored the possibilities for manufacturing and distributing coonskin caps like the ones Crockett would wear on television. Even though almost no American homes had color television sets at that time, Disney producers shot the episodes in color in anticipation of stringing them together and releasing them to theaters as a feature film.

Vince Jefferds, Disney's head of promotion boasted, "I could make a good case that licensing of an article is more profitable than manufacturing it. I often made money out of movies that were a loss at the box office." Shortly before the first episode of the Davy Crockett trilogy was scheduled to air, producers realized that they did not have enough film footage to fill their entire program. They asked the creative staff at the studio to write a song that would enable them to bridge over some gaps in the story, and their creation, "The Ballad of Davy Crockett," went to number one on the hit parade and stayed at the top of the charts for 13 weeks. Merchandisers sold more than 10 million coonskin caps, making them out of rabbits and squirrels when they ran out of raccoon fur.

The filmed portions of the Davy Crockett series cost $700,000 to make with only $300,000 in advertising revenue guaranteed for their dates on the air. But when the episodes were spliced together for theatrical release, they made a profit of almost $2.5 million even though they had already been seen by an estimated 90 million viewers on television. The Davy Crockett phenomenon was perfectly timed for the opening of Disneyland the following summer. The episodes not only enhanced the royalties from record sales and coonskin caps, but they also served as advertising for the "Frontierland" section of the amusement park.

Television provided Disney with the money to finish building Disneyland, and the shows he made for ABC in return worked to advertise his films and amusement park. The second program of the 1954 to 1955 season was a promotional film about the making of the motion picture *20,000 Leagues Under the Sea*, which was soon to be released by Disney Studios. Bolstered by the program-length commercial on the second Disneyland show, *20,000 Leagues Under the Sea* became the biggest grossing live-action Disney film up to that time, earning over $6 million in its first release. "The amazing thing is that nobody complained that we were doing publicity movies," recalls Disney executive Bill Walsh. "Far from it. Our '20,000 League[s]' documentary even won us an Emmy. *And* it brought in sponsorship for our programs, first from Coca-Cola and then from Johnson and Johnson." The deal benefited ABC as well. The network received one-third of the profits generated by Disneyland until Walt Disney Productions exercised its option to buy back the network's one-third share of ownership of Disneyland in 1960 for $7.5 million, a sum 15 times the size of ABC's investment. In addition, the Disneyland television program established ABC as a competitive network for the first time, attracting a flood of national advertisers to its entire schedule.

Television gave Walt Disney the financial resources essential for the construction of Disneyland, and it also served as a marketing device crucial to the success of the park. The rides in the park advertised Disney comic books, cartoons, films, and television programs, and all of Disney's other entertainment and marketing efforts functioned as a commercial for the park. Customers paid money to enter Disneyland and to go on rides that advertised Disney entertainment. They bought souvenir merchandise that further advertised the characters and stories copyrighted by Disney Productions. Furthermore, they bought concessions from corporations that had paid money to Disney for the privilege of associating their products with the fun and frolic at Disneyland.

Walt Disney presided over every decision about Disneyland with an attention to detail that staggers the imagination. He often slept overnight in a small apartment above the fire station on Main Street, and he insisted on training sessions at what he called "the University of Disneyland" for all employees about how to treat the park's visitors. "Always smile," he ordered his staff. "Turn the other cheek to everybody, even the nasty ones. And above everything, always give them full value for their money. If a boat ride is supposed to last 12 minutes and they only get 11 minutes 30 seconds, they've a right to feel cheated. Thirty seconds shy, and they hate us for selling them short. Thirty seconds extra, and they feel they've gotten away with something. That's the way we want them to feel. Contented, even smug." Disney insisted that his staff completely clean the streets with high pressure hoses every night, and he ordered the installation of more than 45,000 signs to communicate with the public.

Most emphatically, Disney pursued uniformity and predictability in the Disneyland experience. He wanted everyone to enter at the same place and to see the same things. As one admiring journalist observed, "He saw the need for Disneyland to flow, as did a movie, from scene to scene." To maintain the "flow" of the Disneyland experience, Disney made sure that all visitors entered by the same gate and started their day with a view of Sleeping Beauty's Castle that served as a visual lure to pull them through the Main Street shops and into the rest of the park. Visual concerns dominated the aesthetics of a day at Disneyland. A corporate publicity brochure boasted about the park's visual clarity, its ability to present visual stimuli in a unified and coordinated manner: "Disneyland was the first to use visually compatible elements working as a coordinating theme avoiding the contradictory 'hodge-podge' of World's Fairs and amusement parks." To preserve the clean visual line of the park and to ensure that maintenance could take place outside the vision of park customers, Disney buried all water, power, and sewer lines beneath the street level. Each theme land (Fantasyland, Adventureland, Frontierland, and Tomorrowland) appeared completely self-contained and could not be seen from any of the other sections of the park. Costumed "characters" in each theme section traveled to their destinations in underground tunnels so they would never be seen in "inappropriate settings." Even on the jungle ride, Disney insisted on mechanical rather than real animals, "so that every boatload of people will see the same thing."

Disney also thought of the park in transitory terms, like a television series that could undergo revisions over time. He complained about the permanence of films, about how they could no longer be changed once they had been released, and he talked longingly of making Disneyland a place that would change constantly. "The park means a lot to me," Disney explained to a reporter. "It's something that will never be finished, something I can keep developing, keep 'plussing' and adding to. It's alive. It will be a live breathing thing that will need changes."

No section of Disneyland carried as much of the burden of Walt Disney's ideals as did Main Street. In that part of the park, Disney drew on his youthful memories of Marceline, Missouri, as well as on the nostalgia for the Gilded Age evident in 1940s films like *Meet Me in St. Louis*. Disney scaled Main Street's buildings slightly smaller at the rear and top to give the illusion that they were bigger than they actually were, creating a perspective that enabled an adult to see the buildings through the eyes of a child.

In a press release, Disneyland's publicists described Main Street as "Walt's and anyone else's home town—the way it should have been." But unlike the real town squares of turn-of-the-century small towns, Disneyland's Main Street offered little space for leisure and none for work. Despite occasional parades by the Disneyland band and scattered benches in public spaces, Main Street's real social life depended on shopping, on funnelling (as rapidly as possible) enormous numbers of consumers into a "comfortable" environment for making purchases. Although buildings appeared to be distinct and separate on the outside, inner passages made it easy to walk from store to store (and difficult to walk back out into the noncommercial space of the street). The meaning of this was not lost on developer and retailer Mel Kaufman, who observed that "Main's Street's purpose is exactly the same as Korvette's [a major department store] in the Bronx, but it manages to make shopping wonderful and pleasant at the same time. I'm sure people buy more when they're happy."

Although its prominence on commercial network television made Disneyland a national phenomenon, its success also stemmed from its strategic role in the cultural life of Los Angeles. Disneyland was most often described as a site specially designed for children, but most surveys showed that adults outnumbered children at the park by ratios of 3 to 1 or 4 to 1. Architect Charles Moore attributed Disneyland's success to its ability to provide Californians with a "public environment" in the midst of a region dominated by the private spaces of suburban subdivisions and automobile interiors. Just as Main Street functioned as the town square of Disneyland, Moore described Disneyland itself as the "town square of Los Angeles."

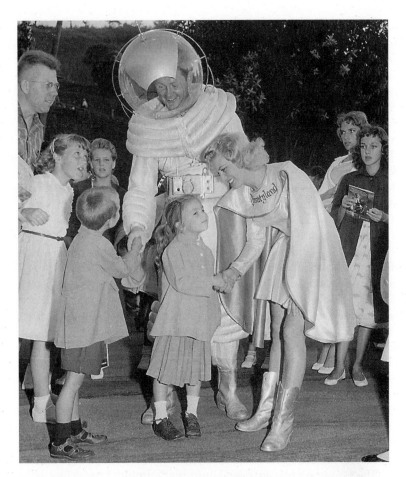

Opened at a time when human space flight had not yet taken place,
Disneyland presented images of space travel in its Tomorrowland
section. Yet the rapid pace of technological change has made this the
part of the park most subject to obsolescence, as its futuristic fantasies
sometimes came true in the present. [Department of Special
Collections, University Research Library, UCLA. Photos are in:
Collection 1429, L.A. Times Negatives. (Neg. no. 111244)]

If there was ever a city in need of a town square it was Los Angeles in the
1950s. Home to the first and largest automobile-oriented highway program in the
country, Los Angeles developed into a major metropolis as a scattered city with
many well dispersed focal points. The city had experienced longer and more sustained population growth than any American city since the 1850s, and it enjoyed
particularly enormous population growth during the 1930s, with 200,000 new
migrants between 1936 and 1939 alone. Defense spending during and after
World War II propelled an even greater expansion. Los Angeles became the second largest industrial center in America during the war (trailing only Detroit),

and between 1940 and 1944 over 780,000 new immigrants entered southern California. This extraordinarily rapid growth continued after World War II. Between 1945 and 1955 more than a million and a half people moved to Los Angeles, a total then equal to the *combined* total populations of Pittsburgh and Baltimore. Figures from the 1950 census reveal that more than 50 percent of the residents of Los Angeles in that year had lived in the city for less than 5 years.

Workers came west to secure employment in Los Angeles's shipyard and aircraft industries during World War II, and massive defense spending for the Cold War in the postwar era fueled even further growth. During the war, blacks, whites, Chicanos, Native Americans, and Asian Americans worked side by side in the defense plants and traveled together on the city's efficient and effective streetcar and bus network.

Cultural interactions enlivened urban life. The city's vibrant popular music mixed Afro-American, Chicano, and Anglo forms in reflection of the increasingly heterogeneous culture of the city. Dances and concerts at El Monte Legion Stadium on the eastern border of the city attracted youths from diverse backgrounds who combined their styles of dress, dance, and speech to form an exciting multicultural youth culture. On the playgrounds and streets of inner-city neighborhoods, in public parks, and at commercial amusement centers at the Long Beach and Santa Monica piers the city's heterogeneous population enjoyed the fun of participating in public play.

But the growth of the postwar suburbs (largely subsidized by tax spending on new highways and the extension of city services including water, gas, electric, and sewer lines) encouraged new forms of isolation and segregation. Racial discrimination by private realtors and developers denied most African Americans and Mexican Americans access to the new suburbs, while the federal government's discriminatory home loan policies effectively subsidized the creation of all-white neighborhoods in the San Fernando Valley and Orange County. The newly dispersed population made public transit less efficient per mile and the numbers of automobiles driven by commuters further slowed the speed of trolleys and buses, thereby providing central city dwellers with even more reasons to move to the suburbs. In less than a decade, Los Angeles's diverse urban space became more segregated than ever, its effective rapid transit system collapsed, and the success of suburbs and freeways only contributed to ever-increasing fragmentation, segregation, and dispersal of the city's population.

Disneyland's emergence corresponded with the increasing suburbanization of Los Angeles. Even though a majority of the park's visitors came from out of town, Disneyland firmly established itself as an important public space in Los Angeles—as the place one took visitors from out of town, as a site for special celebrations like high school proms, and as an emblem of a whole way of life built around suburbanization and the automobile in southern California. The park provided an alternative to the beaches, dance halls, parks, and streets of the city, and it powerfully projected its image of middle-class suburban consumer culture as a norm to which other groups should aspire. Massive in-migration and the city's dispersed physical form left Los Angeles without the kinds of geographic and focal points common to other cities. In addition, dependence on the automobile produced unhealthy and unpleasant smog and brought about traffic jams that inhibited access to the beaches, deserts, and mountains once within easy reach of most local residents. Disneyland came into existence as an easily reachable attraction conveniently located near new freeways in the midst of the region's largest locus of population growth. It redefined the nature of public gathering places, with its location and admission costs making it much more accessible to suburban white families than to ethnic minority residents of the inner city. But its appeal depended on more than accessibility; as a new kind of public space Disneyland contrasted sharply with alternative experiences in the Los Angeles area.

Visitors left their cars in parking lots with more acreage than the park itself, and entered a world with comfortable walkways and efficient rail public transit. The high price of admission and tickets attracted an economically homogeneous crowd and encouraged patrons to devote the entire day or evening to leisurely utilization of the park's facilities. The efficient movement of people through the park and the careful timing of rides and attractions worked against any feeling of overcrowding or stagnation, and the Disney philosophy of viewing visitors as an audience and park personnel as entertainers worked to effectively inculcate passivity in park patrons. A revealing phrase in a Disneyland promotional brochure identifies the kind of social space constructed in the park with startling precision:

> Up until now audience participation in entertainment was almost non-existent. In live theater, motion pictures and television the audience is always separate and apart from the actual show environment. . . . Walt Disney took the audience out of their seats and placed them right in the middle of the action for a total, themed, controlled experience.

Disneyland also spoke to the break with the past that formed an important part of the lives of Los Angeles residents. In a city made up of migrants from all over the country, no common heritage served to underpin individual or collective identity. But by presenting images of familiar figures from television and motion pictures, Disneyland spoke to the commonality of experience made possible by popular culture. People came to Disneyland with a variety of experiences and beliefs, but the reach and scope of electronic mass media guaranteed that they all shared familiarity and knowledge about Disney stories and products.

Disneyland self-consciously promoted itself as an educational institution, as a place, among other things, for learning about the past. Many people admired its successes in that regard. The Freedoms Foundation at Valley Forge awarded Walt Disney its George Washington Medal, and California State Superintendent of Education Max Rafferty lauded Disney as "the greatest educator of this century, greater than John Dewey or James Conant or all the rest of us put together." When Disney died in 1966, California Senator George Murphy claimed that he knew of no individual "who has contributed more to the general welfare of mankind" than Disney did. But Disney himself explained his goals more modestly. "I've always wanted to do American history," Disney explained to an interviewer shortly before the opening of the park. "It's due. We have taken too many things for granted. I'm not really telling history, though. I'm telling about people; history happens to be going on at the time."

Disneyland showed Abraham Lincoln agonizing over the Civil War, but not over slavery. Its "authentic" Frontierland Indians came from reservations in the desert southwest, and had to learn how to handle the "real Indian canoes" from non-Indian park personnel whose knowledge came from their experiences at summer camp. All of its "adventures" replicated the history of white Euro-Americans as they conquered the American or African frontiers. It looked at the conquests of the frontier and the jungle as the spread of European civilization rather than as the plunder of the possessions of indigenous peoples.

In some places, Disneyland's liberties with the past went beyond mere insensitivity. One restaurant featured an "Aunt Jemima" theme echoing the vicious "Mammy" stereotypes of black women that became a staple of popular culture after the Civil War, showing black women invariably as fat, nurturing, childlike, and totally devoted to their white masters. For years the jungle cruise encountered a "humorous trapped safari," which depicted "four red-capped porters, all blacks, who cling bug-eyed to a tree with their white client above them as a menacing rhinoceros stands below." These may seem like innocent errors, mere manifestations of the racism extant in the larger culture of which Disneyland was a part. But Disney's personal prejudices often guided his business practices. He never employed African Americans as studio technicians and did not allow them to work in Disneyland in *any* capacity until pressured to do so in 1963 by civil rights protests. Disney's antisemitism was equally intense; as one writer well acquainted with the details of Disney's life notes, "disappointment and resentment seemed to bring out his latent anti-semitism. He was often heard making snide comments about the Jews, whose success seemed to infuriate him." Disney tried to cloak himself in the American flag and to appropriate for his own purposes the patriotism of his customers. Yet his version of the national narrative was highly selective, prejudiced, and distorted. If his amusement park united its customers in a shared fantasy, it was one tailored to the economic and social interests of a small group of people and not one reflective of the larger shared experience of unity and disunity out of which the complex American nation and society have been forged.

Disneyland management has always tried to present the park as a world apart, as an island of fun in a serious world. Yet no multimillion dollar marketing effort is really cut off from the real world, much less one with the commercial and cultural power of Disneyland. Whether one looks at the lone individual who commented that his first trip to the Mississippi River reminded him of the first part of the Pirates of the Caribbean ride, or to the five high ranking members of the Nixon Administration who received their public relations training handling both the Disneyland and the Richard Nixon accounts for the J. Walter Thompson advertising agency, evidence of Disneyland's influence over American life and culture during the past 40 years has not been hard to find.

Over the years Disneyland has faced strikes ("Disneyland is a kingdom all right, and we're the serfs," complained a worker in a Br'er Bear costume during a 1970 work stoppage), lawsuits over a ban on members of the same sex dancing

"Mouseketeers" from the syndicated "Mickey Mouse Club" television program visit Los Angeles City Hall. As a five-day-a-week afterschool show, "The Mickey Mouse Club" extended the Disney Corporation's popular and commercial influence to the everyday experiences of children. The uniformity of the Mouseketeers' outfits (and ears) hides the symbols of youthful rebellion incorporated into adolescent dress and styles of the day. Adolescence itself disappears as the Mickey Mouse Club appears as a children's "gang" under wholesome adult supervision. [Department of Special Collections, University Research Library, UCLA. Photos are in: Collection 1429, L.A. Times Negatives. (Neg. no. 101369)]

together, and repeated arguments over what constitutes appropriate attire at the park. One particularly vivid example of the links between Disneyland and the "real world" came on August 6, 1970, when 300 "yippies" marked the twenty-fifth anniversary of the dropping of the first atomic bomb on Hiroshima by staging a demonstration in Disneyland. The youths chanted antiwar slogans on the drawbridge to Sleeping Beauty's Castle, followed the Disneyland band down Main Street, and raised a Viet Cong flag over the fort on Tom Sawyer's island. They accused Disneyland of being "a plastic world of fantasy" at odds with the realities outside its walls. Over 100 uniformed Anaheim police officers equipped with riot batons eventually cleared the youths from the park, making nine arrests. Disneyland management closed the park 6 hours early and handed out refunds to 30,000 customers. The next day a *San Diego Union* editorial condemning the disruption of business at the park advised that "smaller folk who need an explanation for what happened at Disneyland Thursday might be told they saw a lifelike reproduction of the pre-historic world—before shaggy creatures with small brains gave way to the human race as we know it today."

In order to further secure the park and to control the nature of its experience, Disney officials began a rigid policy of dress and grooming codes, denying admission to the park to any individuals whose hairstyles or clothing seemed inappropriate to park guards. This policy was based on the idea that there was only one respectable way for people to look and dress, that men should not have long hair or beards, that women should not wear sandals and "love bead necklaces," that black people should not have "Afro" haircuts or be allowed to wear African "dashikis." But as popular styles changed and allowed for more diversity, park guards found themselves facing a losing battle trying to stem the tide of rapidly changing subcultural styles and fashions. Similarly, the park's administrators enforced a policy against men dancing with men or women dancing with women on the grounds that "some patrons might find partners of the same sex offensive," until a lawsuit charging the park with violating the Constitutional rights of its patrons convinced them to drop the policy.

AN INTERPRETATION

Any cultural expression advances one view of reality, and in the process runs the risks of ignoring or erasing other ways of looking at the world. Any struggle over meaning influences struggles over resources, because cultural stories, signs, and symbols help determine what is legitimate and what is illegitimate, what is permitted and what is forbidden, who is included and who is excluded, who speaks and who is silenced. Like many other sites of commercialized leisure, Disneyland provides a useful site for the examination of these larger social questions.

Disneyland initiated and refined distinct cultural practices that characterize much of American society today. It created one of the most important public spaces in our society out of the imperatives of a private profit-making corporation. It redefined public recreation as primarily spectatorship and shopping, and carried the forms and logic of commercial network television outside the home. Its multilayered opportunities for profit-making mixed marketing, merchandising, and advertising into one unified activity, and it broke down barriers between media by blending film, comic book, and television references in the shared space of a theme park. It connected the personal memories of individual childhoods with carefully crafted narratives about the "childhood" of the nation, and it injected a profit-making corporation into the shaping of family life in an unprecedented manner.

In fact, Disneyland is such a microcosm of cultural practices in our society, it is sometimes difficult to view it as a carefully created and manipulated artifact. Like any good ideological cultural work, it seems to flow naturally from the consciousness of the audience and to demand no special investigation. To think of fun as consisting of shopping and spectatorship makes sense in a world of shopping malls and television sets, but these inevitably erode our collective memory of other more sociable, active, spontaneous, and creative ways to have fun. Disney's idea of a park that would always be in flux is a perfect expression of an economic system that is constantly in the service of fashion—changing clothing styles and automobile styles regularly to create "new" needs for what are essentially the same old products. Disney's success at creating a centralized site for recreation that standardizes stories for people around the world speaks powerfully about the forces of homogenization that have undermined localized ethnic and folk traditions that keep alive creative differences among and across diverse populations. Coming into existence at the same time that commercial network television and suburbanization changed the nature of culture and social life in America, Disneyland succeeded at least in part by recognizing that its visitors were likely to watch television and live in suburbs, and that consequently they expected a park that would conform with their other experiences.

Yet asking questions about Disneyland can help us begin to think critically about the world in which we live. It can help us to inquire into the relationships between commerce and art, between labor and leisure, between citizenship and spectatorship, and between our roles as consumers and our lives as community members, gendered subjects, and world citizens.

In 1955, Walt Disney and his corporation established their phenomenally successful amusement park in the wake of the popularity generated by their television films about Davy Crockett. More than 100 years earlier the historical Davy Crockett boasted that "Fashion is a thing I care mighty little about, except when it happens to run just exactly according to my own notion. . . ." Walt Disney created an amusement park, an entertainment empire, a version of American history, and an important element in the lives of many children by getting fashion to run exactly according to his own notion. We know that Disneyland's blend of commerce and art, its exclusion of those outside of mainstream narratives, and its insertion of cash transactions into the operative realities of family life have been the profitable thing, the successful thing, and the effective thing. But we need to think again about their consequences for what we think we know about the American past and for how we live the American present and future.

Sources: The Disneyland story has been told many times from many different points of view. From the wide range of secondary sources on the establishment and development of the amusement park in relation to the larger vision of the Disney Corporation, I have drawn repeatedly on the valuable information and insights presented by Herbert Schiller in *The Mind Managers* (Boston: Beacon, 1973), Michael Real, *Mass Mediated Culture* (Englewood Cliffs: Prentice-Hall, 1977), Richard Schickel, *The Disney Version* (New York: Simon and Schuster, 1968), and Leonard Mosely, *Disney's World* (New York: Stein and Day, 1985). Also useful for descriptions and quotes were Randy Bright, *Disneyland: The Inside Story* (New York: Harry N. Abrams, Inc., 1987), and Bob Thomas, *Walt Disney, An American Original* (New York: Simon and Schuster, 1976). In journals and periodicals, the articles I found most useful were Richard Francaiglia, "Main Street USA," *Journal of Popular Culture* 15 (September 1981), Mark Gottdiener, "Disneyland: A Utopian Urban Space," *Urban Life* 11 (July 1982), and Paul Goldberger, "Mickey Mouse Teaches the Architects," *New York Times Magazine*, October 20, 1972.

13

SHERRI FINKBINE AND THE ORIGINS OF *ROE V. WADE*

Rickie Solinger

Rickie Solinger's story opens in 1962, when Sherri Finkbine sensed that something might be terribly wrong with her pregnancy, and it ends in 1973, with the Roe v. Wade *decision legalizing abortion. The story spans a decade of enormous upheaval and change: war in Southeast Asia, riots among African Americans in the nation's cities, political assassination, protests and violence on the college campuses, a new women's movement. Yet in 1962, when the story begins, it would have required a crystal ball to predict those developments. The U.S. commitment to the war in Vietnam was minimal—a few thousand advisors. John F. Kennedy was still alive. The Berkeley Free Speech movement (the first of the major campus revolts), would not take place until 1964, and the race riots in the Watts section of Los Angeles, a sign of a new, more militant, civil rights movement, not until 1965. The National Organization of Women (NOW), created to help women gain equal rights, was founded in 1966.*

The atmosphere in which Sherri Finkbine struggled to make the most important decision of her life was very much that of the 1950s, an era reflected in George Lucas's classic film, American Graffiti *(1973), set in 1962 and very much aware of how little its characters understood of the future. To be sure, Kennedy, and not his 1960 Republican opponent, Richard M. Nixon, held the White House, but Kennedy had won the office as a typical cold warrior and through most of his presidency had been preoccupied by confrontations with the Soviets over Berlin and Cuba. At Kennedy's urging, Americans rushed to protect themselves by building bomb shelters in their backyards and basements. The civil rights movement, though confrontational and even militant with its freedom rides and lunch-counter sit-ins, remained focused on the South and, led by Martin Luther King, Jr., committed to the method of nonviolence and to the goal of racial integration. On most college campuses, students were subject to curfews, to rules that restricted men's access to women's rooms, and to other regulations intended to shape sexual conduct. Those who lived off campus and were brazen enough to live with a person of the opposite sex, could be subject to disciplinary procedures if discovered. Popular culture, too, remained conservative. Despite the vogue of the twist and other black-inspired dance crazes, especially in New York City clubs, two of the most popular songs of 1962 were "Moon River" and "Days of Wine and Roses," both ballads featuring the weepy, old-fashioned strings of Henry Mancini's orchestra.* Lawrence of Arabia, *a desert epic celebrating empire, won the Oscar for best picture. Among the year's new television series was* The Beverly Hillbillies, *its protagonists a collection of country bumpkins from the fringes of American society suddenly thrust into the consumer mainstream.*

Yet in the midst of this orgy of consensus, there were signs of another sort, signs that might have motivated Sherri Finkbine to understand her situation differently than she would have even a few years before. One, surely, was the publication in 1962 of Rachel Carson's Silent Spring, *an environmental classic that linked the dangerous chemical DDT to rates of economic growth. The American love affair with the automobile, a staple of 1950s popular culture ("See the USA in your Chevrolet"), received a setback from activist Ralph Nader, whose indictment of the popular Corvair was titled* Unsafe at Any Speed. *While the college campuses remained sedate, the groundwork for future activity was being laid by a gathering of students at Port Huron, Michigan, who wrote, debated, and approved a manifesto, the "Port Huron Statement," calling for an end to the Cold War and for a return to social progressivism. Harbingers of the powerful women's movement that would surface later in the decade could be seen in the 1961 "Women's Strike for Peace," in which some 50,000 middle-class American housewives walked away from their jobs to protest Kennedy's confrontational foreign policy; in Kennedy's appointment that same year of the President's Commission on the Status of Women; and in the passage, in 1963, of the Equal Pay Act, which ostensibly guaranteed women equal pay for equal work. And in Grandview, New York, Betty Friedan was putting the finishing touches on* The Feminine Mystique *(1963), a savage critique of the tragic, desperate lot of the unfulfilled, unhappy American housewife—the problem, as she put it, "that has no name."*

It was out of this watershed moment, poised between the social conservatism of the 1950s and the radical social democracy of the 1960s, that Sherri Finkbine pieced together a solution to her problem, a way out of her dilemma. To that problem and that dilemma, and to the way she found, we now turn.

"It was along about mid-July," Sherri Finkbine remembered, placing the opening, shattering moment of her 1962 ordeal. "About then I noticed the first newspaper item. It was in one of the Phoenix morning papers, the *Arizona Republic*." The little item reported how Dr. Frances Kelsey, a pharmacologist at the U.S. Food and Drug Administration, had blocked a Cincinnati drug company from distributing a sleeping pill made out of the compound thalidomide. Sherri Finkbine had looked hard at that small news report. As she put it later, "A tiny alarm bell rang in my mind." According to the paper, this drug could damage a fetus if a woman took it early in her pregnancy. A day or two later, Sherri noticed a second article with essentially the same information, except this time, the newspaper called the drug in question a tranquilizer. Now Sherri was scared.

This young, married mother of four had reason to believe that even though thalidomide pills had never been sold over a drugstore counter in Phoenix or anywhere else in the United States, she had been unlucky enough to have taken as many as 30 or 40 doses over the last month or so. At some point in the spring, the nausea she always experienced with pregnancy had overtaken her, and she realized she was indeed pregnant, for the fifth time. Day after day, as she attempted to keep the nausea at bay, she reached for the brown bottle of pills in her medicine chest.

In the summer of 1962, Sherri Finkbine was 30 years old. Her husband Bob was 31. These two had been college sweethearts at the University of Wisconsin and now, almost 10 years later, they lived busy and happy lives in Scottsdale, a community of young, prosperous families on the edge of the Arizona desert. Bob and Sherri were well on their way to producing the six children they'd agreed to have. And their careers were in good order as well. Bob was a high school history teacher, an athletic coach at school, and gave swimming lessons to local kids at the pool he and Sherri had installed in their backyard. Like many mothers of young children in the early 1960s, Sherri took care of her kids and she had a job. Her perky good looks and personality made her the perfect host of *Romper Room*, the local franchise of the nationally syndicated TV show for preschool children. Sherri loved her job and had won a number of local awards in the months before those innocuous-looking pills took over her life.

What Sherri feared when she read the news item was that the bottle in her medicine cabinet—with the quaint English label reading "Boots Cash Chemist, London"—contained Distaval pills, the commercial name for the tranquilizer thalidomide in Great Britain. These pills had come back from England with Bob the summer before, after he'd led 60 Arizona teenagers on a 10-week European trip. The summer had begun on a harsh note for Bob; nonstop teenage energy and demands were unrelenting, so Bob had asked a doctor in London to write a prescription for something to help him sleep. As it turned out, Bob had taken only a few of the pills because he quickly settled into the role of tour leader, and his sleep smoothed out. The remainder of the medicine came home in Bob's camera case and got stored with the aspirin and nosedrops in the bathroom.

Late in the spring of 1962, after Sherri had run out of the antinausea tranquilizers her own doctor had prescribed, she grabbed for Bob's English supply. "A tranquilizer is a tranquilizer," she told herself guiltily, knowing the rules against taking another person's drugs, but she was still nauseous and interested in saving the few bucks a refill would cost.

Within a few days of reading about the dangerous tranquilizer in July, Sherri visited her doctor, who cabled London for information about those "Boots Cash" pills. The answer was grim and definitive. "You've been taking pure thalidomide," the doctor told her. And he counseled Sherri to get an abortion. "If you were my wife," he said, "I'd see to it that you'd get a therapeutic abortion at a hospital." To make clear to Sherri why this was the only reasonable solution, the doctor showed her terribly disturbing pictures, babies with no arms or legs, and in their place, little flaps of flesh. For months, Sherri particularly remembered one baby, "With only a head and a torso. Nothing else. Absolutely nothing."

Not long afterward, Sherri described how these pictures made her feel, how they caused her to imagine giving birth to a child whose life would be "no more than a living death." She questioned her "right to take the life that was there, but also her right to condemn a human being to live like the baby in the picture." She asked herself whether a baby like this "would look about him at people with arms and legs, at children running, at boys and girls walking hand in hand, and curse her for letting him be born." And she thought deeply about her maternal responsibilities for her healthy children. Taking care of the damaged baby would be so time consuming that she could be only a "partial mother" to the others.

Even while Sherri Finkbine decided that medically and ethically an abortion was the right decision, she was "limp with fear" just thinking about it. That's how pregnant women died in 1962, she thought. Going into the back alley. Perforating their own uteruses and other horrors.

But Sherri's obstetrician reassured her. He said he was talking about a quick, sterile hospital procedure. Sherri just had to write a note to the Good Samaritan hospital's abortion committee, explaining why she had to have an abortion. It was routine. Up to two dozen therapeutic abortions—for women with cancers or heart ailments or psychiatric disorders, for example—were performed in Phoenix each year. "Don't worry," the doctor said. "It's already approved."

So Sherri prepared for her abortion. But before she entered the hospital, she wanted to thank the *Arizona Republic* for publishing the news about the dangers of thalidomide. If not for the stories in the paper, she'd still be carrying a deeply damaged fetus and completely unaware of that fact. And she wanted to amplify the newspaper's warning so that all women living in the Phoenix region would know to avoid this bad drug. Sherri arranged to talk to the newspaper's medical reporter, and soon a frontpage story, PILL CAUSING DEFORMED INFANTS MAY COST WOMAN HER BABY HERE, ran inside an eye-catching black border.

The *Republic* didn't give Sherri's name, but within days, her identity was public knowledge. The *New York Times,* NBC, and news outlets all over the country—and the world—were calling and their reporters swarming down on the Finkbine house. As Sherri put it, "The storm had broken in its fullest fury."

The same day that the newspaper printed the black-bordered story, Good Samaritan Hospital postponed, some said canceled, the abortion. With encouragement from the County Attorney, hospital administrators worried that all the publicity might stimulate someone to sue the hospital for performing an abortion that was not strictly within Arizona law, a statute that permitted abortion only to save the life of the mother. The hospital decided to take the matter to court to ask a judge for a ruling about the hospital's liability.

Sherri and her lawyers were prepared to go into court and make the case that her abortion was justified on psychiatric grounds; giving birth to a profoundly damaged baby could well cause her to become suicidal. The judge, however, felt he could not hold a formal hearing because no one had, in fact, objected to the abortion. Nevertheless, the hospital refused to go ahead with the procedure, afraid of what its spokesman called "distasteful publicity."

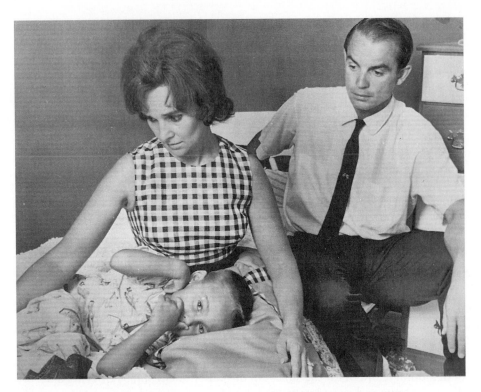

Phoenix, Arizona, July 26, 1962. Sherri and Robert L. Finkbine continued their parental duties last night after filing a court suit aimed at clearing the way for an abortion. Mrs. Finkbine, a Phoenix television performer, says she inadvertently took a drug blamed for the birth of malformed babies. She seeks the abortion rather than risk the birth of such a child. Here, she and her husband tuck into bed one of their four healthy children, 4-year-old Stevie (AP/Wide World Photos). (Original caption)

On July 31, Sherri Finkbine issued a 71-word statement to the press expressing her frustration with the courts, her desire to find a solution that was clearly within the law, and her decision "to seek help in a more favorable climate." That night Sherri put on what she called "a preposterous disguise" to protect herself from the local press and flew from Phoenix to Los Angeles, on her way to Stockholm, Sweden. There she planned to petition physicians for permission to obtain an abortion. In Los Angeles, before boarding the plane that would carry her across the North Pole to Sweden, Sherri held a news conference during which she defined that European nation as more advanced than the United States because there, a woman's abortion was a decision "up to medical men—whereas here, it is up to the courts." The press and millions of Americans tracked Mrs. Finkbine's every move.

Sherri Finkbine captured the attention of America partly because she talked out loud and in public about a subject that women of that day only whispered about to their best friends, their husbands, or their boyfriends. Also, Sherri did

Los Angeles, August 4. As newsmen questioned her about the abortion of the baby she fears may be deformed, Mrs. Sherri Finkbine wipes away a tear at Los Angeles airport today, as she and her husband departed by air for Sweden. Mrs. Finkbine, who presides over a children's television show in Phoenix, Ariz., plans to have the abortion because of her use of a dangerous tranquilizer drug. (AP/Wide World Photos) (Original caption)

not raise thoughts of sex-gone-wrong or even of women's rights. She spoke only in terms of a mother's duty to spare a damaged fetus from a painful life. Even though she didn't say it, she implied that a woman could justifiably make a *choice* about a pregnancy that had already taken hold. In 1962, no American had heard a nice woman suggest such a thing in public.

On the other hand, in 1962 hundreds of thousands if not millions of Americans knew women who had abortions. In 1960 in a statement meant to emphasize the utter failure of state laws banning abortion, the American Medical Association placed the annual number of illegal abortions in the United States at one million. This was a very large number, but across American history, no matter what the law said, girls and women had always looked for and found abortion practitioners in cities and towns all over the country. This was true during the first 150 years of nationhood when abortion was not generally treated as a crime before "quickening," that is, before the pregnant woman announced that she felt the fetus move within her body. And it was true after the middle of the nineteenth century, when in state after state, medical men striving to bolster the status, authority, and client base of obstetricians worked with state legislators to craft anti-abortion statutes.

By 1960, fertility control had become more important to women in this country than ever, partly because in that year over 40 percent of women 16 and older held a job. Fertility control had also become more possible: in 1960, the birth control pill came on the market. More than two-thirds of all white, married women already used some form of contraceptive then, but the birth control pill achieved amazingly quick acceptance. Within 5 years, 6.5 million married women and uncounted but vast numbers of unmarried women were using the pill. (Young, white women were particularly likely to get a prescription. By 1965, 80 percent of white, non-Catholic college graduates 20–24 had done so.) And yet, with so many girls and women employed or in school and interested in planning the timing of their pregnancies and the size of their families—and so many women underpaid, unemployed, unmarried, or impregnated by abusive or irresponsible men—huge numbers found they needed to combine birth control with abortion to achieve a tolerable degree of fertility control.

In 1962, when Sherri Finkbine spoke forthrightly to the press about her determination to get an abortion, the hundreds of thousands of other women also determined to end pregnancies they couldn't manage aimed for a much lower profile. No one knows how many of these women found criminal practitioners to help them. But one surprising fact has emerged from recent studies of the illegal era: relatively few women were killed or even maimed in the so-called back alley, especially after the early 1940s when antibiotics became available and all invasive procedures became safer. The fact is, most practitioners were experienced; many were physicians or other kinds of medical experts such as nurses and naturopaths. Most performed many abortions day in and day out and knew what they were doing.

Putting the back-alley butcher at the center of our "memory" of the illegal era has allowed us to overlook what was arguably the most certain source of danger to women then: the law. (State laws criminalizing abortion, most of them written in the mid-nineteenth century, outlawed the destruction of a fetus and carried various fines and prison sentences for the practitioner and sometimes for the woman herself. The laws typically aimed to protect women from harm and from the "indecency" associated with pamphlets or books that gave women information about how to prevent conception. Historians have shown that the laws were enacted initially as part of an effort to discredit "nonregular" medical practitioners such as midwives, and thereby elevate the standing of the medical profession.) Most essentially, the state antiabortion laws forbade women to control their fertility, their own bodies, probably a dangerous state of affairs for anyone. And the laws certainly created opportunities for some unskilled, ignorant crooks who wanted to make a buck off of women's vulnerability. Some women did die tragically under the hands of such miscreants. According to the stories women have told about their efforts to achieve fertility control through abortion then, being pushed into the space the law allocated

for abortion meant that women were often burdened by the dehumanizing consequences of antiabortion statues: fear and degradation.

Many practitioners understood the basis of that fear. As one Pittsburgh
physician put it, "The problem was that even if you were a competent doctor,
the whole thing meant that you were doing it in your office under dangerous
conditions." And Lawrence Lader, a journalist and prominent early abortion
rights activist wrote about this time, "The media carried 'scare propaganda'
stories suggesting that an abortionist's office was 'where you went to be
killed.'" A great deal of terror must have been stimulated by the sheer degradation of being forced into shameful, shady criminal activity because one had
had shameful sex, because one was willing to mess with what was defined then
as female destiny.

The journey to the abortion practitioner's office was often terrifying.
Women were picked up by arrangement in strangers' cars, forced to wear dark
glasses so they wouldn't know where they were going, sometimes given no
information about what would happen to them on the operating table, and
later blindfolded so they wouldn't see the faces of those who helped them. This
is what the law made necessary. Women worried about the practitioner's com-
petence, about the possibility that the city police might raid the office in the
middle of the abortion, and that they might end up in the public eye despite all
their efforts to hide the abortion. This could happen if a newspaper reporter
snapped their picture in the middle of a raid or if they were forced into court
to testify against the abortion practitioner.

Thousands of pages of transcripts from abortion trials show that after
World War II, the decades-old agreement between abortion practitioners and
the police—"no death, no prosecution"—no longer prevailed in many cities.
Now in the conservative postwar climate, police and district attorneys were
under pressure to show that they were doing their jobs, especially exposing sin
and vice. Abortion raids and trials became important parts of antivice campaigns—presented to the public as spectacles in the morning paper. And these
events announced the new, punishing danger that any woman associated with
abortion could encounter. Sherri Finkbine's deliberate and relatively dignified
journey to Stockholm was quite different from the lurid, degrading experiences
of so many others. The transcripts that remain record courtroom sessions during which the woman who obtained the abortion was typically made to
describe the most intimate details of her sex life. She also had to tell everything
she could remember about the abortion, including how her body was arrayed
on the table, how far apart her legs were spread, and so forth.

In 1962, most abortions performed were illegal. Still, large numbers of
women were too scared to take the risks associated with the criminal abortion
arena, even if they were utterly determined to control their fertility. Many of
those who had resources—money, knowledge, family doctors—applied, like
Sherri Finkbine, to hospital abortion boards for permission to end a pregnancy,
usually because of a physical or mental health problem. These boards were official groups of doctors from which professional, expert diagnoses and decisions
about the cases of individual women could be issued in one voice. No single

doctor had to take on the responsibility of making a decision. The abortion committees gave doctors legal protection and ensured that the "proper" ratio of live births to abortions was maintained by the hospital.

Dr. Alan Guttmacher, a great champion of these committees, described how his committee of doctors worked at this time at Mount Sinai Hospital in New York. "No case is considered unless the staff ob-gyn desiring to carry out the procedure presents affirmative letters from two consultants in the medical field involved. . . . The case is then carefully discussed and if any member of the five on the committee opposes therapeutic interruption, the procedure is disallowed."

Women who went through this ordeal in the 1950s and 1960s remember the experience with the abortion committee as among the most awful of their lives. Many were denied permission; some were granted the abortion. Thousands who were "successful" with the committee found out, to their horror, that they had been given permission to have an abortion only if they were sterilized at the same time. Over 53 percent of teaching hospitals in the United States made simultaneous sterilization a condition of approval for the abortion. In remembering the experience, many women have talked about having been "on trial" before a group of male physicians who did not pay attention to the cardinal principle of the U.S. legal system: they did not assume the woman's innocence.

But what happened in 1962 to a woman who lacked the money, the knowledge or the heart to deal with an illegal practitioner *and* who lacked the resources, the connections, or the willingness to plead her case before a hospital board? What happened to women who, despite these obstacles, determined they were carrying a pregnancy they couldn't manage?

People who saw the results of anti-abortion laws firsthand in the illegal era — the physicians and public health officials who kept tabs on emergency room traffic—were well aware of the fate of this cohort, often the poorest women, often women of color. These were the women who turned to self-abortion. These were the women so desperate and resourceless, so shamed and determined, that they'd take up a hideous array of herbs and implements, despite the specter of damage and death from self-styled abortions that haunted every woman in those days. Dr. Alfred Kinsey, the renowned biologist/sexologist and his colleagues estimated a few years before Sherri Finkbine's ordeal that 75 to 85 percent of septic (infective) abortions were self-induced. An obstetrician in Washington, D.C., observed in 1958 that "attempts to suppress abortion simply raised the self-induced abortion rate and consequently the death rate."

With the sole exception of Sherri Finkbine, then, the very large number of women who sought and obtained abortions in the early 1960s did so secretly, quietly, often desperately. If these women were exposed in a raid, in the pages of the local paper, in court, Americans usually saw the faces of terrified victims. Sherri Finkbine was something new. When she stood before a microphone, in front of hordes of newspaper and radio reporters, she looked pretty, well-dressed, like a sad but very dignified and determined young matron. This did not mean, of course, that Americans loved Sherri in the summer of 1962, but they did feel engaged with her situation. Thousands were moved to tell Sherri directly what they thought about her decision. She received phone calls from strangers, letters, telegrams, recipes for herbal concoctions that would cure the fetus, religious medals, and offers to adopt the baby. One writer prescribed a ride on a roller coaster; another suggested Sherri should smell turpentine fumes. "From New York came the advice of two quarts of gin for three days with hot baths, hard work, no food and no sleep."

People wrote letters to the editor, and Sherri recalled, "One put a black curse on us." Among the hate mail the Finkbines received was a letter accusing Sherri "of starting to campaign for the legalization of unnecessary abortion so that girls who wanted to lead immoral lives could get their babies murdered legally by the thousands." Sifting through the mail, Sherri and Bob Finkbine held fast to their belief that they were doing the right thing. "Yet," Sherri mused later, it was a challenge because "thousands of people sought to judge us and their sickening letters are something that I've had a hard time forgetting."

In part, Americans had so much to say about, and to say to, Sherri Finkbine that summer because they saw a number of their own concerns reflected in the young woman's situation. Of course for many, abortion was the main issue. But Sherri's experience terrified thousands of others who were not thinking about abortion. After all, an innocuous-looking pill swallowed by a perfectly respectable woman had turned out to be a profoundly damaging compound.

Americans had recently become a country of tranquilizer-gulpers. In 1957, physicians wrote 35 million prescriptions for tranquilizers—now called the "wonder drug of the 'fifties"—which represented 1.2 billion doses. In 1960, researchers at Columbia University's medical school estimated that "one in every seven Americans is taking tranquilizers as an escape from anxiety." Some who considered Sherri's plight wondered what the country was coming to, with so much pill popping. A letter-writer to the *New York Times* asked, "What is a little disturbing is the [idea] that taking sleeping pills is a normal thing to do. Is it? Can no one sleep in this mid-twentieth century? Is it worth asking why?"

But others were more concerned about how a bad drug like thalidomide could wind up in a pill, much less in the body of a pregnant woman. Why didn't the U.S. Food and Drug Administration (FDA) know about this disaster-in-the-making? How could a drug manufacturer market it? With so many eager consumers, wasn't the government responsible for protecting Americans from drugs that might harm them?

One prominent pharmacology expert pointed out that the opportunity to make massive profits from tranquilizers and other new drugs had turned drug companies into marketing machines: "A generation ago new drugs, particularly those for relatively minor complaints such as insomnia, only gradually achieved widespread popularity.... Today 'educational' representatives of drug houses visit each physician regularly. Pounds of lavish and expensive drug brochures assault the physician by mail. Most medical journals are crowded with handsome advertisements, many printed in full color on heavy cardboard or metallic paper.... New drugs thus find huge markets within a few months."

According to a former FDA employee in the early 1960s, the drug companies had recently developed skills for manipulating that government agency as well. The FDA had become "merely a service bureau" for the drug industry. The official added in testimony before Congress that sometimes, "orders come 'from above' to medical officers to certify a new drug on the grounds that the drug company itself was the best judge of its safety."

In the case of thalidomide, as we will see, a key government employee did her job well and took steps to protect the public. But nevertheless the agency came off looking irresponsible. It had allowed thalidomide's manufacturer, the Merrell Company in Cincinnati, to distribute the drug for testing purposes to 1,200 doctors scattered across the country, a practice an FDA official later acknowledged "suggested commercialization under the guise of investigational use." The fact was, no one at the FDA had thought of testing thalidomide or other drugs for potential harmfulness to the human embyro, a particularly disturbing omission in 1962, two years after the introduction of the birth control pill, another pharmacological "wonder" that raised questions about a drug's long-term impact on women's reproductive and general health.

When Americans looked at Sherri Finkbine, then, they saw a woman whose innocent drug taking deeply damaged her fetus. When they learned about what had happened to this woman, they also found out about hundreds of other pregnant women, in Germany, France, Great Britain, Belgium, who had in the last couple of years also taken thalidomide as a tranquilizer or sleeping medication and ended up with babies who were damaged or dead. The news created a sense of vulnerability and a deep sense of frustration, as one FDA official put it, about the failure of the Germans to communicate to the British and the British to the Americans.

In 1957, a German drug company, Gruenthal, had introduced a thalidomide compound called Contergan that turned out to be a terrific sedative, causing a deep sleep and no hangover. Soon Germans were taking this drug, which required no prescription, at the rate of 15 million pills a month. Gruenthal mixed thalidomide with aspirin and sold the medication to treat colds, coughs, flu, nervousness, migraine headaches, asthma, and other conditions. The company produced a liquid form for children; some people referred to this version as the country's "babysitter." And Gruenthal marketed the pill as a response to the nausea of pregnancy. In Great Britain, an advertisement stressed the safety of Distoval, the English version, by featuring a picture of a small child taking a bottle from the medicine cabinet.

Soon pediatric clinics in these countries began to report the birth of children with absent or partially absent limbs, deformed ears, various internal deformities including malformed intestines and sometimes, heart defects. Approximately one-third of these babies died. A medical writer in *Scientific American* called these "the luckier ones." At first no one associated these damaged babies with thalidomide. Pediatric experts suggested the cause might be a virus or even radioactive fallout. By early 1962, experts began to notice geographic patterns and to suspect a connection between drug use and damage. In Hamburg, Germany, for example, no cases of this disorder (phocomedlia) had

Frances Kelsey Behind Microphones. Dr. Frances Kelsey, the
Food and Drug Administration medical officer who kept
thalidomide off the American market, is shown as she appeared
before a Senate operations subcomittee here today [August 1,
1962]. The senators called Dr. Kelsey to ask her about pressures
she withstood before the drug was proved dangerous.
(© Bettmann/CORBIS) (Original caption)

occurred between 1949 and 1959. Then one case popped up in 1959. The next
year, 30 babies were born with missing limbs in that city, then 154 in 1961.
Clearly, a new clinical syndrome had appeared.

In the meantime, however, the American manufacturer of thalidomide
took the position that "no causal relationship between thalidomide and [dam-
aged babies] has been established." The drug company pressed the FDA
employee in charge of overseeing the review of the thalidomide application to
complete the investigation so the product could be marketed as soon as possible. The FDA pharmacologist, Dr. Frances Kelsey, described Merrell's pressure
tactics: "They came [to my office] in droves. They wrote letters and they
telephoned—as often as three times a week. They telephoned my superiors and
they came to see them too." The investigation was taking so long because
Dr. Kelsey had worried about the drug even before the news arrived from
Germany.

Among Dr. Kelsey's concerns were questions about the drug's impact on
fetuses. During World War II she had studied the uses of quinine in treating

London: Phillippa Bradourne, 10, an armless thalidomide
victim, uses her toes to present a bouquet to Princess Anne at
Grosvenor House Antiques Fair [June 14, 1972].
(© Bettmann/CORBIS) (Original caption)

malaria. A colleague noted later that Dr. Kelsey had conceived the far-sighted
notion that "the fetus or newborn may be pharmacologically an entirely different organism from the adult." In the end, of course, Dr. Kelsey was correct. She
effectively blocked the release of thalidomide in the United States, and in
August 1962, President Kennedy honored her with the Gold Medal Award for
Distinguished Civilian Service. She was widely considered the heroine of the
whole thalidomide affair.

Dr. Kelsey's scientific caution ended up protecting the pregnancies of
untold but vast numbers of women in the United States. Women all over the
country wrote her letters thanking her and enclosing photographs of their
healthy babies. Yet in 1962, no one had the vocabulary to refer to the matters
involved in this affair as women's rights issues or even gendered issues at all.
Dr. Kelsey, though, unwittingly provided the press with an opportunity to

inject gender matters into coverage of the thalidomide affair. The press stressed the pharmacologist's "two jobs," medical officer with the Food and Drug Administration and "keeping house" for her husband and two daughters, Susan, 15, and Christine, 12. The press also emphasized Dr. Kelsey's tenuous connection to femininity, reporting that she wore suits and low heels, and cut her hair short in a "somewhat mannish style." On the day that Dr. Kelsey was awarded the gold medal, the *New York Times* noted that she wore no lipstick, but approved of her "concession" to femininity; "She left at home her flat-heeled shoes and wore mid-heels." In other words, the thalidomide episode was not defined as a women's issue, but then again, it was.

As for Sherri Finkbine, when Americans looked at her, they could identify with a person who had taken tranquilizers, and they were concerned about a woman whose pregnancy had made her especially vulnerable to a drug company's mistakes and especially dependent on government vigilance. There were also many Americans who paid particular attention to Sherri Finkbine during July and August of 1962 because the ground was shifting so dramatically then around the experience—and the meanings—of sex, pregnancy, and motherhood in the United States. Sherri's ordeal resonated as a significant seismic shiver. What happened confirmed that reproductive politics was a topic for public discussion.

Ever since the birth control pill had come on the market two years before, Americans had struggled to adjust to public discussions of sex and fertility control. Many struggled hardest to adjust to the idea that sex and pregnancy were now easily separated. A woman merely needed to swallow one pill a day for a certain number of days a month, and she could have sex as often as she liked without becoming pregnant. The pill redefined pregnancy and motherhood as choices. Women could now show up in their gynecologist's office, informed and certain about what they wanted. The doctor merely had to fill out a prescription form. These were revolutionary developments.

The widespread use of the pill also clarified the fact that women's bodies were dependent on FDA protection. Throughout the early 1960s, the press and millions of women paid close attention to reports connecting the birth control pill and thromboembolic (related to blood clotting) disease. And the pill made clear that women's reproductive functions were now the target of corporate profits as women became consumers in the domain of fertility control. When Sherri Finkbine stood before the microphone in Phoenix and talked about her damaged pregnancy, it was a remarkable event. But Americans had recently learned that pregnancy—a word that could not be uttered on television in the 1950s—could now be discussed in the "public square" and the country would survive.

Abortion was inching more slowly into the "public square" at the time all eyes were focused on the thalidomide tragedy. Doctors had begun talking among themselves about the fact that many of the therapeutic abortions approved by hospital abortion boards were not strictly within the law since most state laws specified that the only legal justification for abortion was saving a woman's life. Some doctors began to speak out and write articles arguing that abortion should be permitted on humanitarian, psychiatric, and eugenic grounds. Some public health officials began to write in professional journals about the fact that nearly four times as many women of color as white women were victims of abortion-related deaths, mostly self-induced procedures. In 1960 the American Law Institute endorsed liberalized abortion laws which would permit the procedure for physical and mental health reasons, for fetal defects, or when the pregnancy was the result of rape or incest. The same year, the American Medical Association stated publicly that laws against abortion were unenforceable, and soon thereafter, for the first time in the United States, a women's organization, the Society for Humane Abortion in California, explained abortion as a matter of women's right to control their reproductive lives and health. All of these developments shaped the way the public paid attention to Sherri Finkbine and understood what she was talking about.

Even after the Finkbines arrived in Sweden, Americans followed their every move, reading daily newspaper accounts of their progress through that country's medical bureaucracy. And it was a plodding progress, spread out over two weeks and involving interviews with the hospital's "curator of abortions," and with psychiatrists and gynecologists, and a course of x-rays. Afterward, Sherri remembered, "The doctors there were extremely thorough, intensive, and asked probing questions in sessions that lasted hours." All the resulting information was submitted to the 10-person Royal Medical Board of Sweden which met every Friday to consider abortion applications. And then Sherri and Bob Finkbine had to wait.

The Finkbines knew that approval was not certain. In 1961 the Swedish Board had granted half of the abortion requests they reviewed, approximately 2,000 out of 4,000. The Finkbines were worried because they knew that the Swedish government and its physicians did not want to become what Sherri called "a beacon to expectant mothers." So the wait was nerve-wracking: "We had done all we could. We could do nothing else now except wait and pray."

Sherri clearly recalled the moment of decision. She and her husband were sitting in their hotel room. "Then the phone rang," she remembered, "and Bob sprang to answer it. For endless seconds he said nothing, just listened. I thought the decision must be no, that the doctor was explaining why it had gone against us. Then Bob exclaimed, 'Oh Doctor, that's wonderful! Thank you! Thank you very much!'"

The next day, August 18, Sherri had her abortion at Karolinska Hospital in Stockholm, and as it turned out, the fetus had indeed been deeply damaged by thalidomide. The doctor who had performed the surgery firmly counseled Sherri afterward, "It was not a baby. You must think of it as an abnormal growth within you. It would never have been a normal child."

At the end of August, Sherri Finkbine returned to the United States and to her four young children in Phoenix. Then and over the next couple of months as she remained in the public eye, she spoke out about the meaning of her abortion experience. She always pointed out that her ordeal had focused attention on the need for stronger oversight of drug testing and distribution. Indeed,

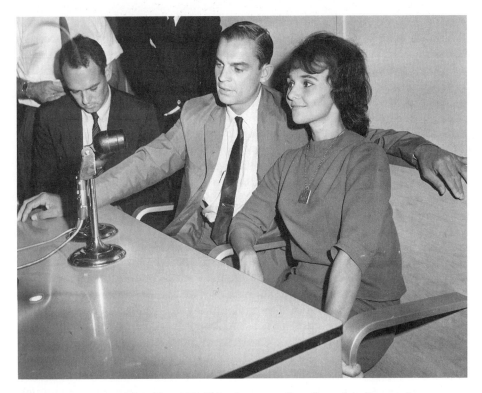

Chicago, August 26. Mrs. Sherri Finkbine has a small smile on her face as she and her husband Robert are interviewed by newsmen after their arrival at Chicago's O'Hare airport on a flight from Stockholm, Sweden, where she underwent a legal abortion. Mrs. Finkbine, who had the operation for fear the expected child would be deformed due to her use of the drug thalidomide, said, "Our initial goal was six children and I don't think we should change." The Finkbines now have four children. (AP/Wide World Photos) (Orignal caption)

Sherri's experience and the experiences of several hundred other American women who took thalidomide and gave birth to damaged babies moved Congress to hold hearings on the FDA drug-approval process and related issues, and moved President Kennedy to recommend a 25 percent increase in FDA staff, and the development of stricter procedures to protect American consumers. In October 1962, the FDA achieved what one analyst defined as an unusual milestone: approving not one new drug during the entire month. The American public was pleased with this inaction. Following the publicity about thalidomide, 76.3 percent of Americans wanted the government to exercise stricter control over drugs than it had.

Sherri Finkbine also made several prominent statements about abortion after she returned from Sweden. She said she hoped that all the attention she got served as a catalyst for abortion reform. "I think," she said, "[my experience] pointed up a real human need and forced people to at least talk about it and to face the issue." And despite the hate mail and a statement from the Pope that associated Sherri with murder, she was willing to publicly express her strongest feelings: "I hope it has hastened the day when our nation, advanced and enlightened in so many other respects, will take a fresh, unprejudiced look at its abortion procedures." Decades later, Sherri Finkbine's daughter Kristin Atwell credited her mother with breaking the silence that surrounded illegal abortion and helping to give birth to the grassroots reproductive rights movement.

Just over 10 years would elapse between the end of Sherri's ordeal and *Roe v. Wade*, the Supreme Court decision that overturned state anti-abortion statutes and legalized abortion nationally. Looking back, Sherri Finkbine becomes a sign of what was to come. Across the 1960s, ever larger numbers of mothers of young children went to work, a condition of life that depended on fertility control. In the late 1960s, women from families like the Finkbines, with incomes over $10,000 a year, worked outside the home at a rate of about 60 percent. By the early 1970s, the majority of mothers of school-age children were working outside the home, most because they were helping to support their families. An increasing number were the sole support of their families. More women than ever were graduating from college during the 1960s and receiving graduate degrees in the 1970s. Becoming educated and having the opportunity to earn a decent salary gave many women the tools to demand a new degree of independence. That included, for growing numbers, a determination to manage their reproductive lives legally, to decide for themselves whether and when to become mothers, and if they became unwed mothers, to decide for themselves whether to raise their own children. This determined sense of independence grew and was nourished during a period of vibrant, multifaceted human rights activities. Women developed language, organizations, and strategies to claim rights to control their reproductive lives at the same time that African Americans, Latinos and Latinas, gays and lesbians, disabled persons, and other marginalized groups were developing the tools and grassroots energy to claim social, economic, and political rights.

Even after Sherri Finkbine gave a public face to the issue, the most vocal proponents of legal abortion were doctors horrified by the deathly parade of self-aborted women in hospital emergency rooms, and population control advocates. In the early 1960s, neither group spoke in terms of *women's rights*. After the Supreme Court's 1965 *Griswold v. Connecticut* decision, which legalized birth control for married couples under a doctrine of "privacy rights," women began to speak out about abortion access as a necessary feature of reproductive privacy. Between 1965 and 1973, many women's groups began to speak out in terms of *abortion rights* and to work for the repeal, not simply the reform of abortion laws.

Grassroots groups such as the Clergy Consultation Service on Abortion begun in New York in 1967 and Jane, an underground abortion services network in Chicago started in 1969, made safe, clandestine abortion available for thousands of women. Colorado, California, North Carolina, New York, Hawaii, and Washington all liberalized, though did not abolish, their abortion statutes in the late 1960s. By 1971, over half of Americans favored legalizing abortion.

A complicated group of developments—demographic trends, including the ongoing movement of women into the workforce; the rise of the population control and antiwelfare movements; the persistence of illegal abortion; the emergence of feminism and grassroots support of abortion reform; the actions of a few state legislatures, and the climate of the era that supported "rights" claims—pushed the medical and legal communities to support formal legalization. *Roe v. Wade* was, in part, a pragmatic response to this complex range of developments.

The *Roe v. Wade* decision was based on four constitutional principles: (a) women have a fundamental, constitutional right to reproductive autonomy and privacy, and governmental restrictions to that right must be subjected to "strict scrutiny"; (b) the government must remain neutral regarding a woman's decision whether or not to have an abortion; (c) in the period before "viability," the government may restrict abortion only in the interests of protecting the woman's health; (d) after "viability" (the point at which the fetus is sufficiently developed to live outside of the woman's womb), the government may prohibit abortion, but laws must make exceptions that permit abortion when necessary to protect a woman's health or life. *Roe* established a "trimester" concept of pregnancy: During the first third of the pregnancy, women have an unimpeded right to abortion; during the following two trimesters, a schedule of increasing restrictions apply.

While no organized anti-abortion groups existed when Sherri Finkbine became a household name in the summer of 1962, or at any other time before *Roe v. Wade*, such organizations began to form immediately following the Supreme Court's decision.

AN INTERPRETATION

When Sherri Finkbine made it clear to her husband, her doctor, her employer, a judge, a slew of reporters, and the American public that she was going to abort her pregnancy, no matter what the law said, she became a historical, transitional figure. Before Sherri had the operation, she kept her public statements focused on motherhood and the responsibilities of a good mother. At all public appearances, she had her husband, Bob Finkbine, by her side, lending his support, his approval, and his protection.

Sherri Finkbine was a white, middle-class matron of her times: recognizable and respectable, unremarkable and unthreatening. When she spoke to Americans, she was addressing a people increasingly saturated by media. And the packagers of news then increasingly recognized that the individual dramas of ordinary people helped Americans to understand the world they lived in, and sold the news.

Sherri addressed the consumers of news. At the same time, she *represented* the American consumer in several crucial ways. Her experience brought attention to the ubiquity and vulnerability of drug consumers. Also, in the dawn of the era of choice—an era ushered in by the birth control pill—Sherri Finkbine suggested that even for pregnant women pregnancy could be a choice, especially for women who had the resources to be choice-makers.

In an entirely new way, Sherri Finkbine's statements and actions suggested the complicated proposition that middle-class American women, the world's most careful consumers, had the right to give birth to perfect babies. In the end, many Americans understood and approved of Sherri's actions because, with the rise of the adoption market and other postwar developments, even newborns and children had become commodities of sorts. As a white woman with enough money to be a legitimate choice maker, Sherri Finkbine could make a winning case that, as such, she deserved a high-quality child.

Sherri Finkbine did open the door to public discussions of abortion and to the idea that a woman's life need not be in danger for that woman to decide that she could not manage a particular pregnancy. The more than one million women a year who were getting illegal and therapeutic abortions in the United States surely felt vindicated or at least represented honorably by Sherri Finkbine. The girls and women who arranged for illegal abortions over the next decade may have felt more justified and determined because for a moment in 1962, a well-dressed wife and mother had told everybody that she was going to get an abortion, and afterward, her life went on.

Sherri Finkbine was perhaps most importantly, a transitional figure because she framed her need for an abortion as more than an individual crisis. As a woman of her time, she didn't mention women's rights, and may not even have thought in term of "rights" at all. She did not direct her remarks to politicians or other public figures because, in the early 1960s, abortion was not a topic that politicians or other prominent leaders discussed in public. But she did take on the task of explaining to the American public that this was a problem any woman could face, and she wanted to save every woman from such a tragic ordeal. In this sense, she foreshadowed both the feminist politics of abortion and the strategy of speak-outs, events in which women who had illegal abortions stood up in public in the late 1960s and early 1970s, and told their own stories as a way to speak for themselves and for all women—to make the case that abortion rights were crucial if women were to achieve the status of full citizens in the United States.

Sources: The United States Congress holds hearings on a wealth of subjects every year. The published records of congressional hearings include expert and citizen testimony, reprinted news articles, and analyses from mass media and professional publications, relevant studies, and other materials. These hearings are extremely rich sources of information about many subjects, including the ordeal of Sherri Finkbine and the thalidomide tragedy. The hearings on thalidomide and related matters, conducted between January and August of 1963 ("Interagency Coordination in Drug Research and Regulation, Hearings before the Subcommittee on Reorganization and International Organizations of the Committee on Government Operations," U.S. Senate, 88th Congress, 1st and 2nd sessions), are bound into five volumes and can be obtained from libraries that are designated "government respositories." During July and August of 1962, the *New York Times* closely covered the thalidomide story, including Sherri Finkbine's predicament.

Sherri Finkbine told her story several times in the period immediately following the events recounted in this essay. See: "The Lesser of Two Evils," Sherri Finkbine, in *The Case for Legalized*

Abortion Now, ed. Alan F. Guttmacher, M.D. (Berkeley, CA: Diablo Press, 1967) and "The Baby We Didn't Dare Have," Sherri Finkbine as told to Joseph Stocker, *Redbook,* January 1963.

For information about women seeking and obtaining abortions—and about the state of reproductive politics in the United States before the legalization of abortion in 1973—see the following: Leslie J. Reagan, *When Abortion Was a Crime: Women, Medicine, and Law in the United States, 1867–1973* (Berkeley: University of California Press, 1997); Carole Joffe, *Doctors of Conscience: The Struggle to Provide Abortion before and after Roe v. Wade* (Boston: Beacon Press, 1995); Rickie Solinger, *The Abortionist: A Woman against the Law* (New York: Free Press, 1994), and *Beggars and Choosers: How the Politics of Abortion Shapes Adoption, Abortion, and Welfare in the United States* (New York: Hill and Wang, 2001). An indispensable volume for understanding reproductive politics in this country is Rosalind Pollack Petchesky, *Abortion and Women's Choice: The State, Sexuality, and Reproductive Freedom,* rev. ed. (Boston: Northeastern University Press, 1990).

14

THE IRANIAN HOSTAGE CRISIS

Walter LaFeber

During the 444 days in 1979 to 1981 that Americans waited for the return of 76 American hostages, held by Iranian militants, they were entertained by a song by country artist Kenny Rogers. It was called "Coward of the County," and it told the story of a young man named Tommy and his efforts to deal with a menacing trio of local punks called the Gatlin boys. Raised by his father to believe that one could achieve manhood without fighting, Tommy had always walked away from trouble—and, in the process, had become known as the "coward of the county." But when the Gatlin boys gang-rape Tommy's girlfriend, Becky, Tommy takes his father's picture down from above the fireplace, finds the Gatlin boys in a bar, and avenges Becky's rape with a fury born of righteous indignation and "twenty years of crawling." Of course, from then on no one called Tommy the "coward of the county."

It was a good song, and no doubt would have been popular under any circumstances. But it had special appeal in 1980 because its parable seemed so closely to parallel the American experience with the Iranian hostage crisis. To many Americans, the conduct of the Iranian militants seemed no less barbaric and no more explicable than that of the Gatlin boys; indeed, the holding of American hostages seemed a violation as complete and horrifying as that Becky had experienced. According to Rogers's story, Tommy's problem—and the American nation's—was fundamentally one of the spirit, something inside Tommy, rather than a matter of some exterior condition that Tommy was helpless to deal with. In his July 15, 1979, television address, President Jimmy Carter had interpreted the American condition in much the same terms: as a "moral and spiritual crisis," a crisis of the "national will." And like Tommy, Carter and his advisors attempted to resolve this spiritual crisis through action—the rescue mission of April 1980—only to discover that the world no longer yielded to the brawling barroom tactics of the Wild West.

Walter LaFeber's narrative confirms this view of the Iranian hostage crisis as a moment in which an ignorant American people acted badly. But it also tells another, more encouraging story, a story of a nation's first, begrudging adjustment to the changing distribution of economic, political, and military power in the world. The Carter administration was, of course, in charge of this process of adjustment, and the conflicts and disagreements over foreign policy that are apparent in LaFeber's account are indicative of the nation's divided sensibilities at a difficult moment in its history. To open a dialogue with the Ayatollah Khomeini or prop up the Iranian shah; to allow or refuse the shah access to the United States; to let the hostage crisis take its course or to intervene militarily—at every turn, policymakers disagreed over what ought to be done. Carter, too—Carter, especially—appeared unsure and even confused, a champion of human rights toasting the leadership of one of the world's great tyrants.

Hoping to find a way out of its confusion, the nation turned in 1980 to Ronald Reagan. His foreign policy—a reinvigorated Cold War—seemed to give Americans a welcome sense of direction. But many of Reagan's initiatives, including the invasion of the tiny Marxist country of Grenada in 1983, failed to measure up to the Berlin airlift, the naval blockade of offensive weapons into Cuba, or other compelling moments in the epic of the Cold War. As Carter and then Reagan would discover, the post-Vietnam era of the 1970s and 1980s was no longer what Time *magazine publisher Henry Luce had described in 1941 as "The American Century."*

On November 4, 1979, 400 screaming Iranian youths stormed the stone walls surrounding the United States Embassy in Iran's capital city of Tehran. They then invaded the embassy itself, captured 100 people, including 66 Americans, and declared that the Americans would be held hostage for the crimes of the "Great Satan"—the United States—against the Iranian people. Elizabeth Montagne, an American working as an embassy secretary, soon faced an Iranian holding a gun. He put a single bullet into the pistol's chamber, pointed it at Montagne's temple, and demanded the combination to an embassy safe. When she replied she did not know the combination, he began pulling the trigger on the empty chambers one by one. There was one more click to go. "Do you think I'll pull the trigger?" he asked her. "We stared at each other," Montagne recalled, and then he put the gun down. "He said: 'OK, so you don't know the combination.' I just kind of collapsed."

Montagne's horror was relived in other ways by the American hostages during the 444 days they endured captivity. The world, especially tens of millions of Americans who followed the hostages' fortunes almost hourly on television, watched the ordeal with wonder and fear. Americans soon learned, however, that the story did not actually begin that rainy November afternoon in Tehran. Like all historic events, it had deep, tangled roots. In this case the story went back to 1941 at least, when a thin 22-year-old, Muhammad Reza Pahlavi, became shah, or king, of Iran. He was made shah by the United States, Great Britain, and the Soviet Union. These nations removed his father from power because the old dictator had moved his strategically located, rich oil-producing nation too close to the Nazis. From the beginning, therefore, the young shah owed his kingdom to foreign powers. By 1946 he especially owed his throne to the United States, which that year forced the Soviets to leave Iran. The Americans then replaced the British as the dominant foreign power. When the shah's rule was threatened by a nationalist, antiforeign movement in 1953, the U.S. Central Intelligence Agency (CIA) played a key role in overthrowing the threatening movement. In partial thanks, the next year the shah allowed American oil companies to begin extracting the black gold for the first time.

By the mid-1950s the world and especially the Iranians, who had the best view, saw the young shah and the powerful Americans as political bedfellows. In 1964, the relationship was almost stretched too far. The shah agreed to a Washington request that U.S. troops stationed in Iran be liable only to U.S. law, not Iranian law—even if they committed a crime against an Iranian. The 62-year-old, bearded Ayatollah (or Islamic religious leader) Ruhollah Khomeini bitterly attacked the deal. The shah and the Americans, Khomeini declared, "have reduced the Iranian people to a level lower than that of an American dog." "The dignity of Iran," he concluded, "has been destroyed." Khomeini's influence, already immense in this nation that had followed the Shi'ite Muslims since the sixteenth century, became even greater—so great that the shah's police threw the Ayatollah out of the country. Khomeini spent 15 years of exile in Turkey, Iraq, and finally France. But whatever the distance, his influence continued to grow in Iran.

That was proved in 1970 when the shah announced that a group of visiting American investors, led by David Rockefeller of Chase Manhattan Bank, would receive large investment opportunities. Anti-American riots erupted as Khomeini condemned the deal from exile in Iraq. One of his students, Muhammad Reza Sa'idi, publicly condemned the American group. Shortly after, the shah's dreaded secret police, SAVAK, tortured the young student to death. When other Islamic leaders mounted protests, the shah cracked down with arrests, more torture, and imprisonment of the protesters and their religious leaders. In 1974 the head of Amnesty International (a London-based organization that later won the Nobel Prize for Peace for its work on behalf of human rights around the world), announced that Iran had the globe's worst human rights record.

This announcement did not cool the United States' relationship with the shah. By 1974 it grew even warmer because President Richard Nixon concluded he desperately needed Iran. Because of overspending (especially in Vietnam) and too many overseas commitments, the United States no longer had the resources to defend its allies everywhere. Nixon begged the shah to help protect vital U.S. interests in the Middle East. Americans' need for Iran, moreover, grew dramatically in 1973 and 1974, when Arab oil producers protested Israel's invasion of their ally, Egypt, by cutting off petroleum shipments to Israel's closest ally, the United States. The shah was willing to help Nixon, but for a price: almost unlimited access to the non-nuclear U.S. military arsenal. Nixon happily obliged.

With his immense oil wealth generating revenues that jumped five times to $20 billion in only a matter of months, the shah increased his defense spending seven times to nearly $10 billion between 1973 and 1977. He bought military goods, as one historian phrased it, "with the abandon of an alcoholic using a credit card in a liquor store." Thus at the very moment the shah used force against his country's powerful religious leaders, the United States was publicly sending him all the weapons he could buy. Then, in 1975 and 1976, Iran's oil revenues flattened out. The economy began to decline. The already wide gap between poor rural and well-off urban incomes greatly widened. As many

Iranians resorted to criminal activities to make a living, corruption became so rampant that the shah was advised not to begin an anticorruption campaign because, as one advisor suggested, "people will laugh."

Conditions were ripening for revolution. The first small revolutionary bands had actually appeared in 1971. Between 1972 and 1975 the country endured more than 400 bombing acts of terrorism. Americans soon became targets. Three U.S. military officers and three American civilians had been murdered by late 1976. Even the U.S. Peace Corps office, as well as the U.S. Embassy, had been blasted by bombs.

When President Carter assumed power in January of 1977, he was determined to restore American moral authority at home and abroad by emphasizing human rights—supporting, in his words, "the idealism of Jefferson" instead of the right-wing monarchs and military dictators the United States had too long supported just as long as they were anticommunist. In Iran's case, however, Carter was trapped. If he demanded that the shah stop the arrests and torture, the Iranian ruler might be overthrown and the cornerstone of U.S. military policy in the Persian Gulf region removed. The President tried to escape the trap by continuing to talk publicly about human rights, but at the same time sending over half of all American arms sales to the shah. The king was too important, revenue from the $5.7 billion in arms sales too vital for the U.S. economy, to anger the occupant of Iran's Peacock Throne.

When the shah again cracked down brutally on protesters in 1977 and 1978, Iranians believed (wrongly) that it happened with Carter's consent, if not on United States orders. Their belief seemed confirmed when President Carter visited Iran on New Year's Eve of 1977, and delivered one of the most stunning, and unfortunate, banquet toasts in recorded history. "Iran, because of the great leadership of the shah," Carter began, "is an island of stability in one of the more troubled areas of the world. This is a great tribute to you, Your Majesty, and to your leadership and to the respect and the admiration and love which your people give to you. . . . We have no other nation with whom we have closer consultations on regional problems that concern us both. And there is no leader with whom I have a deeper sense of personal gratitude and personal friendship."

Within 10 days after Carter spoke those words, massive antishah riots, led by Islamic clergy and religious students, erupted in the holy city of Qum. The police killed at least 24 people, including religious leaders. The shootings ignited a chain-reaction of protests. By November and December 1978, literally thousands of demonstrations were erupting. The death toll reached 10,000. Nearly all the dead were unarmed protesters whose only strengths were in numbers and the hot conviction that the shah had to be overthrown. "For more than a year," two close observers wrote, "literally millions of Iranians faced [the shah's] tanks and machine guns with little more than moral outrage."

Islamic religious leaders guided the demonstrators, but those leaders were divided. On one side was a small fundamentalist group that hated the shah's Western friends. This group wanted to turn Iran into a fully religious state shorn of all possible Western influence. A much larger and more powerful group of clergy wished to modernize Iran and bring it fully into the late twentieth century, but under religious direction. These moderates were less opposed to the shah's vast plans to modernize (the "White Revolution" as it became known) than to driving peasants off their land and destroying communities; the changes that only made the rich much richer and the poor desperate; and the shah's ideas that seemed to be turning the country over to nonreligious, non-Iranian developers from the West, especially from the United States. These critics pointed out that even when the shah tried to meet some of their demands by reorganizing his government in 1977, his new advisors were Iranians who, suspiciously, held degrees from universities in California, Colorado, Nebraska, Kentucky, Utah, and New York.

This growing fear of Western control even brought many educated Iranian women over to the antishah side. Their decision seemed especially remarkable because Islam required that they wear veils (*chadurs*) in public and have a traditional, and inferior, role in society. But these women were first of all Iranian and aware of the shah's devastating policies. They were also young: Half the country's population was under 16 years of age, and two-thirds was under 30 years of age. As unemployment and educational problems increased, the young, both men and women, became more radical. As the protests grew, however, they cut across age, geographical area, and class. The Islamic clergy became the steering wheel but not the engine of the revolution. As one Western expert on Iran explained: "The causes of the revolution, and its timing, were economic and political; the form of the revolution, and its pacing, owed much to the tradition of religious protest."

Americans understood none of this. Most read little or nothing about Iran or other foreign policy problems. They received their view of world events from easily digested television programs. But in the six years of growing revolution between 1971 and 1977, the three United States television networks spent an average of only five minutes per year on events in Iran. The most respected national newspaper, the *New York Times,* closed its Tehran office in 1977. Not one regular U.S. reporter remained in Iran. American experts on Iran were few, and those few were either overlooked or ignored when they tried to explain the deep economic, religious, and anti-U.S. roots of the revolution.

The upheaval confused even some observant Americans. Throughout much of the twentieth century, they had judged the anti-American sentiment of most revolutionaries by their communist ties. But Islamic fundamentalists hated atheistic communism. The revolutionaries' rallying cry was "Neither East nor West!" Soviet leaders, sharing a 1,600-mile border with Iran, and nervously watching millions of Muslims inside their own country, were nearly as fearful of the revolution as were Americans. The U.S. media, however, had long viewed the shah as a close anticommunist ally, so it began to characterize his opponents with other stereotypes—"religious fanatics," "Muslim fundamentalists," even "Islamic Marxists"—in order to discredit the revolutionaries. Columnist Meg Greenfield of *Newsweek* was one of the few exceptions. "No part of the world is more important to our well-being at the moment," she wrote in early 1979, "and no part of the world is more hopelessly and systematically and stubbornly misunderstood by us." She compared American ignorance of the Islamic Middle East with Columbus's ignorance when he landed in the New World and thought he was in India.

Greenfield and other close observers of President Carter also realized that confusion and ignorance paralyzed United States official policy. Carter's administration divided sharply between his secretary of state, Cyrus Vance, and the national security advisor in the White House, Zbigniew Brzezinski. Vance believed the problem was wholly Iranian and that the shah had to come to terms with the revolutionaries. His position would lead him to favor contact with Ayatollah Khomeini, who was now orchestrating the revolution from exile in Paris where he put his instructions on audiotapes that secretly circulated throughout Iran. Brzezinski, on the other hand, feared the shah's fall would have ramifications far beyond Iran: It could lead to a pro-Soviet Iran and a major U.S. defeat in the Cold War. Brzezinski urged that the shah establish a military regime that would ruthlessly crush the uprising. Carter could not make up his mind whether to follow Vance or Brzezinski.

By January of 1979, the shah himself could not make up his mind. Increasingly weakened by cancer of the lymph glands, which had been discovered several years earlier, and unable to destroy the revolution through either mass killings or political reforms, the king waited for advice and help from his longtime friends in Washington. But little of either advice or help appeared. Brzezinski continued to push a military solution. He even wanted to use force to prevent the plane carrying Khomeini back to Tehran from landing. But it was too late. The Iranian military, with its Muslim soldiers and its ranks infiltrated with Islamic leaders, simply disintegrated as a thousand and more troops defected each day.

On January 16, 1979, the shah and his family climbed aboard a blue-and-silver Boeing 707 and flew into exile in Egypt. Celebrations erupted on Iranian streets. On February 1, Khomeini landed in Tehran to be welcomed by two million followers. The United States, American Ambassador William Sullivan reported, was now linked in Iranian minds with "evaporating institutions." A new Iran was arising. On February 2, 45,000 U.S. citizens began to leave. Despite crowds that surrounded the U.S. Embassy shouting "Death to the Great Satan," Carter ordered 75 American diplomats to remain at their posts. Rumors spread through Tehran that the Americans were harboring hated agents of SAVAK. On February 14, Iranians, some armed, broke into the embassy, seized 70 Americans, and demanded that Carter return the shah for punishment. The Americans, however, were quickly released.

Khomeini's role in all this was not clear. He seemed to hold ultimate power, although he did not occupy a government post. Khomeini despised the United States for its long friendship with the shah, but he did not want an immediate, possibly armed, confrontation with the world's most powerful nation. It was not clear whether Khomeini controlled the mob, many of whom were political leftists and not devout followers of the Islamic clergy. He also worked with a badly divided government. Several top officials, including the new Iranian president and prime minister, were moderates. They hoped to restore some relations with Washington because they believed Iran especially needed American spare parts and other help for the nation's wrecked economy. Other Iranian leaders, however, notably those among the clergy and in the streets, hated the United States. They hoped to use the Iranian fear of the Great Satan to gain control over the revolution and the country. In May of 1979, 50,000 marched to the U.S. Embassy shouting "Death to Carter!"

The United States had no contact with either the radical left or the religious right wing in Iran. Americans talked only with the relative moderates at the top of the government, but these officials obviously did not control the street mobs. Washington knew too little about what was occurring. "We simply do not have the bios [biographies], inventory of political groups, or current levels of daily life as it evolves at various levels in Iran," the top State Department expert on the country, Henry Precht, wrote in July 1979. "Ignorance here of Iran's events is massive. The U.S. press does not do a good job but in the absence of [U.S.] Embassy reporting, we have to rely on inexperienced newsmen" for information.

Amid this "ignorance," Carter was touching a low point in his presidency during the autumn of 1979. The American economy was slipping badly, the victim of inflation and the loss of six million barrels of Iranian oil that were no longer available each day on the international market. Americans suddenly paid nearly twice the regular price for gasoline—or they did after sitting for hours in lines at the pumps. Carter's relations with both the Soviet Union and his own allies, as well as with Iran, steadily worsened. As prices jumped and gasoline supplies slumped, and both angry Democrats and Republicans circled Carter to wait for a political kill in the 1980 elections, the President escaped to his Camp David mountaintop retreat to ponder the American, and his own, decline.

He emerged to give a nationally televised address on July 15, 1979, that is unsurpassed in presidential messages for its pleading and pessimism. "It's clear that the true problems of our nation are much deeper—deeper than gasoline lines or energy shortages, deeper even than inflation or recession," he declared. "And I realize more than ever that as President I need your help." He spoke of "a moral and a spiritual crisis," a "fundamental threat to American democracy" that "strikes at the very heart and soul and spirit of our national will." The President became specific: "There is a growing disrespect for government and for churches and for schools, the news media, and other institutions." He noted the murders of John F. Kennedy, Robert Kennedy, and Martin Luther King, Jr., and how peoples' confidence in their economy had been shattered by "10 years of inflation" and the post-1973 years "when we had to face a growing dependence on foreign oil." Americans, Carter lamented, looked to the federal government for help but "found it isolated. . . . Washington, D.C. has become an island." After this litany of sadness, the president had few solutions to offer except a vague national energy plan and the hope that Americans would overcome their "crisis of confidence." Critics quickly responded that the problem was less in the American people than in their leader's confusion.

Amid this bleakest time of Carter's presidency, the shah urgently asked that he be allowed to enter the United States for treatment of his cancer.

Brzezinski, supported by two close friends of the shah—former Secretary of State Henry Kissinger and Chase Manhattan Bank President David Rockefeller—pressured Carter to grant the request. At first the President refused and, as Brzezinski recalled, "made the prophetic comment that he did not wish the shah to be here playing tennis while Americans in Tehran were being kidnapped or even killed" by mobs tearing down the U.S. Embassy. Brzezinski noted that when he objected that "we should not be influenced by threats from a third-rate regime [like Iran], and that at stake were our traditions and national honor, both Vance and Carter . . . became quite angry" with him. Three months later Vance and Carter changed their minds.

The Brzezinski–Kissinger–Rockefeller pressure, and the realization that the shah's life depended on quick medical help, led the President to reverse himself. On October 22, 1979, the shah's Gulfstream aircraft roared to a stop in the darkness of New York's LaGuardia Airport. Carter had given in, however, only after high Iranian officials had guaranteed the safety of the U.S. Embassy in Tehran during the shah's temporary stay in New York. Brzezinski then went much further. He tried to open talks with the Iranian moderates. Flying to North Africa, he met secretly with top officials, including Prime Minister Mehdi Bazargan. The secret quickly leaked. Iranian mobs (and perhaps Khomeini), concluded that Bazargan was trying to make deals with the Great Satan. On November 1, 1979, Khomeini issued a statement: "It is therefore up to the dear pupils, students and theological students to expand their attacks against the United States and Israel, so that they may force the U.S. to return the deposed and criminal shah."

At 3:00 A.M. Washington time (10:30 A.M. Tehran time) on Sunday, November 4, 1979, the Department of State's Operations Center's telephone rang. Voices in the U.S. Embassy in Tehran reported that a large mob of youths was storming the building. The mob was later estimated at about 400. The embassy was unprotected. The Iranian government had pulled its guard from around the building, but Carter was not concerned because he had been assured by Bazargan's government that the building would be safe during the shah's stay in the United States. Sixty-six Americans found themselves held hostage. Six others managed to escape and secretly lived in the Canadian Embassy until courageous Canadian officials helped sneak them out of Iran in January 1980. The mobs fell upon top-secret documents that the embassy staff had not had time to destroy. Other documents were found in small pieces in shredding machines. The Iranians painstakingly began to fit these together. Ultimately they had enough formerly secret U.S. documents to fill 60 published volumes.

More immediately, the documents revealed that since the shah had fled, the CIA had developed two operations in which it planned to work closely with the moderates. Within 48 hours after the storming of the embassy, Bazargan and other moderate leaders were driven from power. The new Iranian regime was more militant and anti-American, but neither it nor its spiritual leader, Khomeini, could fully control the youths who now occupied the embassy. Khomeini did convince them to release eight African-Americans and

The beginning of an ordeal. Within hours after Iranian militants stormed and occupied the U.S. Embassy in Tehran on November 4, 1979, American hostages are blindfolded and paraded by the mob outside the embassy.
(© Bettmann/CORBIS)

five women (including Elizabeth Montagne) because of Iran's professed respect for "oppressed" blacks and women. Otherwise, Khomeini—who apparently had at first quietly disapproved of the occupation and then changed his mind when he discovered the widespread support for it—found that the occupiers included different leaders of competing political factions. They had few common goals except to humiliate both the United States and the Iranian moderates.

The militants succeeded far more than they had hoped. Television cameras quickly showed the world graphic pictures of triumphant Iranians leading blindfolded, apparently confused Americans through the streets as crowds shouted insults. When the militants discovered that a global audience, and especially the United States, seemed to be hanging on their every word, their every burning of a U.S. flag, and their every success at putting thousands into the streets shouting antishah and anti-American slogans, they also discovered how valuable the hostages had become for their cause. Americans who could not have located Iran on a map before November 4 now became addicted to watching such daily programs as ABC-TV's *America Held Hostage* (later to become the popular *Nightline*), with Ted Koppel, an influential late-night news show created to follow the crisis in the embassy.

Carter at first profited politically. As is usual during foreign policy crises, Americans rallied around their leader as they expressed fury and frustration. In Denver three teenagers hurled a rock at a window of an Iranian; he fired a shot in return and killed one of them. The International Longshoremen's union ordered all members not to load vessels bound for Iran. A Kansas wheat farmer declared, "I'm beginning to think we should either seize [Iranian] oilfields or destroy them if we can." A New York truck driver concluded, "We might as well write off the hostages; they're going to be killed no matter what we do. We should bomb the hell out of the country so it will be a long time before anyone else does the same thing." Even the president's mother, Lillian Carter, was quoted as telling a New Hampshire men's club: "If I had a million dollars to spare, I'd look for someone to kill [Khomeini]." The men cheered. Carter's approval rating shot up from a lowly 32 percent just before the hostage seizure to 61 percent in December.

The President understood, however, that both his nation's honor and his own political future depended on freeing the hostages quickly, and certainly before the presidential elections only 11 months away. A Palo Alto, California, resident expressed the views of many Americans: "The political booby prize of 1979 should be shared by President Carter and Secretary Vance for giving a visa to the shah of Iran. . . . The United States cannot afford to have a president with such poor judgment." As one of his top aides later told the Phil Donahue television show, Carter developed an "emotional obsession" about the hostages, especially as he feared the Iranians might begin to execute one hostage each day until Carter met their demands. Those demands included the shah's return to stand trial, and the return of the shah's fortune that was variously estimated at $50 million to $250 million. The President had no intention of meeting either demand. He instead retaliated by cutting off imports of Iranian oil, froze Iran's assets (estimated at $18 billion) in U.S. banks, and ordered the aircraft carrier *Kitty Hawk* and five other warships to steam from their station in the Philippines to the Arabian Sea close by Iran.

As it became clear that the militants did not intend to surrender the hostages, American anger grew even more passionate. The *Wall Street Journal* urged a military solution that would use paratroopers and a helicopter attack to rescue the captives. Inside the privacy of the White House, Brzezinski also pushed again for military action. On December 27, 1979, however, he changed his mind when the Soviets suddenly invaded their neighbor, Afghanistan, to prop up a wobbly Communist regime. Carter was astounded and deeply angered by the invasion. He and many Americans believed it meant the Soviets were willing to use force to establish their dominance over Afghanistan and perhaps neighboring Iran. Brzezinski understood that using U.S. troops in Iran could possibly lead to a confrontation with the Soviet Union, so he reconsidered. But he and Carter, and to a lesser extent Secretary of State Vance, were now prepared to warn Moscow leaders that if the Red Army moved toward Iran and the oil-rich Persian Gulf, the United States was ready to respond with force. The president announced this "Carter Doctrine" in a nationally televised speech before Congress. Critics quickly claimed correctly that the United States did not have enough conventional power to stop any Soviet drive toward Iran. That realization led many to fear that the turmoil in Iran and the invasion of Afghanistan were setting the two superpowers on a dead-end course to nuclear war.

As tension grew, Iranian moderates recaptured some of their lost power when Abolhassan Bani Sadr was elected president. Determined to end the hostage crisis, on February 11, 1980, Bani Sadr set conditions for the captives' release: The United States must admit its "past crimes" against Iran and promise never to "interfere" again, while also recognizing Iran's right to seize the shah and recover his fortune. Carter continued to refuse to negotiate the fate of the shah, who by now had flown off to refuge in Panama. In any case, the militants were refusing to surrender the hostages to the moderate government. The Tehran power struggle became more heated. A United Nations Commission arrived in January of 1980 with the hope of negotiating the hostages' release. It was forced instead to view crippled and maimed Iranians tortured by SAVAK, was told by Bani Sadr that he sided with the militants, was threatened by street mobs, and finally decided to give up the mission.

Carter continued to seek a peaceful solution. His frustration, however, was becoming a torment. "What choices do we have," he blurted out to his close advisors in late January. "Those bastards have held our people for two months now. Nothing we have tried diplomatically has worked. The UN can't do anything, our allies have tried and struck out, everything imaginable has been attempted. We've got to take some risks." His popularity began to sink as the presidential primaries opened for the 1980 elections. "I say one thing," Carter bitterly remarked privately in March 1980, "Khomeini says another—and who does the American press believe? Khomeini!" But by trying to use the crisis for his own political gain, he gravely wounded his own credibility. On April Fool's Day, 1980, the day of a key primary in Wisconsin, Carter faced powerful opposition for the Democratic Party nomination from Senator Edward Kennedy of Massachusetts. That day, Carter called an unusual early morning press conference to announce that the hostages were about to be transferred from the militants to the more moderate Bani Sadr government. He implied this could lead to their release. Actually the prisoners' situation did not change, and Carter knew nothing about any possible release, but he scored a victory over Kennedy in Wisconsin. The President soon learned that the transfer of the captives to Bani Sadr's care had been vetoed by Khomeini. As one White House insider observed, now "there was a sense that the diplomatic route was closed." Carter angrily broke diplomatic relations with Iran. He vowed not to leave the White House to campaign until the hostages were released.

On April 11, the beleaguered President summoned his National Security Council to discuss a rescue plan. It had begun to be developed by Brzezinski and U.S. military leaders just 48 hours after the hostages had been seized. Vance condemned the plan. He believed that Khomeini, for his own interests, would not allow the hostages to be killed, but that they could be shot during a

An American perspective on Ayatollah Khomeini. This poster, with the Iranian
leader serving as a bull's-eye, became a best-seller in the United States as
frustration grew after the Iranian seizure of the U.S. Embassy and hostages in
November 1979. (© Bettmann/CORBIS)

rescue attempt. Vance also feared that the use of U.S. military power would not
only endanger American interests throughout the Islamic world, but anger
close allies in Western Europe and Japan who were now willing to squeeze Iran
economically, but wanted no use of military force.

At the decisive April 11 meeting, Vance was absent. He had flown off for
several days of rest in Florida. His top aide, Deputy Secretary of State Warren
Christopher, did attend. As Brzezinski viewed it, only three options existed:
Continuing "negotiating ad infinitum, even if the Iranians gave no indication
of a willingness or ability to accommodate"; undertake a major military operation to punish Iran severely—a strike that could, however, lead the Iranians to
kill the hostages or perhaps even ask the Soviets for help; or, finally, try a quick
but highly risky rescue mission. Christopher outlined possible nonmilitary
options. He was quickly overruled by Defense Secretary Harold Brown and
Vice President Walter Mondale. Both of them favored the rescue mission.
Brzezinski himself argued that it was time "to lance the boil." After a discussion lasting 1 hour and 50 minutes, the President announced, "We ought to go

ahead without delay." Convinced that the plan would not work, and that the attempted use of force could deeply injure relations with allies, Vance believed he had to resign. He became the first Secretary of State to resign on an issue of principle in 65 years. Brzezinski, however, privately concluded simply that Vance "is the ultimate example of a good man who has been traumatized by his Vietnam experience." (During the mid-1960s Vance had been involved in policymaking that expanded the tragic conflict with Vietnam.)

At a press conference a week later, Carter indirectly revealed one reason for his secret decision. He announced that reports had been received that Khomeini would not release the hostages until after the U.S. presidential election. Carter would not elaborate on the reports, but he reemphasized his determination not to apologize to Iran for U.S. relations with the shah.

The president had triggered a rescue plan that was as dramatic as it was dangerous. Six giant C-130 transport planes were to carry 130 army Green Berets, Rangers, drivers, and Iranian translators, along with 50 air crewmen, from an Egyptian air base to a secret landing strip in Iran—"Desert One"—260 miles from Tehran. At Desert One this force would be joined by eight Sea Stallion helicopters that had left three hours earlier from the U.S. aircraft carrier *Nimitz* sailing in the Arabian Sea. The troops were to transfer to the helicopters, fly to "Desert Two," a secluded mountain 50 miles from Tehran, then board trucks for a ride into the capital. Just before midnight, some would storm the compound where the hostages were held, while others would break into the Iranian Foreign Ministry where three other Americans were hostages. Forty minutes later they were all to board helicopters flown into the embassy compound or, if the compound was insecure, into a nearby soccer stadium. If mobs threatened the operation, two C-130H Spectre gunships, circling overhead, were to use any necessary force. The helicopters would then rendezvous with transport planes south of Tehran, the helicopters were to be destroyed, and everyone would fly off to safety in Egypt.

The Delta Force, as the special troops were called, had undergone special training since 1977 to combat terrorists. Colonel Charles A. Beckwith, better known to his military colleagues as "Chargin' Charlie," would lead Delta Force. Fifty-one years old, former University of Georgia football player, a veteran of the wars in Korea and Vietnam, Beckwith had become a legend among his fellow soldiers. In Vietnam he had survived a supposedly fatal chest wound. On his desk was a sign: "Kill 'em all. Let God sort 'em out."

Carter had emphasized that he wanted to "avoid wanton killings" in the rescue. The President lost sleep over the possibility of hostages dying. Beckwith held a different view: "When we went into that embassy, it was our aim to kill all Iranian guards . . . and we weren't going in there to arrest them; we were going in there to shoot them right between the eyes, and to do it with vigor!" As a military expert later observed, Beckwith's men were trained to kill anyone with a weapon, and "there would be no time for recognition of any hapless American holding a gun in the shadows." Carter wanted the hostages' lives saved, this expert continued, but "he had authorized a raid in which there was a good possibility that some of them might die."

The President's caution vividly appeared 24 hours before the attack was to begin on April 24, 1980. Brzezinski had urged that the rescue be accompanied by an air force strike against Tehran. The strike would either help the mission or, if the rescue failed, the United States would at least have punished the Iranians. Carter, however, pulled back the air attack because he wanted no needless killings and feared it would severely hurt U.S. relations with other Middle East states. Brzezinski nevertheless wrote in his journal at the last minute: "I feel good about [the mission]. I realize that if it fails I will probably be blamed more than anybody else, but I am quite prepared to accept that. If it is a success, it will give the United States a shot in the arm, which it has badly needed for twenty years."

During early dawn of April 24, Delta Force reached Desert One. But two of the eight helicopters from the *Nimitz* never made it. One suffered mechanical problems. The others ran into a dust storm that one pilot likened to "flying into a bowl of milk." A helicopter used too much gas avoiding the dust, had mechanical difficulties, and returned to the *Nimitz*. Only six helicopters remained, the minimum number Beckwith demanded for the mission. Then, after they landed at Desert One, another helicopter was disabled by a hydraulic system failure. With only five choppers left, Beckwith radioed that the mission had to be aborted. His words were relayed to Carter, who was monitoring the operation minute by minute in the White House. He approved Beckwith's decision. Now, Beckwith recalled, "the only thing on my mind was, 'We've failed, and I've got to get my soldiers out of here.' "

As a helicopter pilot lifted away, his spinning rotor sliced through the fuselage of a C-130 loaded with troops. Beckwith "looked out to my left and a C-130 all of a sudden exploded. It was one hell of a fire. . . . The munitions went off. The heat from the [burning] aircraft forced the helicopter pilots out of their cockpits." Three Marines on the helicopter and five Air Force crewmen in the transport plane died instantly. Beckwith quickly decided that the intense heat, along with the rising sun (which made it probable the Iranians would soon discover his force), made it impossible to stay until the eight bodies could be recovered. The survivors climbed into the remaining C-130s and flew off. Beckwith put his head in his hands and cried.

Carter went on television at 7:00 A.M. to reveal the disaster. Republican presidential candidates George Bush and Ronald Reagan, as well as Edward Kennedy, quickly supported the rescue attempt and asked for national unity. By a margin of 4 to 1, Americans backed the President's decision to try the mission. But the failure helped seal Carter's political fate. Detroit Mayor Coleman Young, who led the President's campaign in Michigan, declared flatly, "Unless the hostages are rescued, it's a no-win situation for Carter." Publicly, the closest U.S. allies in Western Europe and Japan sympathized with the President. Privately some were seething. They had reluctantly gone along with U.S. demands for squeezing Iran economically in the belief that Carter would not then resort to military action. Now they feared their Middle East oil supplies could be endangered by angry Arab producers. A top West German official declared privately (and was soon quoted in *Time* magazine): "The incompetence that permeates this Administration is incredible."

This map of the Middle East shows Iran and the routes of the attempted U.S. rescue mission in April 1980. Note the proximity of the Soviet Union and also of Afghanistan, which Soviet troops had invaded four months earlier.

Within the map:

MediterraneanSea

TURKEY

SYRIA

LEBANON

ISRAEL

JORDAN

IRAQ

Baghdad ✪

U.S.S.R.

④ One helicopter fails leaving five in operation. Carter cancels the mission. During takeoff one helicopter crashes into a C-130, both burst into flames.

● Tabas

DESERT ONE

Caspian Sea

Tehran ✪

IRAN

③ Two helicopters develop mechanical trouble. One is left in the desert, one returns to the *Nimitz*.

AFGHANISTAN

PAKISTAN

Arabian Sea

② Eight RH-53 helicopters take off from the *Nimitz*.

OMAN

Strait of Hormuz

Persian Gulf

KUWAIT

BAHRAIN

QATAR

Riyadh ✪

SAUDI ARABIA

UNITED ARAB EMIRATES

① The C-130s proceed to Iran.

EGYPT

Red Sea

SUDAN

The end of a failed rescue mission. At "Desert One" charred remains of
Americans lie among the wreckage of C-130 transports and the destroyed U.S.
helicopters on April 24, 1980. (© Bettmann/CORBIS)

In Iran, Khomeini declared that the president had "lost his mind," and that
the disaster proved whose side was favored by heaven. On April 26 the
charred, unrecognizable bodies of the dead Americans were publicly displayed
in Tehran. The government announced that the bodies would be returned to
relatives, but through an organization such as the Red Cross, not through the
U.S. government. The Iranians had also captured secret maps, photographs,
and lists of radio frequencies that had been left behind in the abandoned helicopters. As for the hostages, the Iranians separated and moved some of them
outside Tehran so another rescue mission would not be attempted.

Negotiations for their release went into a dead stall. The lack of movement
was due partly to the rescue tragedy, but it was especially due to turmoil in
Tehran. In what a French reporter called a "witch-hunt atmosphere," militants
conducted a feverish search for moderates, "CIA agents," leftists, rightists, anyone suspected of having cooperated with the rescue plans. In early July, the
hostage number dropped to 52 as Richard Queen was released because of illness; the Iranians had clearly decided they wanted no hostage to die in their
hands. In late July, the shah passed away in Cairo. Tehran radio rejoiced that
"the bloodsucker of the century has died," but quickly added that the hostages
would nevertheless continue to be held until the United States delivered both
apologies and as much as $24 billion.

Carter defeated Kennedy for the Democratic presidential nomination in August, but public opinion polls showed an astounding 77 percent of the voters giving Carter a negative rating. By 79 to 19 percent, they also condemned him for his handling of the Iranian crisis. There had been an incredible negative swing of 47 points in just 7 months over his handling of the hostages. The President, one congressman believed, "couldn't get the Pledge of Allegiance through Congress."

Republican presidential nominee Ronald Reagan declared that he would never "negotiate with terrorists," but otherwise he stressed Carter's economic failures and said little about the hostages. He did not have to say much; television kept the suffering of the hostages and their relatives in the United States before millions of viewers every night. The Republicans did worry about published reports that the Iranians and Carter were preparing an "October surprise": The hostages would supposedly be released on the eve of the election to ensure the President's victory. Republicans were especially worried about this after Carter's attempt to spring his "April Fool's Day surprise" against Kennedy during the Wisconsin primary. Nine years later, British reporters found evidence that the Republicans had sent former President Richard Nixon on a secret mission to the Iranians to prevent such a "surprise."

In April 1991, Gary Sick, who had been Carter's White House expert on Iran, dropped a bombshell. Sick announced that his investigations had turned up evidence to suggest that Reagan's campaign chair, William J. Casey, had met secretly with Iranians in July and August 1980. Casey, so witnesses told Sick, had sent $150 million of arms to Iran in return for the Iranians' assurance that the hostages would not be freed until Reagan was safely elected. Reagan and his advisors heatedly denied Sick's allegations. (Casey could not respond. He had died of a brain tumor just as the Iran-Contra scandal broke in 1986—a scandal in which he, as director of the CIA, had secretly sold arms to Iran in 1985 in return for the release of several other hostages. Throughout the 1980s, Reagan publicly denied that he would ever deal with terrorists who held hostages.) Evidence and public outcries nevertheless built up until, in 1991, Congress had to begin investigating the possibility that 11 years before, a small group of campaign officials had seized U.S. foreign policy and kept 52 men hostage for 5 extra months so Reagan could be elected President. Whatever Nixon's and Casey's activities, the hostages were not released. Reagan won a landslide victory, taking 44 states. "The voters," Carter recalled, "expressed their disgust with our nation's apparent impotence in the face of several disturbing problems—Iran foremost."

After early November, the defeated President no longer faced a political timetable for producing a settlement. It was becoming clear to the Iranians that a deal could be struck with Carter. As the hostages were losing their political value to Tehran officials, talks became serious in December 1980. One Iranian diplomat declared, "The hostages are like a fruit from which all the juice has been squeezed out." Another reason for the release, however, also now existed. In September 1979, Iraq attacked Iran to begin a struggle to decide which nation would control the Persian Gulf area. The conflict turned into one of the longest and bloodiest in the post-1945 era. Iran needed at least relief from U.S. pressures and even, if possible, western help.

Tehran officials suggested, and Carter accepted, that Algeria become an intermediary to help in the talks. Deputy Secretary of State Warren Christopher flew to Algiers and on January 18, 1981, a settlement appeared. Iran had demanded $24 billion, but finally accepted Carter's offer of $5.5 billion, released out of frozen Iranian assets, in exchange for the hostages. The remaining frozen assets and the American counterclaims against Iran were to be decided through arbitration.

Throughout the night before he was to surrender the White House to Reagan, Carter remained awake in his office surrounded by his close advisors. He prayed that Iran would release the hostages during his presidency. Khomeini, however, squeezed out the last drop of "juice": The hostages became free shortly after noon on January 20, 1981, just minutes after Reagan took the oath of office.

AN INTERPRETATION

The hostage crisis was not only one of the most frustrating and embarrassing chapters in American history. It encapsulated major themes of the 1970s that mark the decade as part of a turning point in the nation's experience as a great world power. Between 1945 and the 1970s the United States controlled world affairs in a manner unmatched by any nation in history. In the 1970s, however, Americans finally lost the war in Vietnam, realized that the Soviet Union had the capacity to destroy them in a nuclear exchange, and had to tolerate the rise of a radical Sandinista government in Nicaragua (a country long considered by the United States to be in its "backyard"). They also, of course, lost the shah's cooperation, oil resources, and military intelligence listening posts in Iran. As Christopher declared in 1978, the "absolute power" of such great nations as the United States "is growing," but "the relative power of any single nation has been reduced."

Americans had to come to terms with that relative decline during the hostage crisis. In a real sense they had to understand that the 1945-to-1970 years were aberrations, an era never to be repeated because the unique conditions that made the United States so powerful after World War II would never—if human civilization is fortunate—be repeated with another such war. In the 1970s, history began to return to normal as a more multipolar world emerged, the kind of world that interestingly resembled the pre-1939 or even pre-1914 years more than 1945 to 1970.

Americans also discovered that although they had spent trillions of dollars developing weapons that could destroy all civilization, they could not negotiate a quick political settlement, or mount a successful rescue mission, to release Americans held in chains by a much weaker nation. Power other than simply military was working in the world. Indeed, the religious belief embodied in Ayatollah Khomeini's cause not only was organizing a new Iran, but neutralizing vast U.S. military and economic power. Vaunted American technology, which the nation had proudly paraded since the days of Samuel Colt's revolver and Henry Ford's Model-T, even came into question. The nation was suffering disastrous unfavorable trade balances with Japan and Western Europe because Americans were having difficulty competing in tough world markets.

The nation's most basic assumptions about how the world worked became so fundamentally questioned that its educational system, as well as its top decision-making apparatus, became suspect. Most Americans knew nothing about Iran or its neighbors, although these same Americans utterly depended on these distant nations for an energy supply. Those in the press and government who did think they knew Iran too easily assumed, as Frances FitzGerald pointed out, "that the shah was the only person who counted . . . ; that the country, being underdeveloped, had no politics in the sense that advanced countries do; and that Iranians, being apolitical, would simply accept a dictatorship as necessary and good for them. The [U.S.] foreign-policy establishment," FitzGerald emphasized, "has traditionally made similar assumptions about almost all Third World countries."

Americans' assumptions about how easily they could burn up energy were also undermined. Since 1945 they had burned or melted about 40 percent of the world's nonrenewable materials. The world consumed 30,000 gallons of petroleum each second; with 6 percent of the world's population, the United States burned 33 percent of those gallons. In 1973 and 1974, and again in 1979 and 1980, severe energy shortages not only inconvenienced American motorists, but increasingly expensive petroleum made costs skyrocket until the United States found its goods less competitive on the world market and millions of its people newly out of work.

A psychological, as well as an economic, depression also set in. "For the first time in its history," influential *Business Week* magazine declared in late 1979, "the United States is no longer growing in power and influence among the nations of the world. In fact, the United States is now in steep decline." Ronald Reagan rode that pessimism into power. Three of four Americans polled in 1980 believed Reagan would ensure that the United States would be respected by other nations. As noted above, the hostages were indeed released minutes into his presidency.

From 1990 to 1992 President George Bush led a U.S.-dominated coalition that waged war during another Middle East crisis. But this crisis, triggered by Iraqi dictator Saddam Hussein's invasion of oil-rich Kuwait, ended with a massive victory for Bush and the coalition's half-million troops and thousands of high-technology weapons. Republicans noted sarcastically that 11 years earlier Carter could not even get "eight helicopters across a desert." The victory of 1991, however, did not lessen the importance of learning from the events of 1978 to 1981. Saddam Hussein's threat was a more traditional military aggression that the United States and its allies could overwhelm with superior firepower. Americans did not need to understand his culture to repulse his aggression. But the Iranians had posed a more subtle threat that could not be dealt with by conventional forces and high-tech wonder weapons. The

Ayatollah represented a cultural and religious force in a world increasingly shaped by cultural pluralism and nonmilitary power. Neither the Ayatollah Khomeini's ideas nor the hostages' situation could have been dealt with successfully by military weapons, no matter how high-tech. What the United States needed was an understanding of the Iranians before 1979, the limits of U.S. military power, and the new international arena in which the United States had to act. Whether the basic conditions that led to the hostage crisis and its intense frustrations have fundamentally changed remains a central question of today's United States.

Sources: The best scholarly treatment of the background is Gaddis Smith, *Morality, Reason, and Power: American Diplomacy in the Carter Years* (New York: Hill and Wang, 1986). Especially useful for understanding the crisis and its backdrop are three revealing memoirs: Jimmy Carter, *Keeping Faith* (New York: Bantam, 1982); Cyrus R. Vance, *Hard Choices* (New York: Simon and Schuster, 1983); and, most notably, Zbigniew K. Brzezinski, *Power and Principle* (New York: Farrar, Straus and Giroux, 1983). A number of fine studies on post-1973 U.S.-Iranian relations have appeared that focus on the hostage crisis: James A. Bill, *The Eagle and the Lion: The Tragedy of American–Iranian Relations* (New Haven: Yale University Press, 1988); Gary Sick, *All Fall Down: America's Tragic Encounter with Iran* (New York: Random House, 1985); William H. Sullivan, *Mission to Iran* (New York: Norton, 1981), by the embattled U.S. Ambassador. Paul Ryan, *The Iranian Rescue Mission: Why It Failed* (Annapolis: Naval Institute Press, 1985) is a good analysis of that tragedy. The Iranian background is in R. K. Ramazani, *The United States and Iran* (New York: Praeger, 1982). The important beginnings of the relationship are traced in Mark H. Lytle, *The Origins of the Iranian–American Alliance, 1945–1953* (New York: Holmes and Meier, 1987).

15

SEX, LIES, AND STEREOTYPES: THE POLITICS OF THE HILL–THOMAS HEARINGS

Michael May

Elaine Tyler May

While some remember where they were the day John F. Kennedy was shot, or when Neil Armstrong set foot on the moon, this editor can recall a sunny day in October, 1991, spent putting up storm windows and doing other household tasks, while keeping one eye on the television, where a dignified, earnest black woman named Anita Hill was telling a Senate committee about some of the embarrassing things her former employer, an intense black man named Clarence Thomas, had said to her. If true—and I was sure they were—these claims amounted to sexual harassment and (so I thought) spelled defeat for Thomas, who was on the cusp of being confirmed as a justice of the United States Supreme Court. As things turned out, Thomas survived to take his seat on the court, and I had learned another lesson in American politics.

The issue of sexual harassment that was the core of Hill's testimony was controversial, in part because the law of sexual harassment was so new and, for some people, so odd. Based on Title VII of the Civil Rights Act of 1964, which prohibited discrimination in employment, the form of sexual discrimination now called harassment was not recognized by the courts until 1976, and not until 1986 did the U.S. Supreme Court hold that harassment could occur even in situations that produced no direct financial injury. The law of sexual harassment appears odd because charges of sexual harassment depend on context rather than simple behavior. Put another way, what a man may say to a woman depends on whether or not the man and woman have a relationship based on formal power. That is, a man may legally tell a woman he finds her attractive if that woman is only an acquaintance or a friend, but the same comment becomes illegal if the woman is his employee. The distinction (which some men, and some women, believe violates human nature and something like the right to "court," the right to pursue one's appropriate sexual desires) became socially significant and enforceable only in the late twentieth century, when large numbers of upwardly mobile, middle-class women entered the workplace and, through the feminist movement, secured the means to enforce their right to a nondiscriminatory working environment. Anita Hill was one of those women.

Yet sexual harassment was not the only issue, nor even, perhaps, the most important one, presented to the all-white cast of the Senate Judiciary Committee. Indeed, the story told by Michael May and Elaine Tyler May has at its center not Anita Hill but Clarence Thomas, depicted here as a man unworthy of a seat on the nation's highest tribunal, and one whose deficiencies would have proved self-defeating had not Hill charged "harassment" and distracted the lot of us—me, anyway, putting up my storm windows—from focusing on the nomination itself. That said, Thomas was more than a jurist of doubtful talent. In an age in which the forces of de-industrialization had deprived average black men of the opportunity to work in factories, join unions, and earn decent wages, Thomas was a personal example of exceptional upward mobility, a black man who had made it, the American dream incarnate. He represented, too, the wave of ideological and political conservatism, the calls for "free markets" and "limited government" that helped carry Ronald Reagan to the presidency in 1980 and George Bush to the same office in 1988, and that in 1994 would produce the first Republican Congress in a generation. Across from a phalanx of white men that could hardly be said to be a panel of his peers, he could credibly and, perhaps, reasonably, assume the role of the black victim, humiliated by the powerful one more time. And in October, with Anita Hill as an adversary, he was somehow also just a man, with a man's desires, caught in the act of having expressed them to the wrong woman.

On October 11, 1991, Anita Hill, an African-American law professor at the University of Oklahoma, sat before the Senate Judiciary Committee and accused Clarence Thomas, her former boss and the second black Supreme Court nominee in history, of sexual harassment. Hill told the all-white-male committee that Thomas had repeatedly asked her out, despite her polite refusals, and had humiliated her by discussing pornographic movies "involving women with large breasts and engaged in a variety of sex with different people, or animals," even though the conversations clearly made her uncomfortable.

When Thomas testified that evening, he was livid. Emphatically denying all of Hill's accusations, he implied that the white establishment had engaged in a conspiracy to destroy him. "This is a high-tech lynching for uppity blacks who in any way deign to think for themselves, to do for themselves, to have different ideas," he said, "and it is a message that, unless you kow-tow to an old order, this is what will happen to you, you will be lynched, destroyed, caricatured by a committee of the U.S. Senate, rather than hung from a tree."

In the end, Thomas would be confirmed, but Hill's testimony, and the efforts of Republican senators to destroy her credibility, would spark a national debate about sexual harassment, the overwhelmingly male composition of the Senate, investigations into the private lives of public servants and the stereotyping of black men.

This explosion was the last thing that President George Bush anticipated when he nominated Thomas to the court that July. It was also the final controversy in a nomination that was controversial from the beginning. The sexual harassment

Clarence Thomas takes the constitutional oath to become a
justice of the United States Supreme Court during an outdoor
ceremony on the South Lawn at the White House in
Washington, D.C., Friday, Oct. 18, 1991. Looking on at left is
U.S. President George Bush. Holding the Bible is Clarence's
wife, Virginia Lamp Thomas. (Marcy Nighswander/AP/Wide
World Photo)

issue ultimately overshadowed all other issues in the case. But there were many
other problems with the Clarence Thomas nomination. Bush wanted to appoint a
conservative acceptable to the right wing of the Republican party, and he also
wanted to appoint an African American to replace Thurgood Marshall, the first
and only black Supreme Court justice. With Thomas, Bush found one of the very
few jurists in the nation who could meet both of these criteria.

Clarence Thomas was not the first Supreme Court nominee selected for
political reasons, nor would he be the last. Politics certainly influenced the selection of Thomas's predecessor, Thurgood Marshall. In the 1960s, at the height of
the civil rights movement, President Lyndon Johnson wanted the distinction of

appointing the first African American to the nation's highest court. But unlike Bush, Johnson insisted that his nominee have impeccable judicial credentials that would silence any critics who might claim that the appointment was merely opportunistic. He selected Marshall, a lawyer for the Legal Defense and Education Fund of the National Association for the Advancement of Colored People (NAACP), who had successfully argued the 1954 case of *Brown v. Board of Education of Topeka, Kansas.* That landmark Supreme Court decision toppled the Jim Crow system of segregation in the South. Although Marshall was also a controversial nominee—particularly irksome to Southern segregationists—his qualifications were beyond reproach, and he was confirmed.

George Bush wanted to replace Marshall with a black justice—although one of distinctly different political leanings. Bush needed to appease right-wing Republicans who were sorely disappointed with Bush's first Supreme Court appointment, David Souter, a judge known as a free thinker rather than as a conservative ideologue. But he also had to be careful to avoid repeating the disaster that unfolded in 1987 when President Ronald Reagan nominated Robert Bork, a controversial conservative with a rigid strict-construction approach to constitutional issues. After a bitter battle, the Senate refused to confirm Bork's nomination, on the grounds that his views of the constitution and the law were too extreme. Marshall's resignation gave Bush an opportunity to appoint a black conservative who might, he hoped, gain acceptance by liberals who would be reluctant to oppose a black nominee.

Marshall, who was 82, had hoped to resign when a Democratic president could replace him, but failing health and his increased isolation on the conservative-leaning court persuaded him to resign during the Bush administration. During his tenure on the court, Marshall worked tirelessly to advance the cause of civil rights. He made it clear that protecting this legacy was much more important to him than having a black justice replace him. "My dad told me way back," he told the media the day after his resignation, "there's no difference between a white snake and a black snake. They'll both bite." Obviously, Marshall had anticipated the strategy of the Bush administration.

On July 1, Bush nominated Clarence Thomas, a black judge who hoped to tear down much of what Marshall had helped to build. In the 1980s, President Ronald Reagan had appointed Thomas head of the Equal Employment Opportunity Commission [EEOC], an agency whose mission was to enforce affirmative action policies and civil rights laws, precisely because Thomas opposed those policies and would work to minimize the effectiveness of the agency.

Among the policies the EEOC was charged to enforce were affirmative action codes and sexual harassment laws—both of which Thomas opposed. Thomas believed that sexual harassment laws were too vague and led to trivial lawsuits, and that affirmative action amounted to nothing more than "quotas" for educated women and the black elite. Ignoring the many ways that affirmative action policies had helped people of color—including himself—to break through racial barriers, he remarked, "If quotas help you—fine. If they help you get a BMW or Mercedes, say that is why you want quotas. Man, quotas are for the black middle class. Look what is happening to the masses. They are my people. They are just where they were before any of these policies."

Thomas and the Bush administration downplayed the ways that the nominee had benefited from those very same affirmative action policies and instead portrayed him as a classic self-made man. Born into abject poverty, Thomas claimed to have overcome adversity through talent and sheer determination. When Bush officially announced the nomination from his seaside estate in Kennebunkport, Maine, he made a point of claiming that Thomas was the "best man" for the job, and "the fact that he was black and minority had nothing to do with this." In a follow-up question, Bush—against his handlers' wishes—blurted out that Thomas was also the "best-qualified" candidate.

Thomas was not the "best-qualified" nominee. He had served as a federal judge for less than two years, and, in that time, had not written any substantial constitutional opinions. The American Bar Association (ABA) gave Thomas the lowest rating of any confirmed Supreme Court justice in history. Of the 15 members of the panel, two rated Thomas as "unqualified," while the others in attendance rated him as "qualified." None rated Thomas as "well qualified," which is the typical rating for Supreme Court nominees. The panel unanimously rated Souter, for example, as "well qualified," compared to the rejected candidate Robert Bork who received four "unqualified" ratings.

To divert attention from Thomas's mediocre credentials, the Bush administration tried to keep the focus on his life story. Thomas was born in a rural wooden shack on the edge of a swamp in Pin Point, Georgia, a Gullah-speaking community near Savannah. The family had no electricity or plumbing. Clarence's father, M. C. Thomas, abandoned Thomas and his brother and sister when he was barely a year old, forcing his mother, Leola Williams, to work long days as a servant for a white family. When Thomas was six, he and his brother accidentally burned down their shack when some curtains had ignited on the wood stove. The family was then rendered homeless as well as destitute.

This tragedy turned out to be a turning point in young Thomas's life. Out of desperation, Williams asked her father, Myers Anderson, to take care of the boys. Unlike his daughter and grandchildren, Anderson was not poor. He was a successful distributor of oil, coal, and ice in Savannah. He was also a strict guardian who believed strongly in education. He sent Thomas and his brother to a demanding Catholic school and forced them to study every night. In contrast, their sister stayed in Pin Point, went to a mediocre public school, and worked in the crab shelling factories after school in order to survive. The elder Anderson's largess did not extend to his daughter and granddaughter, but it made a huge difference in the life chances of the two boys. Clearly, Thomas's frequently noted humble beginnings told only part of the story.

Thomas's good fortune in being raised by his grandfather gave him the education and skills that he would need to get ahead. In an earlier day, that training would have done little to help Thomas crack into previously all-white institutions. It might have helped him become a successful businessman, like his grandfather, but it never would have enabled him to enter the world of the white elite. Affirmative action policies, however, were opening up those arenas to people of color just as Thomas came of age.

After graduating from the Catholic high school, Thomas was admitted to Holy Cross, a Jesuit college in Worcester, Massachusetts, shortly after the school began an aggressive affirmative action plan to recruit black students in the wake of Martin Luther King's assassination. Upon graduation Thomas was admitted to Yale Law School soon after it implemented an affirmative action policy aiming to boost black enrollment to 10 percent—precisely the type of "quota" system Thomas would later oppose. Thurgood Marshall "would shake his head in wonderment that a black man who grew up in Jim Crow Georgia, and who had benefited from a thousand affirmative actions by nuns and others, and who attended Yale Law School on a racial quota, could suddenly find affirmative action so destructive of the character of black people," said Carl Rowan, a journalist who frequently interviewed Marshall.

In his youth, Thomas was neither a brilliant student nor a political activist. Like most of his peers he opposed the Vietnam War and supported civil rights. He graduated from Yale Law School with an undistinguished record and applied for jobs in the nation's largest law firms, which were still overwhelmingly white. He did not receive a single offer. Then John C. Danforth, Missouri's Republican attorney general and a Yale Law School alumnus, visited his alma mater looking for a black attorney to join his office. For Danforth, "Clarence embodied the American dream: he had ascended from humble origins in Pinpoint [sic], Georgia." Thomas accepted Danforth's offer and soon joined the Republican party.

With Danforth's patronage, Thomas's career was well on its way. Except for two years as a lawyer for the Monsanto corporation, Thomas would spend his entire career working for the government. When Danforth was elected senator in 1977, Thomas joined his staff as a legislative assistant. By the time Ronald Reagan was elected president in 1980, Thomas had gravitated to the ideas of Thomas Sowell, a senior fellow at Stanford University's Hoover Institute, and had moved well to the right of Senator Danforth. Sowell was among a small group of black conservatives who fused left-wing black separatist ideas of leaders like Malcolm X to right-wing economic theories of white conservatives like Milton Friedman. Sowell argued that government programs such as welfare and affirmative action served to weaken the black community, co-opting and corrupting those whom the well-intentioned programs intended to help, including welfare recipients as well as the liberal black bourgeoisie. For Thomas, Sowell's ideas were "like pouring a half a glass of water on the desert. I just soaked it up."

Shortly after Reagan was elected, Thomas told the *Washington Post* that he would not accept any job in the administration which dealt with racial matters because "I would have to prove that I didn't have the job because I am black." Yet when offered a job as assistant secretary for civil rights in the Department of Education, Thomas accepted the position. Shortly thereafter, he hired Anita Hill to be his personal assistant.

Like Thomas, Hill grew up in a poor, rural environment. She was born in 1956 in Lone Tree, Oklahoma, the youngest of 13 children. Her parents were farmers, and Hill spent hours before and after school working on the farm.

Friends and family described her as very serious and ambitious from an early age. "My childhood was one of a lot of hard work and not much money," she would later tell the Judiciary Committee. "But it was one of solid family affection as represented by my parents."

Hill attended segregated schools until the ninth grade, when she went to the largely white Morries High School, graduating as valedictorian. She then attended Oklahoma State University in Stillwater on a full scholarship. In 1977, Hill went on to Yale Law School on a full scholarship funded by the NAACP. After graduating Hill worked for a few months with a law firm before Thomas hired her to join him at the Department of Education. At this point, the public and private versions of Hill's and Thomas's relationship diverge. To most observers, these ambitious young African-American lawyers were both rising stars. On the surface, there was no evidence of tension during the many years that they worked together. But according to Hill's later testimony, things were very different behind closed doors.

Hill had always wanted to work in the field of civil rights, and working for Thomas was a prestigious position for a 25-year-old recent law school graduate. But after three months on the job, Hill later told the Senate Judiciary Committee, her job became much more difficult when Thomas asked her out on a date. "I declined the invitation to go out socially with him," she said. "I thought it would jeopardize what at the time I considered to be a very good working relationship."

While Hill acknowledged that she never explicitly told Thomas that she was not romantically interested in him, she assumed that her polite refusal would be sufficient. But over the next few months, Hill claimed, Thomas continued to pressure her into going out with him, and instigated crude conversations about pornography and kinky sex. Not wanting to jeopardize her job or her future, she continued to work for him, made no formal complaint, and told only a few close friends about Thomas's sexual harassment.

In February 1982, Reagan named Thomas chair of the Equal Employment Opportunity Commission (EEOC). The EEOC was charged with enforcing civil rights laws—including affirmative action policies and sexual harassment codes—that both Reagan and Thomas opposed. Thomas accepted the job, and Hill agreed to continue as his assistant at the EEOC.

Hill later explained to the Senate Judiciary Committee that in the months before she accepted the job at the EEOC, Thomas had stopped harassing her. "I needed to face the question of whether to go with him," she explained. "I was asked to do so and I did. The work itself was interesting and, at the time, it appeared that the sexual overtures, which had so troubled me, had ended." However, according to her testimony, the conversations began again during the fall of 1982, and they became so distressing that Hill was hospitalized for five days with "acute stomach pain." She later testified, "I was really upset. I felt like my job could be taken away or at least threatened. . . . That this person who had some power in the new Administration would make it difficult for me in terms of other positions." She said that her hospitalization "was related to the stress that I felt because of this." When she was offered a teaching position at Oral Roberts University in the summer of 1983, she accepted immediately. Thomas took her out for dinner on her last day at the EEOC and, according to Hill, said that "if [she] ever told anyone of his behavior it would ruin his career."

At the time, Thomas had other things to worry about as well. Thomas was a maverick within the Reagan administration. Conservatives frequently claimed that affirmative action was unnecessary because racism was a thing of the past. Thomas also opposed affirmative action, but he disagreed about racism. He believed that racism was alive and well, and he often quoted the militant black separatist Malcolm X on the need to resist it. Thomas told the *Atlantic Monthly* in 1987, "There is nothing you can do to get past black skin. I don't care how educated you are, how good you are at what you do—you'll never have the same contacts or opportunities, you'll never be equal to whites."

Thomas argued that African Americans needed self-discipline and strength in order to stand up to white America: "My view is that the most vulnerable unit in our society is the individual. And blacks, in my opinion one of the most vulnerable groups, should fight like hell to preserve individual freedoms so people can't gang up on us." He opposed affirmative action because "playing the group game builds up racial conflict," and, the way he saw it, African Americans would always lose when pitted against other minorities.

Thomas also opposed welfare, and he gained the wrath of many African Americans when he denounced his own sister. "She is so dependent," he told the *Washington Post*, "she gets mad when the mailman is late with her welfare check." His sister, who had none of the advantages given to Clarence by his grandfather and various affirmative action programs, replied to the rebuke by noting that she no longer received public assistance but worked double shifts for $2.35 per hour minimum wage at a nursing home in Savannah. She had been on welfare in part because she had to quit her job to take care of their elderly and incapacitated aunt, with no assistance from Thomas.

African Americans also criticized Thomas for his actions at the EEOC, where he rejected all class-action suits and only accepted complaints brought by individuals. Civil rights leaders felt especially betrayed as Thomas ignored the laws they had worked to enact. But conservatives were delighted. At Thomas's reappointment in 1986, he was joined by three of the most right-wing Republican ideologues: Attorney General Edmund Meese III, Senator Strom Thurmond (R-SC), and William Bradford Reynolds, assistant attorney general for civil rights. Reynolds congratulated Thomas with a back-handed compliment: "Clarence Thomas is the epitome of the right kind of affirmative action working in the right way." Thomas looked away, stung by the comment, which proved how little his Republican colleagues understood him. Although his political agenda brought him into the inner circle of the conservative movement, he would never feel altogether at home there. He found himself in the awkward no-man's-land between white Reaganites, many of whom he considered to be racists, and black liberals who considered him a traitor.

Nevertheless, Thomas set his sights on a seat on a federal court, and he began the deft balancing act of courting allies in both the far right and the civil rights movement. In 1990 he was sworn in to the Washington, D.C., Circuit Court. Barely 20 months later, Justice Marshall retired from the court and the

Bush administration began to look for a replacement. While the administration openly decried racial preferences, Attorney General Richard Thornburgh told *Meet the Press* that Bush wanted the court to "reflect the diversity of our society." The short list for Marshall's replacement, he said, included "qualified women, blacks, Hispanics, persons with disabilities and the like."

When seeking to appease the right wing, Bush looked to the increasingly powerful think tanks at the forefront of the conservative movement. So when Marshall retired, Bush's chief of staff, John Sununu, turned immediately to Thomas Jipping, who worked on legal issues for the conservative Free Congress Foundation. Jipping responded with an enthusiastic endorsement of Thomas, stating that "the entire conservative movement not only supports him but believes in him."

Bush also needed to be assured that the civil rights community, especially the NAACP, would not oppose Thomas's nomination. They turned to Arch Parsons, a friend of Thomas and a black reporter for the *Baltimore Sun*, who then lobbied Benjamin L. Hooks, executive director of the NAACP. On June 30, Parsons assured the Bush administration that Hooks would not oppose Thomas, saying that having a black justice on the court was more important than his politics.

Assuming that he had the support of both the civil rights community and the conservatives, Bush nominated Thomas on July 1, 1991. In accepting the nomination, Thomas said, "Only in America could this have been possible. As a child I could not dare dream that I would ever see the Supreme Court, not to mention be nominated to it." The White House then began the campaign to ensure Thomas's confirmation and hired Kenneth Duberstein, the powerful lobbyist who had secured the Souter nomination, to oversee the process. Duberstein brought Thomas into the office for a confidential interview. He wanted to defuse any potential scandals linked to the candidate. Duberstein carefully leaked to sympathetic reporters the potentially harmful facts that Thomas had smoked marijuana and avoided the Vietnam draft, guaranteeing that they would not emerge later to disrupt the nomination.

One thing that Duberstein could not explain away was Thomas's record. When the NAACP took a closer look at Thomas's opposition to key civil rights legislation, it became clear that Thomas was not going to win endorsement by the NAACP at their board meeting on July 31. As *Washington Post* reporter Juan Williams noted years earlier, "[Thomas] is a Republican, a long-time supporter of Ronald Reagan, opposed to the minimum wage law, rent control, busing and affirmative action. How a black man can say no to those policies is a mystery to most black people." On the same day as the NAACP vote, the Bush administration imported a busload of blacks from Thomas's hometown of Pin Point to arrive in Washington for a seemingly spontaneous show of support. The ruse had the desired effect—the news media divided their coverage between the Pin Point demonstrators and the NAACP vote.

Far away from the spin doctors in Washington, D.C., however, a story was brewing that would grab the public's attention. The long-hidden allegations of sexual harassment were soon to emerge. In the final week prior to the confirmation hearings before the Judiciary Committee, acting on information leaked quietly from friends of Hill, aides of Senator Howard Metzenbaum (D-OH) and Senator Edward M. Kennedy (D-MA) called Hill. As the hearings began, Hill told her story, under conditions of anonymity, to Harriet Grant, chief of nominations for the Judiciary Committee.

Meanwhile, the Judiciary Committee grilled Thomas on his controversial opinions. Rather than vigorously defending his positions, as he had done in many interviews, he did his best to appear noncontroversial. He was not completely opposed to affirmative action, he said, but thought it should apply to disadvantaged kids of all races. He explained away as merely "theoretical discussions" his frequent endorsement of libertarian ideas, and his support of an activist Supreme Court to promote these ideas. When asked his opinion on the highly charged subject of abortion, the normally opinionated Thomas insisted that he had never discussed it and reserved his right to maintain "impartiality" if *Roe v. Wade* was ever reconsidered by the Court.

Many observers at the time felt that Thomas's answers to these questions should have disqualified him from consideration. "Here was a man who benefited from federal legislation based on race but who assailed that policy for the benefit of the highest bidder. Here was a man who incredulously professed no prior thought on abortion or *Roe v. Wade*, who was poised to ascend to the highest court," noted African-American historian Earl Lewis. "Many I spoke to thought he perjured himself."

Thomas did well maneuvering around political questions, but he fumbled when asked to discuss "landmark" Supreme Court decisions handed down since his graduation from law school. Thomas could name only one. He made no mention of the Supreme Court's 1986 ruling that sexual harassment constituted a form of discrimination covered under the 1964 Civil Rights Act, even though he was head of the EEOC at the time and it was his agency's job to enforce the ruling. Erwin Griswold, a well-respected Republican lawyer, was a witness against Thomas. "I do not question that the president has a right to take ideological factors into consideration," he said. "But that is no reason for this committee or the Senate approving a presidential nominee who has not demonstrated any clear intellectual or professional distinctions."

The Judiciary Committee continued to debate the merits of Thomas's nomination. Meanwhile, on September 23, just days before the committee was scheduled to vote, Hill spoke to FBI investigators and provided the details of her story. When the FBI contacted Thomas about the allegations, he expressed outrage and categorically denied Hill's charges. Thomas's response worried the few Democrats who knew about the allegations. Senator Joseph Biden (D-DE), chair of the Judiciary Committee, was reluctant to make Hill's statement an issue in the hearings for fear of appearing intent on smearing Thomas's reputation with unsubstantiated accusations. As a result, although Hill assumed that all members of the Judiciary Committee would read her carefully detailed statement, the report was not distributed to the full committee. When the committee did vote on September 27, before the release of the FBI report, it split down the middle 7–7.

At this point, before Hill's testimony had reached the full committee or the media, the senators on the committee opposing Thomas had enough ammunition to push their cause in the full Senate. In the report of the initial hearings, Senator Kennedy and Senator Paul Simon (D-IL) provided evidence that Thomas had lied to the committee about his previous record, writings, and opinions, noting that Thomas "attempted to cloak himself with more moderate views than his record supports" on issues such as abortion, and that Thomas's "extreme statements" demonstrated that President Bush was trying to "pack the Supreme Court with Justices who share a single one-dimensional view of the Constitution." Senator Metzenbaum pointed to Thomas's "extensive and controversial record on a wide range of important legal and policy issues," and he noted that his "discussion of his record before the committee was evasive, unresponsive, implausible and, at times, simply unbelievable. Stated simply, Judge Thomas ran from his record. His refusal to discuss his record with the committee in a candid, thorough and straightforward manner was the single biggest factor which led to his inability to obtain an endorsement from the committee."

Thomas's opponents had strong evidence and solid arguments to bring before the full Senate as well as the court of public opinion before the Senate was scheduled to vote on October 8. A month before the vote, public opinion polls showed that only 24 percent of Americans supported confirmation, and 10 percent were opposed. Among African Americans, support was even weaker: Only 22 percent indicated support and fully 22 percent were opposed—double the opposition among whites. But the majority of all groups were undecided. The vote was fairly predictable in the Senate, but close enough that a highly publicized debate of Thomas's record in the full Senate might have tipped the balance of public opinion and possibly affected the outcome of the vote.

But the Hill controversy was about to boil over, derailing the effort to reject Thomas using solid evidence from his record and focusing attention on the murky and ultimately unprovable accusations of sexual harassment. Timothy Phelps of *Newsday* eventually broke the story. He had known about it for months, but Hill would not confirm the story unless a senator first provided Phelps with her statement. "Anita Hill was one of the more reluctant people I have ever tried to interview," he later wrote. Then, just days before the Senate vote, he found someone willing to confirm, off the record, that Hill's statement had been given to members of the Judiciary Committee. It was enough. On Sunday, October 6, newspapers across the country covered the allegations, and Anita Hill was catapulted into the limelight. Public opinion immediately changed. Fully 87 percent of those polled had heard about Hill's accusations; 63 percent said that if the charges were true, it would be reason enough for the Senate to reject his nomination.

That Monday morning, October 7, the nation was in an uproar. Inside the Judiciary Committee, Republican Senator Orin Hatch (UT) accused Democratic Senator Metzenbaum of orchestrating the leak. The Republicans claimed that Hill's accusations were part of an eleventh-hour attempt by the Democrats to derail the nomination. That afternoon, Hill held a press conference and explained that she had only "responded to the Committee's approach" and "resent[ed] the idea that people would blame the messenger rather than looking at the content of the message itself." The Senate vote was still set for the following afternoon.

On Tuesday at around noon, seven congresswomen entered the room where the Democratic senators were in caucus, and stood there in protest. "The thing everyone miscalculated was the reaction of the women, the girls' vote," a Bush advisor later commented. That afternoon, the Senate agreed to postpone the vote for a week. Anita Hill and Clarence Thomas would testify in front of the committee on October 11.

The White House and the Republicans were prepared to stand by their man. That meant not simply defending Thomas against Hill's accusations, but destroying Hill's credibility. This was not going to be easy, because there was no compelling motive for Hill to lie about these events. She was not known to be particularly liberal; indeed, she had defended Robert Bork's nomination. Nevertheless, the Republicans pressed on. Meanwhile, although Hill's lawyers worried that exposing the raunchy details might backfire in the Senate, they decided that Hill should provide as many specifics as possible. But Hill's advisors were unprepared for how aggressively the Republican Senators would protect Thomas, and how pale the Democratic defense would be.

On the morning of October 11, in a nationally televised live broadcast, Democratic Senator Joseph Biden opened the hearings in the lavish Senate Caucus Room. Biden sat in the center of a long table, flanked on both sides by the all-white-male members of the Judiciary Committee. Facing the committee, in the fulcrum of the senators' gazes, was the table where Thomas and Hill would sit and defend themselves in the coming days. "The Committee is not here to put Judge Thomas or Professor Hill on trial," Biden said in his opening remarks. "Certain subjects are simply irrelevant to the issue of harassment, namely, the private conduct of out-of-the-workplace relationships, and the intimate lives and practices of Judge Thomas, Professor Hill, and any other witness that comes before us. . . . [The] primary responsibility of this committee is fairness. That means making sure that we do not victimize any witness who appears here and that we treat every witness with respect. And without making any judgment about the specific witnesses we will hear from today, fairness means understanding what a victim of sexual harassment goes through, why victims often do not report such crimes, why they often believe that they should not or cannot leave their jobs." As the hearings unfolded over the next three days, the Republicans on the committee flagrantly violated Biden's ground rules.

Thomas gave a brief opening statement, filled with passion: "I have never in all my life felt such hurt, such pain, such agony. My family and I have been done a grave and irreparable injustice. During the past two weeks, I lost the belief that if I did my best all would work out. I called upon the strength that helped me get here from Pin Point, and it was all sapped out of me. It was sapped out of me because Anita Hill was a person I considered a friend, whom I admired and thought I had treated fairly and with the utmost respect. . . . Mr. Chairman, in my forty-three years on this Earth, I have been able, with the help of others and with the help of God, to defy poverty, avoid prison, overcome segregation, bigotry, racism, and obtain one of the finest educations available in this country. But I have not been able to overcome this process. This is worse than any obstacle or anything that I have ever faced."

Senator Orin Hatch makes a point at the hearing about allegations of sexual harassment made by former aide Anita Hill, Washington, D.C., October 11, 1991. Senators Strom Thurmond and Joseph Biden listen to the proceedings. Senator Ted Kennedy, face on hand, is at the far right. Although some hoped that Kennedy would prove a spirited defender of Ms. Hill, he proved to be a cautious supporter. The Senator was haunted by an incident in 1969, when a car he was driving plunged off a bridge on Chappaquiddick Island, killing 28-year-old Mary Jo Kopechne, a volunteer staff worker in the Robert Kennedy 1968 presidential campaign. (Reuters/Hulton Archive/Getty Images)

When Hill presented her opening statement, her strained voice betrayed her nervousness, but she nonetheless maintained her composure as she explained how Thomas had repeatedly harassed her, first during her tenure at the Department of Education and later at the EEOC. She said that Thomas had repeatedly asked her out in spite of her refusals; boasted that his penis was "larger than most"; described pornographic videos starring "Long Dong Silver"; and at one point during a meeting had picked up his soda can and asked, "Who has put pubic hair on my Coke?" Hill testified that it was these sorts of comments that she found particularly harassing, much more than being asked out by her boss. "The conversations about sex, I was much more embarrassed and humiliated by," she told the committee. "The two combined really made me feel sort of helpless in a job situation, because I really wanted to do the work that I was doing; I enjoyed the work. But I felt that that was being put in jeopardy by the other things going on in the office. And so, I was really, really very troubled by it and distressed over it."

According to federal law, "Harassment on the basis of sex is a violation of section 703 of title VII. . . . Unwelcome sexual advances, requests for sexual favors, and other verbal or physical conduct of a sexual nature constitute sexual harassment when (1) submission to such conduct is made either explicitly or implicitly a term or condition of an individual's employment, (2) submission to or rejection of such conduct by an individual is used as the basis for employment decisions affecting such individual, or (3) such conduct has the purpose or effect of unreasonably interfering with an individual's work performance or creating an intimidating, hostile, or offensive working environment." Hill accused Thomas of behavior that fell under the third condition for harassment: creating an offensive working environment. She did not claim that his behavior, upsetting as it was, interfered with her work performance, and she did not attempt to charge him with criminal behavior. Thomas's supporters, however, did not debate the fine points of the law. They simply set out to discredit Hill and her story.

After Hill's opening statement, the Republican members of the Committee attacked her credibility. They suggested that Hill was attracted to Thomas. They grilled her about two visits and eleven phone calls she made to Thomas between 1984 and 1987—an average of fewer than four calls a year. "Well, it

Despite the sometimes hostile questioning by members of the Senate Judiciary Committee, Oklahoma law professor Anita Hill remained poised and composed. October 11, 1991. (Reuters/Rick Wilking/Hulton Archive/Getty Images)

just seems incredible to me that you would have visited with him twice after that period," said Senator Alan Simpson (R-WY). "And after he was no longer able to manipulate you or destroy you, that you then not only visited with him, but took him to the airport, and then eleven times contacted him. That part of it appalls me." She explained that most of the calls were at the request of colleagues to help arrange a guest lecture at the University of Oklahoma. Although these few calls hardly reflected someone in ardent pursuit, Senator Simpson claimed that they provided evidence that Hill pursued Thomas, rather than the other way around.

The strategy was to portray Hill as a "woman scorned," and that this was her attempt at revenge. In many ways, the hearings showed the white male senators in a worse light than either Thomas or Hill. The Republican senators accused Hill of having fantasies and of being mentally unstable. At one point Senator Simpson motioned to the inside pockets of his coat, asserting that he had a number of letters, which never surfaced, from people in Oklahoma warning him to watch out for Anita Hill. This image evoked the fanatical anticommunist Senator Joe McCarthy, who, in the early days of the Cold War, waved pieces of paper before TV cameras and claimed they were lists of communists working in the government. Senator Arlen Specter (R-PA) appeared mean and heartless as he pounded away at Hill's credibility. "The question is why with an experienced lawyer in the position being concerned about women's rights," Specter said, peering down at Hill, "do you leave a man, Clarence Thomas, as chairman of the EEOC for years, when according to your testimony he has been guilty of sexual harassment himself? Now, I do see explanations at every turn. And I have wondered about the quality of those explanations, candidly." Senator Ted Kennedy looked foolish and passive, his own history of sexual misbehavior silencing him. For the most part, Thomas let the senators do the character assassination, but at one point he described Hill's behavior at work as "unyielding to the other members of the staff, and then storming off or throwing a temper tantrum of some sort that either myself or the chief of staff would have to iron out."

The Republicans also pressed Hill repeatedly to explain why she hadn't charged Thomas with sexual harassment at the time, and why she had followed him to the EEOC. Hill explained that, as a young woman starting her career, she did not want to "invoke any kind of retaliation against me professionally." Explaining why she had not come forward earlier, she echoed Senator Biden's opening remarks: "One does have to really understand something about the nature of sexual harassment. It's very difficult for people to come forward with these things, these kinds of things. It wasn't as though I rushed forward with this information. . . . Telling the world is the most difficult experience of my life."

After Hill had completed her testimony and when the TV audience was at its prime-time peak, Thomas returned to the room. In a steady firm voice filled with rage, he called the hearings a "high-tech lynching." "Mr. Chairman, I am a victim of this process and my name has been harmed, my integrity has been harmed, my character has been harmed, my family has been harmed, my

Caught here in a reflective moment, Clarence Thomas took an aggressive stance in his testimony to the Senate Judiciary Committee, denying the charges of sexual harassment brought by Anita Hill and calling the proceeding a "high-tech lynching." (Greg Gibson/AP/Wide World Photos)

friends have been harmed. There is nothing this committee, this body or this country can do to give me my good name back, nothing. I will not provide the rope for my own lynching or for further humiliation. I am not going to engage in discussions, nor will I submit to roving questions of what goes on in the most intimate parts of my private live [sic] or the sanctity of my bedroom. These are the most intimate parts of my privacy, and they will remain just that, private."

The Democrats did little to defend Hill. Another former employee of Thomas at EEOC, Angela Wright, had come forward to say she had experienced similar harassment by Thomas and was willing to testify. But when Thomas attacked her credibility the Democrats lost their nerve. Thomas said that Wright wanted revenge because he had fired her from the EEOC: "I summarily dismissed her. . . . I felt her performance was ineffective, and the office was ineffective. And the straw that broke the camel's back was a report to me from one of the members of my staff that she referred to another male member of my staff as a faggot." The unsubstantiated hearsay was enough. Angela Wright, who had an entirely different version of the events, never testified.

The Democrats also decided against calling several witnesses to the committee who were prepared to testify that Thomas consumed pornography. The fact that Thomas had kept stacks of *Playboy* magazines and rented X-rated movies was presumably his private business, no matter how relevant the facts might be. Respect for private matters, however, did not stop another witness, John N. Doggett III, a management consultant from Austin, Texas, from asserting, "Ms. Hill's fantasies about my sexual interest in her were an indication of the fact that she was having a problem with being rejected by men she was attracted to. Her statements and actions in my presence during the time when she alleges that Clarence Thomas harassed her were totally inconsistent with her current descriptions and are, in my opinion, yet another example of her ability to fabricate the idea that someone was interested in her when in fact no such interest existed." Although Hill said that she could barely recall who Doggett was, raising questions about whose fantasy Doggett described, these unsubstantiated claims about Hill's private life were fair game. However, testimony that would corroborate aspects of her story was off-limits.

The attempts to destroy Hill's credibility worked. Public opinion polls throughout the hearings showed that most Americans were following the news, and that a majority of Americans believed Thomas over Hill. Yet more than two-thirds of those polled said that if the charges were true, Thomas should not be confirmed. When the Senate voted on October 15, Thomas won confirmation on a vote of 52–48. It was the closest confirmation vote for a Supreme Court nominee in history. The official swearing in was to be on November 1. However, when the White House learned that several reporters were about to go public with further evidence that witnesses saw Thomas renting pornographic movies starring "Long Dong Silver," as Hill had described, they decided to have a private swearing in before the allegations surfaced.

The issues raised during the Hill–Thomas hearings would reverberate far into the future. A year later the tide had turned and most now believed that Hill was telling the truth. Then, in 1993, Hill's reputation took a beating with the publication of David Brock's bestseller, *The Real Anita Hill*, in which he described her as "a little bit nutty and a little bit slutty." Nearly a decade later, in a book entitled *Blinded by the Right: The Conscience of an Ex-Conservative*, Brock admitted that he had falsely slandered Hill: "To protect myself and my tribe from the truth and the consequences of our own hypocrisies, smears, cover-ups and falsehoods, I consciously and actively chose an unethical path. I continued to malign Anita Hill and her liberal supporters. . . . I knowingly published a lie. I falsified the record."

Evidence of lies after the fact did nothing to alter the result. But there was other fallout from the case. The spectacle of these aging white men who had no understanding of sexual harassment attacking Anita Hill angered many viewers, especially women. "A lot of men do not understand how devastating this is, be it physical harassment or verbal or visual," Dottie Jones, assistant director of the United Auto Workers' women's department, told *Newsday*. "When the real deal goes down, boys will be boys and they stick together. And here, you're talking about what we consider the most exclusive all-male, white club

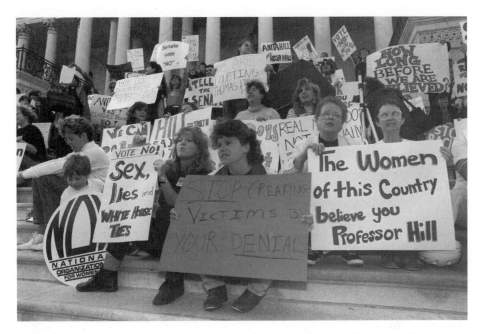

Demonstrators against U.S. Supreme Court nominee Clarence Thomas rally on the steps of the U.S. capitol building shortly before a U.S. Senate vote, October 15, 1991, in Washington, D.C. (Agence France Presse)

in America—the U.S. Senate." In the next election women came out to vote in droves and helped to elect four new women senators—including Carol Mosely Braun, the first African-American woman senator—as well as a record number of women to Congress who called themselves "the Anita Hill class." The hearings also raised awareness about sexual harassment and emboldened women to come forward with complaints. The number of sexual harassment cases brought before the EEOC in the first half of 1992 increased by 50 percent over the previous year. Hill, for her part, was a reluctant symbol, and she remained silent for more than a year. However, in 1992 she began to speak out against sexual harassment. "We need to be sure that we can go out and look anyone who is a victim of harassment in the eye and say, 'You do not have to remain silent any more,'" she told a crowd of 2,000 at a women's rights conference at Hunter College.

Under a barrage of criticism, members of the Judiciary Committee indulged in public acts of repentance. Senator Simpson acknowledged that he had been too hard on Hill in order to protect Thomas. Senator Kennedy admitted that his own checkered past had interfered with his ability to be an effective politician during the hearings. Senator Metzenbaum, plagued by accusations that he had leaked the Hill story, retired from the Senate. Even Senator Danforth, Thomas's long time friend and mentor, admitted that he had not been fair to Hill.

The effect of the Hill-Thomas hearings was particularly painful for the black community. Long before Hill's accusations became public, black citizens divided among themselves over Thomas. James W. E. Dixon III, an African-American pastor, noted, "Black people are divided over Clarence Thomas, even divided inside themselves." Some opposed him because of his political views. Retired black postal worker James Douglas resented Thomas, saying, "He benefited from all the civil rights battles, but now he says we don't need that any more." The situation became even more complicated after Hill's allegations became public. Robert Lane, of the National Organization of Concerned Black Men, objected to Thomas casting Hill's accusations as an example of racism: "I see it as one woman accusing one man of reprehensible acts; I don't see it as furthering old stereotypes." Eleanor Holmes Norton, congresswoman from Washington, D.C., concurred: "A black woman raised these questions, not a white woman or white men." Black feminist Barbara Smith noted, "Ironically, there are probably a lot of black people who believe Anita Hill's charges, but who still think it's more important to stand behind a black man even when he has utter contempt for the struggles of African Americans, than it is to support a black woman's right not to be abused."

AN INTERPRETATION

Perhaps the most unfortunate legacy of the confirmation process was that the intense focus on Hill's accusations diverted attention away from the most salient and critical issue relevant to Thomas's appointment to the Court: his legal judgment. Thomas's behavior since his confirmation vindicates those who questioned his qualifications long before Anita Hill came forward. Despite his assurance during the hearing that he believed that Supreme Court justices should "put ideologies away," Thomas has not done that. He has proved himself among the most ideologically rigid members of the Court, sitting mostly silent but voting with the unabashed conservative Antonin Scalia. In contrast to his sworn testimony that he was "impartial" on the issue of abortion, he and Scalia have been the only two justices who consistently voted to erode women's reproductive freedom and to undercut the *Roe v. Wade* decision. Thomas has also violated the Judicial Code, which forbids justices from attending political events, by appearing frequently as a guest and speaker for several conservative legal groups. Thomas later acknowledged that he had misrepresented himself during the hearings, explaining, "If you are yourself, like Bob Bork, you're dead."

The battle between Hill and Thomas was no mere "he said–she said" volley of accusations. It represented one of the most bitter and controversial moments in the political and cultural wars that have unfolded since the social upheavals of the 1960s. Those turbulent days witnessed the civil rights movement, which destroyed the system of legal segregation in the South and opened doors previously closed to African-American citizens. In the wake of the civil rights movement came many other movements for social justice and equality, including the powerful feminist movement. Early feminist activists emerged from the civil rights movement where they developed their political skills—at the same time encountering sexism within the very movement that fought to abolish racism. Historically, movements for racial and gender equality have been linked, usually in common cause but sometimes in competition. During the confirmation process of Clarence Thomas to the Supreme Court, these issues came together and exploded, because it seemed to many as if the goals of the women's movement were standing in the way of a black Supreme Court nominee.

These two movements—feminism and civil rights—achieved profound and lasting changes in American society, from laws and public policies to the intimate levels of daily interaction at home and at work. But both movements contained a great deal of disagreement and diversity within their own ranks. Civil rights, with its emphasis on integration and political equality, gave way to black power by the late 1960s, with its more militant and separatist emphasis. Among black leaders there were also political differences. Some favored liberal policies of government spending and welfare, while others believed that black people should organize themselves into strong communities, work to eliminate racial barriers, and promote individual achievement of the sort that Clarence Thomas seemed to represent.

Feminists also disagreed among themselves over goals, strategies, and philosophy. Some favored political equality, arguing that the nation's laws and policies should treat women and men the same. Others believed that women were fundamentally different from men, and worked to establish separate institutions for women to meet their particular needs. Feminists also disagreed over issues such as pornography, with some arguing that pornography and sexual exploitation degraded and oppressed women, while others claimed that women's liberation should include sexual liberation and an end to prudery. Black women— among them Anita Hill—endeavored to balance their advocacy of women's rights against their solidarity with black men in the struggle against racism.

Thomas claimed that he was the victim of a "high-tech lynching," but of course nothing of the kind took place. He was not a victim; he became one of the most powerful men in the nation. Moreover, he misused the metaphor. Black men were lynched if they were suspected of desiring or raping white women. Black women were also lynched, especially if they accused a white man of rape. As historian Estelle Freedman points out, "No black man was ever lynched for assaulting a black woman. White men historically did not give a damn about the honor or purity of black women; nor . . . given the outcome of the hearings, do those in the United States Senate today."

In the end, the Thomas confirmation was disastrous not so much because of what he may have done to Anita Hill, but because he never should have been nominated in the first place. Bush selected Thomas because of his race, with no regard for his qualifications, in direct violation of affirmative action statutes. According to federal codes established in 1978, there is a clear distinction between *recruitment* of job candidates and *selection* criteria: "While such affirmative action programs may in design and execution be race, color, sex, or ethnic conscious, selection procedures under such programs should be based upon the ability or relative ability to do the work." Bush violated these codes by focusing on race in the selection of his nominee rather than on Thomas's "ability or relative ability to do the work." Even Bush's own aides acknowledged that Thomas was not the best-qualified candidate for the Supreme Court.

In terms of Anita Hill's allegations, because her supporters failed to bring witnesses and evidence that would corroborate her story, there was nothing but her word against his. Hill testified that she tolerated behavior that she found extremely stressful and upsetting in order to continue doing work she enjoyed and to advance her career. However, Hill's treatment at the hands of the all-white-male Judiciary Committee proved that her reluctance to speak about Thomas's harassment was well founded, highlighting the fact that the person making sexual harassment accusations often suffers the consequences more than the alleged perpetrator.

Ultimately, the liberals who hoped to discredit Thomas deserve the blame for the outcome. In the first place, they should have stuck to what really mattered and where they had solid evidence: Thomas's qualifications to serve on the Supreme Court. In the end their strategy of bringing in Hill's accusations diverted the nation's attention from the substantial reasons Thomas should not have been confirmed. Second, once they opened up the sexual harassment issue, they brought no evidence, witnesses, or facts to corroborate Hill's testimony. They sat by meekly while Thomas's defenders on the committee pilloried her and smeared her reputation. Hill's supporters' reluctance to play hardball gave the advantage to their foes. Moreover, by deciding that she should describe Thomas's sexually explicit remarks in detail, her supporters actually placed her in an awkward situation. In front of the cameras, it was Hill, not Thomas, who uttered the offensive words, with the ironic result that those words became associated with Hill in the public mind, rather than with Thomas. Last, by their decision to bring the sordid details of Hill's allegations into the glare of the media, they opened the door for conservatives in Congress to come back later in the decade to expose the sexual misbehavior of the Democratic President, Bill Clinton, leading to his impeachment and near removal from office. And the same David Brock who falsely smeared Anita Hill led the charge against Clinton, confessing his lies and apologizing to both after the fact. But the era of X-rated prime-time news had arrived. When the Starr Report detailing President Bill Clinton's dalliance with a White House intern hit the limelight, the resulting media circus made the Hill–Thomas hearings look like a mere warm-up act.

Sources: On the Hill–Thomas controversy see the hearing transcripts, compiled in Anita Miller, ed., *The Complete Transcripts of the Clarence Thomas–Anita Hill Hearings* (Chicago: Academy of Chicago Publishers, 1994), and videotapes of the televised hearings. Much has been written about the case in its immediate aftermath and in the decade since. Among the many works that we used for this story are Jane Mayer and Jill Abramson, *Strange Justice: The Selling of Clarence Thomas* (New York: Houghton Mifflin, 1994); Robert Chrisman and Robert L. Allen, *Court of Appeal: The Black Community Speaks Out on the Racial and Sexual Politics of Clarence Thomas vs. Anita Hill* (New York: Ballantine Books, 1992); Toni Morrison, ed., *Race-ing Justice, En-gendering Power: Essays on Anita Hill, Clarence Thomas, and the Construction of Social Reality* (New York: Pantheon, 1992).